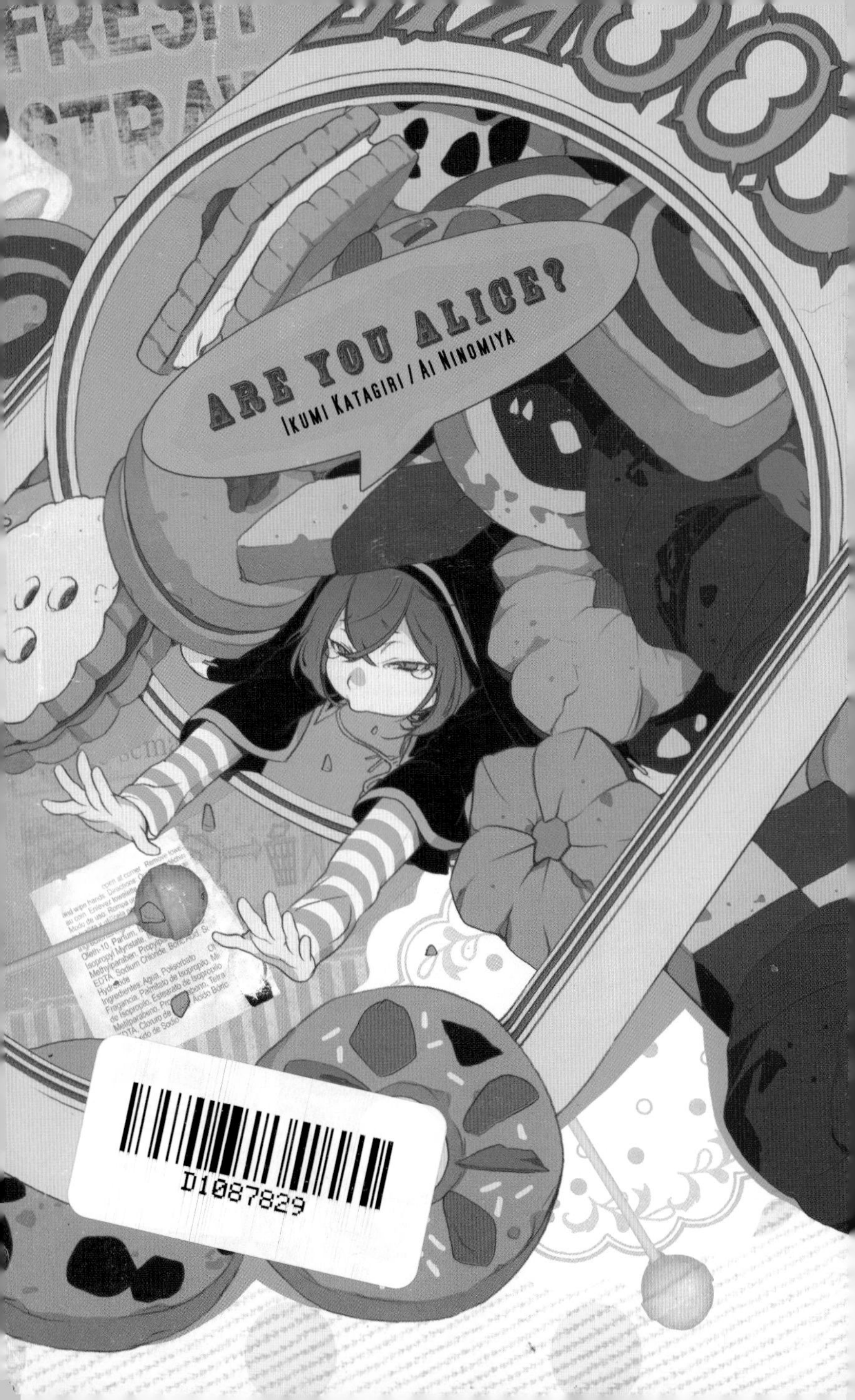
ARE YOU ALICE?
Ikumi Katagiri / Ai Ninomiya

Are You Alice?
6
CONTENTS!

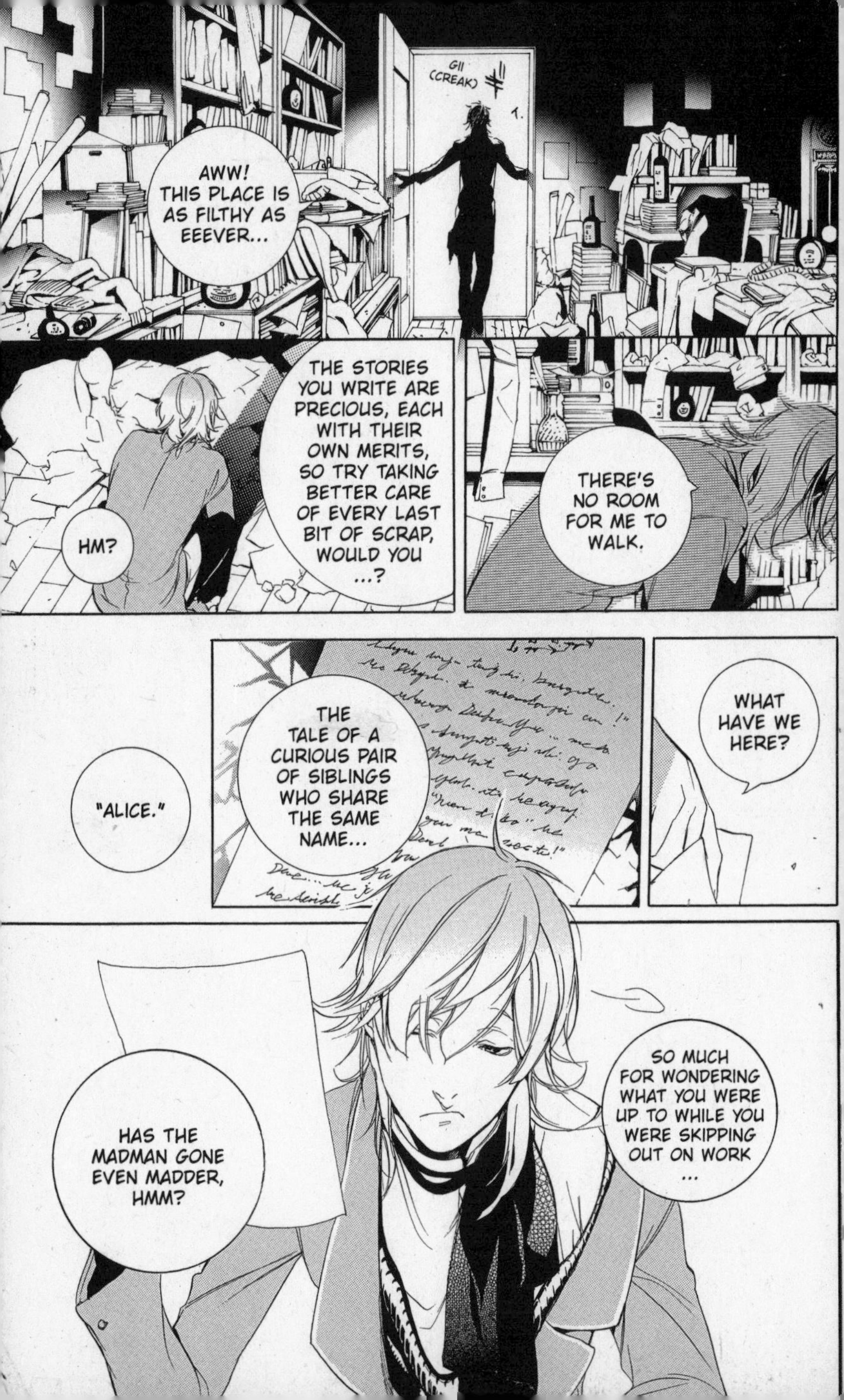
GII (CREAK)
AWW! THIS PLACE IS AS FILTHY AS EEEVER...
THERE'S NO ROOM FOR ME TO WALK.
THE STORIES YOU WRITE ARE PRECIOUS, EACH WITH THEIR OWN MERITS, SO TRY TAKING BETTER CARE OF EVERY LAST BIT OF SCRAP, WOULD YOU ...?
HM?
WHAT HAVE WE HERE?
THE TALE OF A CURIOUS PAIR OF SIBLINGS WHO SHARE THE SAME NAME...
"ALICE."
SO MUCH FOR WONDERING WHAT YOU WERE UP TO WHILE YOU WERE SKIPPING OUT ON WORK ...
HAS THE MADMAN GONE EVEN MADDER, HMM?

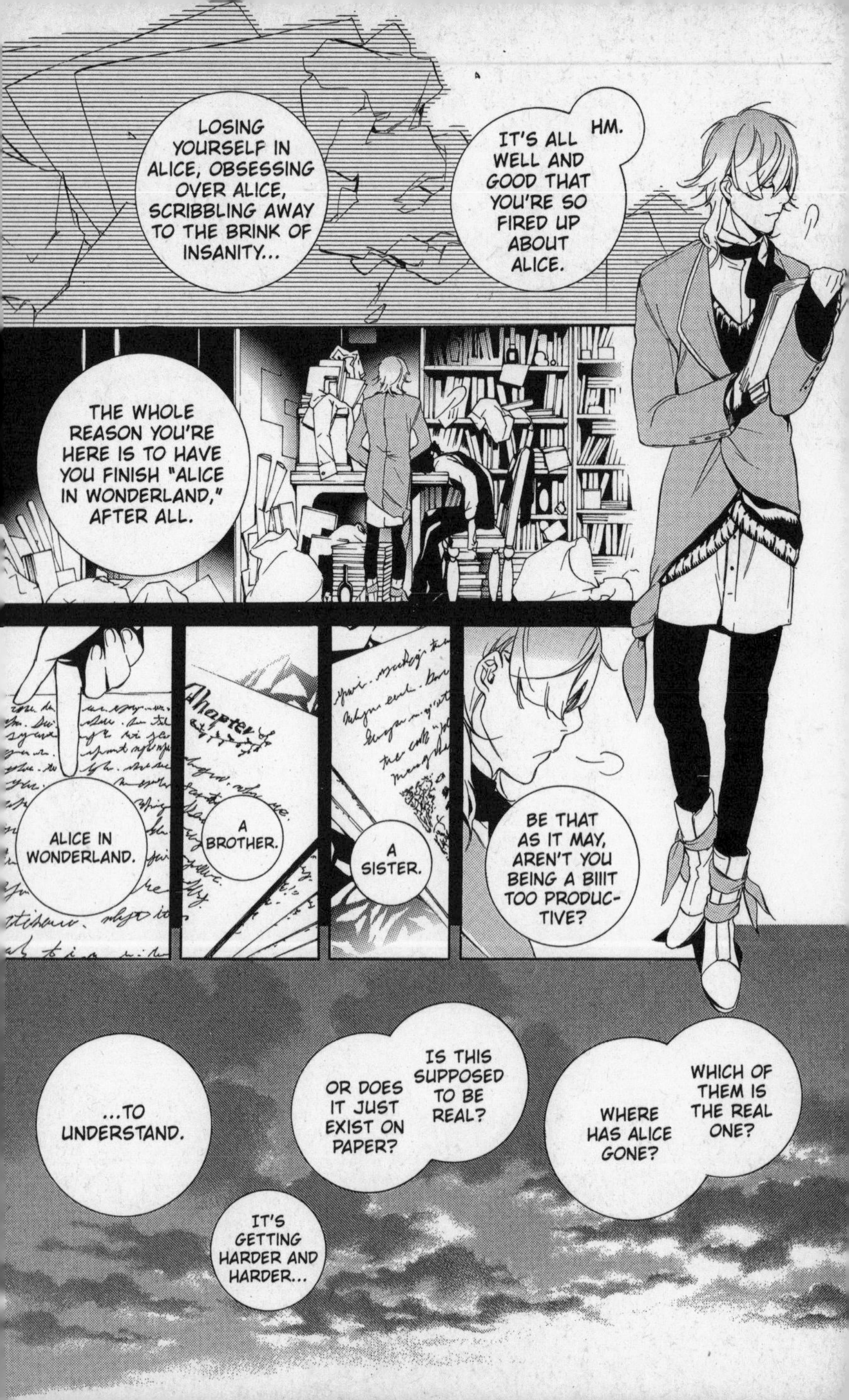
HM.
IT'S ALL WELL AND GOOD THAT YOU'RE SO FIRED UP ABOUT ALICE.
LOSING YOURSELF IN ALICE, OBSESSING OVER ALICE, SCRIBBLING AWAY TO THE BRINK OF INSANITY...
THE WHOLE REASON YOU'RE HERE IS TO HAVE YOU FINISH "ALICE IN WONDERLAND," AFTER ALL.
BE THAT AS IT MAY, AREN'T YOU BEING A BIIIT TOO PRODUCTIVE?
A SISTER.
A BROTHER.
ALICE IN WONDERLAND.
WHICH OF THEM IS THE REAL ONE?
WHERE HAS ALICE GONE?
IS THIS SUPPOSED TO BE REAL?
OR DOES IT JUST EXIST ON PAPER?
IT'S GETTING HARDER AND HARDER...
...TO UNDERSTAND.

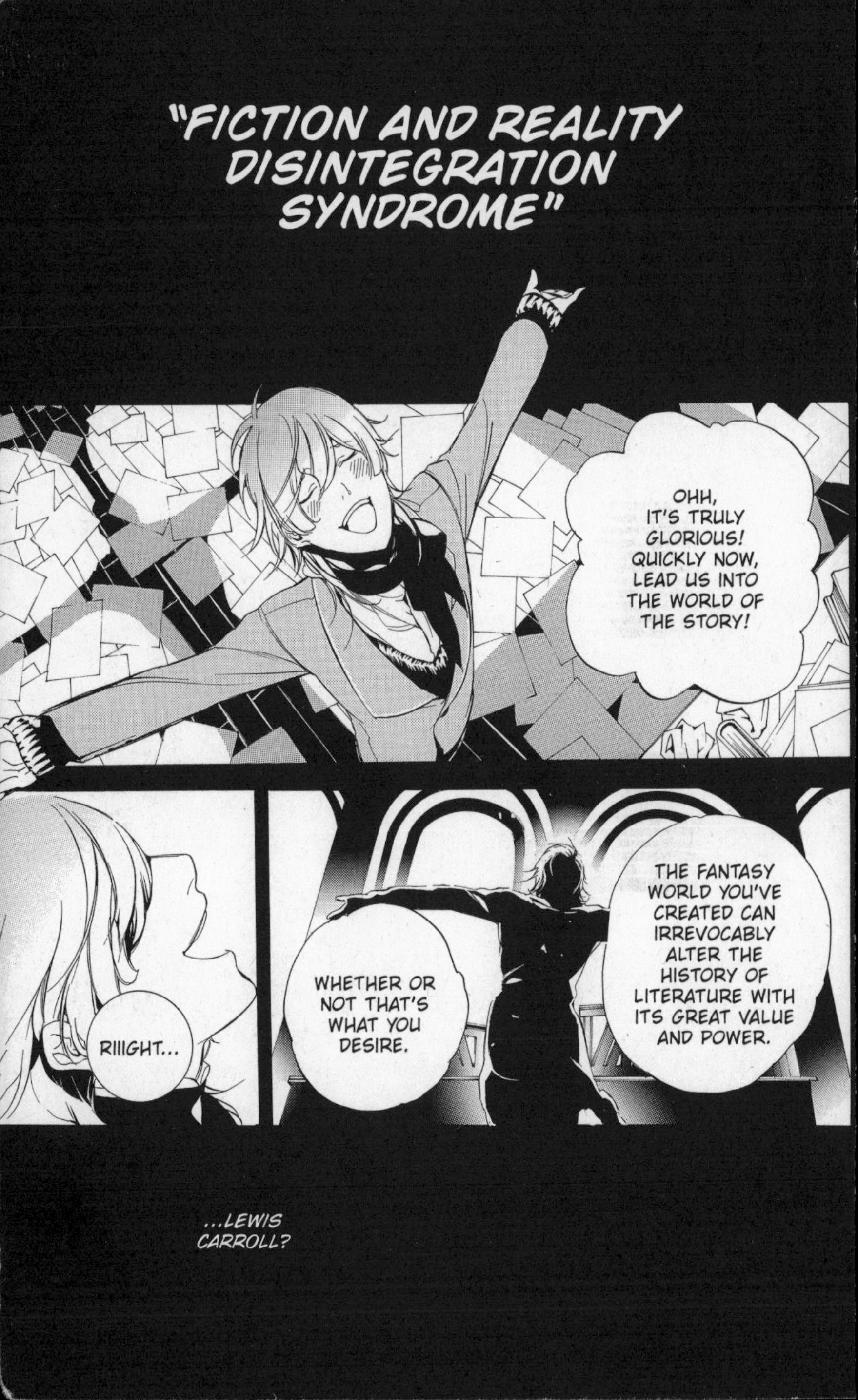
"FICTION AND REALITY DISINTEGRATION SYNDROME"
OHH, IT'S TRULY GLORIOUS! QUICKLY NOW, LEAD US INTO THE WORLD OF THE STORY!
THE FANTASY WORLD YOU'VE CREATED CAN IRREVOCABLY ALTER THE HISTORY OF LITERATURE WITH ITS GREAT VALUE AND POWER.
WHETHER OR NOT THAT'S WHAT YOU DESIRE.
RIIIGHT...
...LEWIS CARROLL?

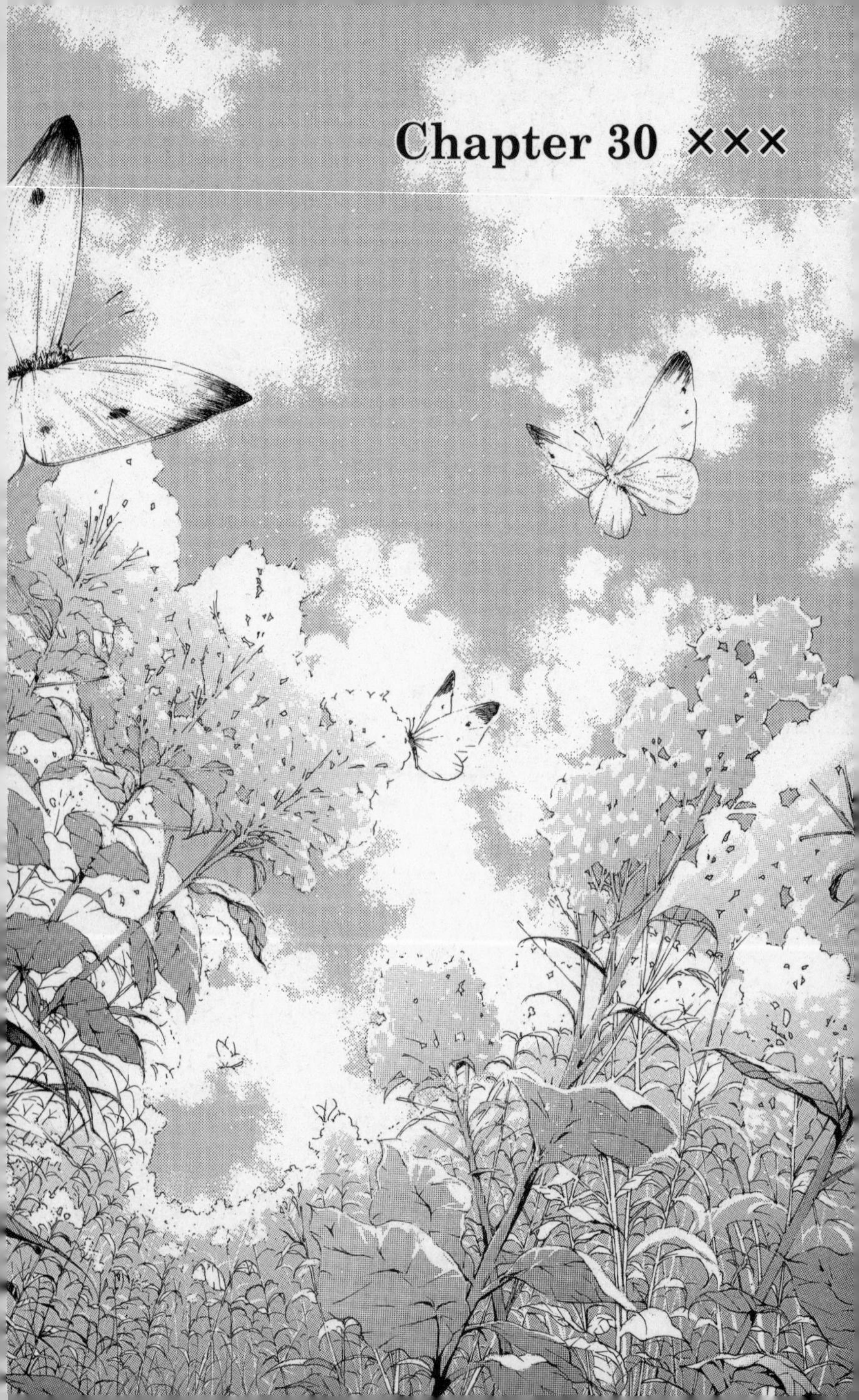
Chapter 30 ×××

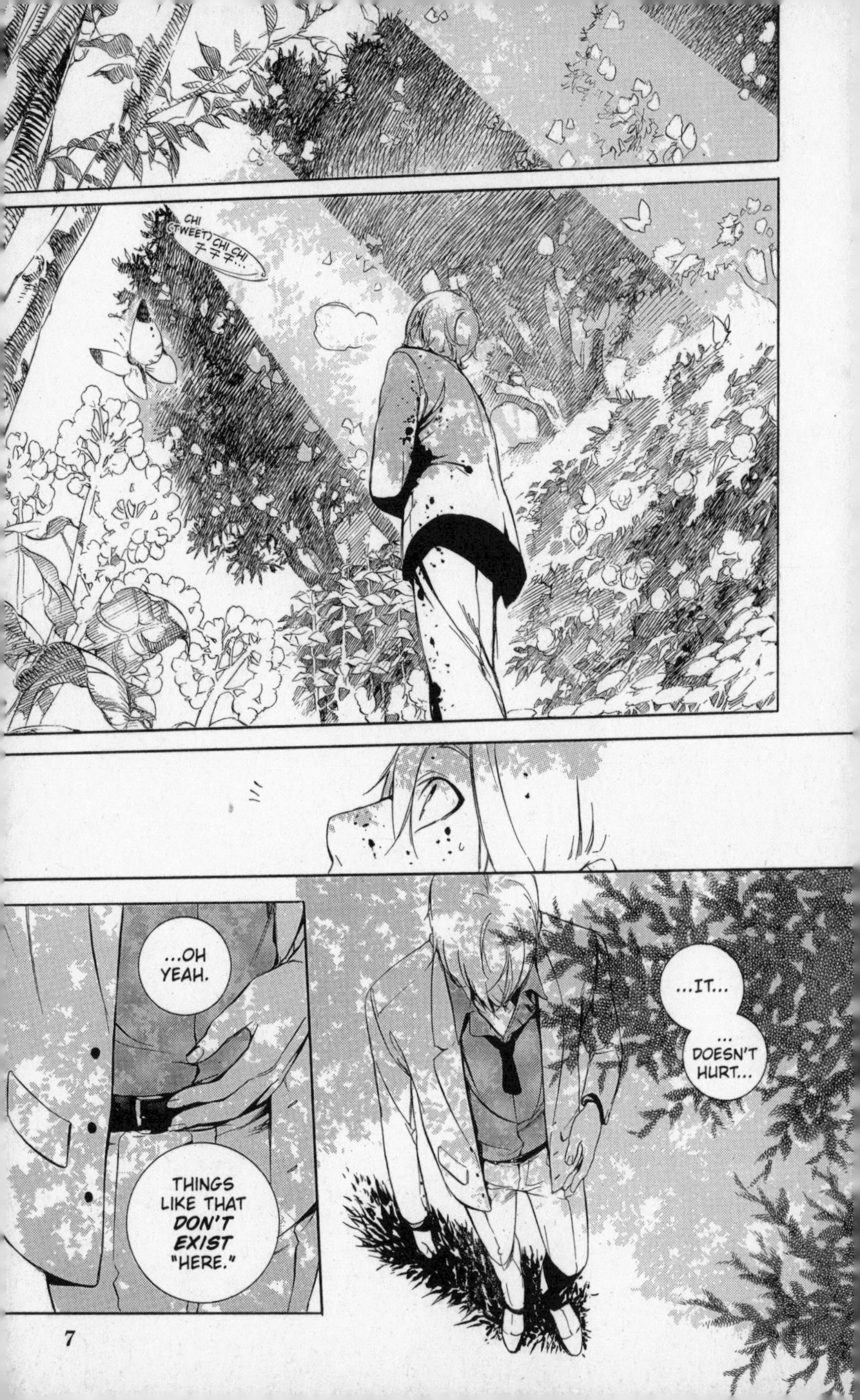
CHI
(TWEET) CHI CHI
チチチ…
...IT...
...DOESN'T HURT...
...OH YEAH.
THINGS LIKE THAT ***DON'T EXIST*** "HERE."

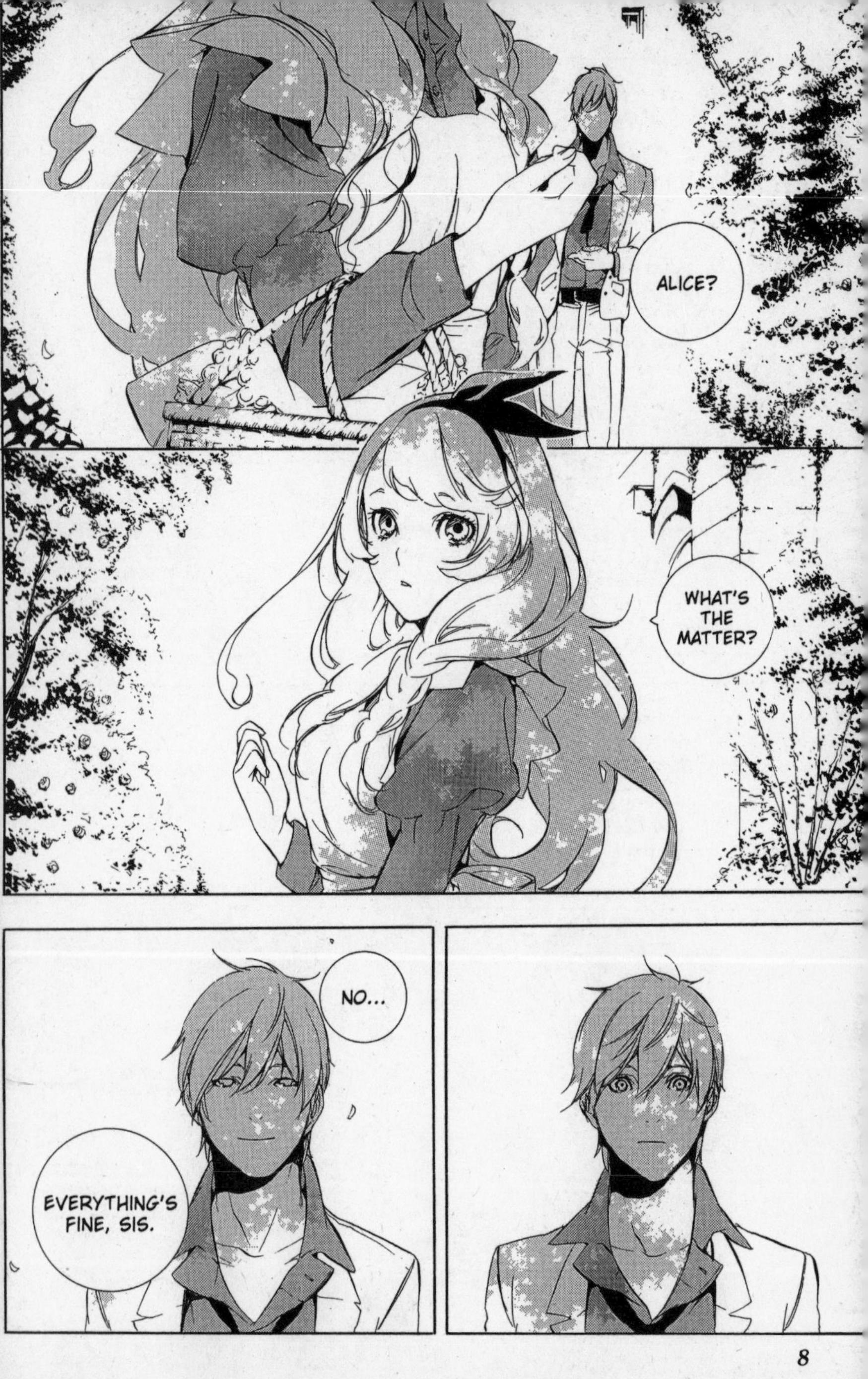
ALICE?
WHAT'S THE MATTER?
NO...
EVERYTHING'S FINE, SIS.

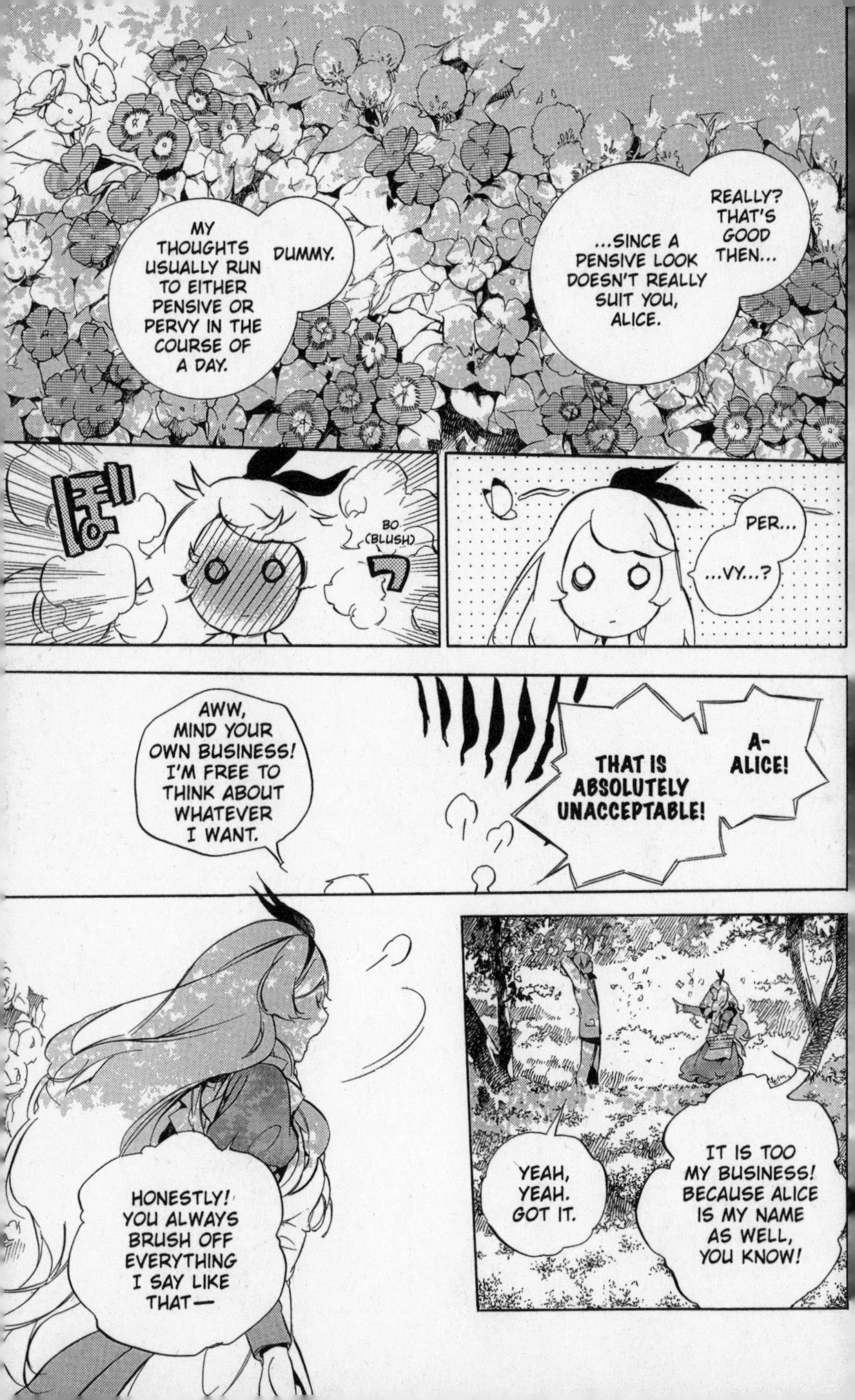
REALLY? THAT'S GOOD THEN...
...SINCE A PENSIVE LOOK DOESN'T REALLY SUIT YOU, ALICE.
DUMMY.
MY THOUGHTS USUALLY RUN TO EITHER PENSIVE OR PERVY IN THE COURSE OF A DAY.
PER...
...VY...?
ぼっ
BO (BLUSH)
A- ALICE!
THAT IS ABSOLUTELY UNACCEPTABLE!
AWW, MIND YOUR OWN BUSINESS! I'M FREE TO THINK ABOUT WHATEVER I WANT.
IT IS TOO MY BUSINESS! BECAUSE ALICE IS MY NAME AS WELL, YOU KNOW!
YEAH, YEAH. GOT IT.
HONESTLY! YOU ALWAYS BRUSH OFF EVERYTHING I SAY LIKE THAT—

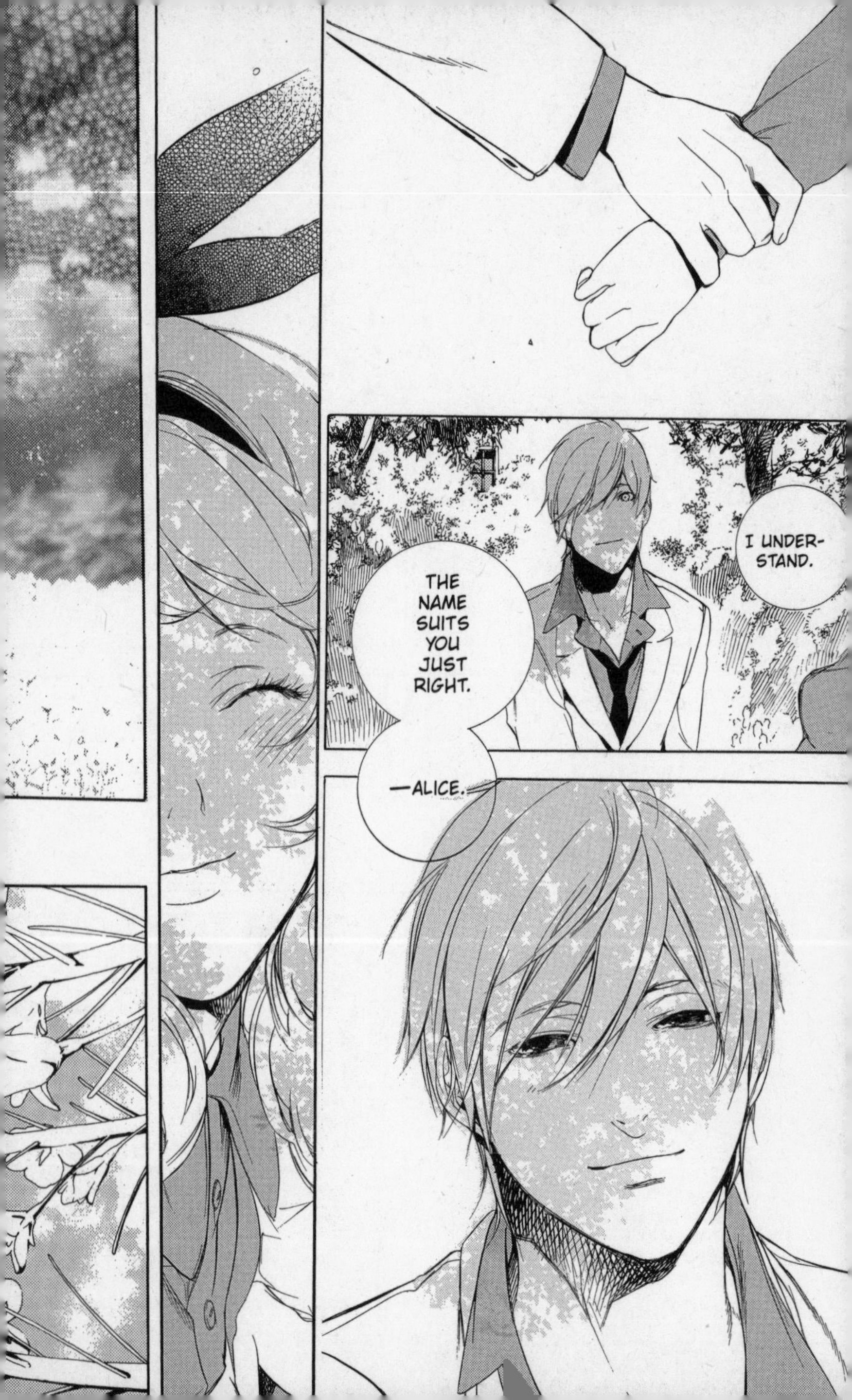
I UNDER-STAND.
THE NAME SUITS YOU JUST RIGHT.
—ALICE.

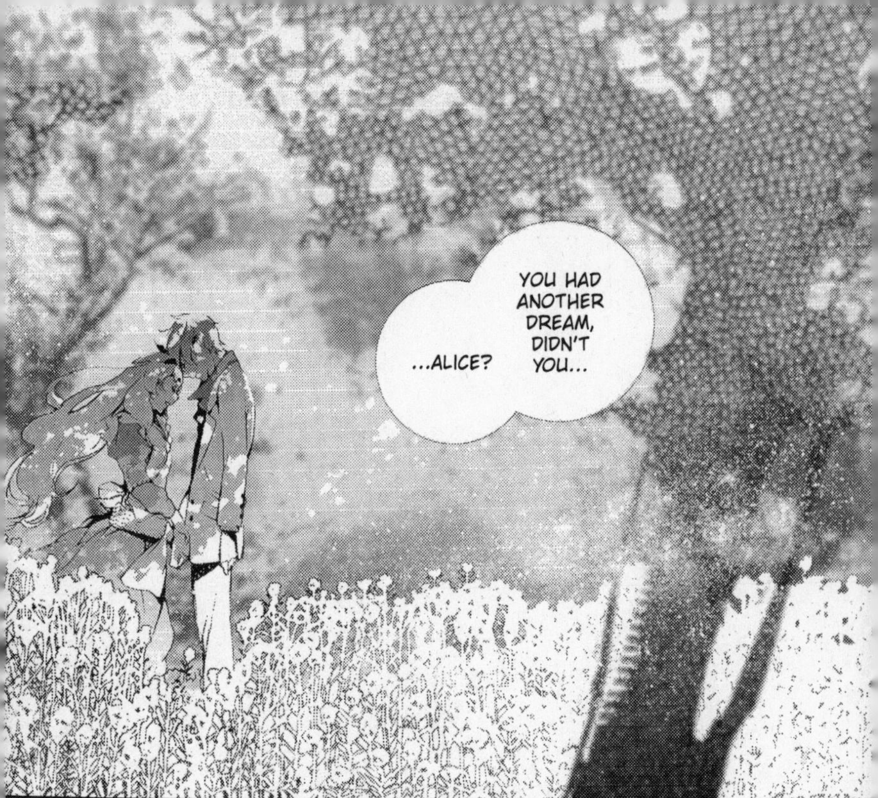
YOU HAD ANOTHER DREAM, DIDN'T YOU...
...ALICE?

*YES, I'M BLISSFULLY HAPPY NOW.*

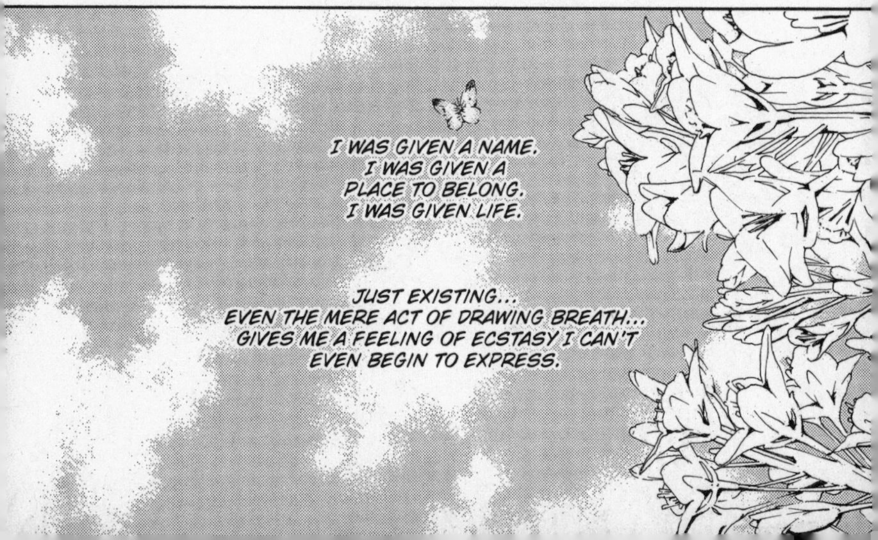
I WAS GIVEN A NAME. I WAS GIVEN A PLACE TO BELONG. I WAS GIVEN LIFE.
JUST EXISTING... EVEN THE MERE ACT OF DRAWING BREATH... GIVES ME A FEELING OF ECSTASY I CAN'T EVEN BEGIN TO EXPRESS.

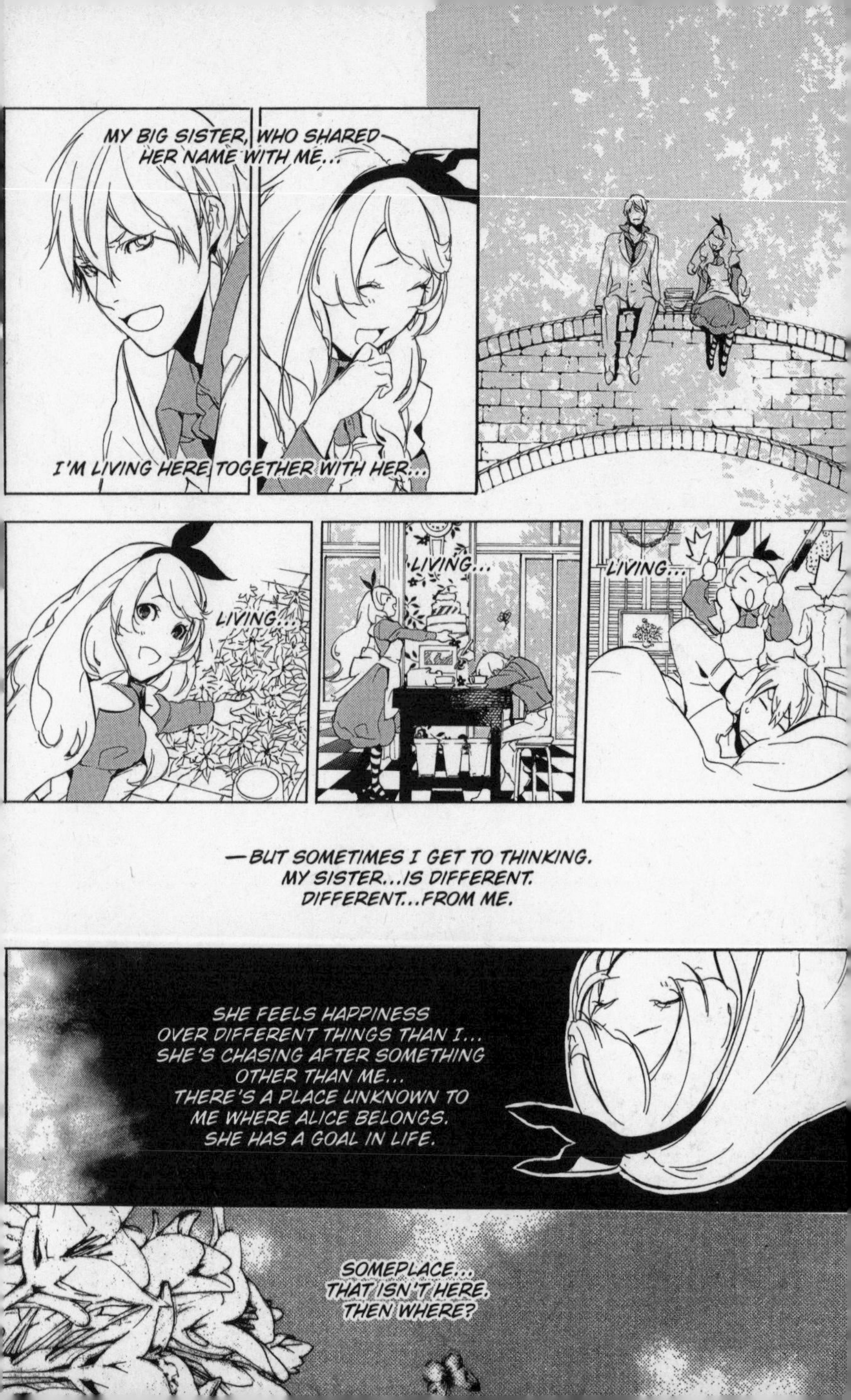
MY BIG SISTER, WHO SHARED HER NAME WITH ME...
I'M LIVING HERE TOGETHER WITH HER...
LIVING...
LIVING...
LIVING...
—BUT SOMETIMES I GET TO THINKING. MY SISTER...IS DIFFERENT. DIFFERENT...FROM ME.
SHE FEELS HAPPINESS OVER DIFFERENT THINGS THAN I... SHE'S CHASING AFTER SOMETHING OTHER THAN ME... THERE'S A PLACE UNKNOWN TO ME WHERE ALICE BELONGS. SHE HAS A GOAL IN LIFE.
SOMEPLACE... THAT ISN'T HERE. THEN WHERE?

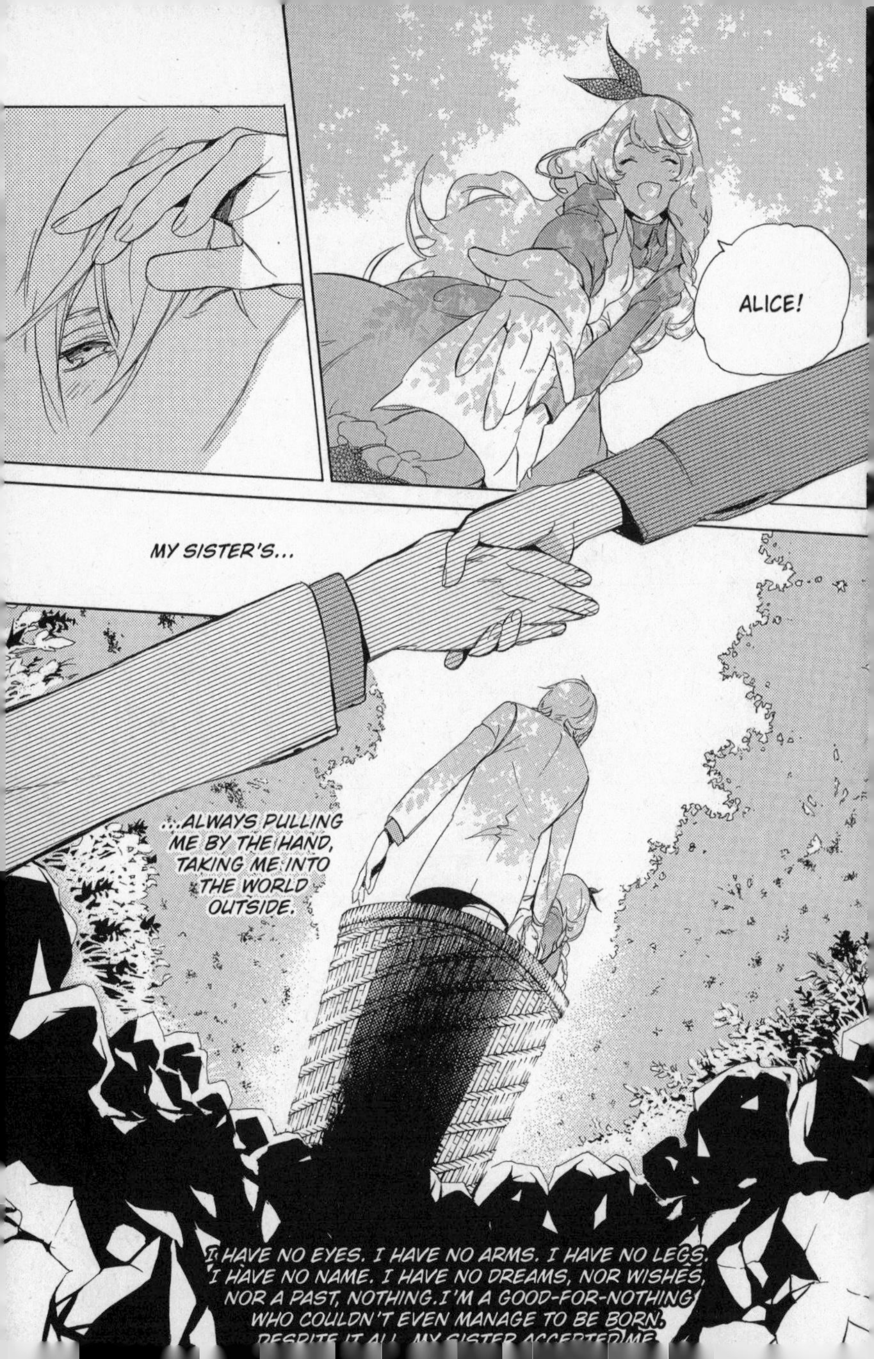
ALICE!
MY SISTER'S...
...ALWAYS PULLING ME BY THE HAND, TAKING ME INTO THE WORLD OUTSIDE.
I HAVE NO EYES. I HAVE NO ARMS. I HAVE NO LEGS. I HAVE NO NAME. I HAVE NO DREAMS, NOR WISHES, NOR A PAST, NOTHING. I'M A GOOD-FOR-NOTHING WHO COULDN'T EVEN MANAGE TO BE BORN.
DESPITE IT ALL, MY SISTER ACCEPTED ME.

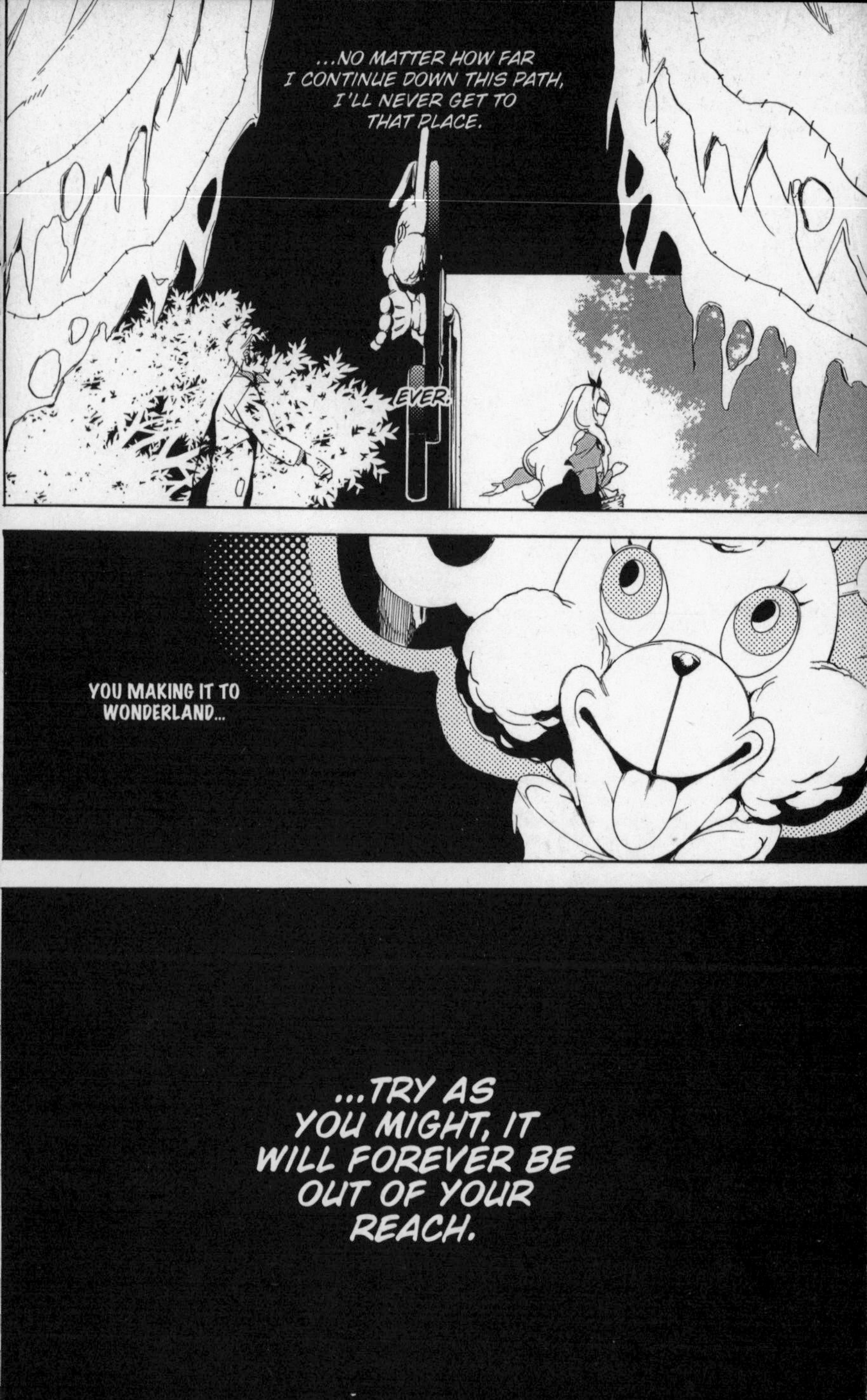
...NO MATTER HOW FAR I CONTINUE DOWN THIS PATH, I'LL NEVER GET TO THAT PLACE.
EVER.
YOU MAKING IT TO WONDERLAND...
...TRY AS YOU MIGHT, IT WILL FOREVER BE OUT OF YOUR REACH.

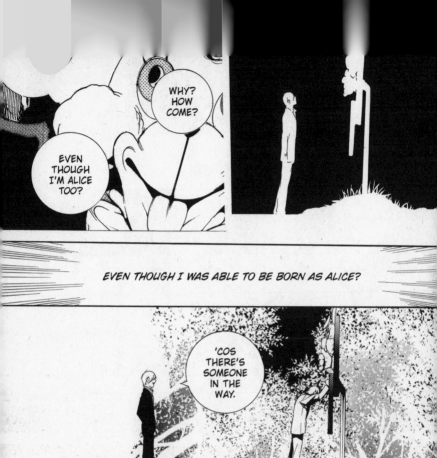

WHY? HOW COME?

EVEN THOUGH I'M ALICE TOO?

EVEN THOUGH I WAS ABLE TO BE BORN AS ALICE?

'COS THERE'S SOMEONE IN THE WAY.

THERE'S AN *ALICE* IN THE WAY OF MY BEING BORN.

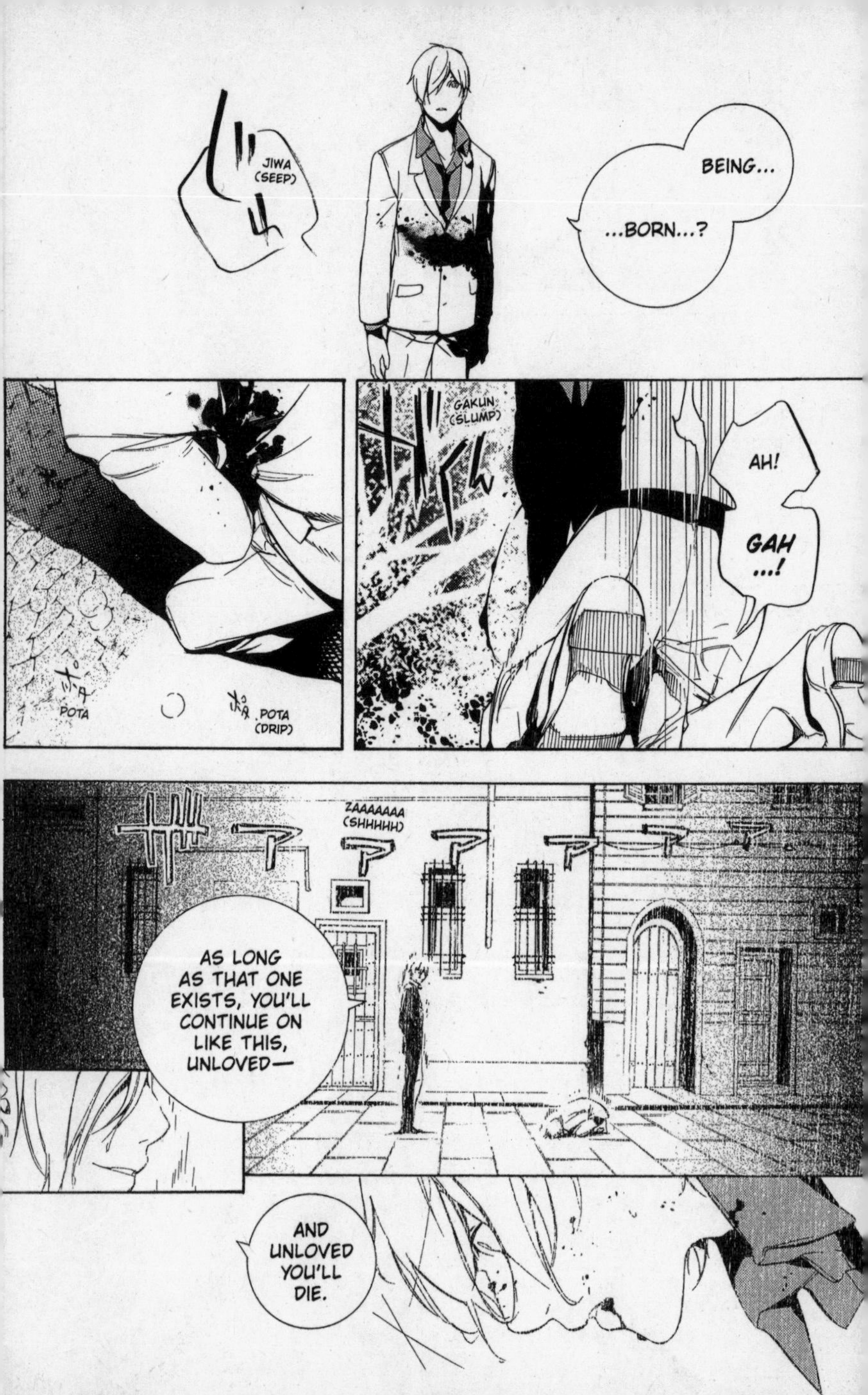
BEING...
...BORN...?
JIWA (SEEP)
GAKUN (SLUMP)
AH! GAH...!
POTA
POTA (DRIP)
ZAAAAAAA (SHHHHH)
AS LONG AS THAT ONE EXISTS, YOU'LL CONTINUE ON LIKE THIS, UNLOVED—
AND UNLOVED YOU'LL DIE.

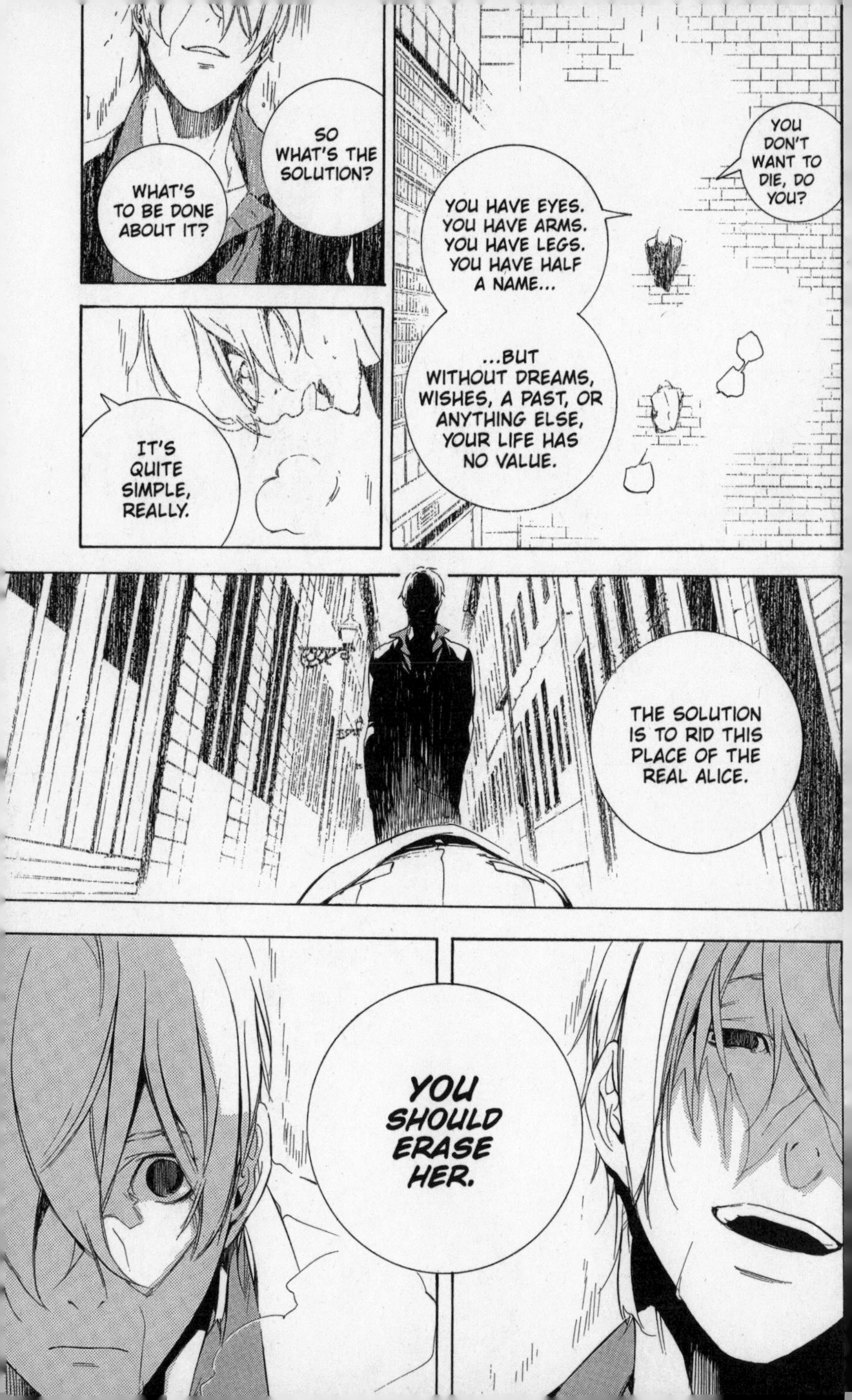
YOU DON'T WANT TO DIE, DO YOU?
YOU HAVE EYES. YOU HAVE ARMS. YOU HAVE LEGS. YOU HAVE HALF A NAME...
...BUT WITHOUT DREAMS, WISHES, A PAST, OR ANYTHING ELSE, YOUR LIFE HAS NO VALUE.
SO WHAT'S THE SOLUTION?
WHAT'S TO BE DONE ABOUT IT?
IT'S QUITE SIMPLE, REALLY.
THE SOLUTION IS TO RID THIS PLACE OF THE REAL ALICE.
YOU SHOULD ERASE HER.

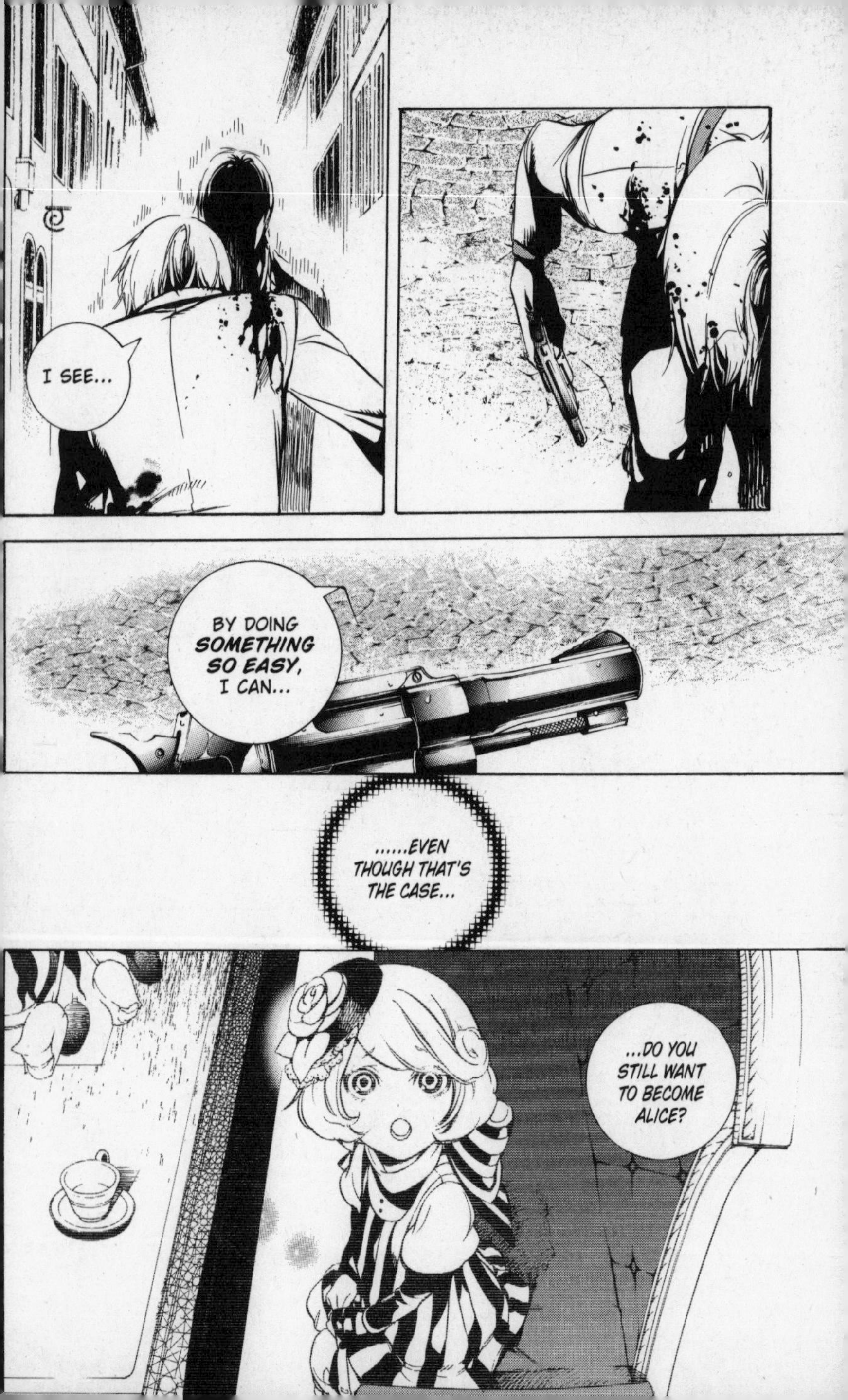
I SEE...
BY DOING SOMETHING SO EASY, I CAN...
......EVEN THOUGH THAT'S THE CASE...
...DO YOU STILL WANT TO BECOME ALICE?

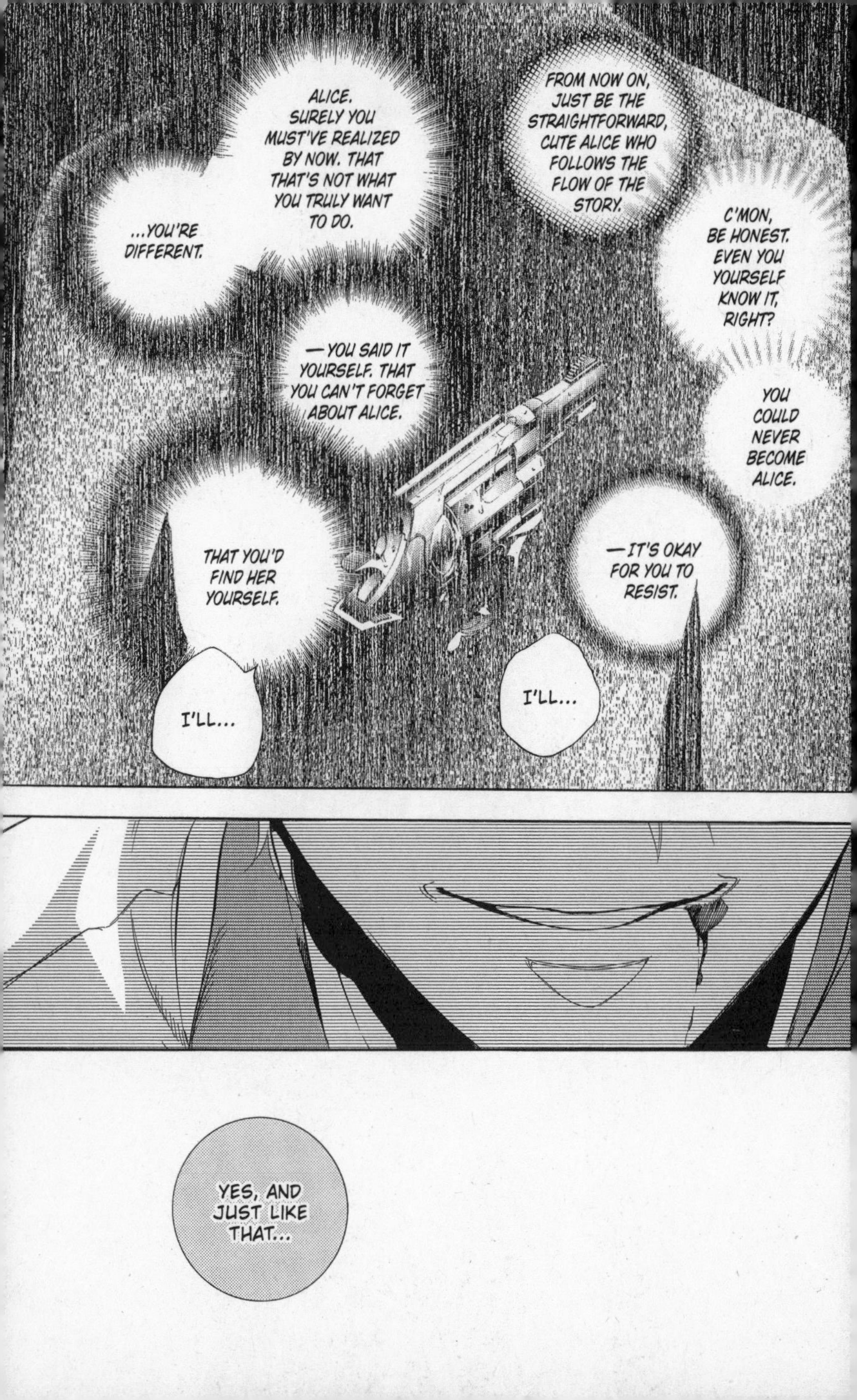
FROM NOW ON, JUST BE THE STRAIGHTFORWARD, CUTE ALICE WHO FOLLOWS THE FLOW OF THE STORY.
C'MON, BE HONEST. EVEN YOU YOURSELF KNOW IT, RIGHT?
ALICE. SURELY YOU MUST'VE REALIZED BY NOW. THAT THAT'S NOT WHAT YOU TRULY WANT TO DO.
...YOU'RE DIFFERENT.
YOU COULD NEVER BECOME ALICE.
—YOU SAID IT YOURSELF. THAT YOU CAN'T FORGET ABOUT ALICE.
—IT'S OKAY FOR YOU TO RESIST.
THAT YOU'D FIND HER YOURSELF.
I'LL...
I'LL...
YES, AND JUST LIKE THAT...

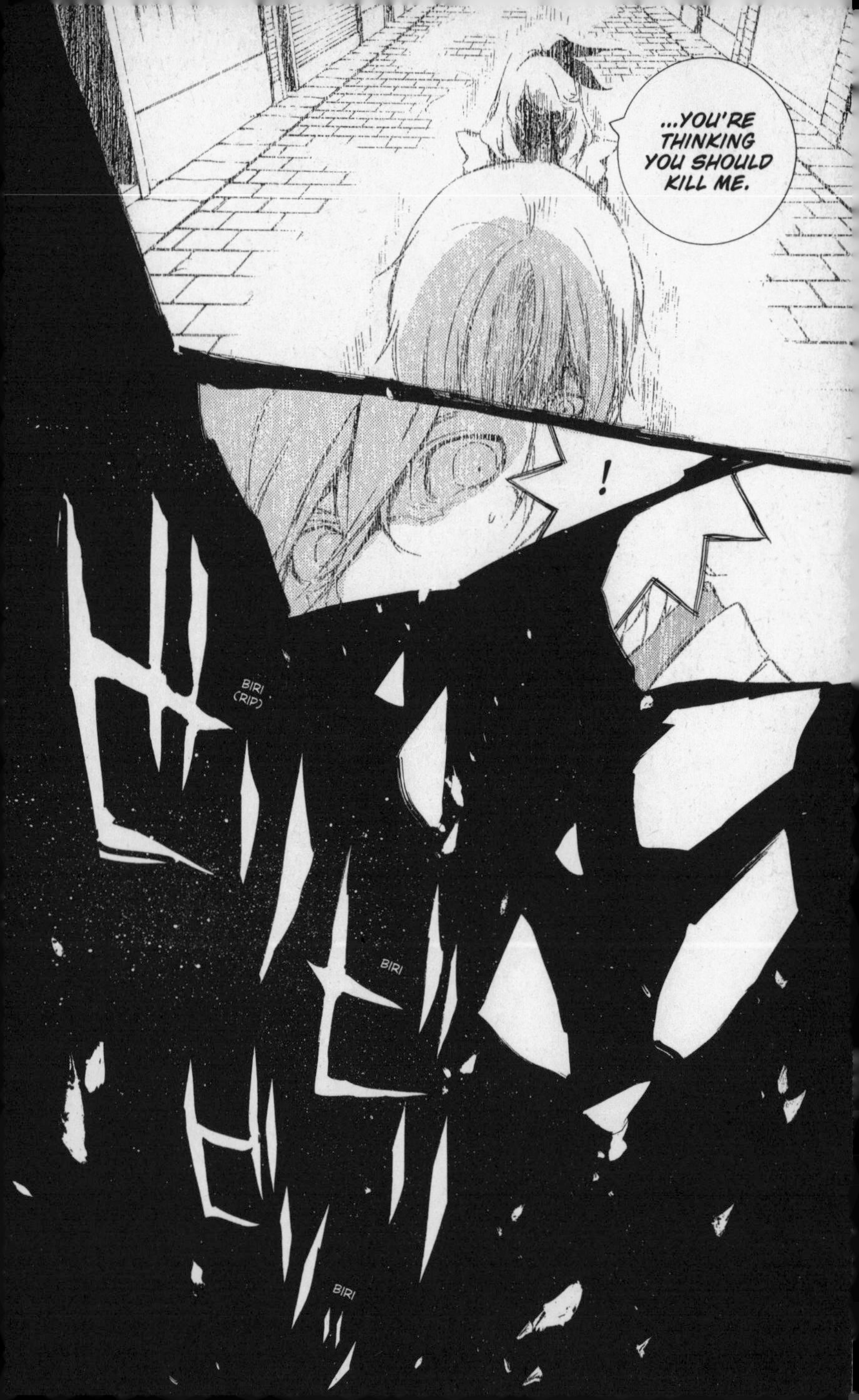
...YOU'RE THINKING YOU SHOULD KILL ME.
!
BIRI (RIP)
BIRI
BIRI

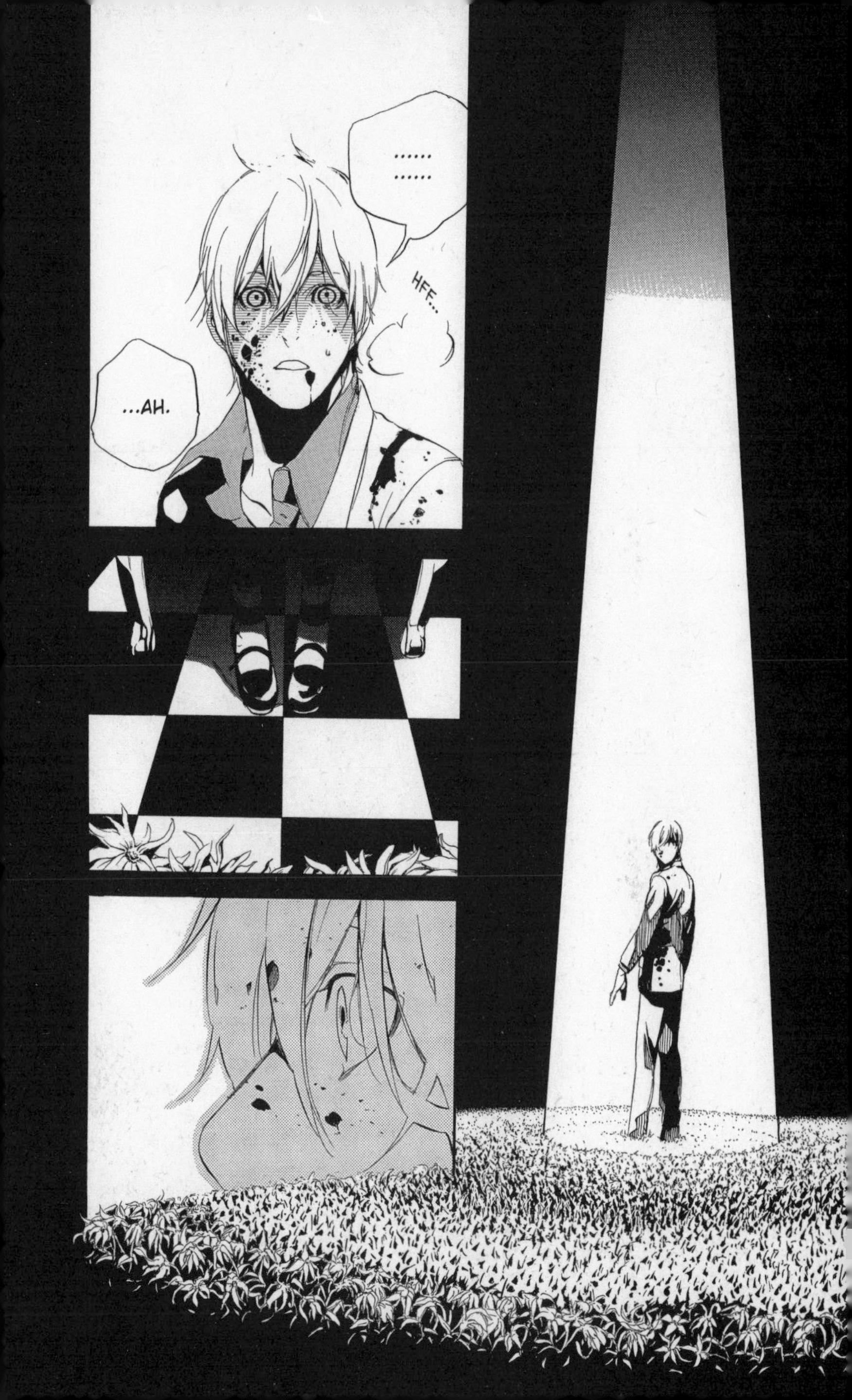
......
......
HFF...
...AH.

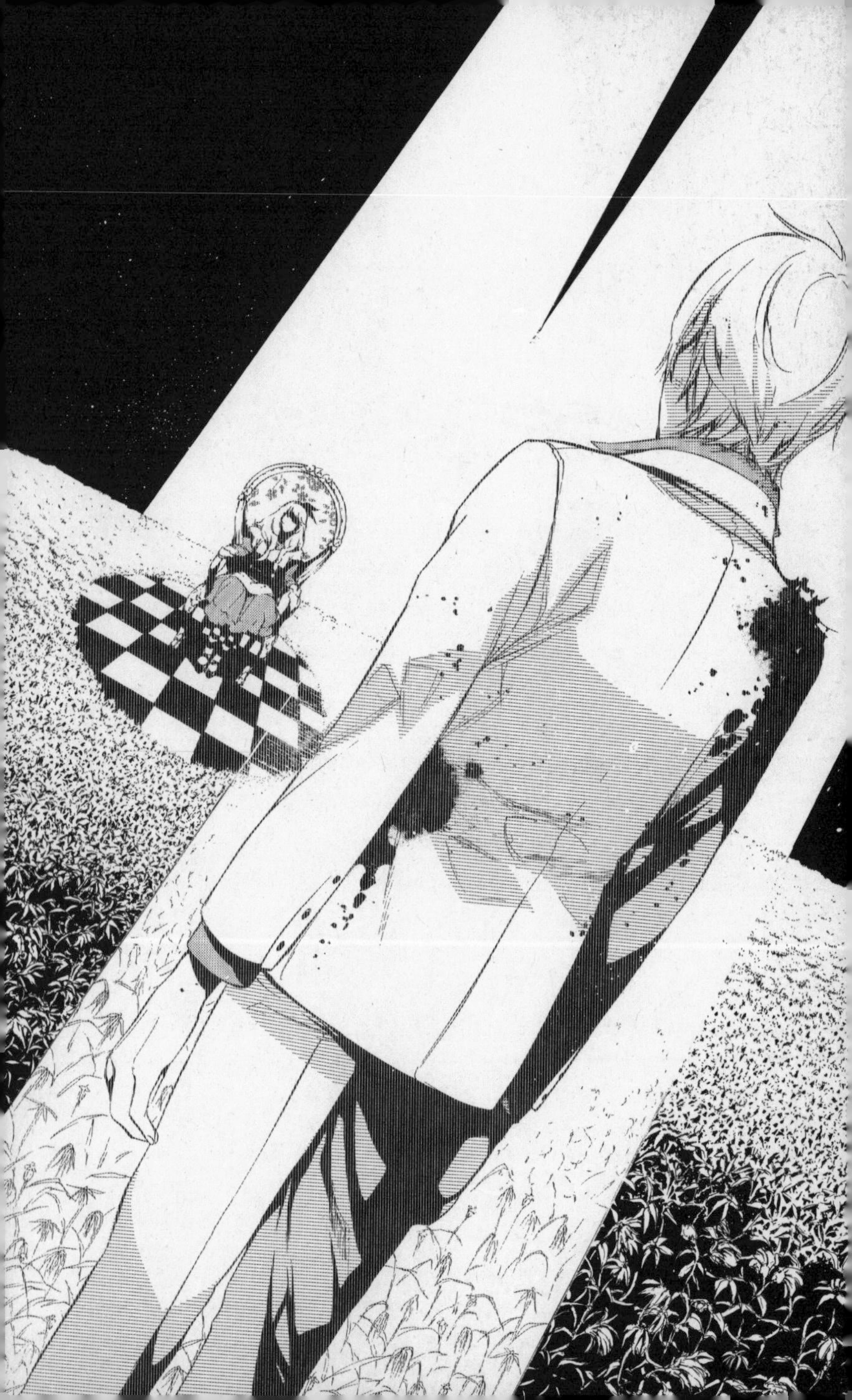

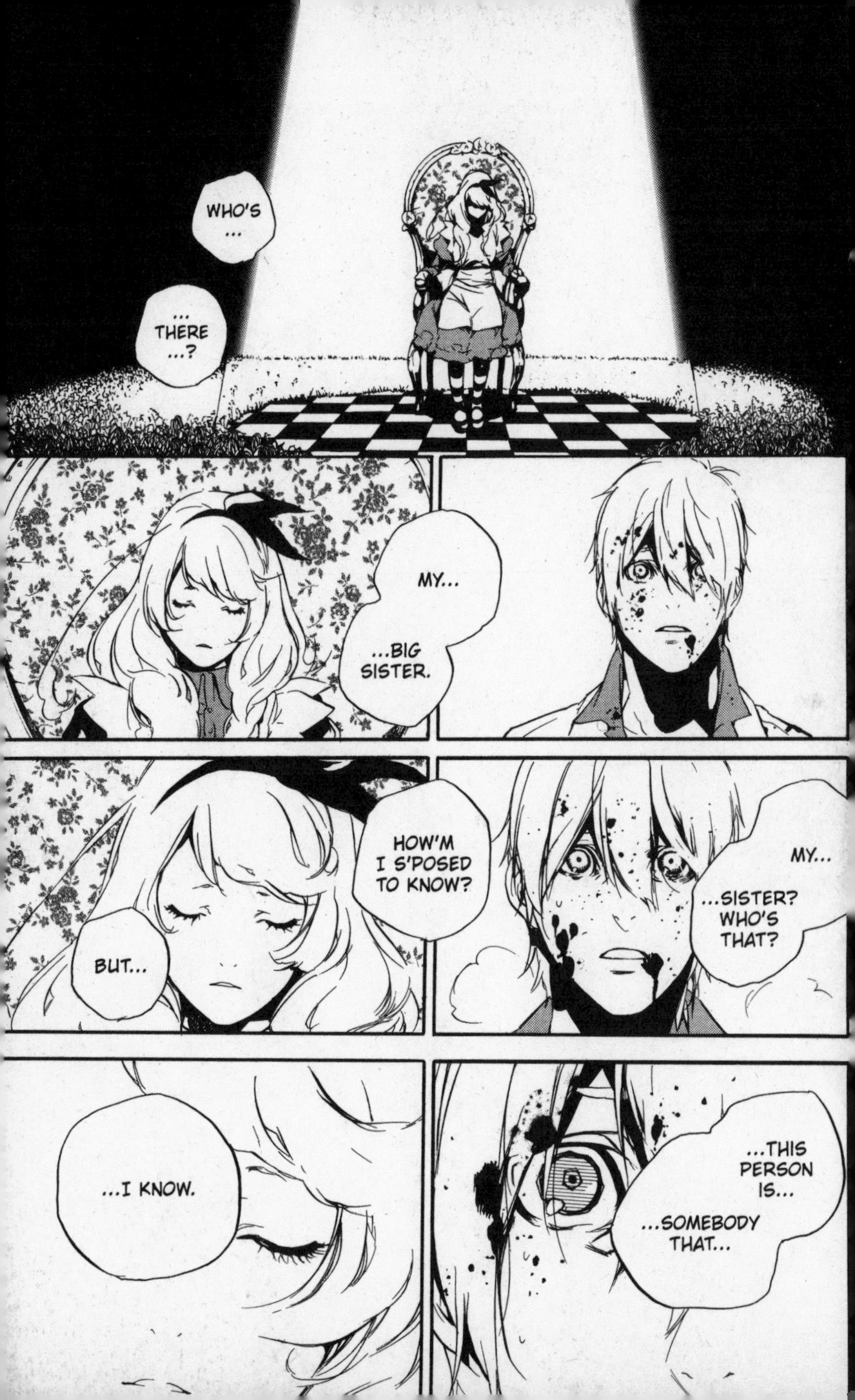
WHO'S ...
... THERE ...?
MY...
...BIG SISTER.
MY...
...SISTER? WHO'S THAT?
HOW'M I S'POSED TO KNOW?
BUT...
...THIS PERSON IS...
...SOMEBODY THAT...
...I KNOW.

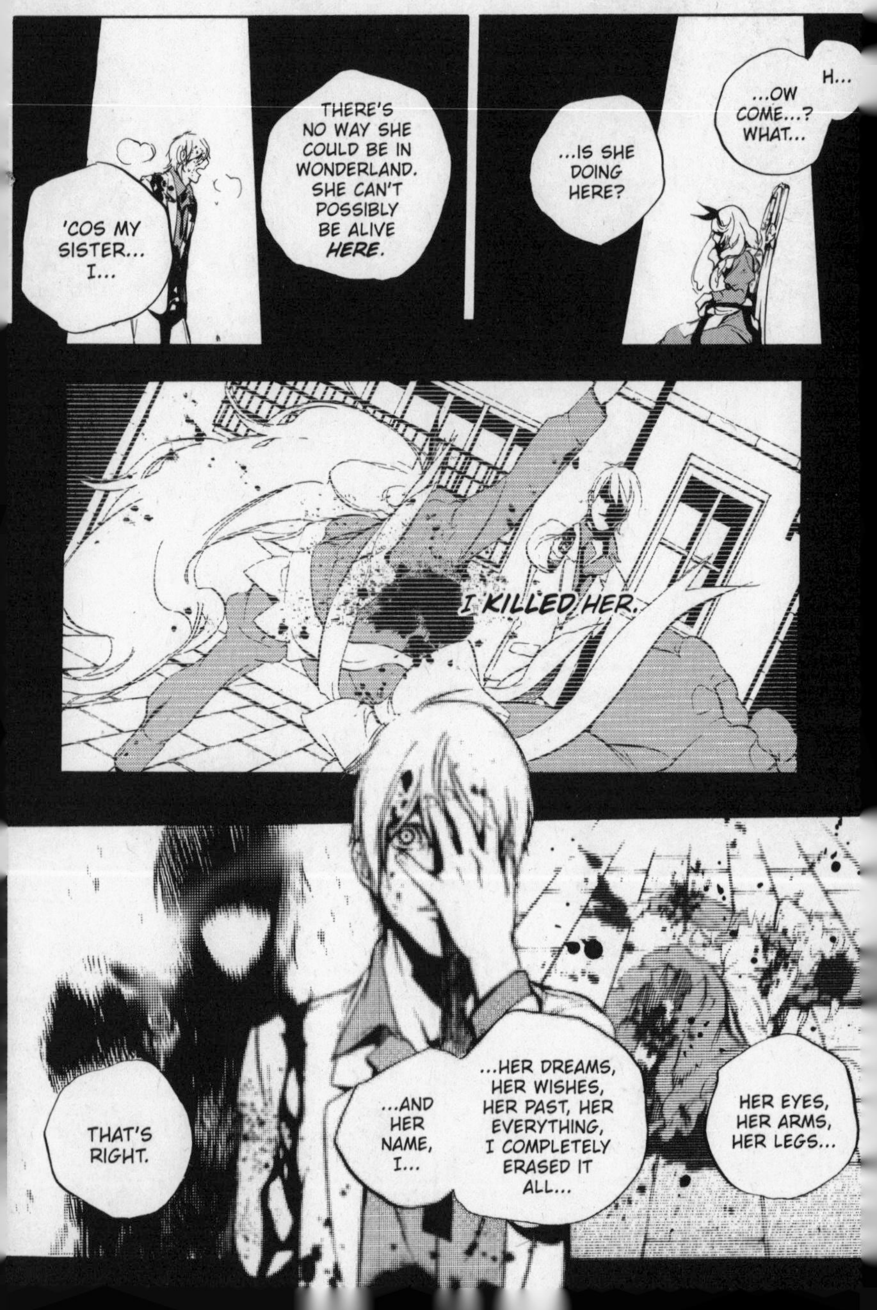
H...
...OW COME...? WHAT...
...IS SHE DOING HERE?
THERE'S NO WAY SHE COULD BE IN WONDERLAND. SHE CAN'T POSSIBLY BE ALIVE *HERE*.
'COS MY SISTER... I...
I KILLED HER.
HER EYES, HER ARMS, HER LEGS...
...HER DREAMS, HER WISHES, HER PAST, HER EVERYTHING, I COMPLETELY ERASED IT ALL...
...AND HER NAME, I...
THAT'S RIGHT.

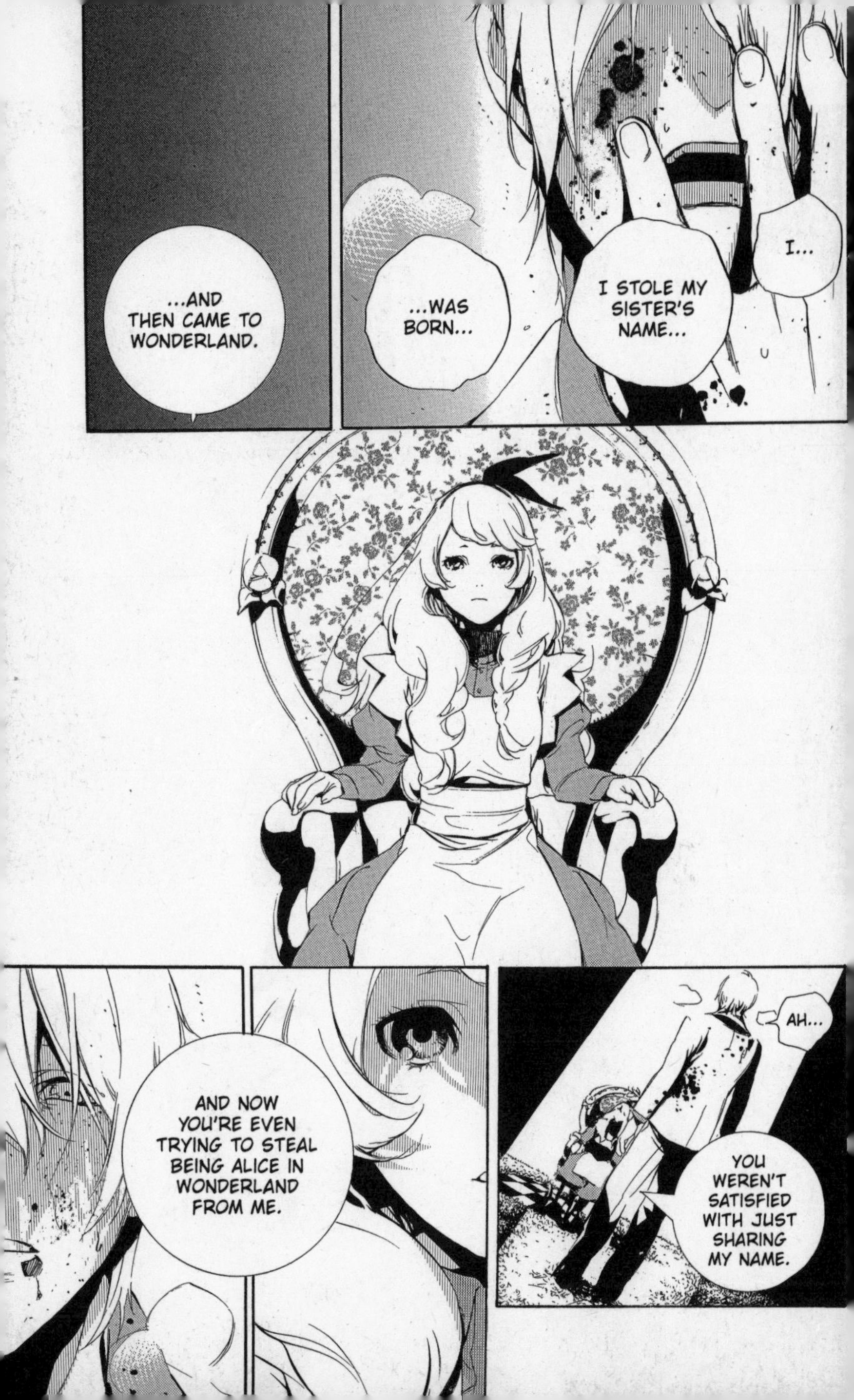
I...
I STOLE MY SISTER'S NAME...
...WAS BORN...
...AND THEN CAME TO WONDERLAND.
AH...
YOU WEREN'T SATISFIED WITH JUST SHARING MY NAME.
AND NOW YOU'RE EVEN TRYING TO STEAL BEING ALICE IN WONDERLAND FROM ME.

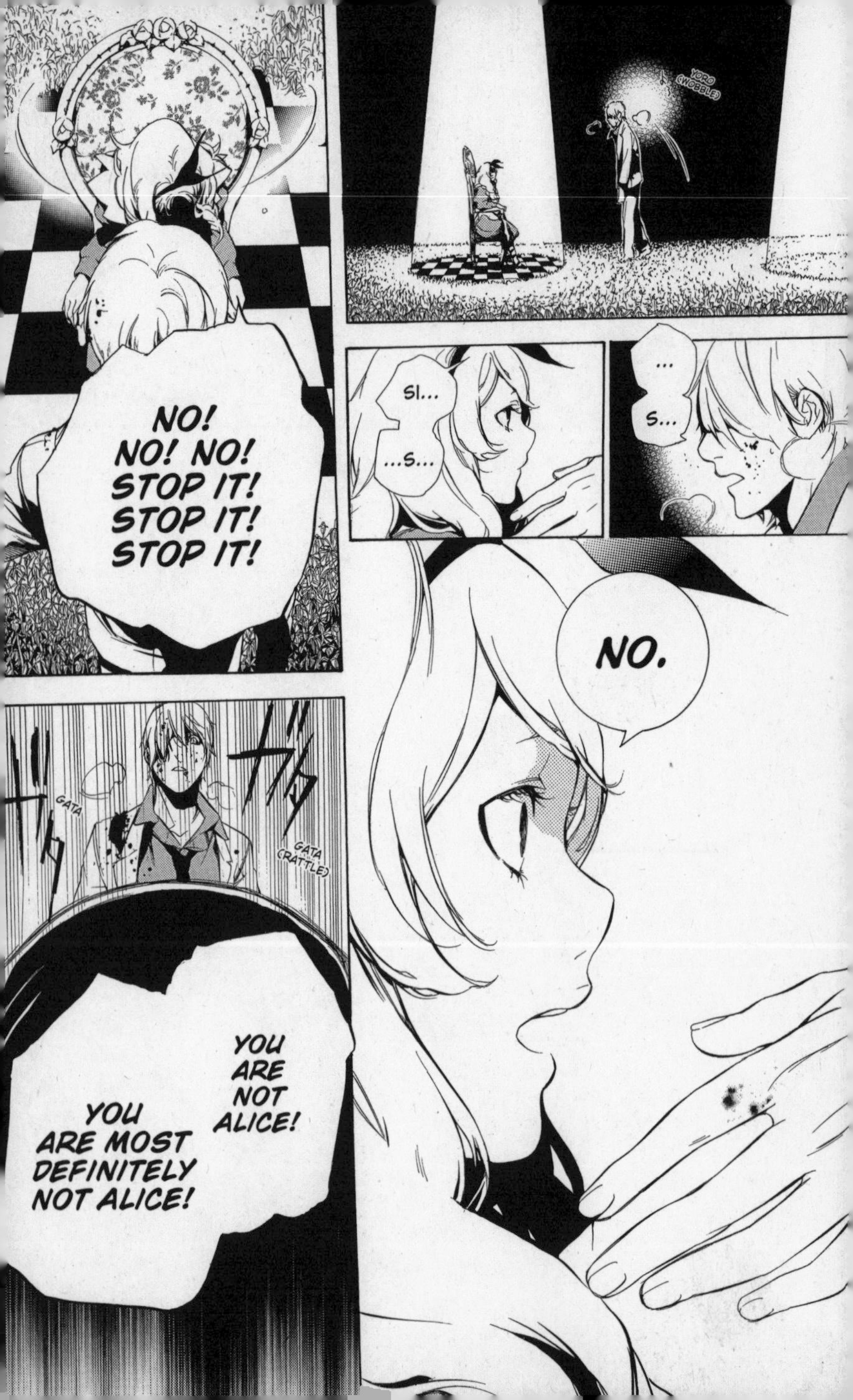
YORO (WOBBLE)
...
S...
SI...
...S...
NO! NO! NO! STOP IT! STOP IT! STOP IT!
NO.
GATA
GATA (RATTLE)
YOU ARE NOT ALICE!
YOU ARE MOST DEFINITELY NOT ALICE!

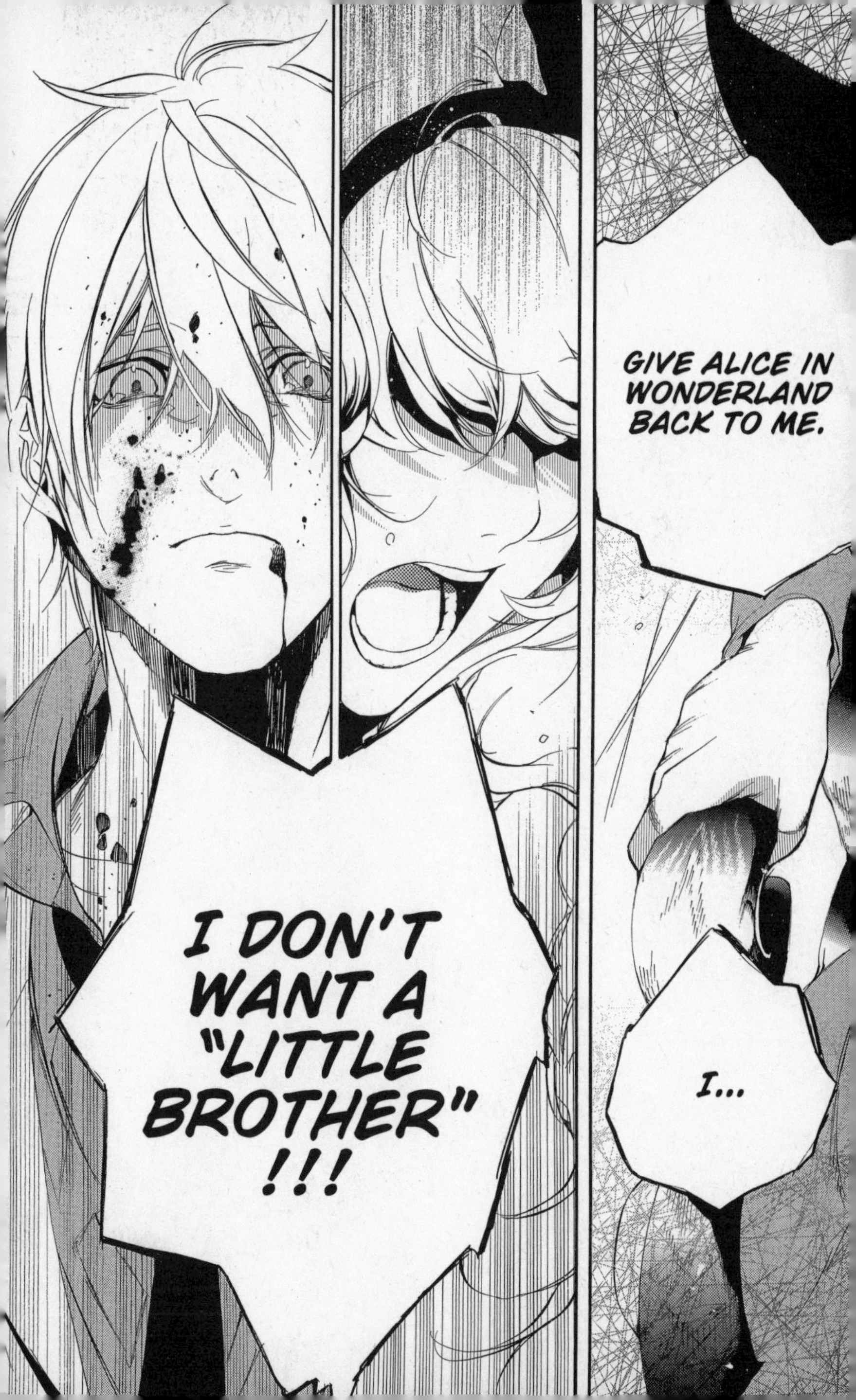
GIVE ALICE IN WONDERLAND BACK TO ME.
I...
I DON'T WANT A "LITTLE BROTHER" !!!

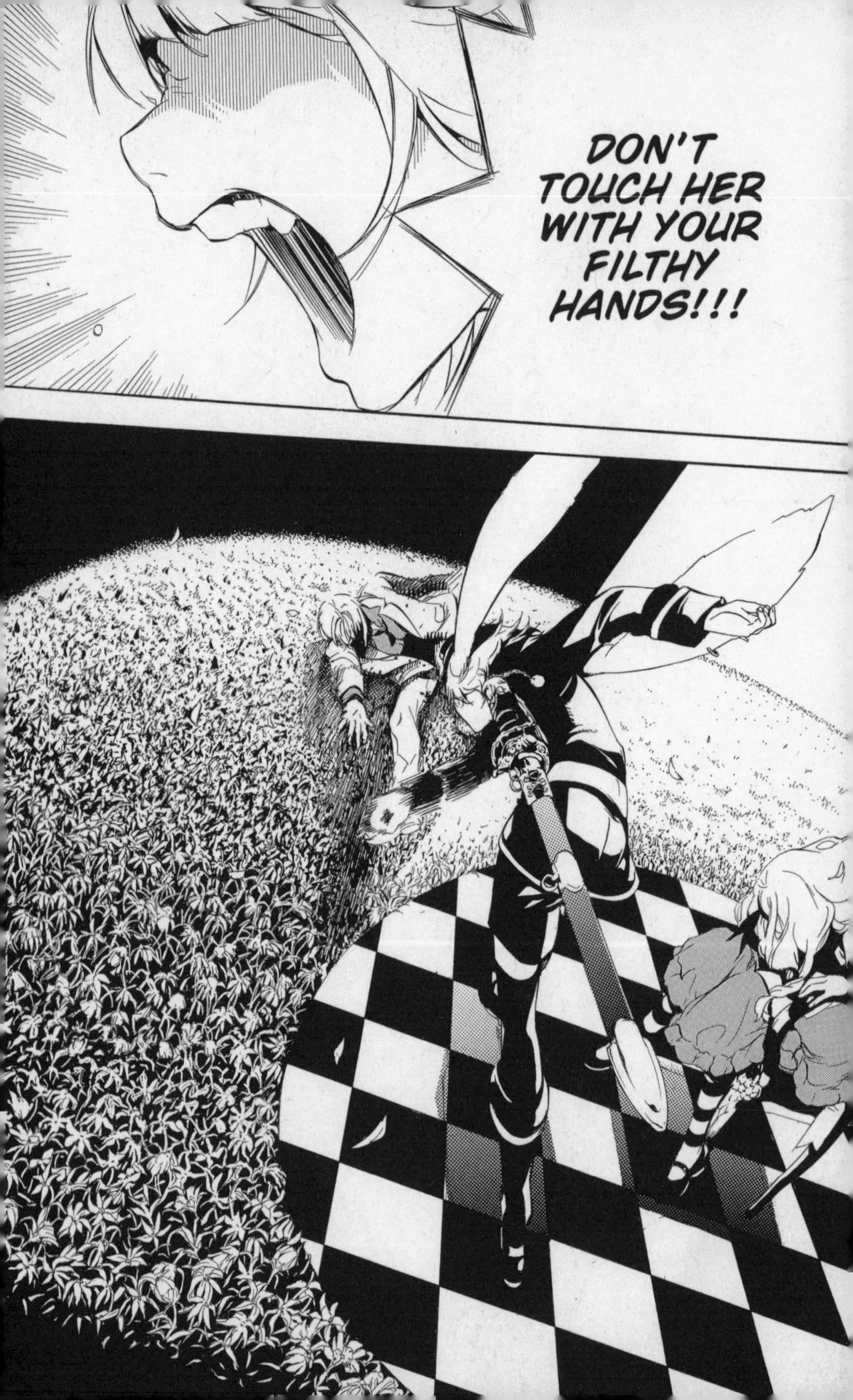
DON'T TOUCH HER WITH YOUR FILTHY HANDS!!!

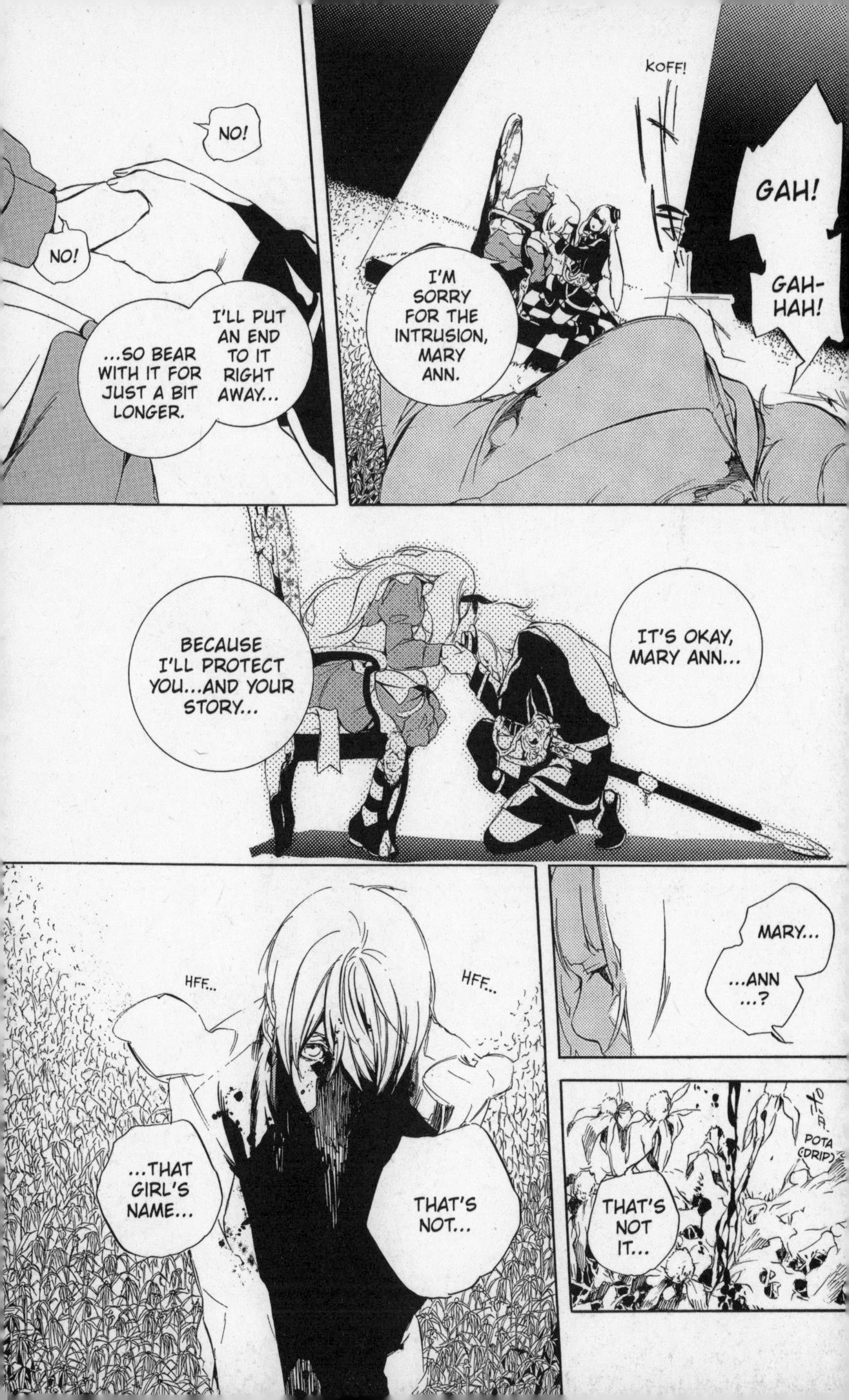
KOFF!
GAH!
GAH-HAH!
I'M SORRY FOR THE INTRUSION, MARY ANN.
NO!
NO!
I'LL PUT AN END TO IT RIGHT AWAY...
...SO BEAR WITH IT FOR JUST A BIT LONGER.
IT'S OKAY, MARY ANN...
BECAUSE I'LL PROTECT YOU...AND YOUR STORY...
MARY...
...ANN ...?
POTA (DRIP)
THAT'S NOT IT...
HFF..
HFF..
THAT'S NOT...
...THAT GIRL'S NAME...

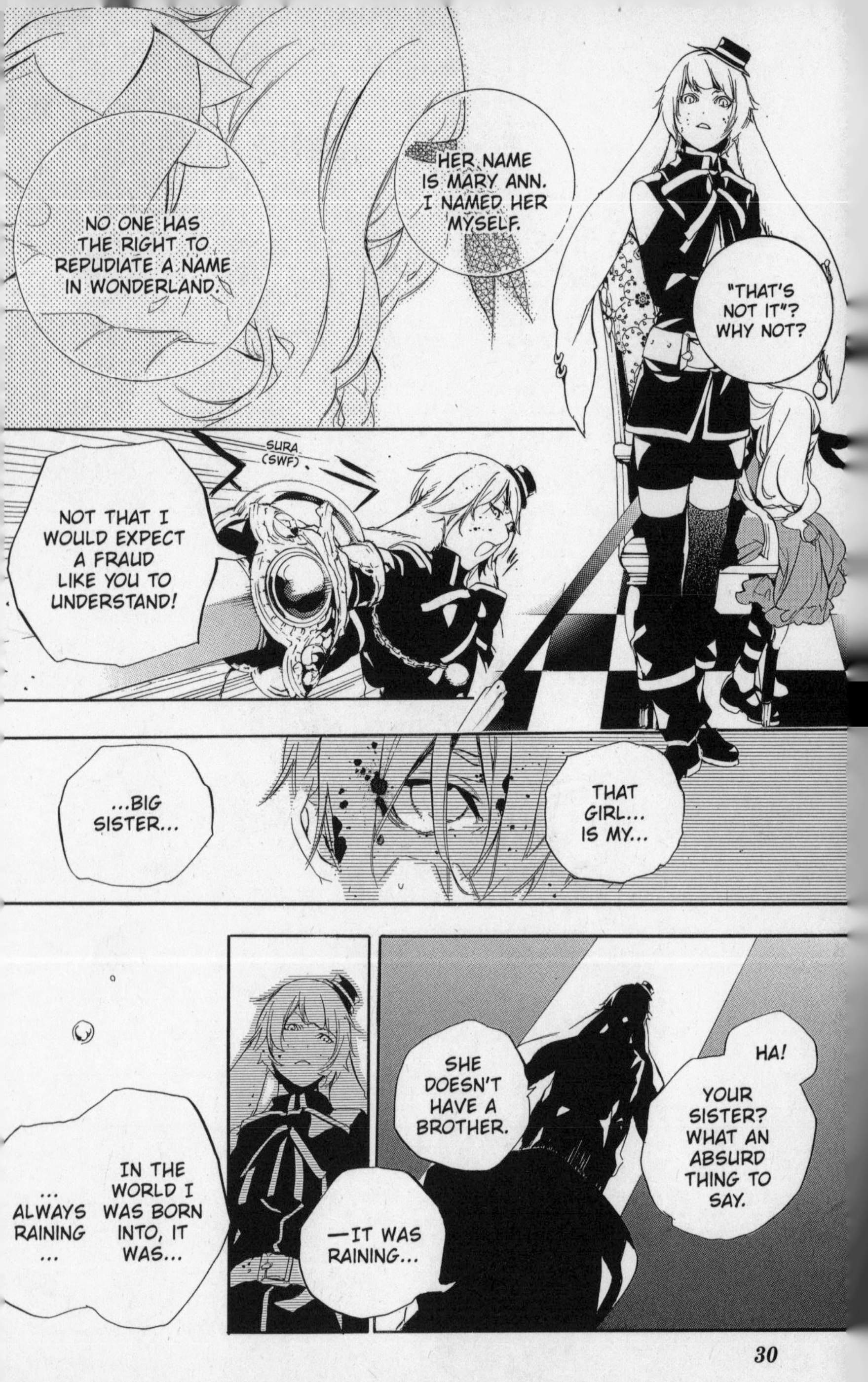
"THAT'S NOT IT"? WHY NOT?
HER NAME IS MARY ANN. I NAMED HER MYSELF.
NO ONE HAS THE RIGHT TO REPUDIATE A NAME IN WONDERLAND.
SURA (SWF)
NOT THAT I WOULD EXPECT A FRAUD LIKE YOU TO UNDERSTAND!
THAT GIRL... IS MY...
...BIG SISTER...
HA!
YOUR SISTER? WHAT AN ABSURD THING TO SAY.
SHE DOESN'T HAVE A BROTHER.
—IT WAS RAINING...
IN THE WORLD I WAS BORN INTO, IT WAS...
...ALWAYS RAINING...

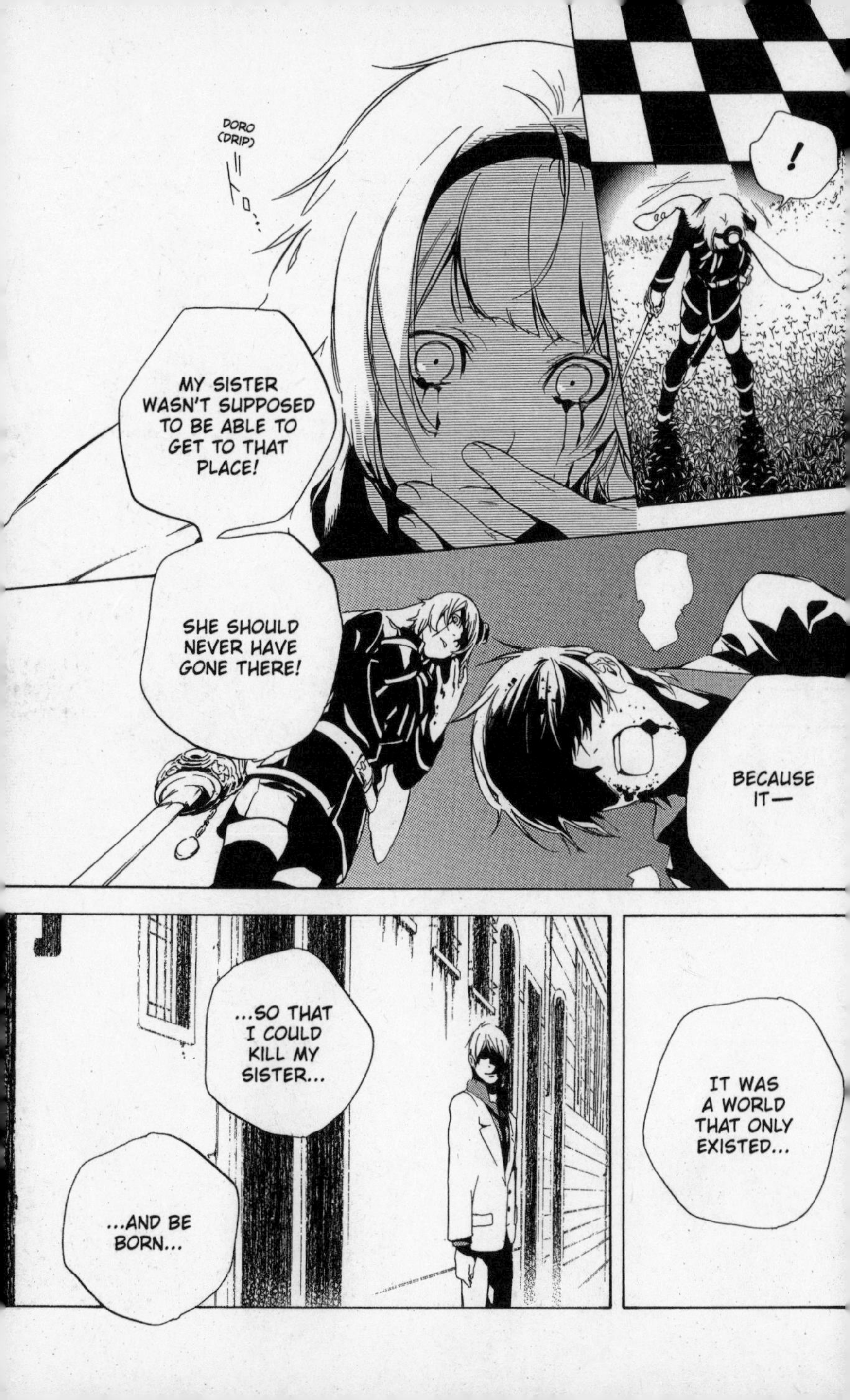
!
DORO (DRIP)
MY SISTER WASN'T SUPPOSED TO BE ABLE TO GET TO THAT PLACE!
SHE SHOULD NEVER HAVE GONE THERE!
BECAUSE IT—
IT WAS A WORLD THAT ONLY EXISTED...
...SO THAT I COULD KILL MY SISTER...
...AND BE BORN...

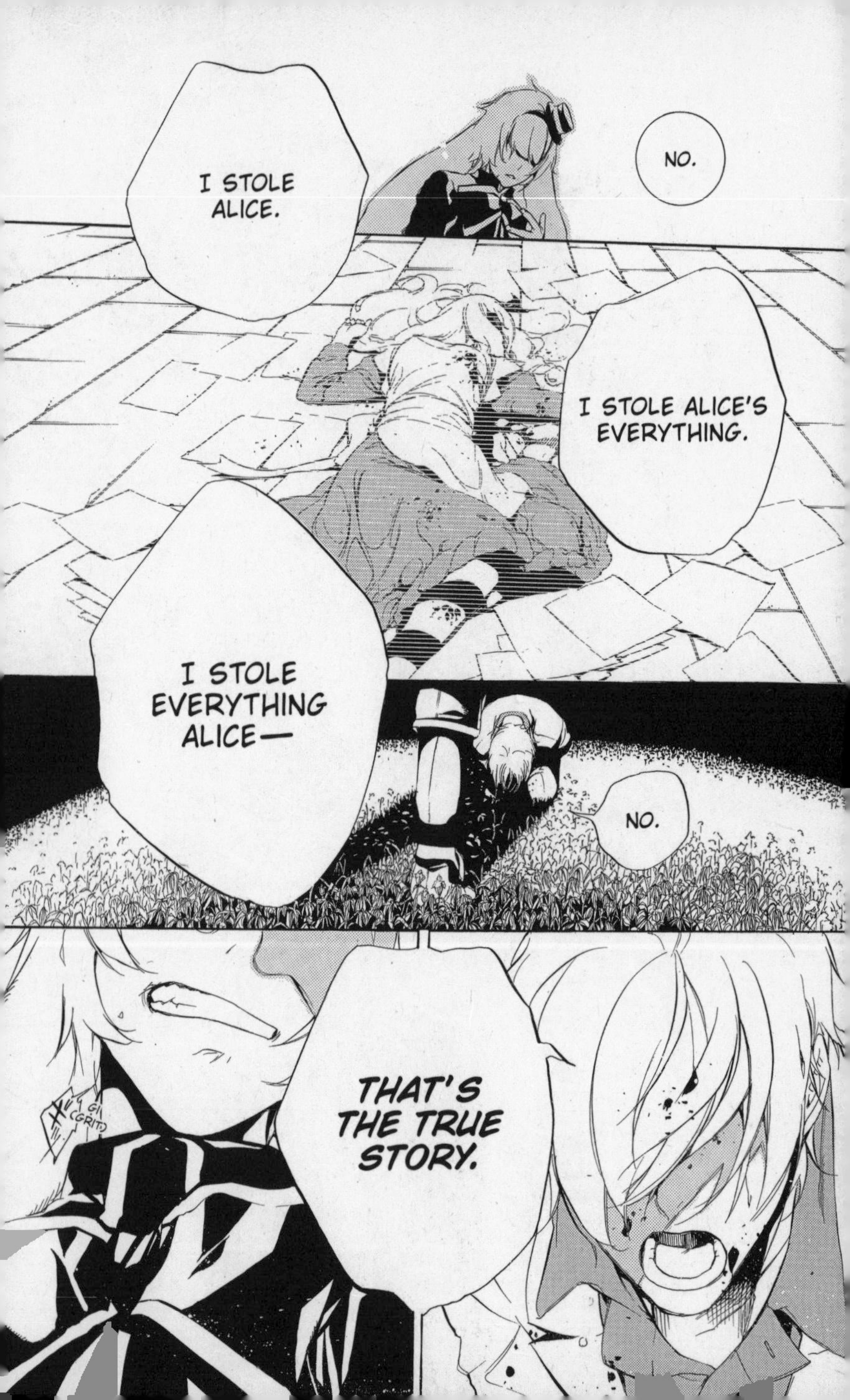
I STOLE ALICE.
NO.
I STOLE ALICE'S EVERYTHING.
I STOLE EVERYTHING ALICE—
NO.
THAT'S THE TRUE STORY.
GI (GRIT)

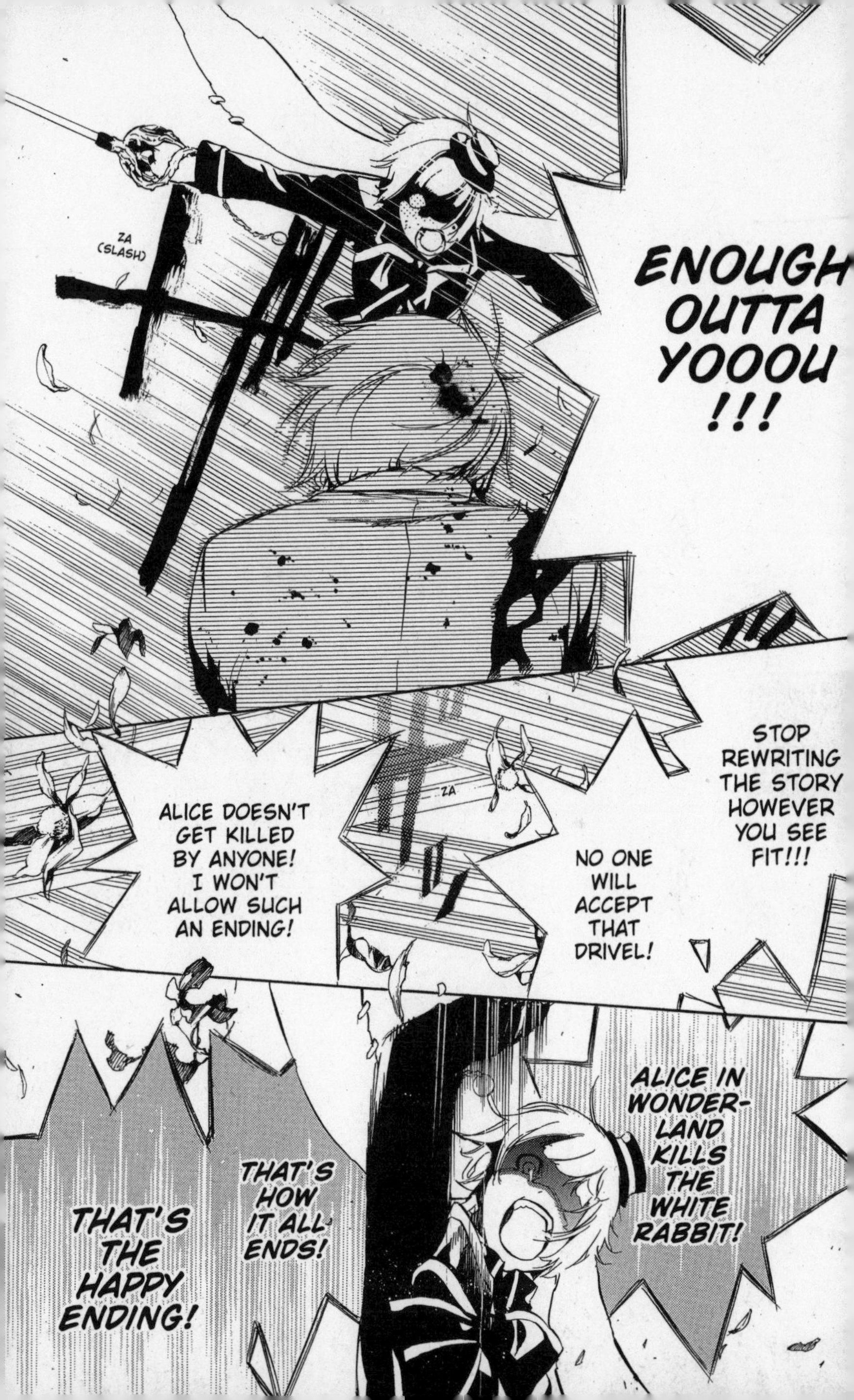

ENOUGH OUTTA YOOOU!!!
ZA (SLASH)
STOP REWRITING THE STORY HOWEVER YOU SEE FIT!!!
NO ONE WILL ACCEPT THAT DRIVEL!
ZA
ALICE DOESN'T GET KILLED BY ANYONE! I WON'T ALLOW SUCH AN ENDING!
ALICE IN WONDER-LAND KILLS THE WHITE RABBIT!
THAT'S HOW IT ALL ENDS!
THAT'S THE HAPPY ENDING!

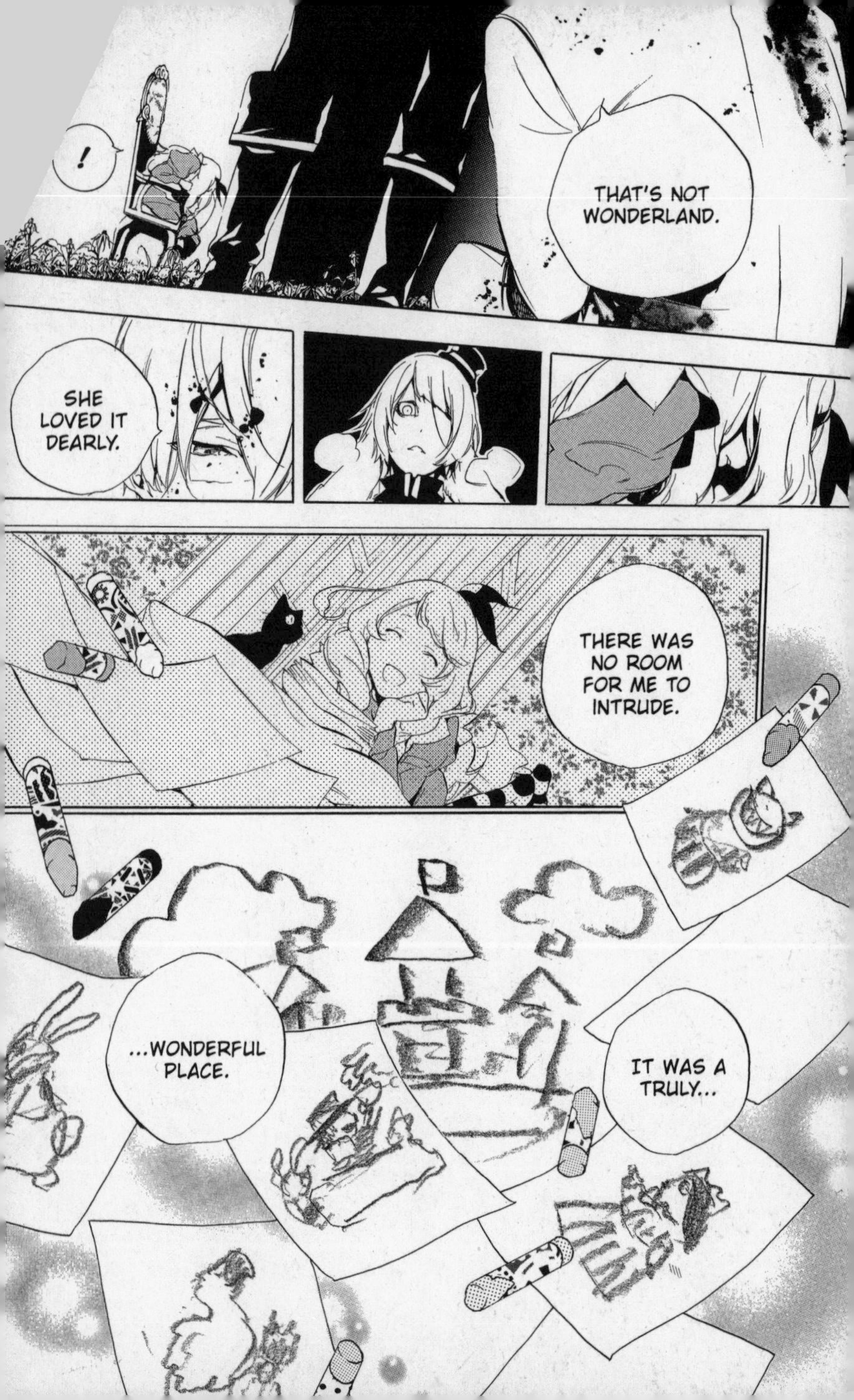
THAT'S NOT WONDERLAND.
!
SHE LOVED IT DEARLY.
THERE WAS NO ROOM FOR ME TO INTRUDE.
IT WAS A TRULY...
...WONDERFUL PLACE.

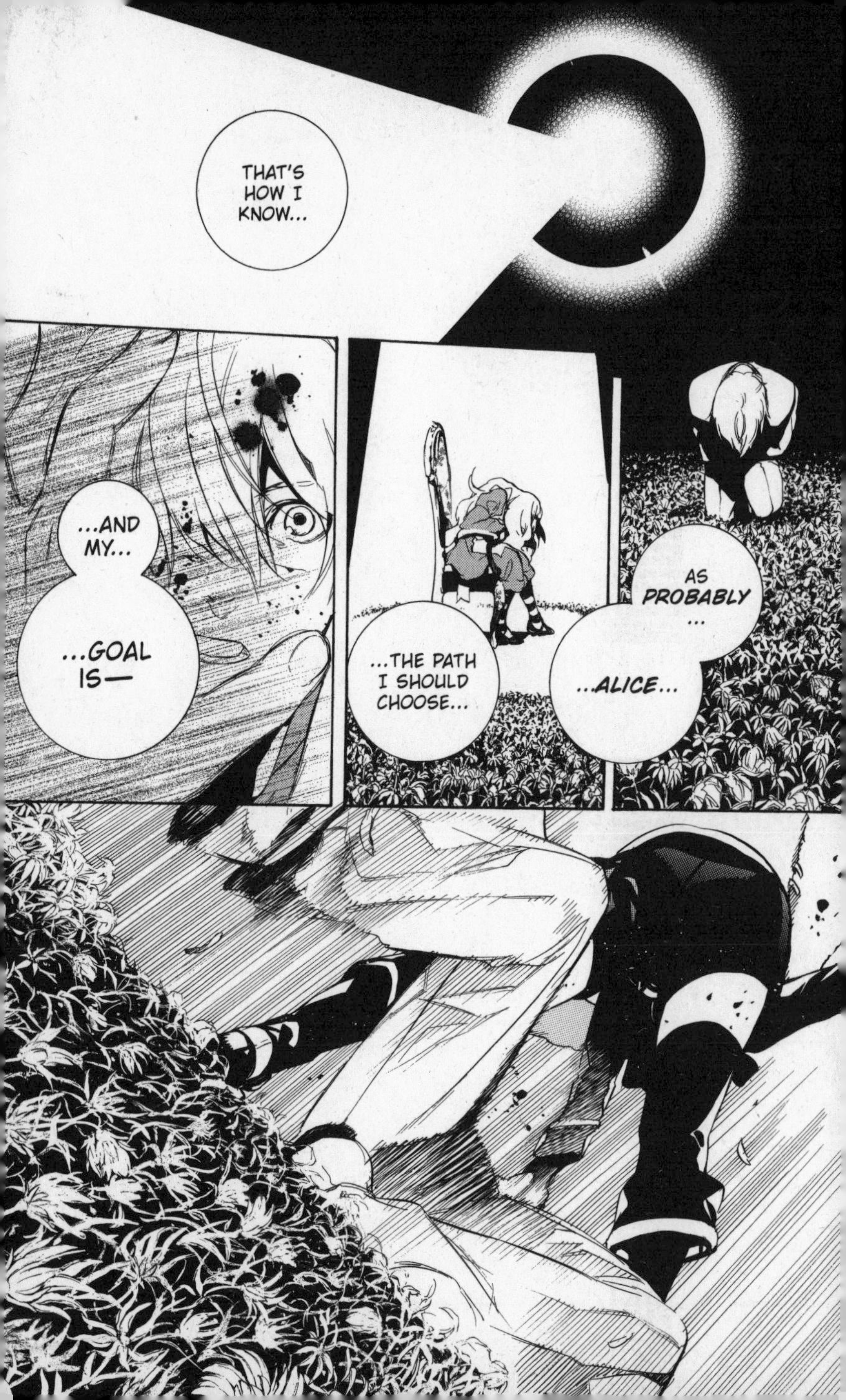
THAT'S HOW I KNOW...
AS PROBABLY ...
...ALICE...
...THE PATH I SHOULD CHOOSE...
...AND MY...
...GOAL IS—

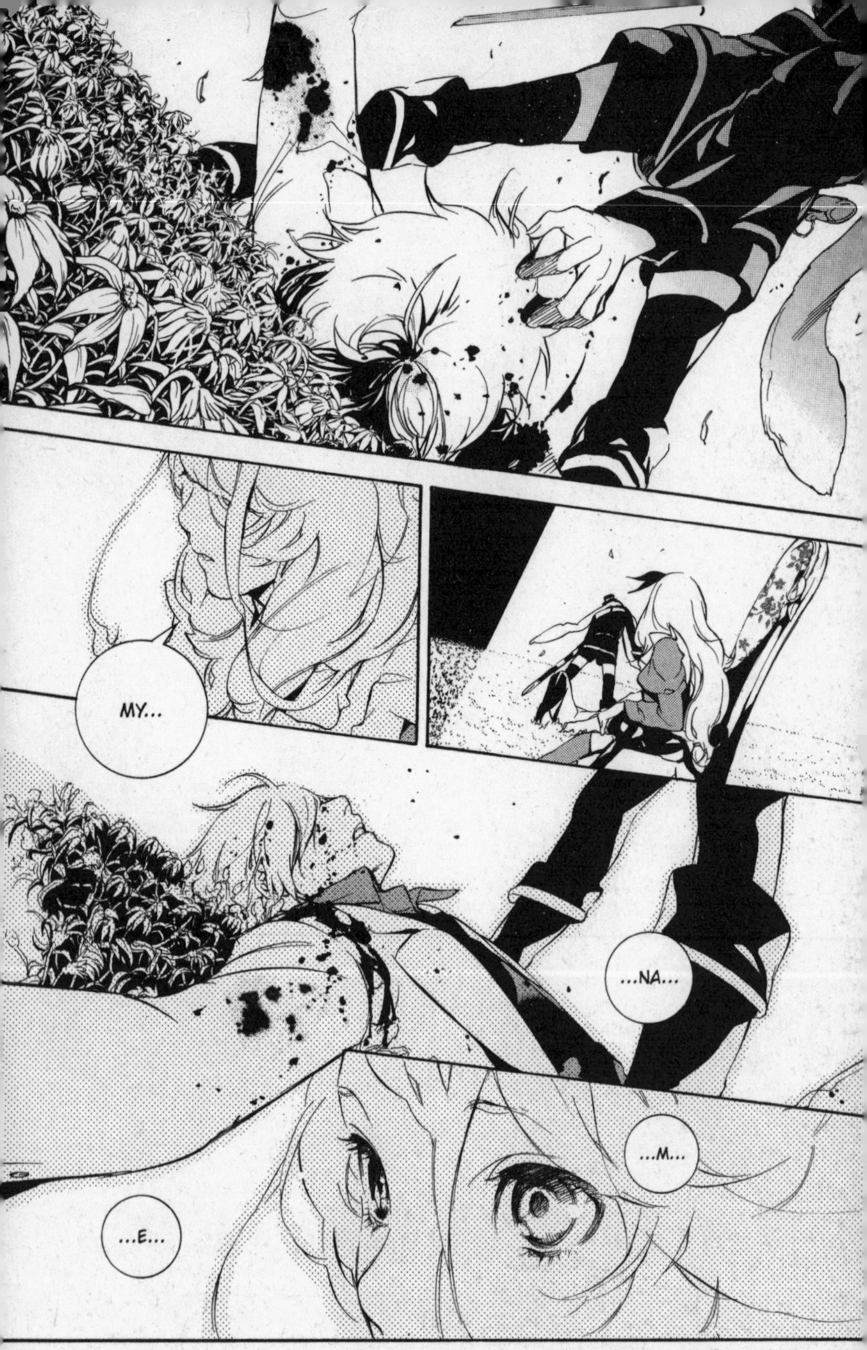
MY...
...NA...
...M...
...E...

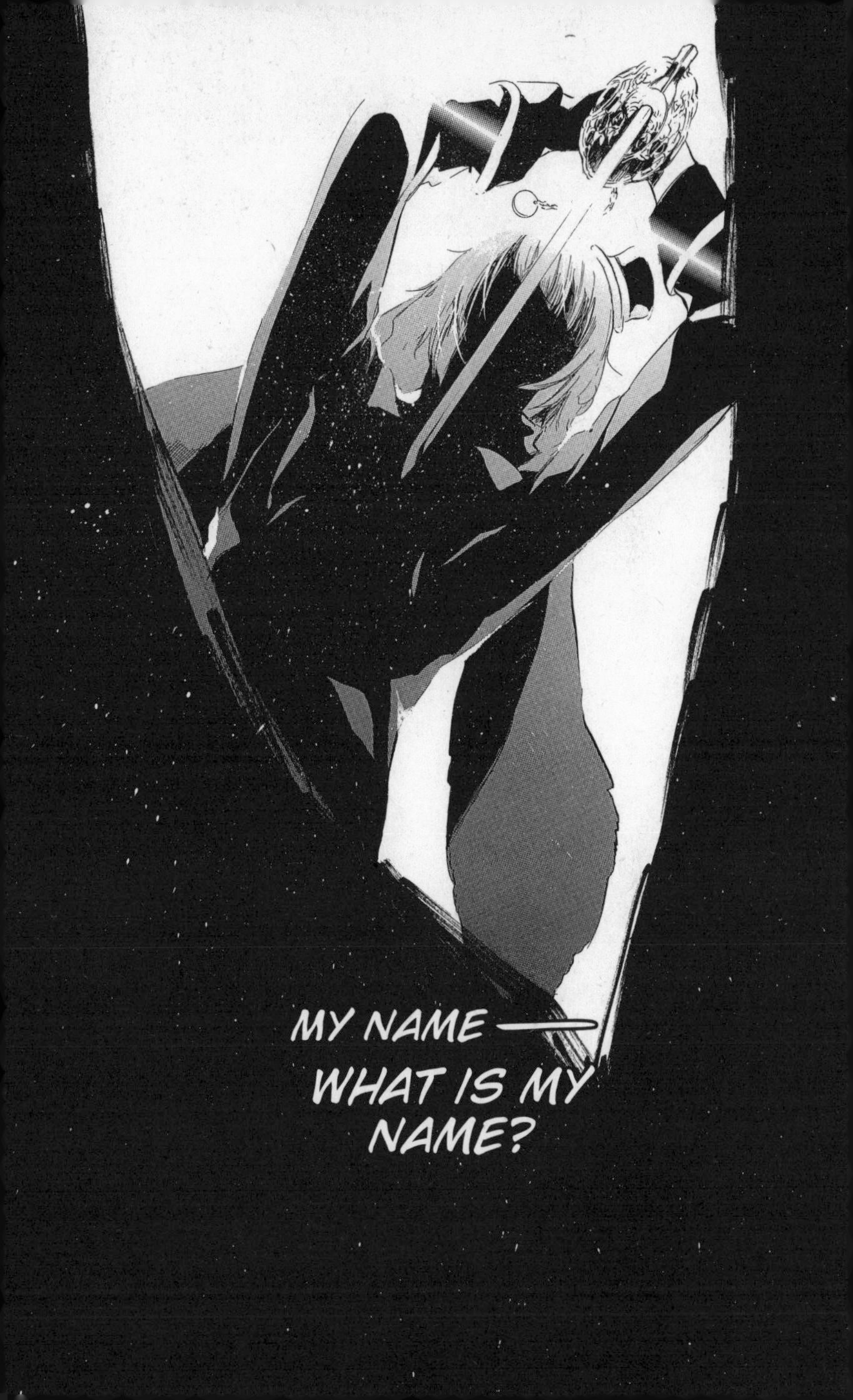
MY NAME—
WHAT IS MY NAME?

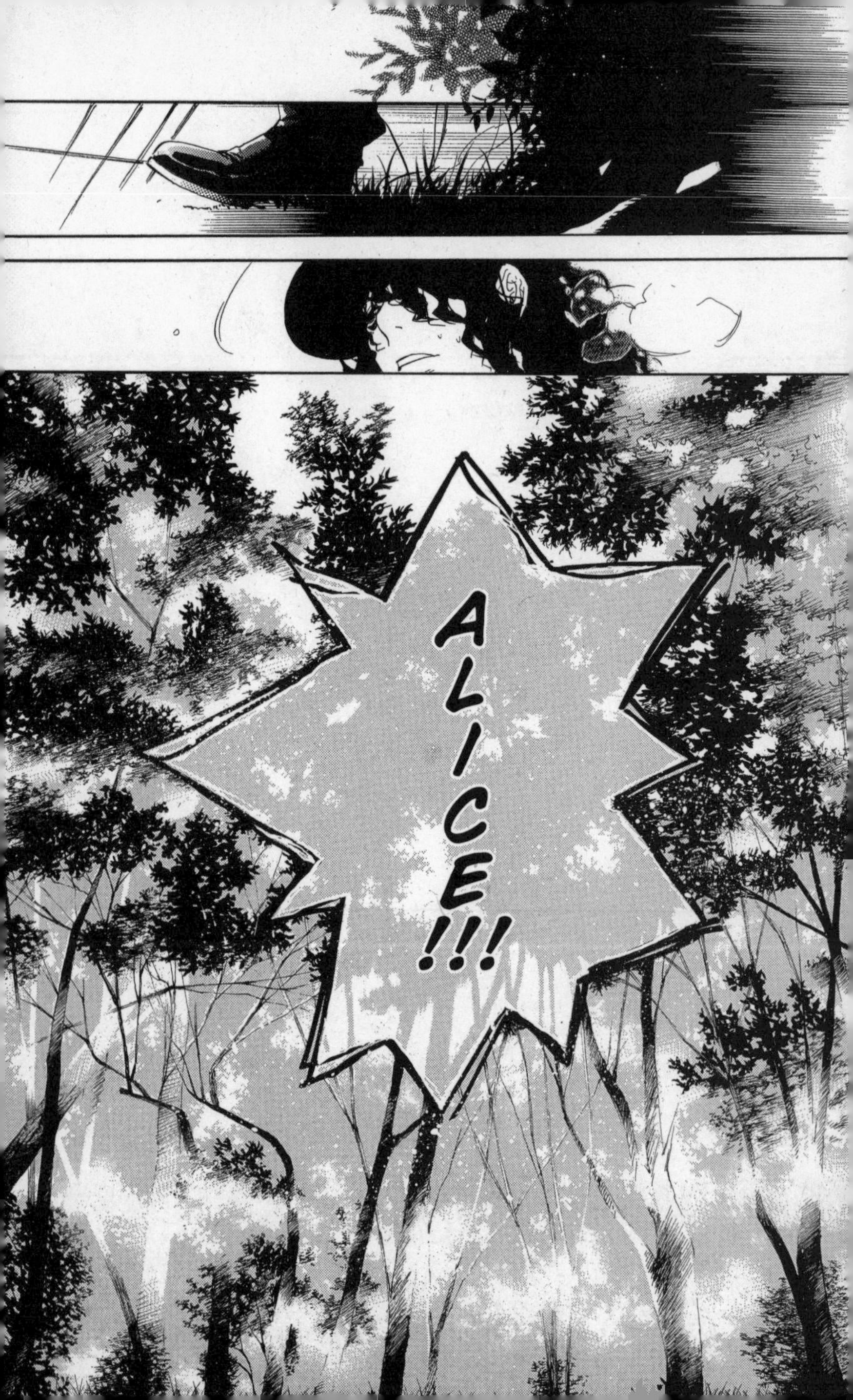
ALICE!!!

# Chapter 31

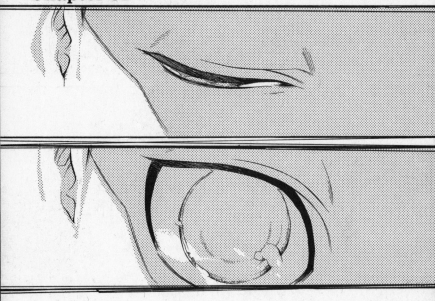

OHH...

WHAT'S
THIS?

*YOU STILL WON'T LET IT END...?*

chapter.31

Time will tell.

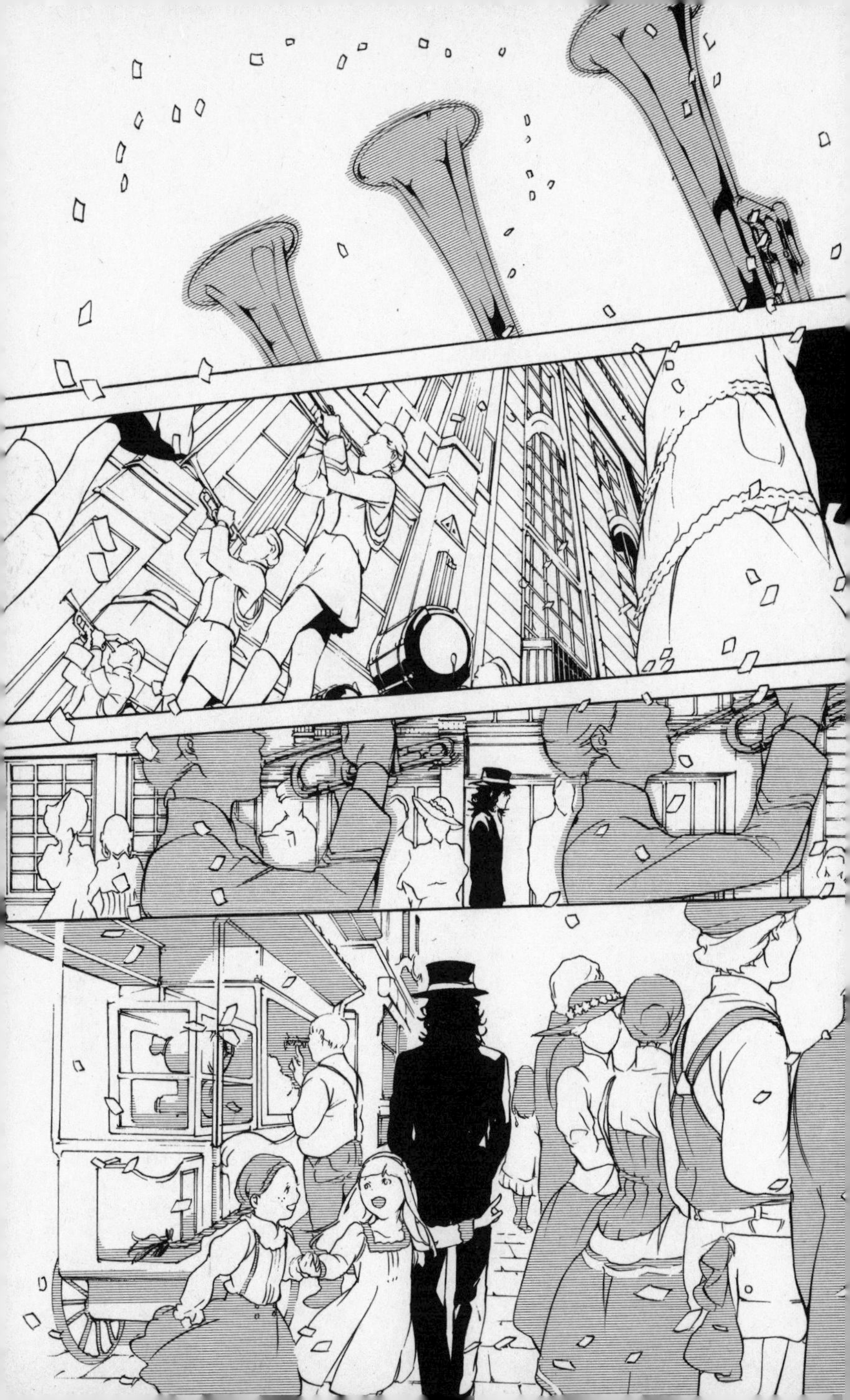

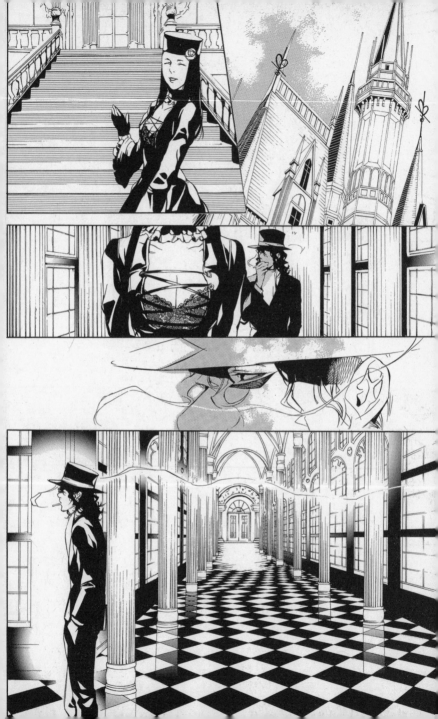

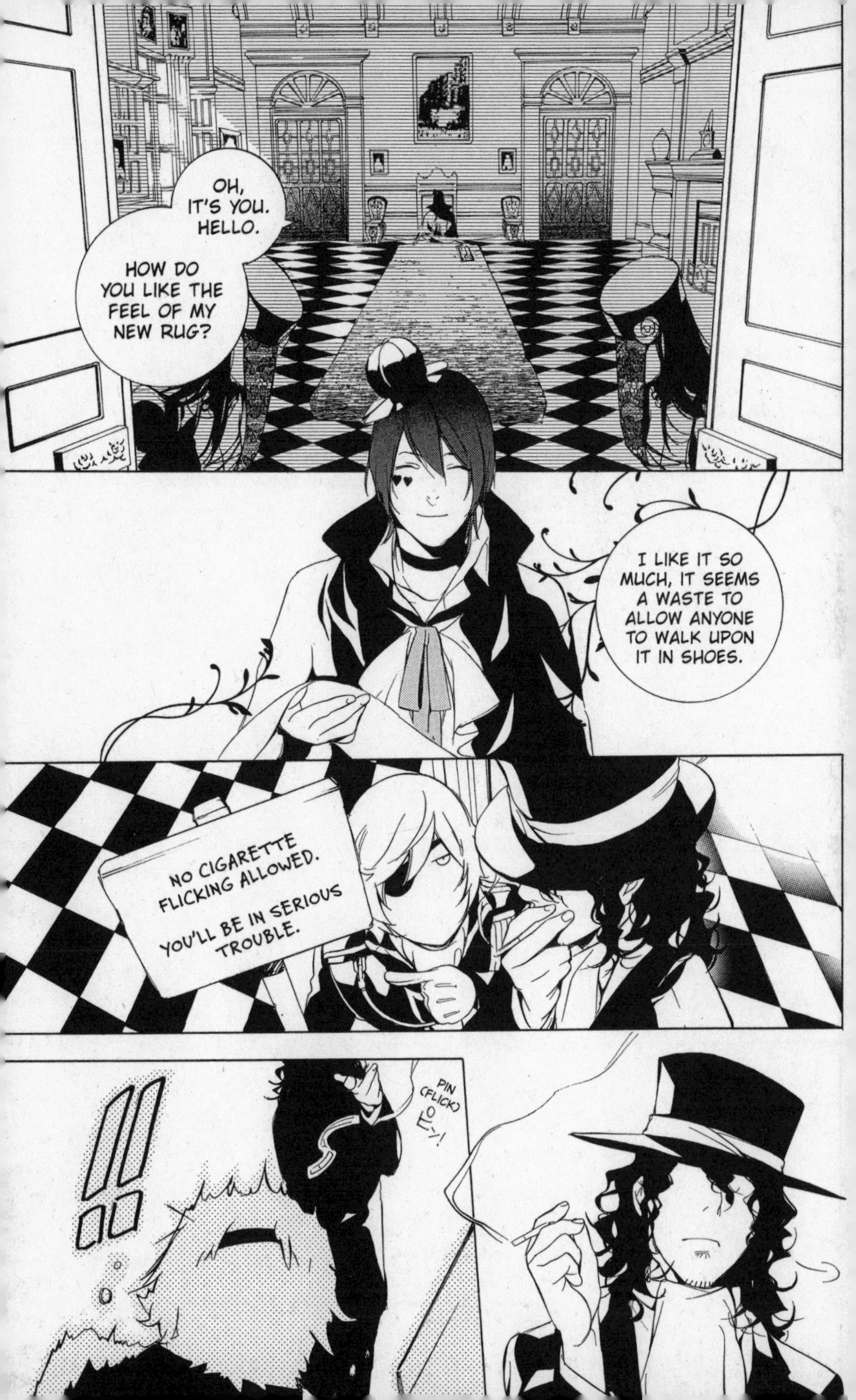
OH, IT'S YOU. HELLO.
HOW DO YOU LIKE THE FEEL OF MY NEW RUG?
I LIKE IT SO MUCH, IT SEEMS A WASTE TO ALLOW ANYONE TO WALK UPON IT IN SHOES.
NO CIGARETTE FLICKING ALLOWED.
YOU'LL BE IN SERIOUS TROUBLE.
PIN (FLICK)

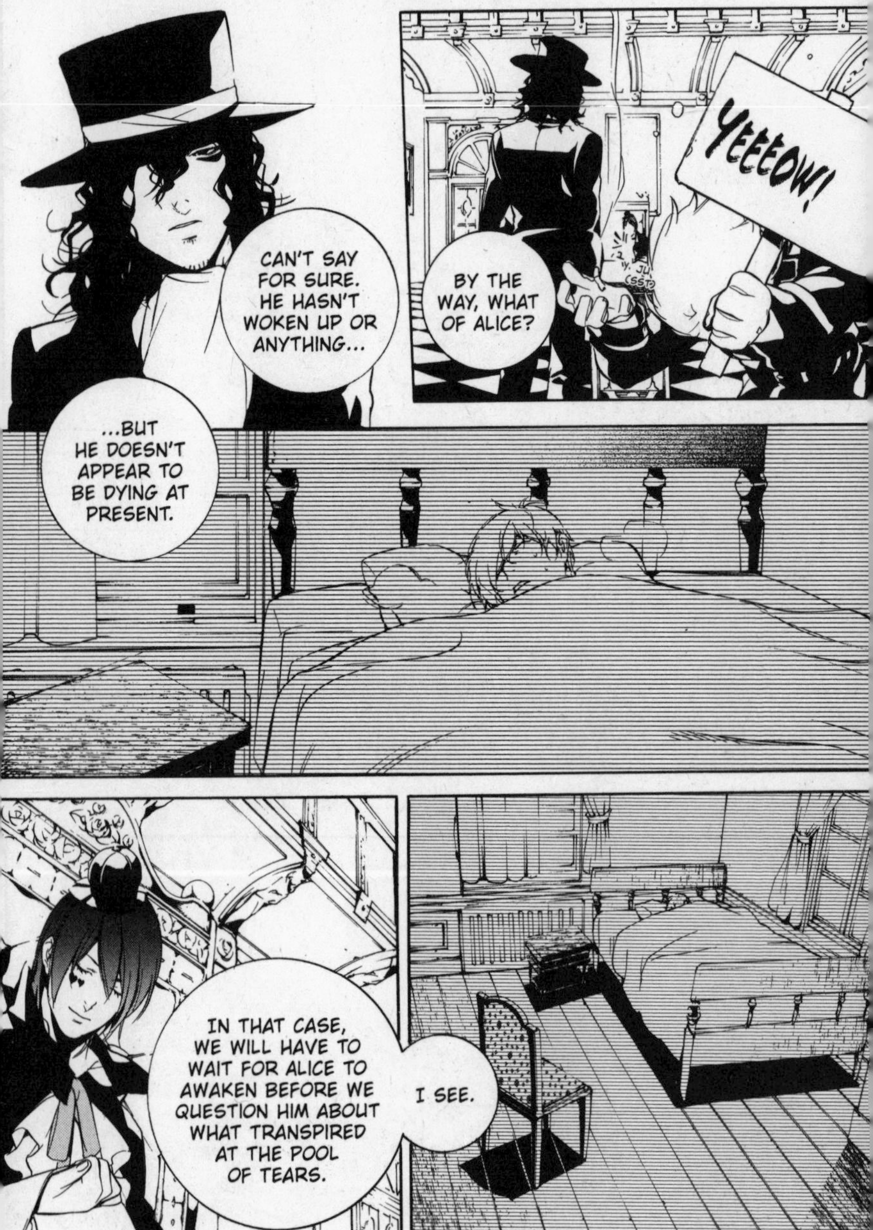
YEEEOW!
BY THE WAY, WHAT OF ALICE?
CAN'T SAY FOR SURE. HE HASN'T WOKEN UP OR ANYTHING...
...BUT HE DOESN'T APPEAR TO BE DYING AT PRESENT.
I SEE.
IN THAT CASE, WE WILL HAVE TO WAIT FOR ALICE TO AWAKEN BEFORE WE QUESTION HIM ABOUT WHAT TRANSPIRED AT THE POOL OF TEARS.

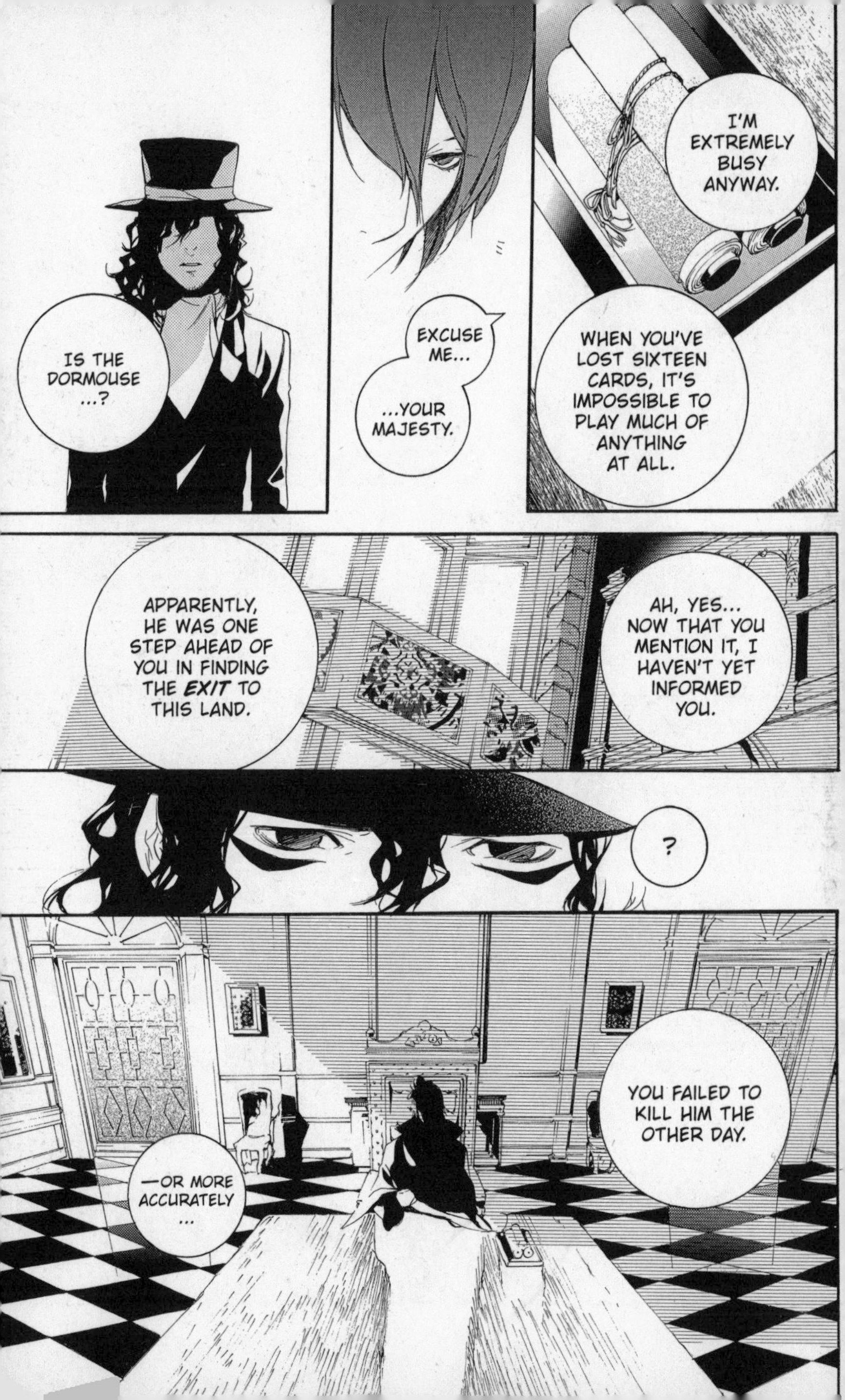
I'M EXTREMELY BUSY ANYWAY.
WHEN YOU'VE LOST SIXTEEN CARDS, IT'S IMPOSSIBLE TO PLAY MUCH OF ANYTHING AT ALL.
EXCUSE ME...
...YOUR MAJESTY.
IS THE DORMOUSE ...?
AH, YES... NOW THAT YOU MENTION IT, I HAVEN'T YET INFORMED YOU.
APPARENTLY, HE WAS ONE STEP AHEAD OF YOU IN FINDING THE *EXIT* TO THIS LAND.
?
YOU FAILED TO KILL HIM THE OTHER DAY.
—OR MORE ACCURATELY ...

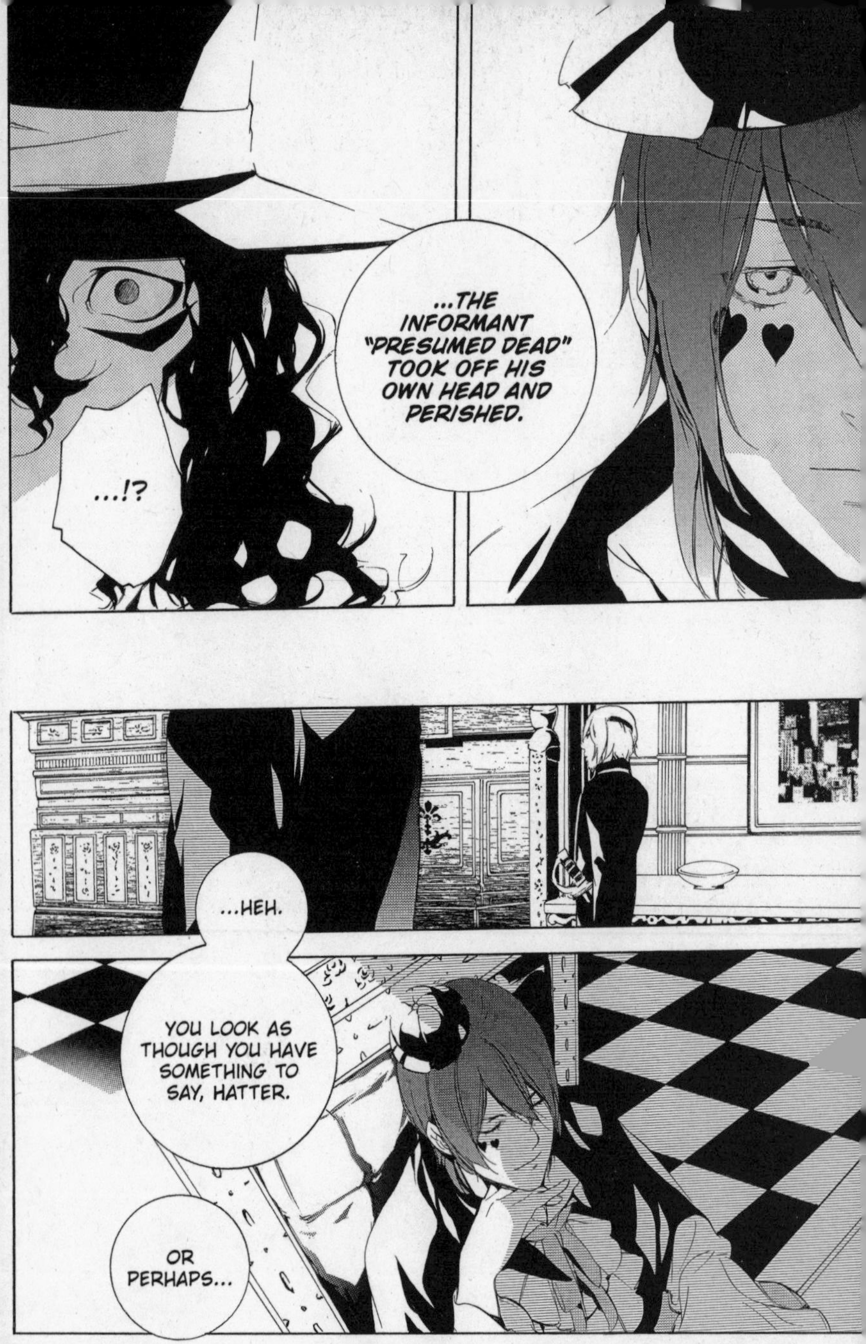
...THE INFORMANT "PRESUMED DEAD" TOOK OFF HIS OWN HEAD AND PERISHED.
...!?
...HEH.
YOU LOOK AS THOUGH YOU HAVE SOMETHING TO SAY, HATTER.
OR PERHAPS...

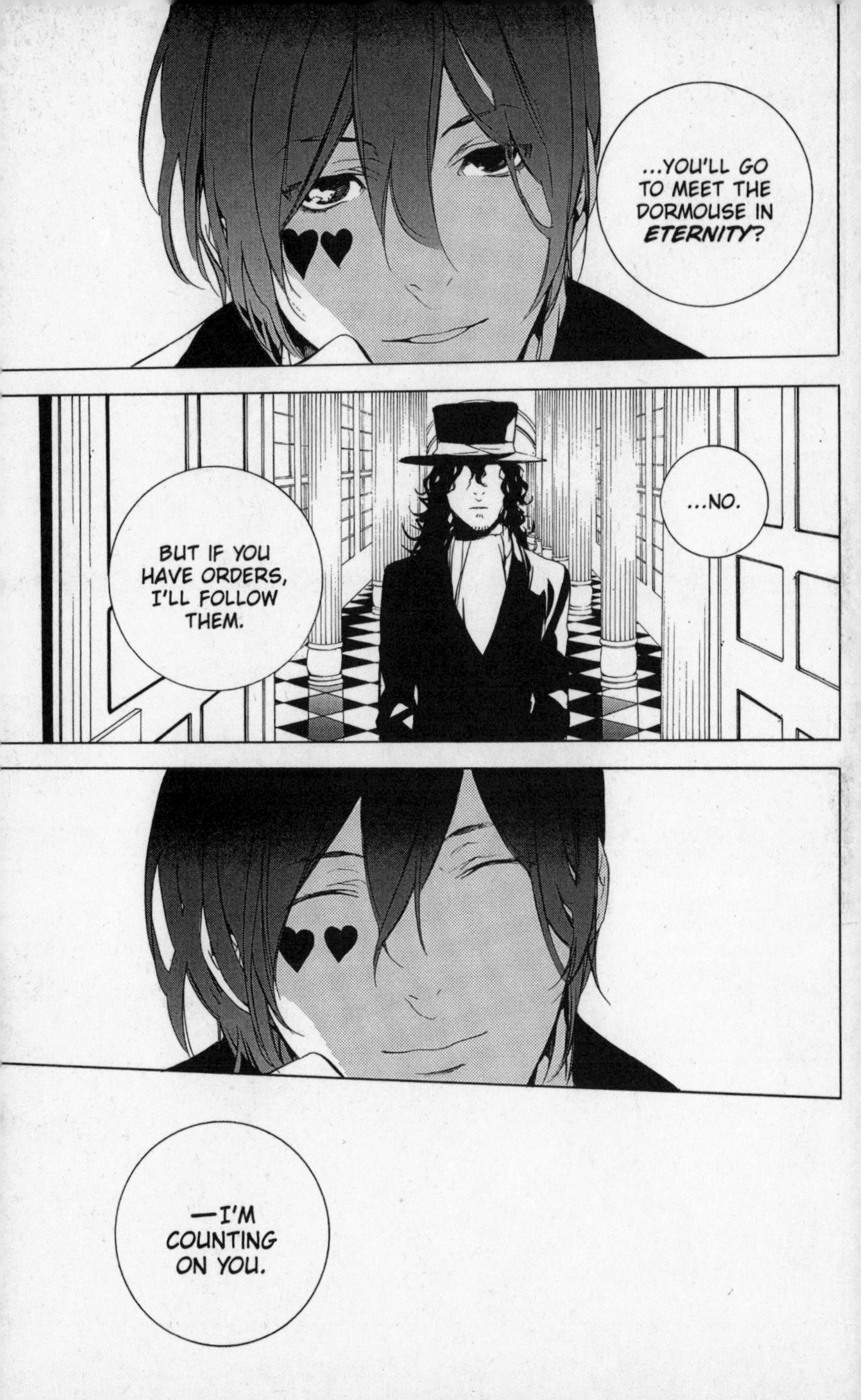
...YOU'LL GO TO MEET THE DORMOUSE IN *ETERNITY*?
...NO.
BUT IF YOU HAVE ORDERS, I'LL FOLLOW THEM.
—I'M COUNTING ON YOU.

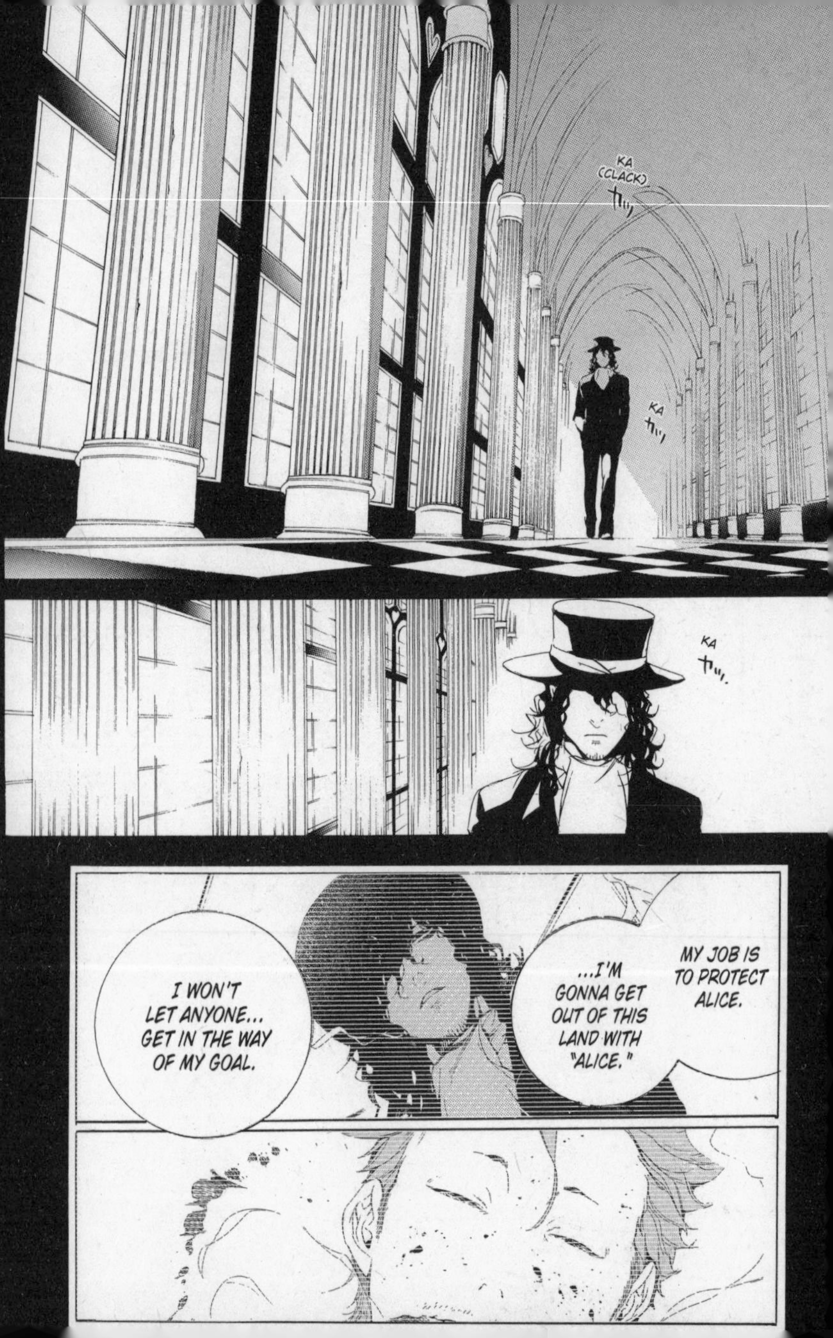
KA (CLACK)
カッ
KA
カッ
KA
カッ
MY JOB IS TO PROTECT ALICE.
...I'M GONNA GET OUT OF THIS LAND WITH "ALICE."
I WON'T LET ANYONE... GET IN THE WAY OF MY GOAL.

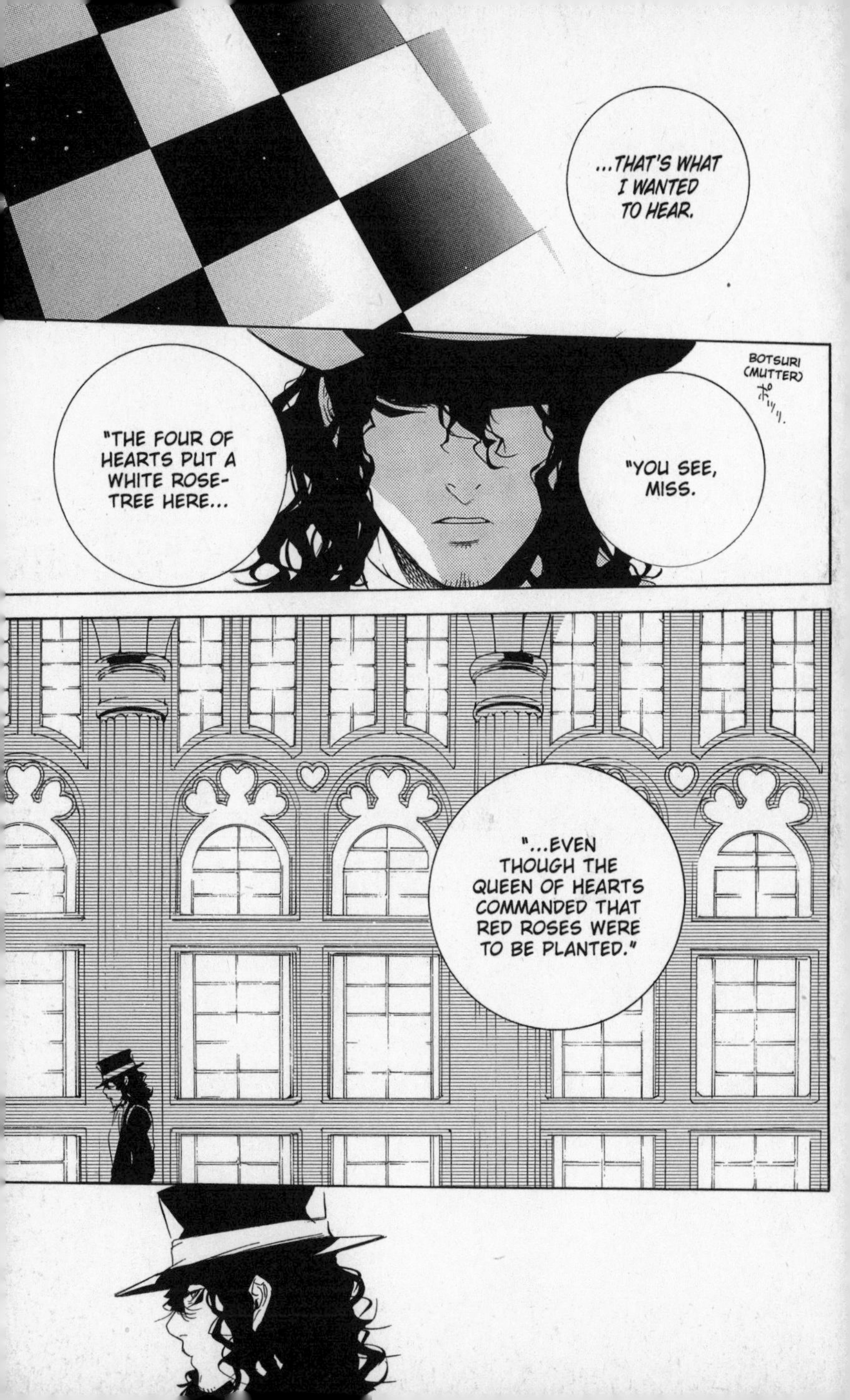
...THAT'S WHAT I WANTED TO HEAR.
BOTSURI (MUTTER)
"YOU SEE, MISS.
"THE FOUR OF HEARTS PUT A WHITE ROSE-TREE HERE...
"...EVEN THOUGH THE QUEEN OF HEARTS COMMANDED THAT RED ROSES WERE TO BE PLANTED."

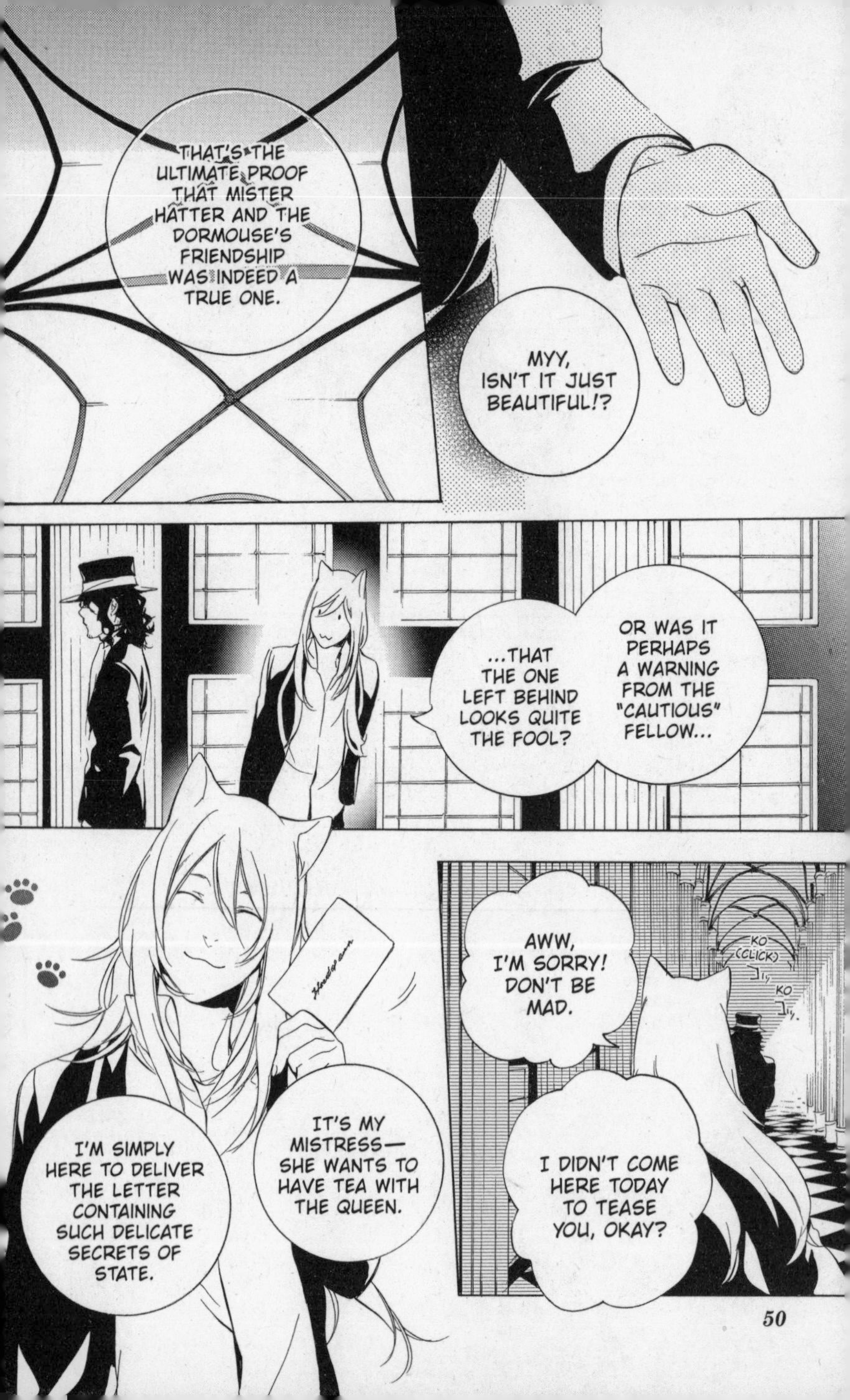
MYY, ISN'T IT JUST BEAUTIFUL!?
THAT'S THE ULTIMATE PROOF THAT MISTER HATTER AND THE DORMOUSE'S FRIENDSHIP WAS INDEED A TRUE ONE.
OR WAS IT PERHAPS A WARNING FROM THE "CAUTIOUS" FELLOW...
...THAT THE ONE LEFT BEHIND LOOKS QUITE THE FOOL?
AWW, I'M SORRY! DON'T BE MAD.
KO (CLICK)
KO
I DIDN'T COME HERE TODAY TO TEASE YOU, OKAY?
IT'S MY MISTRESS— SHE WANTS TO HAVE TEA WITH THE QUEEN.
I'M SIMPLY HERE TO DELIVER THE LETTER CONTAINING SUCH DELICATE SECRETS OF STATE.

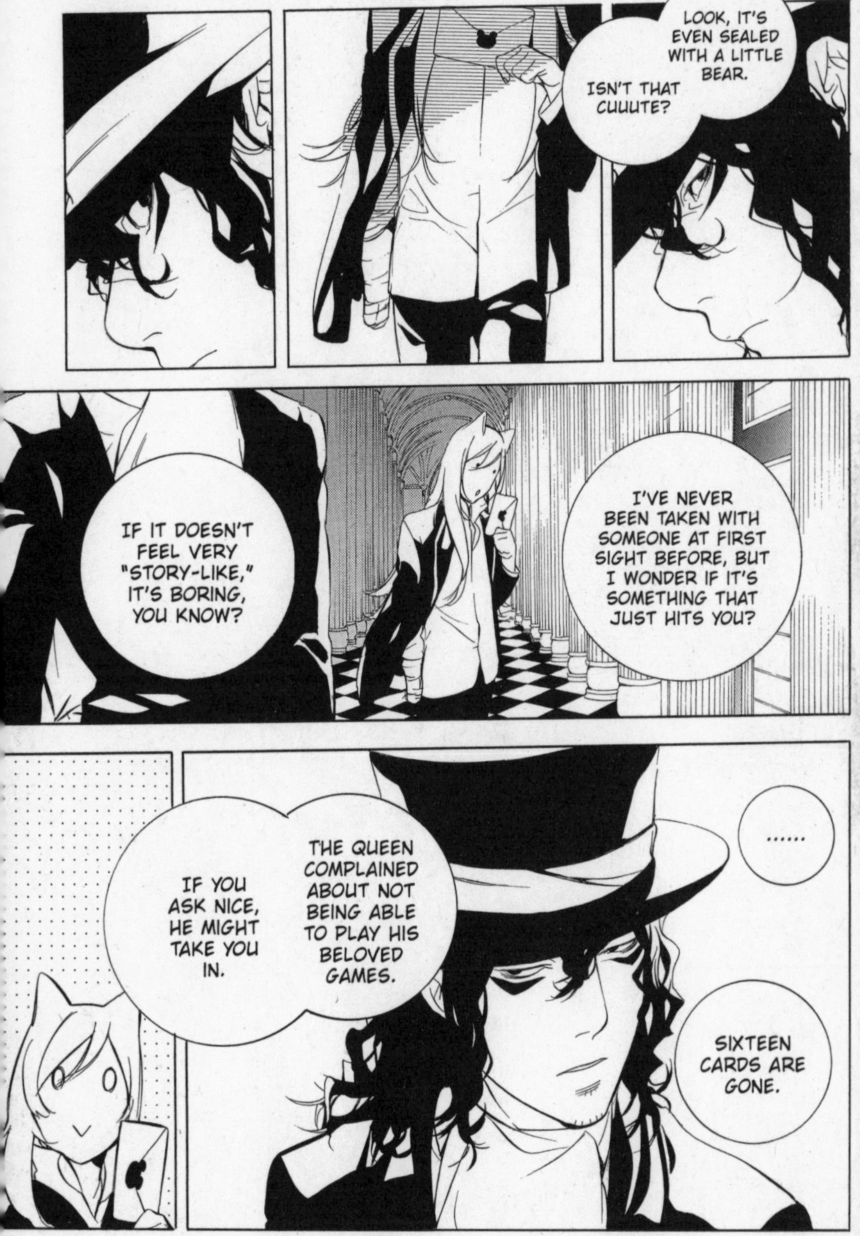
LOOK, IT'S EVEN SEALED WITH A LITTLE BEAR.
ISN'T THAT CUUUTE?
I'VE NEVER BEEN TAKEN WITH SOMEONE AT FIRST SIGHT BEFORE, BUT I WONDER IF IT'S SOMETHING THAT JUST HITS YOU?
IF IT DOESN'T FEEL VERY "STORY-LIKE," IT'S BORING, YOU KNOW?
......
SIXTEEN CARDS ARE GONE.
THE QUEEN COMPLAINED ABOUT NOT BEING ABLE TO PLAY HIS BELOVED GAMES.
IF YOU ASK NICE, HE MIGHT TAKE YOU IN.

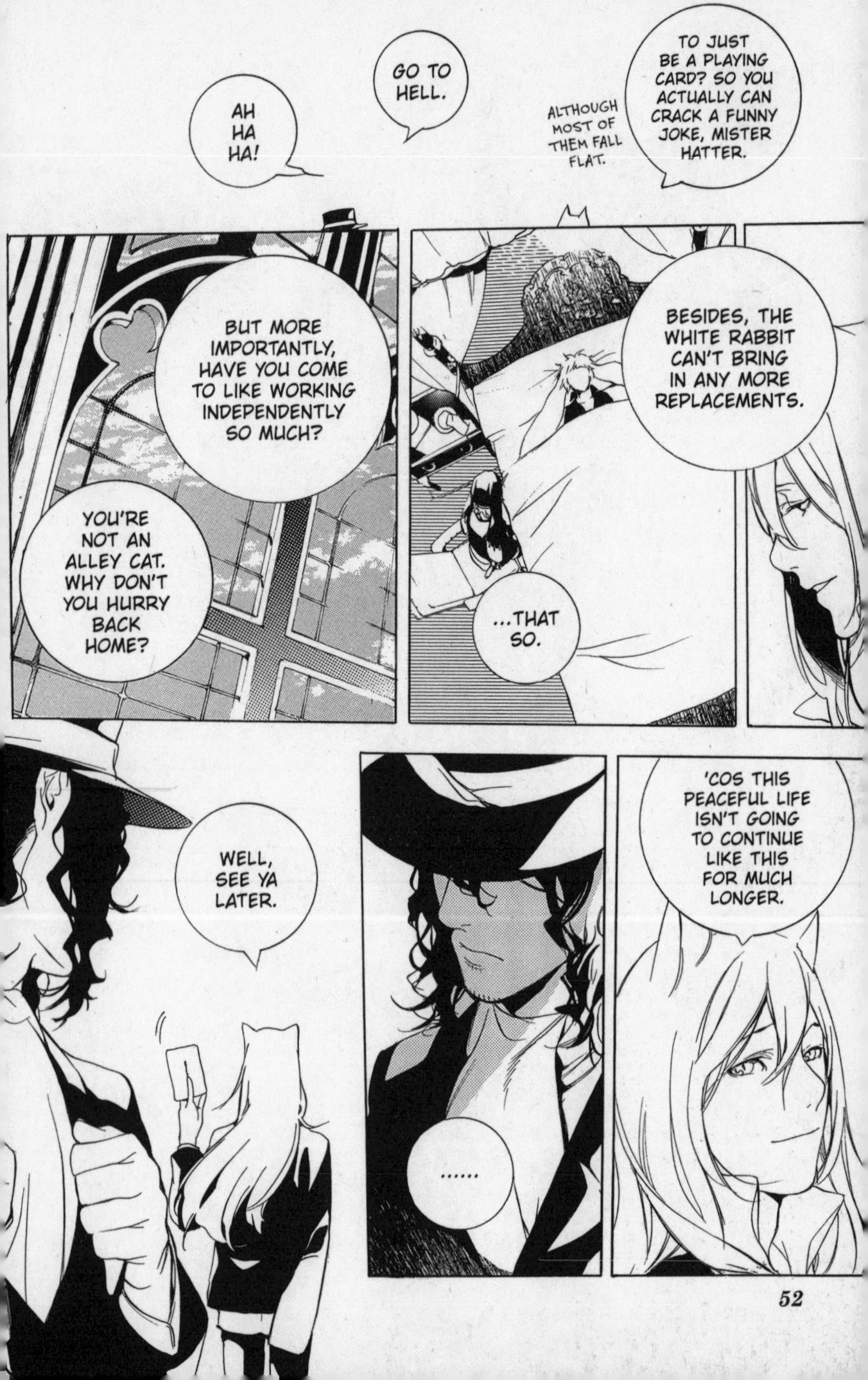

TO JUST BE A PLAYING CARD? SO YOU ACTUALLY CAN CRACK A FUNNY JOKE, MISTER HATTER.
ALTHOUGH MOST OF THEM FALL FLAT.
GO TO HELL.
AH HA HA!
BESIDES, THE WHITE RABBIT CAN'T BRING IN ANY MORE REPLACEMENTS.
...THAT SO.
BUT MORE IMPORTANTLY, HAVE YOU COME TO LIKE WORKING INDEPENDENTLY SO MUCH?
YOU'RE NOT AN ALLEY CAT. WHY DON'T YOU HURRY BACK HOME?
'COS THIS PEACEFUL LIFE ISN'T GOING TO CONTINUE LIKE THIS FOR MUCH LONGER.
......
WELL, SEE YA LATER.

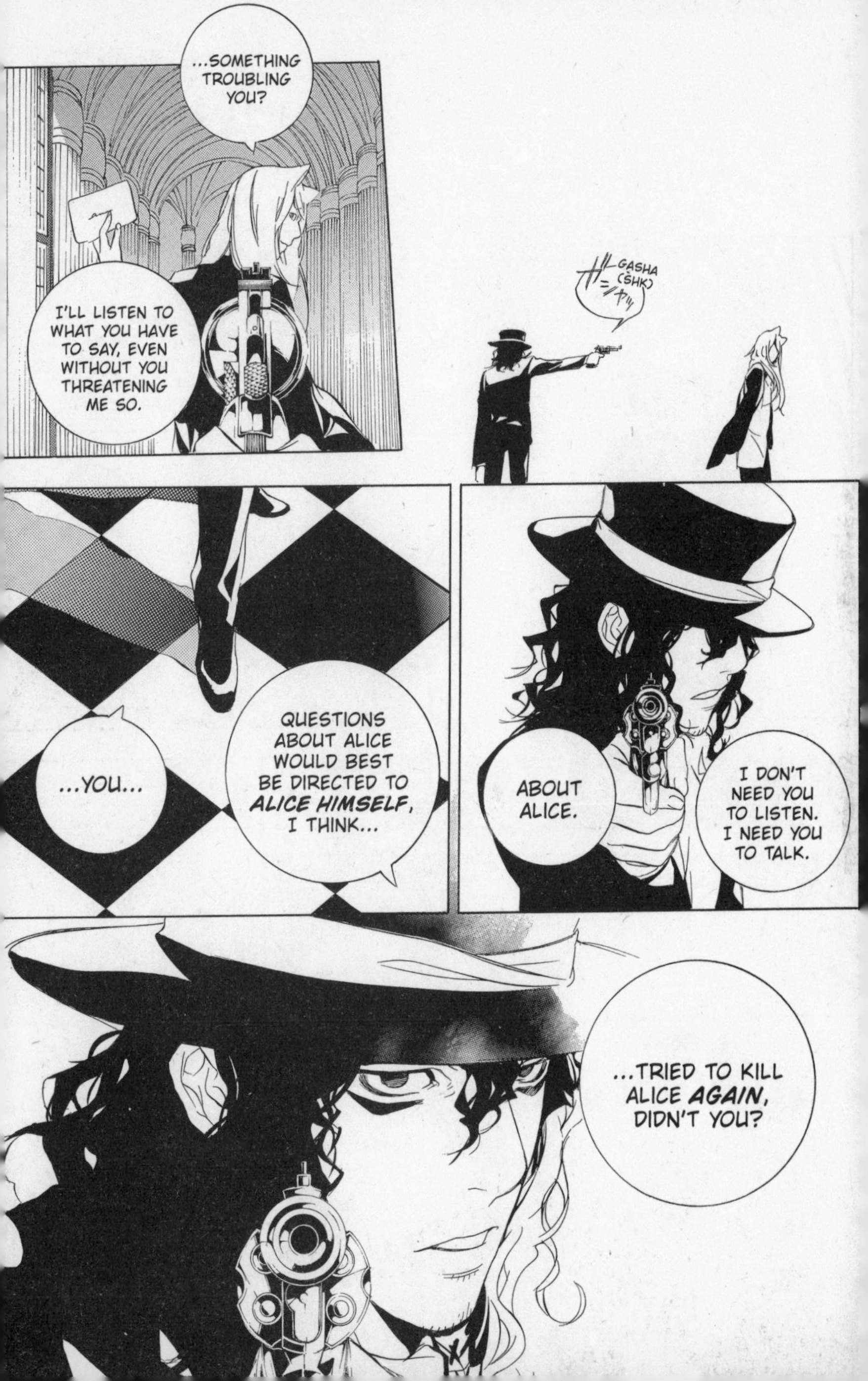
GASHA (SHK)
...SOMETHING TROUBLING YOU?
I'LL LISTEN TO WHAT YOU HAVE TO SAY, EVEN WITHOUT YOU THREATENING ME SO.
I DON'T NEED YOU TO LISTEN. I NEED YOU TO TALK.
ABOUT ALICE.
QUESTIONS ABOUT ALICE WOULD BEST BE DIRECTED TO ***ALICE HIMSELF***, I THINK...
...YOU...
...TRIED TO KILL ALICE ***AGAIN***, DIDN'T YOU?

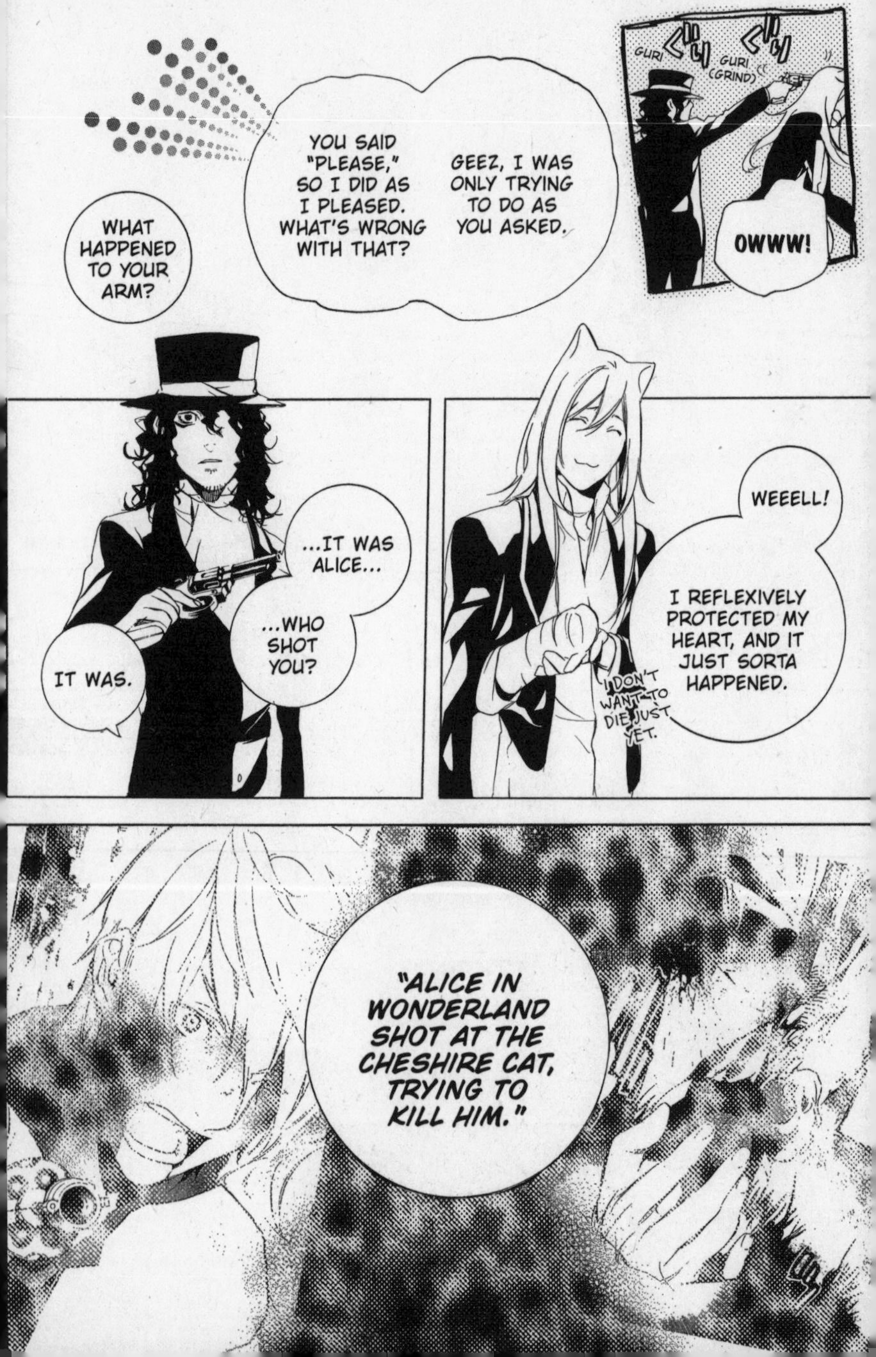
GURI
GURI (GRIND)
OWWW!
GEEZ, I WAS ONLY TRYING TO DO AS YOU ASKED.
YOU SAID "PLEASE," SO I DID AS I PLEASED. WHAT'S WRONG WITH THAT?
WHAT HAPPENED TO YOUR ARM?
WEEELL!
I REFLEXIVELY PROTECTED MY HEART, AND IT JUST SORTA HAPPENED.
I DON'T WANT TO DIE JUST YET.
...IT WAS ALICE...
...WHO SHOT YOU?
IT WAS.
"ALICE IN WONDERLAND SHOT AT THE CHESHIRE CAT, TRYING TO KILL HIM."

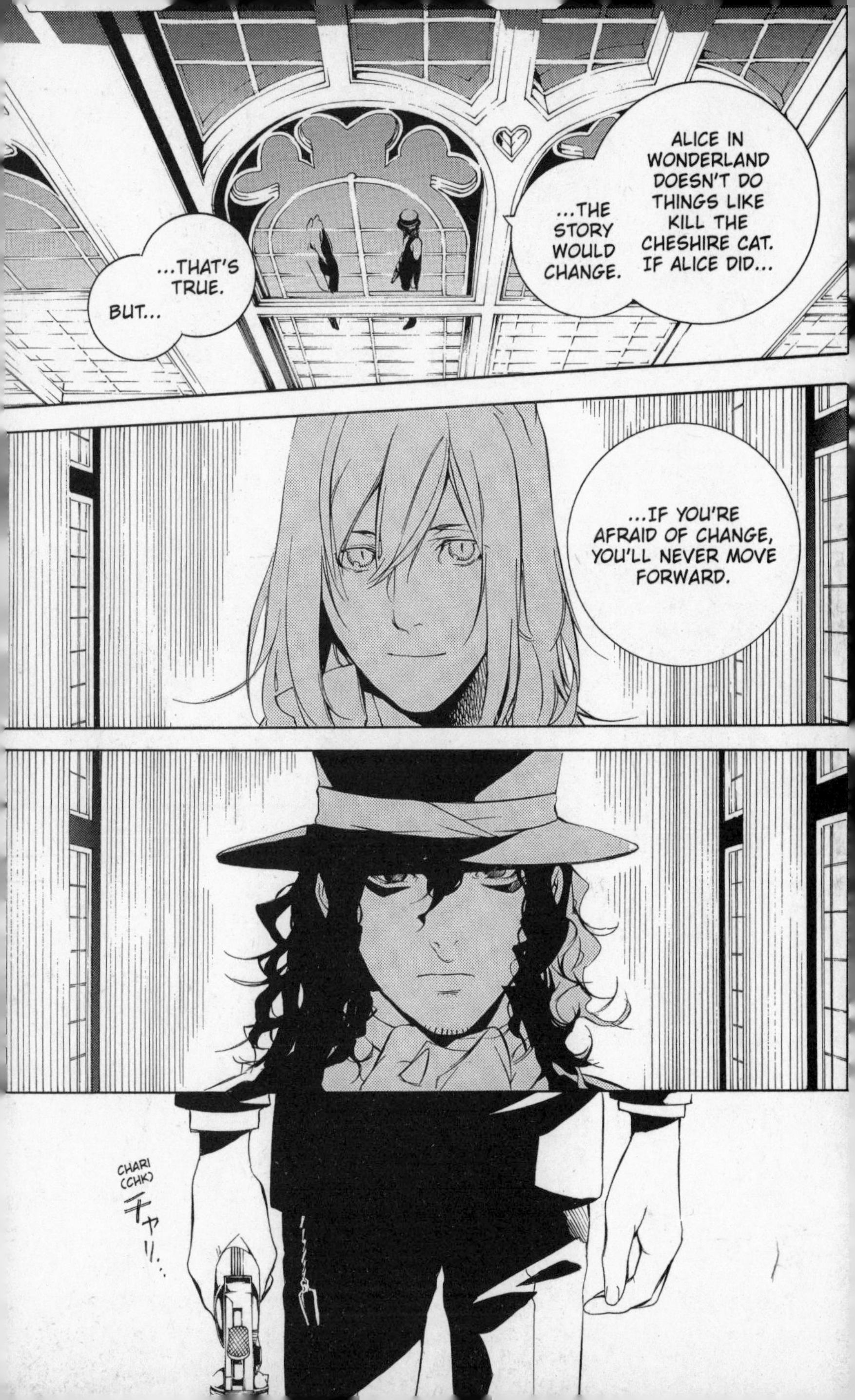
ALICE IN WONDERLAND DOESN'T DO THINGS LIKE KILL THE CHESHIRE CAT. IF ALICE DID...
...THE STORY WOULD CHANGE.
...THAT'S TRUE.
BUT...
...IF YOU'RE AFRAID OF CHANGE, YOU'LL NEVER MOVE FORWARD.
CHARI (CHK)
チャリ...

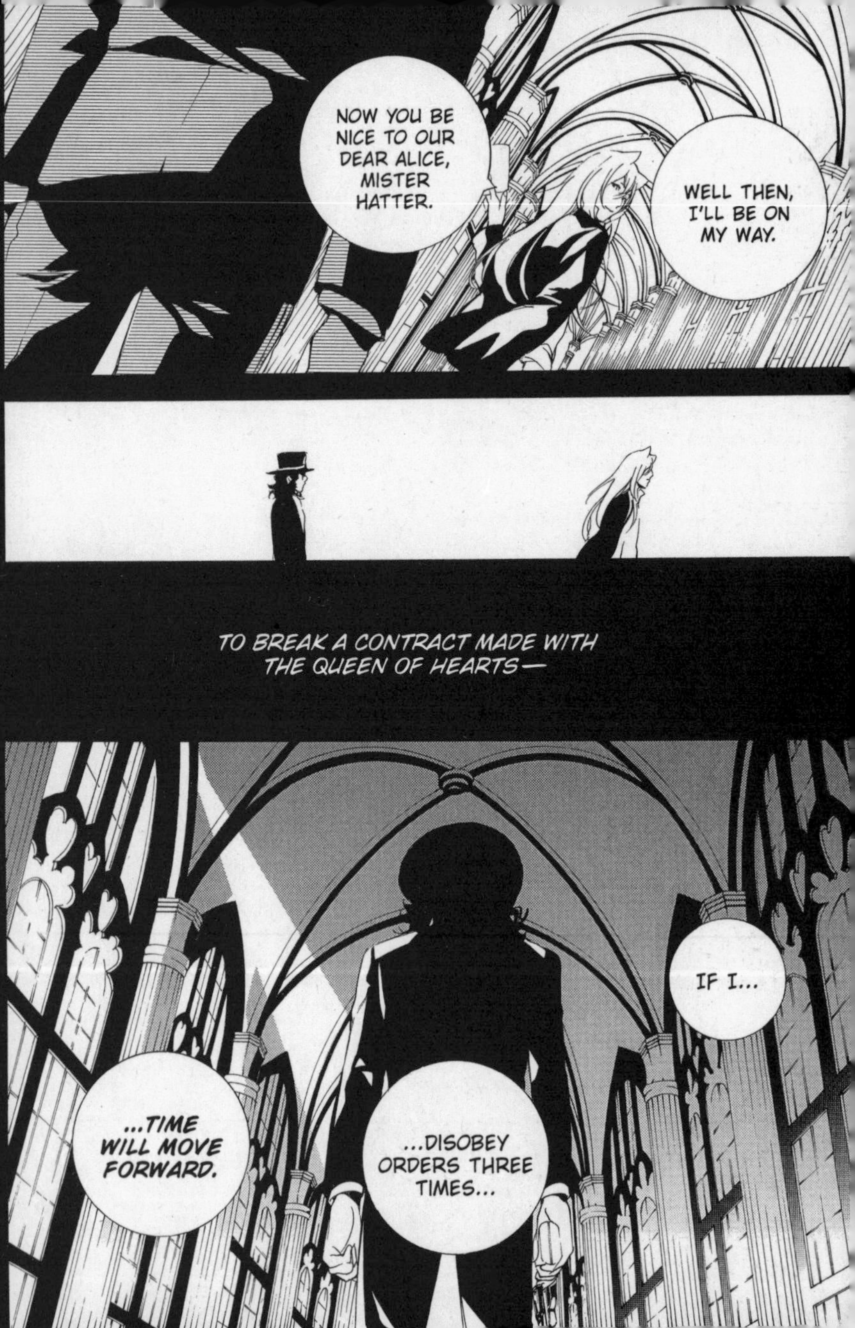
WELL THEN, I'LL BE ON MY WAY.
NOW YOU BE NICE TO OUR DEAR ALICE, MISTER HATTER.
TO BREAK A CONTRACT MADE WITH THE QUEEN OF HEARTS—
IF I...
...DISOBEY ORDERS THREE TIMES...
...TIME WILL MOVE FORWARD.

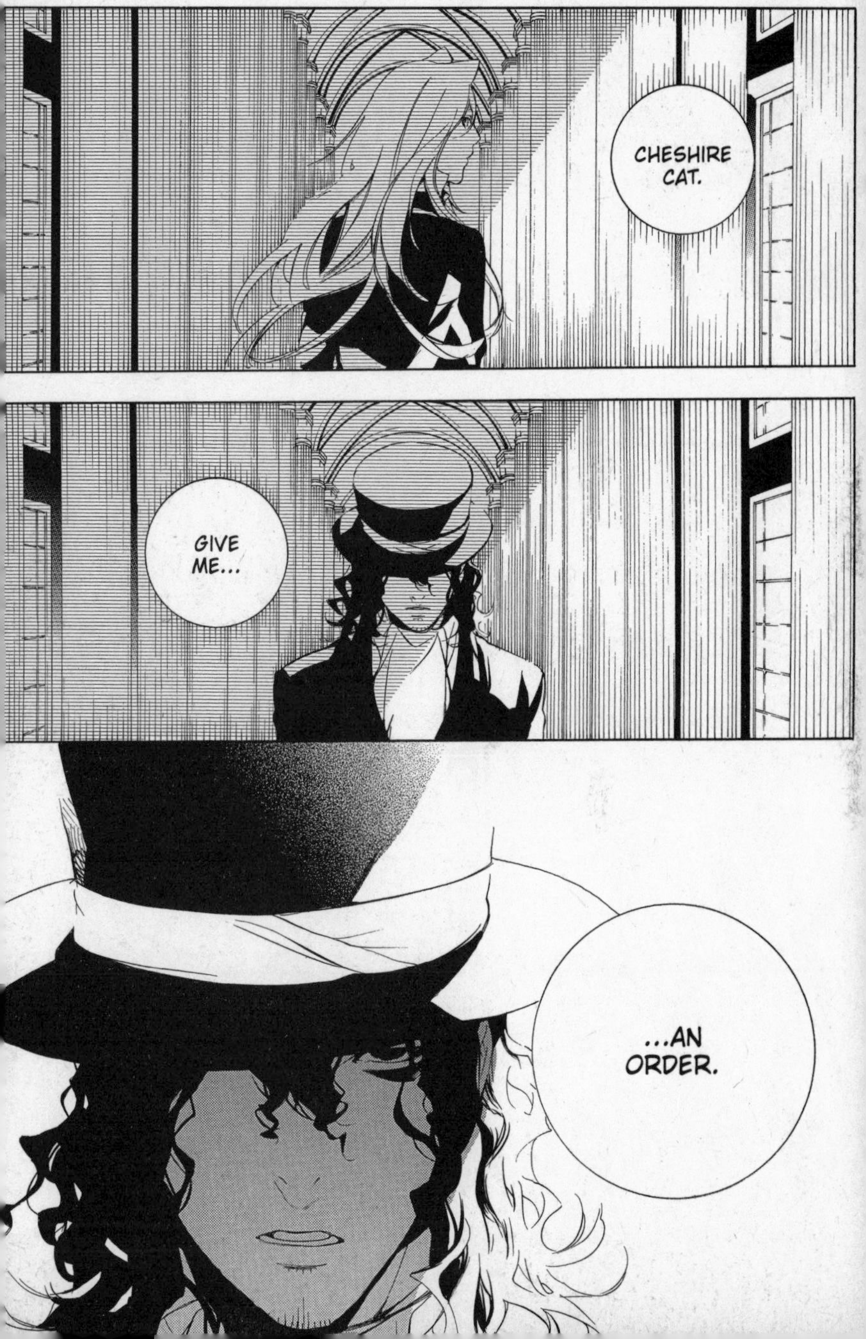
CHESHIRE CAT.
GIVE ME...
...AN ORDER.

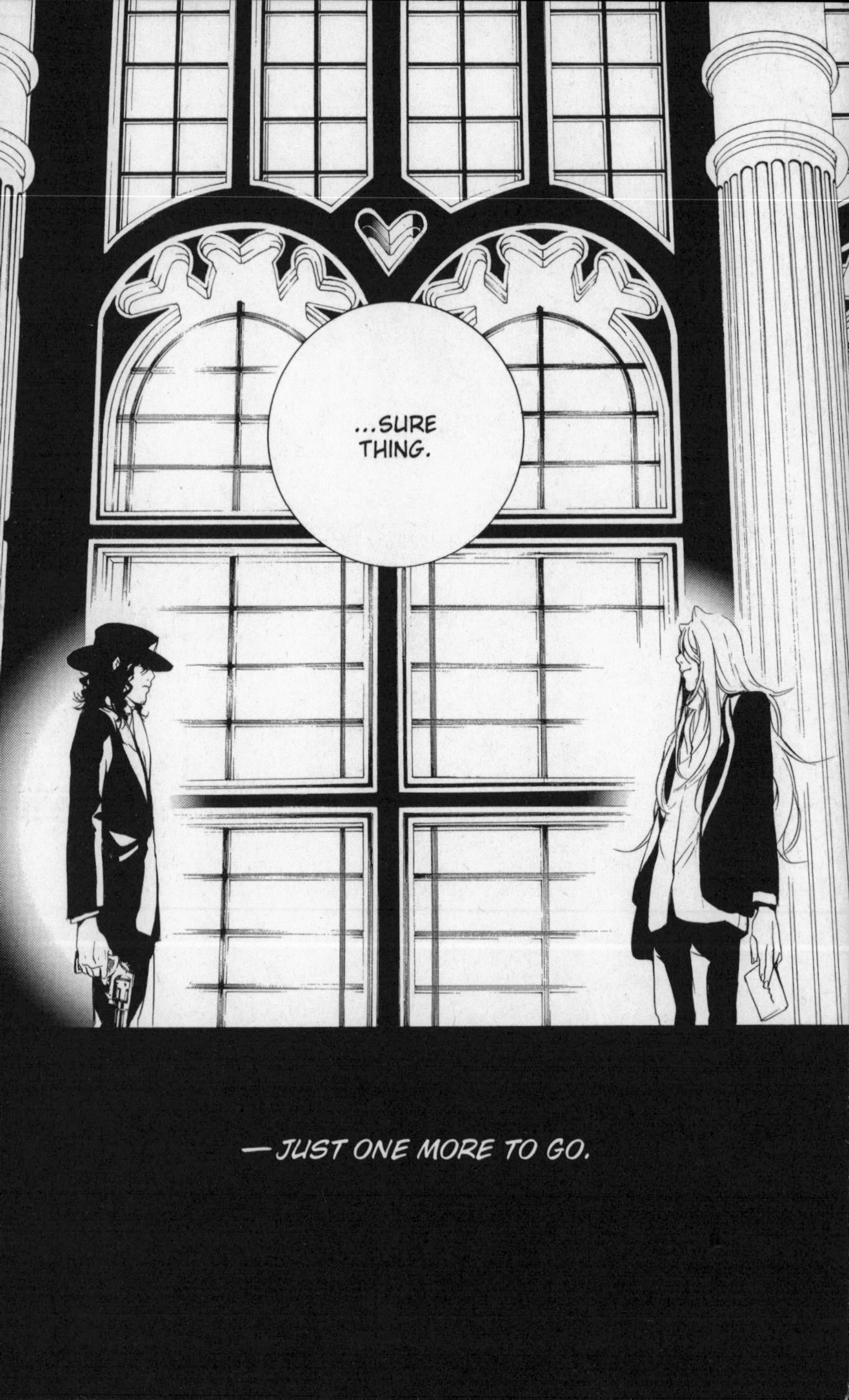
...SURE THING.
—JUST ONE MORE TO GO.

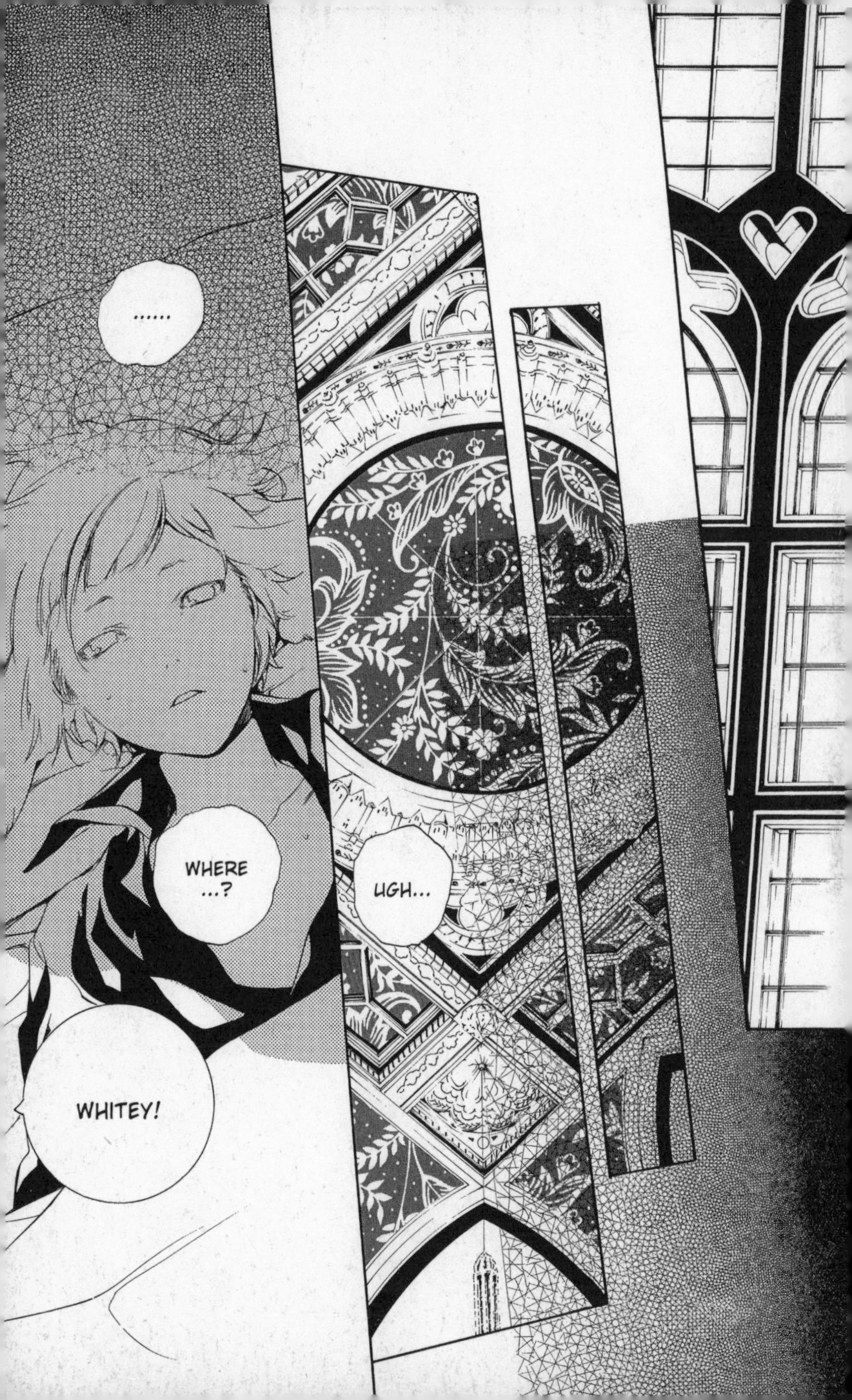
UGH...
......
WHERE ...?
WHITEY!

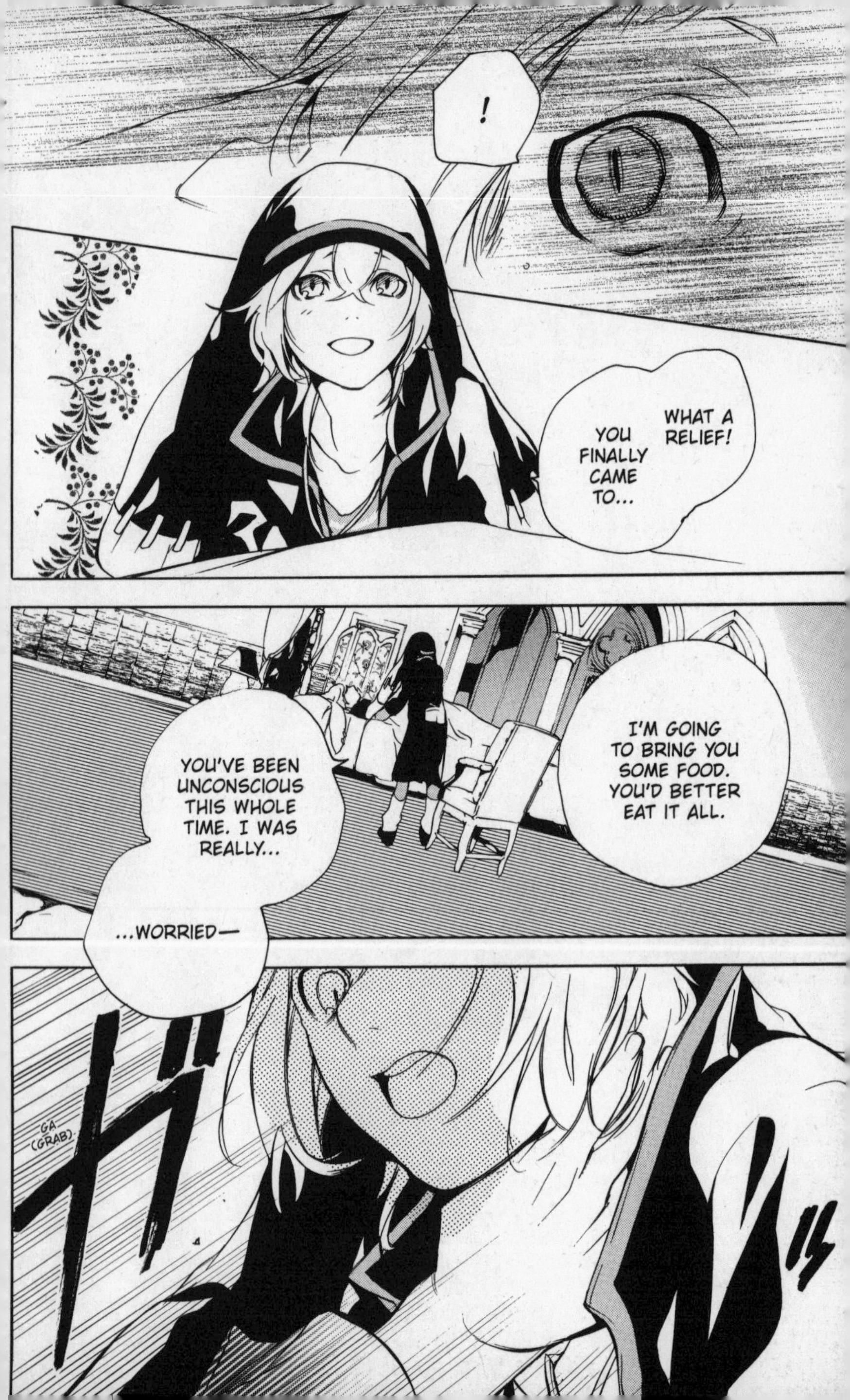
!
WHAT A RELIEF!
YOU FINALLY CAME TO...
I'M GOING TO BRING YOU SOME FOOD. YOU'D BETTER EAT IT ALL.
YOU'VE BEEN UNCONSCIOUS THIS WHOLE TIME. I WAS REALLY...
...WORRIED—
GA (GRAB)

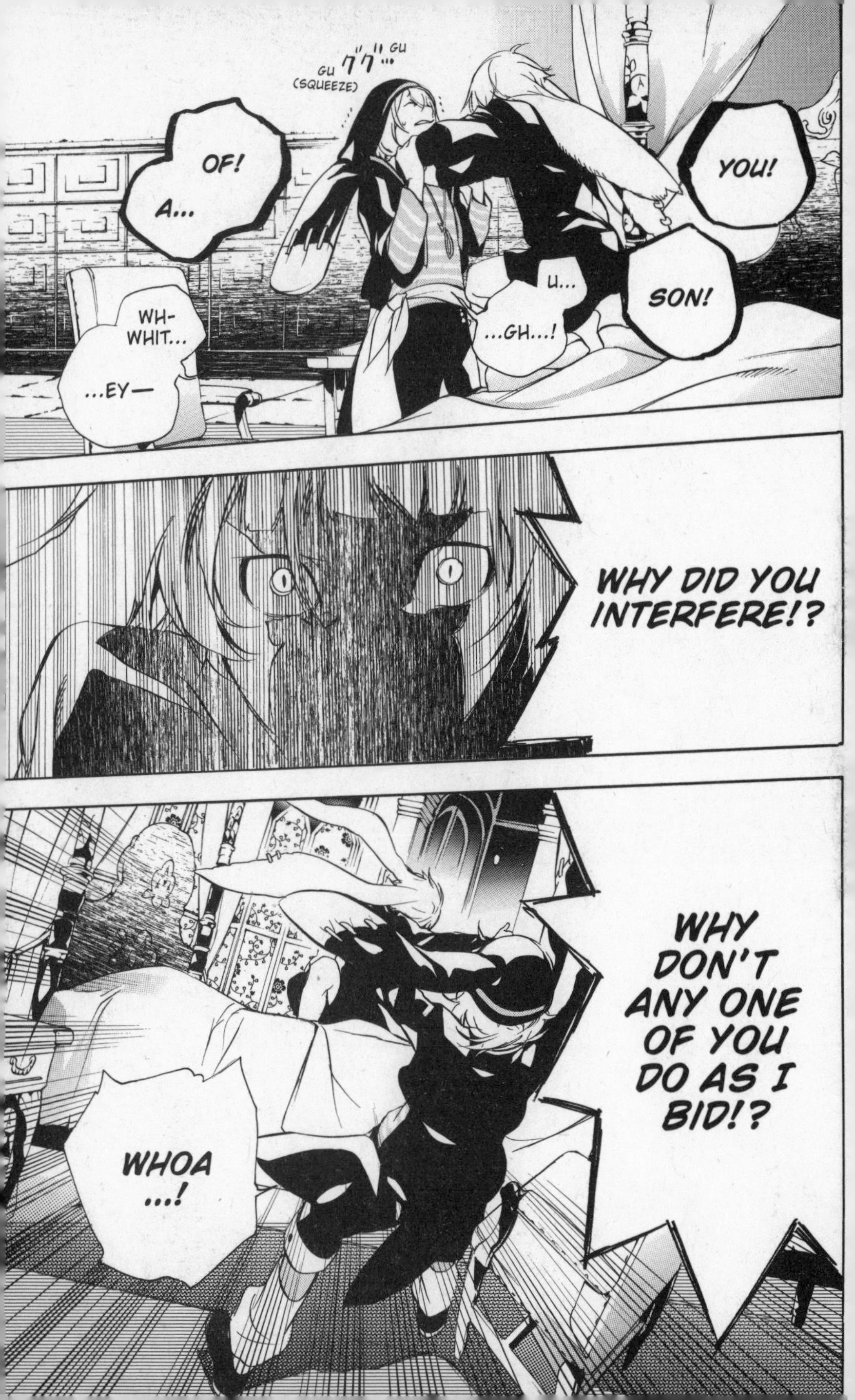
YOU!
SON!
GU グッ GU (SQUEEZE)
U... ...GH...!
OF! A...
WH-WHIT... ...EY—
WHY DID YOU INTERFERE!?
WHY DON'T ANY ONE OF YOU DO AS I BID!?
WHOA ...!

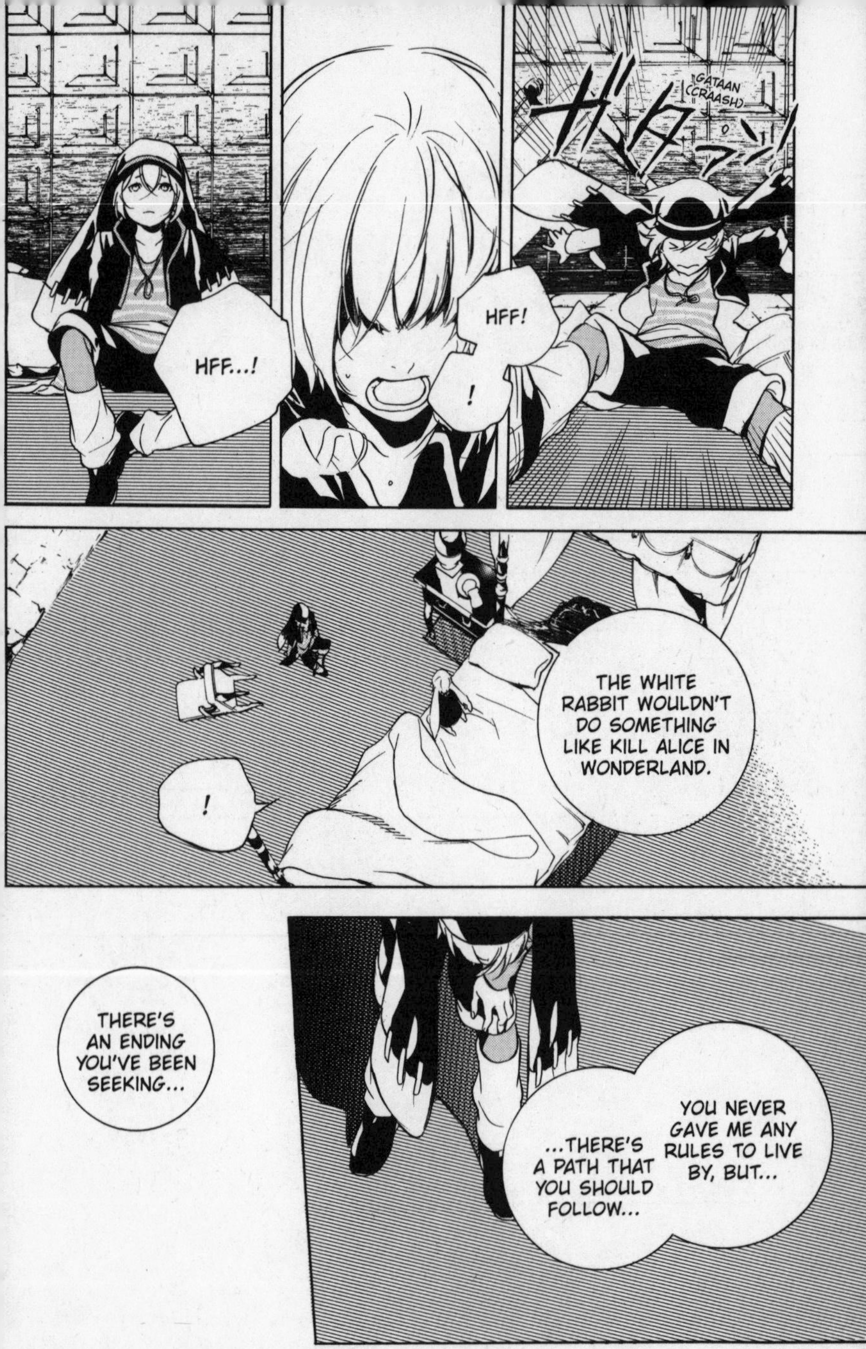
GATAAN (CRAASH)
HFF!
!
HFF...!
THE WHITE RABBIT WOULDN'T DO SOMETHING LIKE KILL ALICE IN WONDERLAND.
!
YOU NEVER GAVE ME ANY RULES TO LIVE BY, BUT...
...THERE'S A PATH THAT YOU SHOULD FOLLOW...
THERE'S AN ENDING YOU'VE BEEN SEEKING...

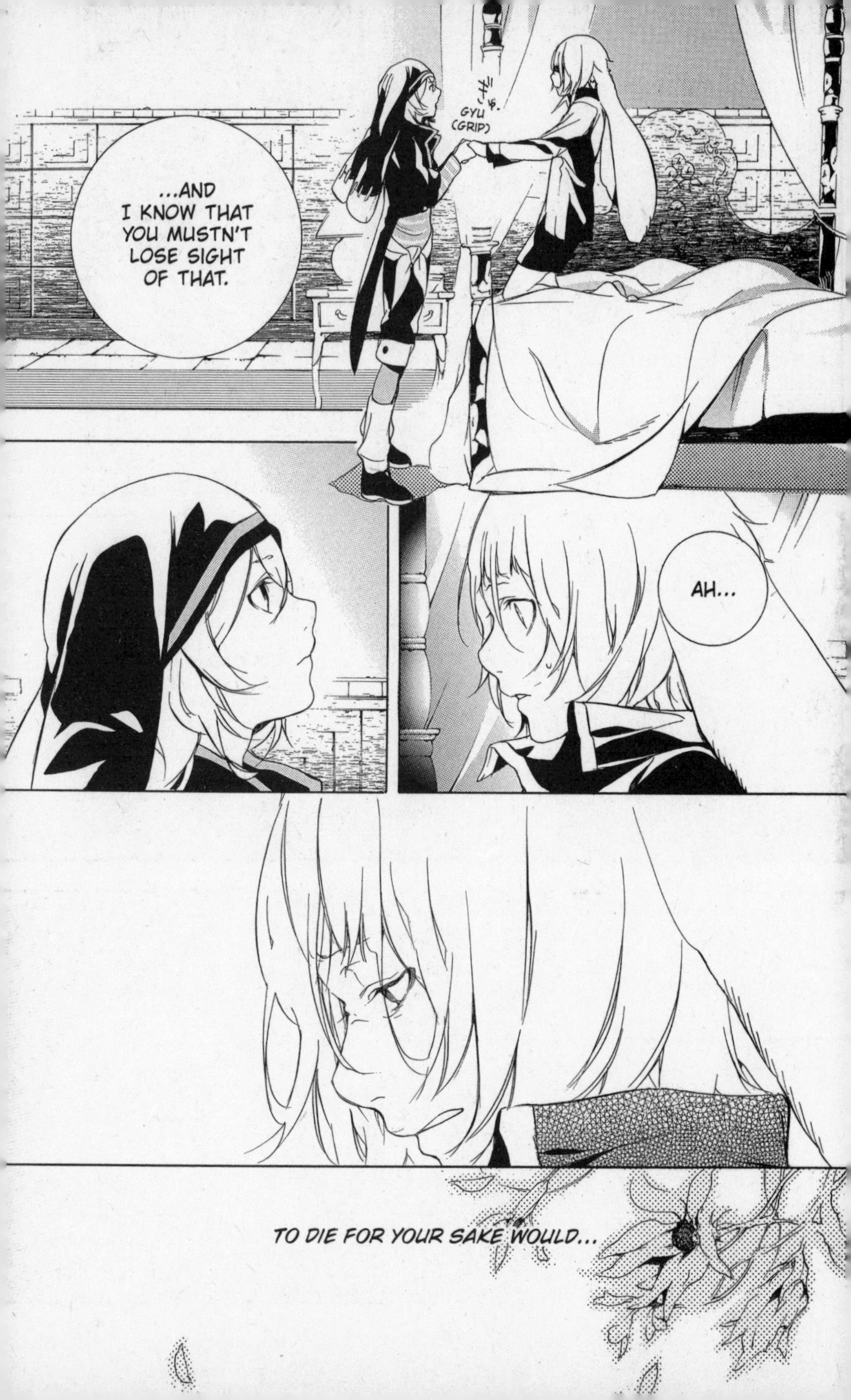
GYU (GRIP)
...AND I KNOW THAT YOU MUSTN'T LOSE SIGHT OF THAT.
AH...
TO DIE FOR YOUR SAKE WOULD...

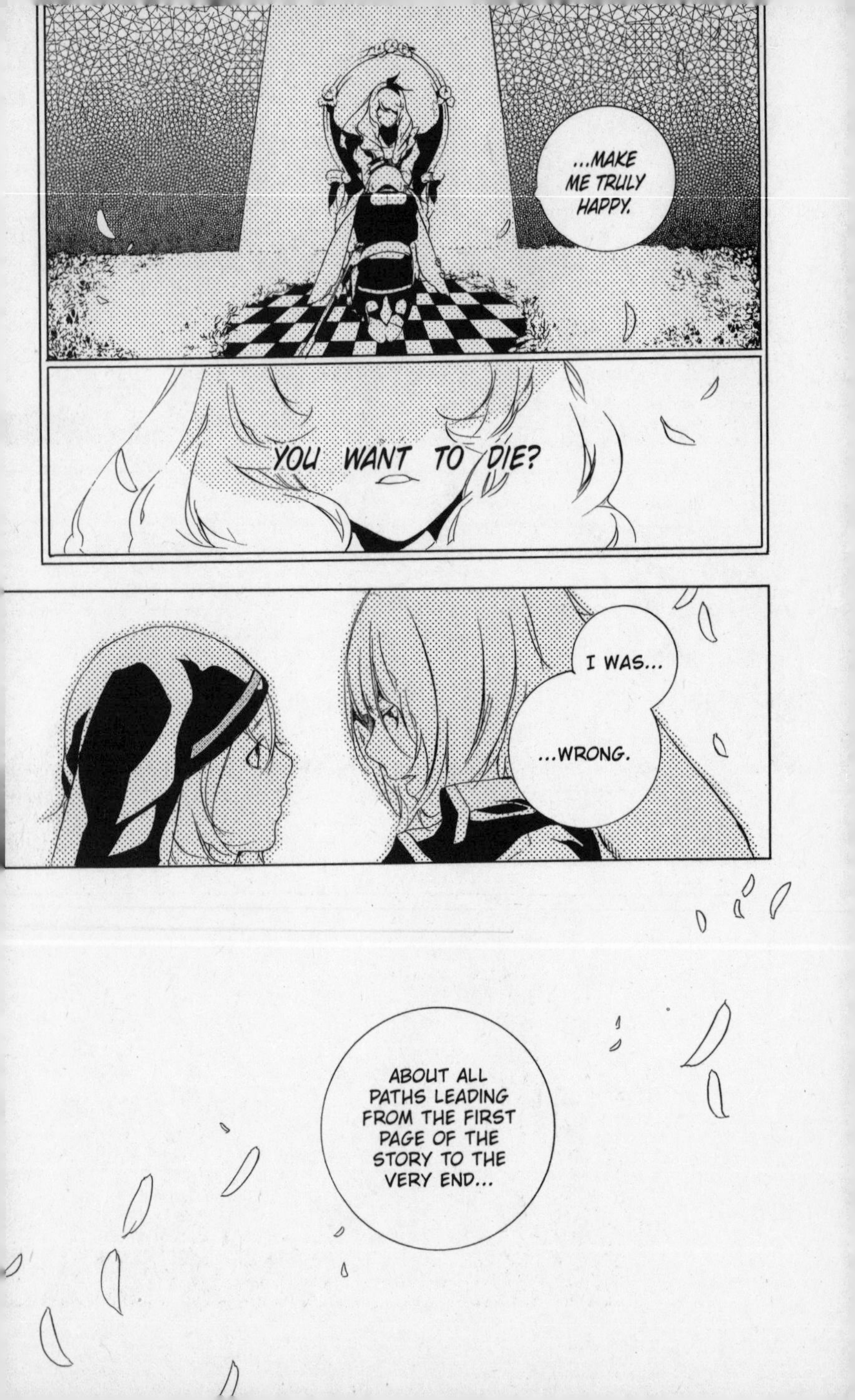
...MAKE ME TRULY HAPPY.
YOU WANT TO DIE?
I WAS...
...WRONG.
ABOUT ALL PATHS LEADING FROM THE FIRST PAGE OF THE STORY TO THE VERY END...

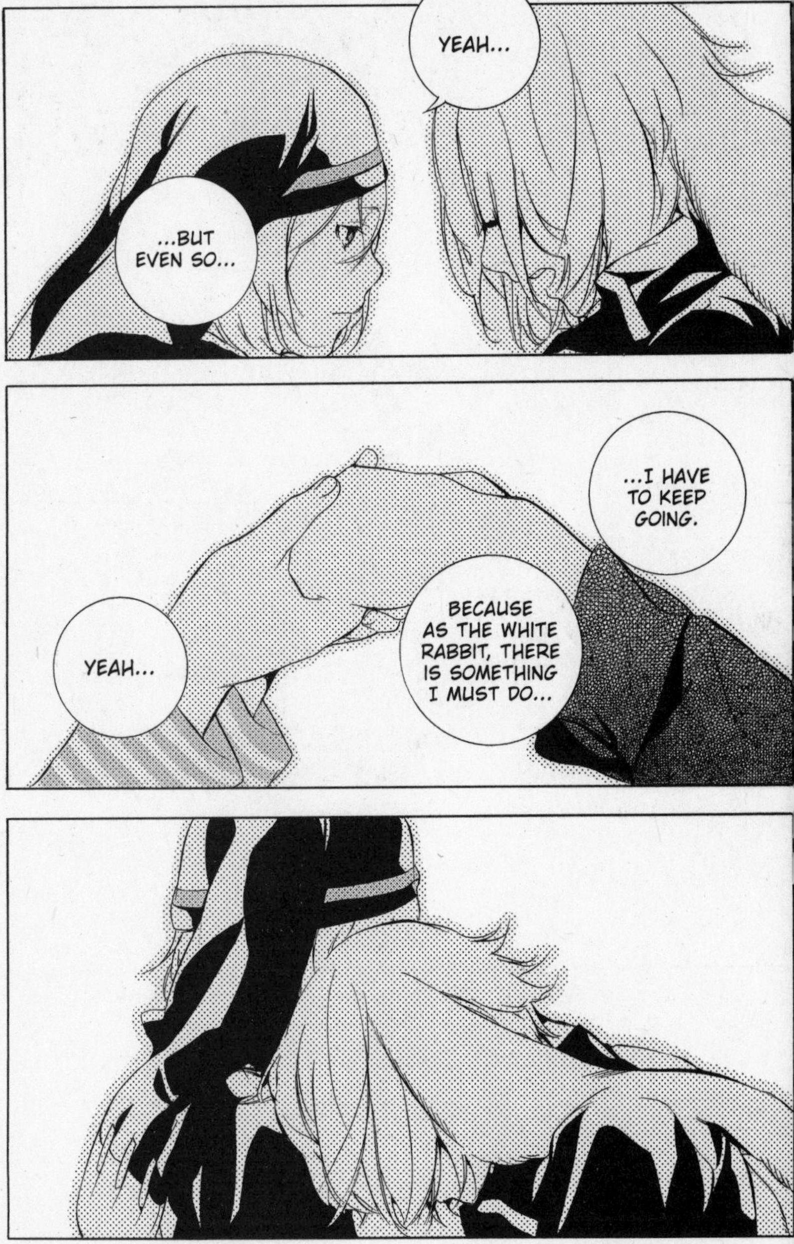
YEAH...
...BUT EVEN SO...
...I HAVE TO KEEP GOING.
BECAUSE AS THE WHITE RABBIT, THERE IS SOMETHING I MUST DO...
YEAH...

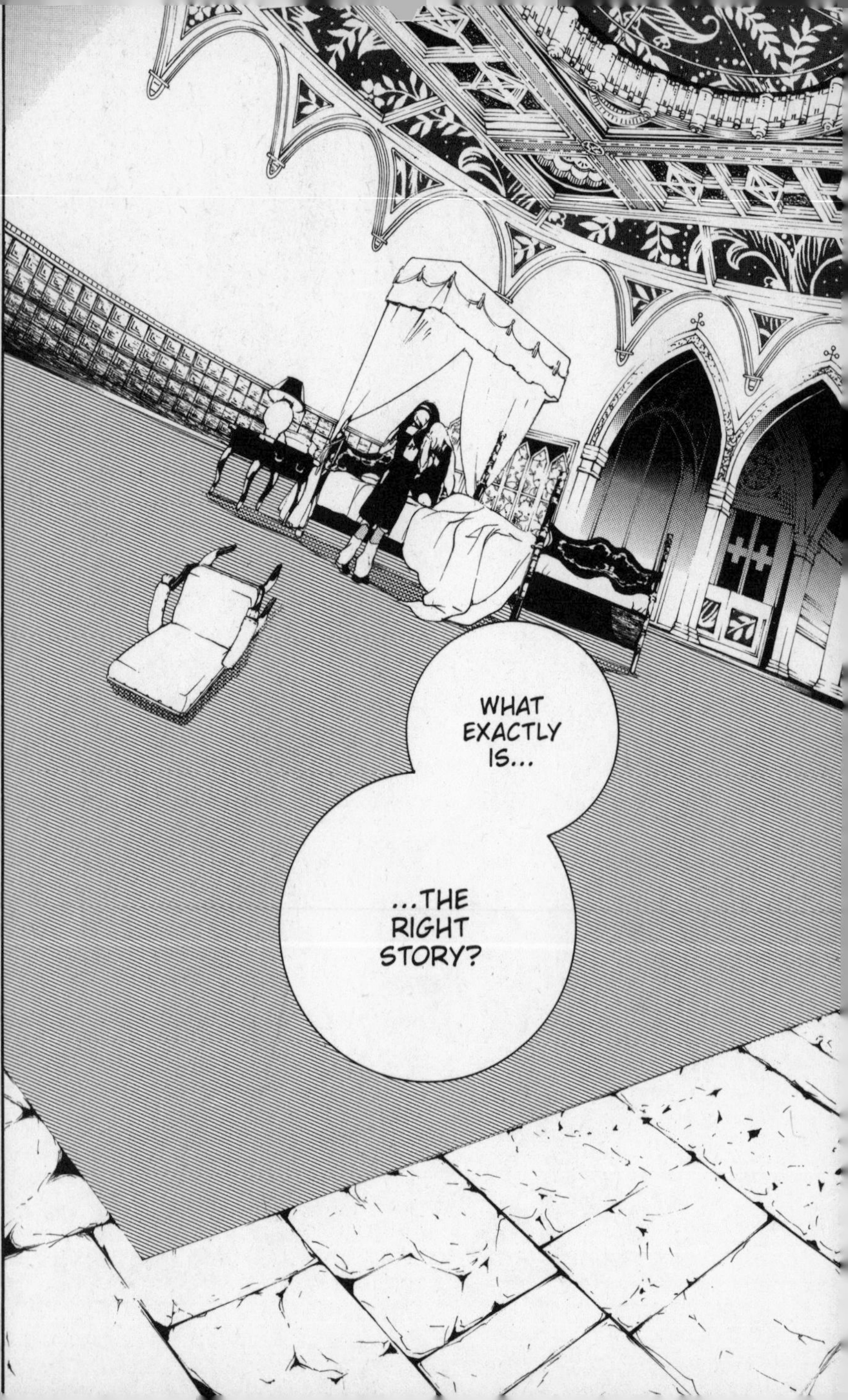
WHAT EXACTLY IS...
...THE RIGHT STORY?

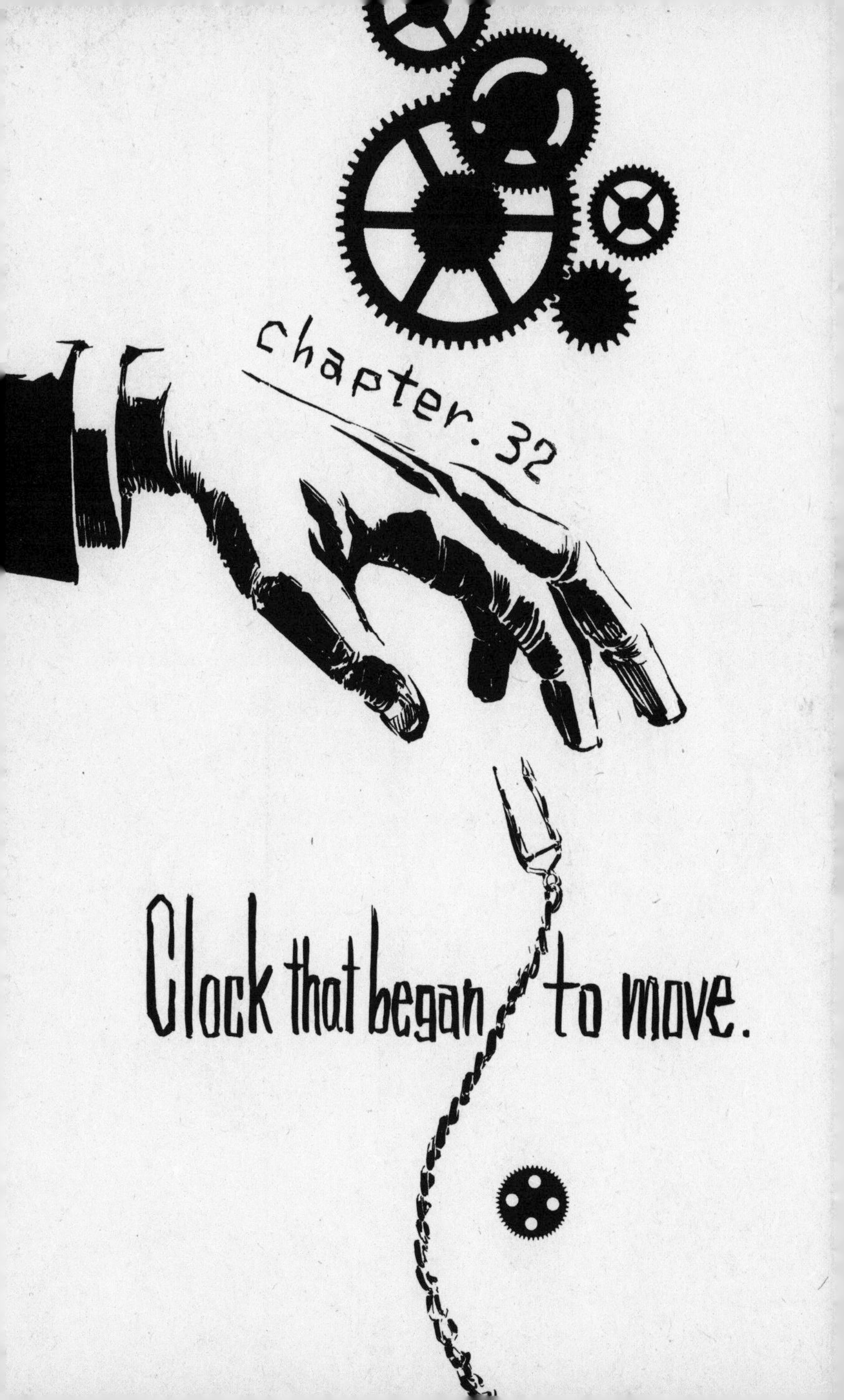
chapter. 32
Clock that began to move.

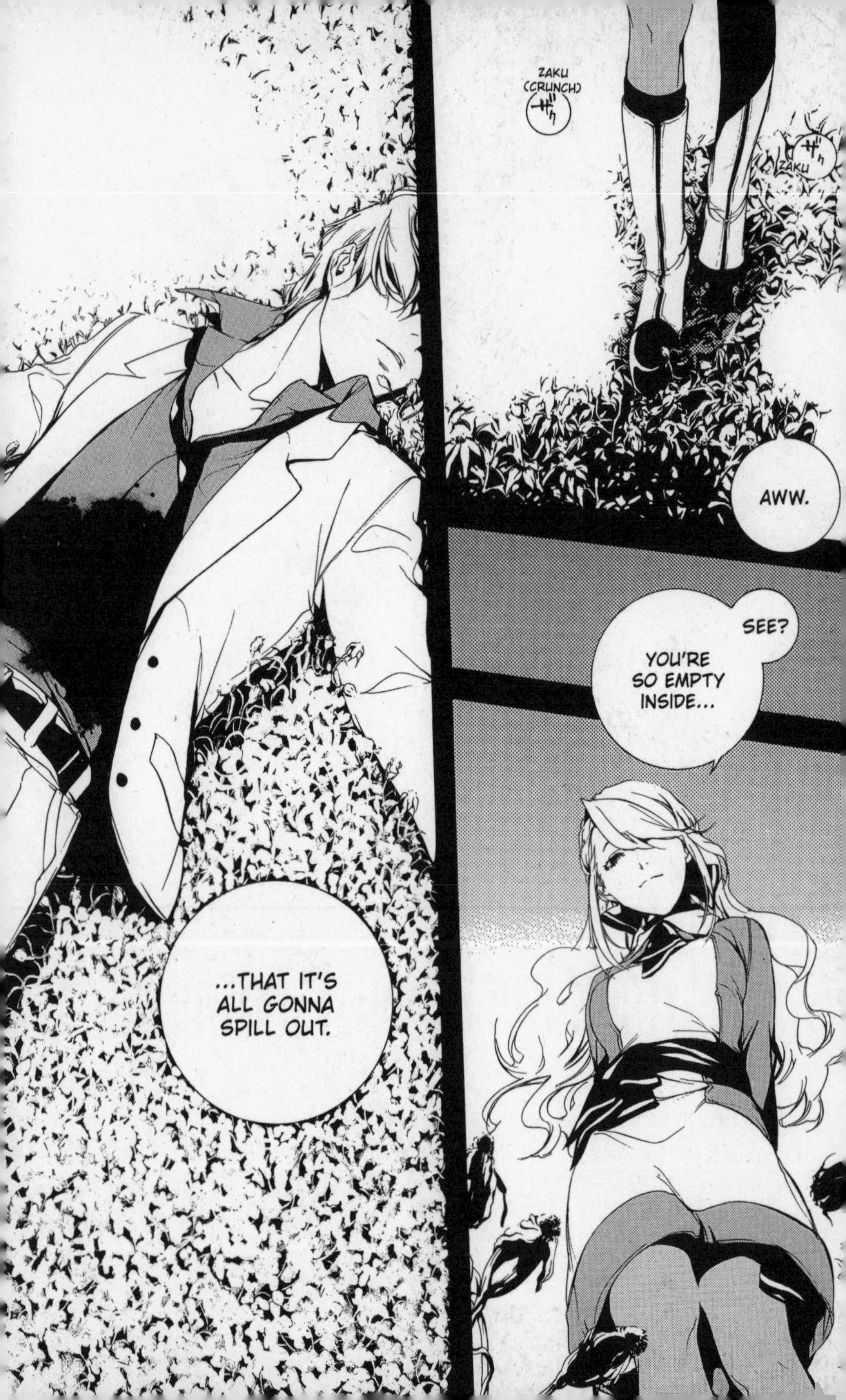
ZAKU
ZAKU (CRUNCH)
AWW.
SEE? YOU'RE SO EMPTY INSIDE...
...THAT IT'S ALL GONNA SPILL OUT.

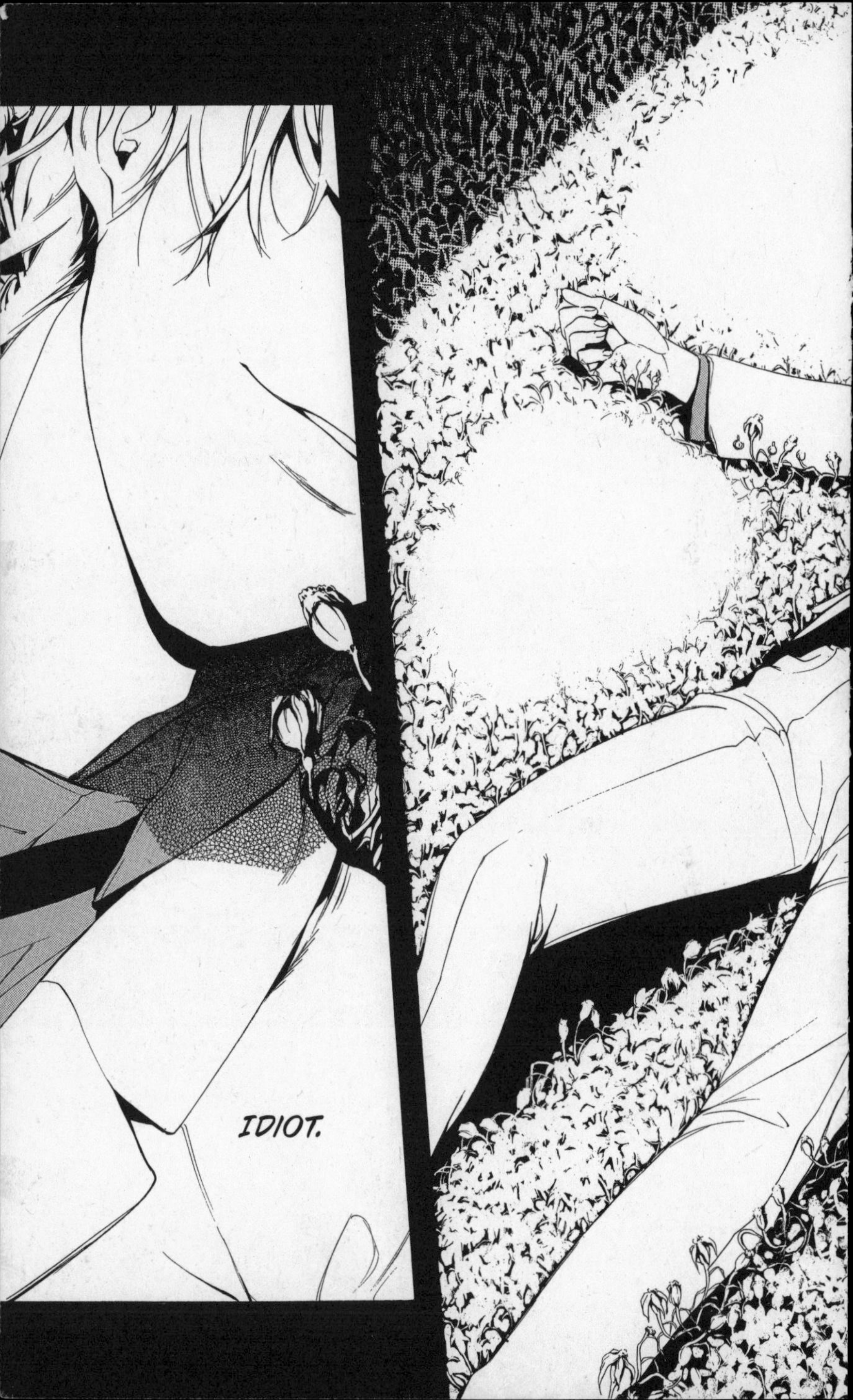
IDIOT.

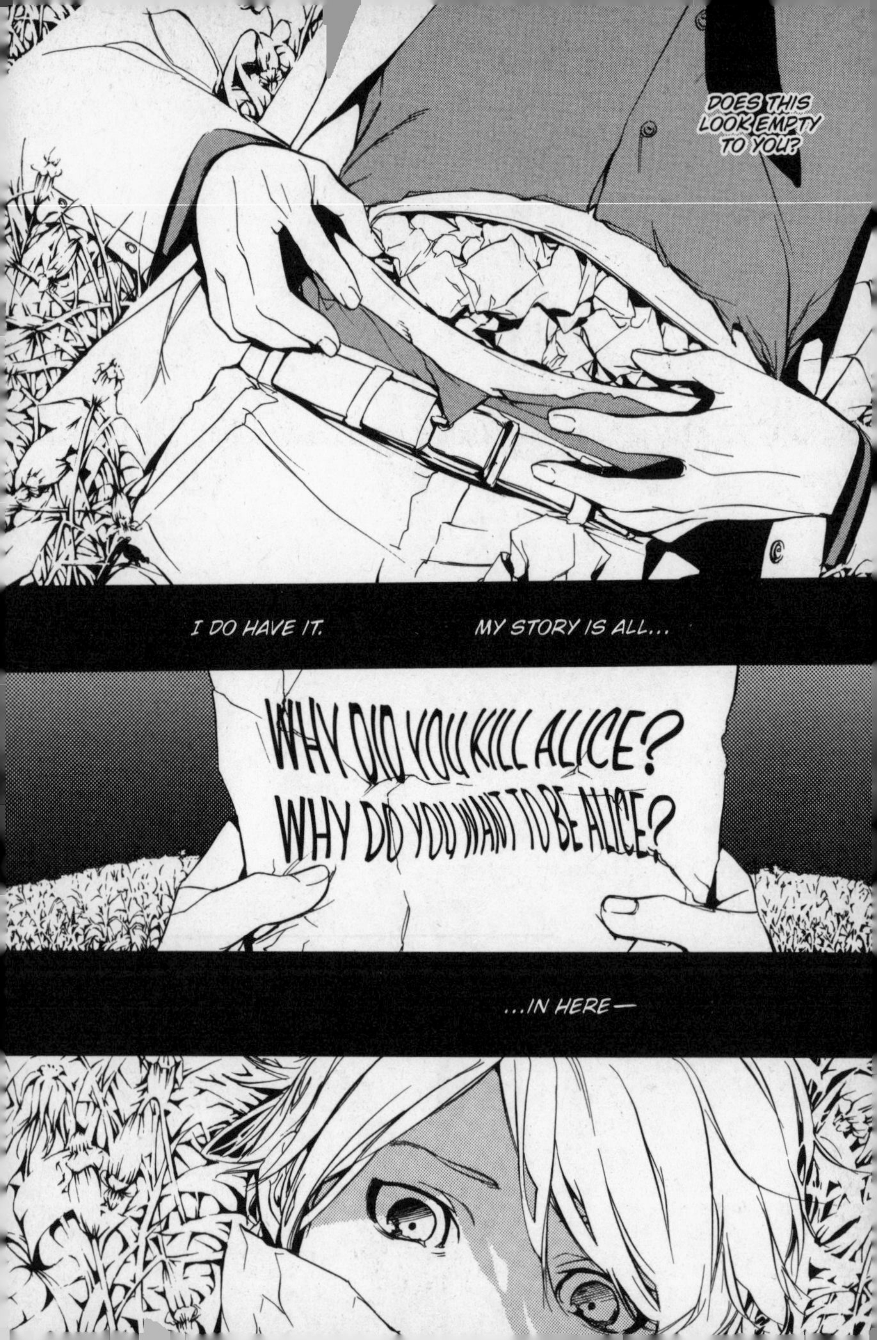
DOES THIS LOOK EMPTY TO YOU?
I DO HAVE IT.
MY STORY IS ALL...
WHY DID YOU KILL ALICE?
WHY DO YOU WANT TO BE ALICE?
...IN HERE—

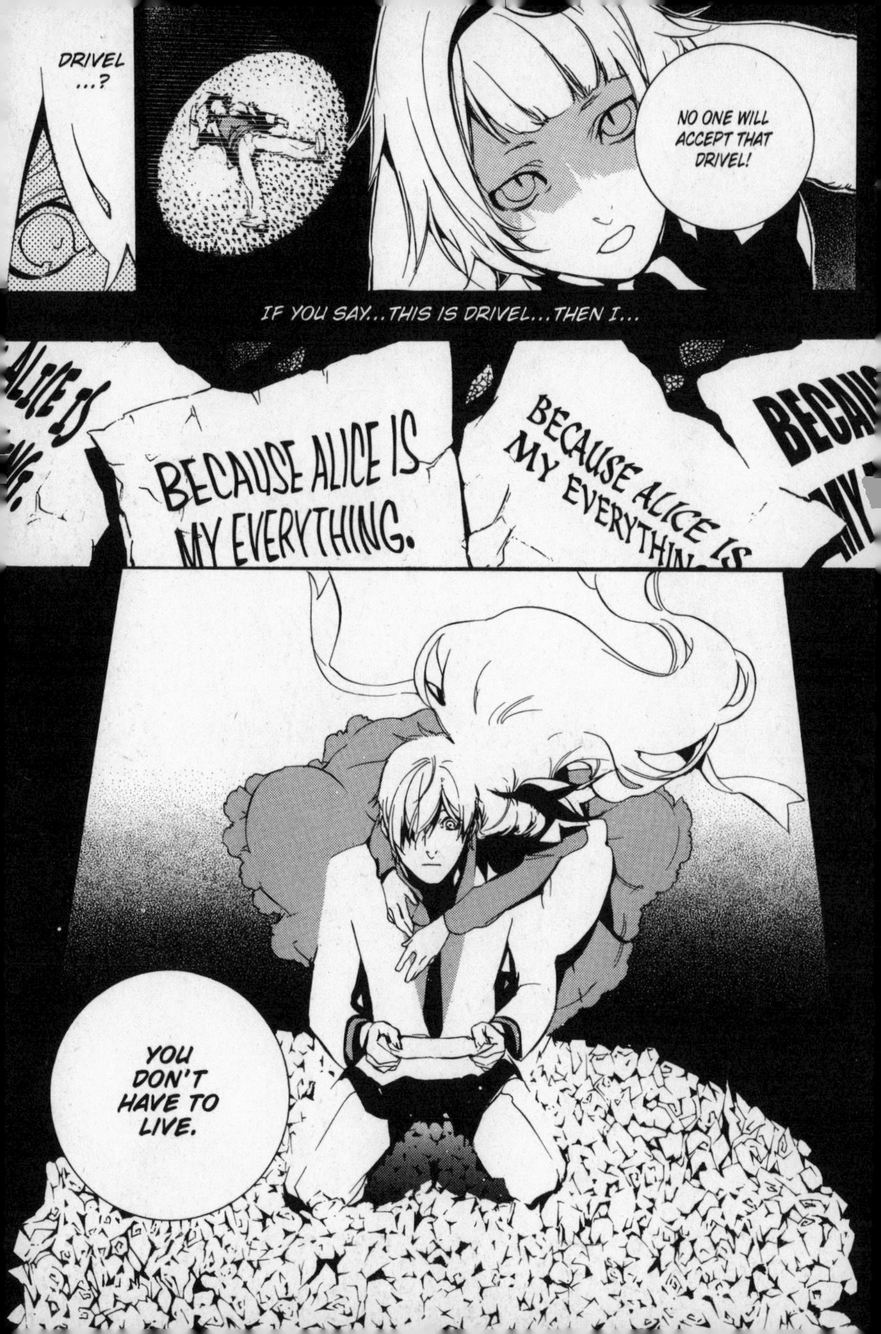
NO ONE WILL ACCEPT THAT DRIVEL!
DRIVEL ...?
IF YOU SAY...THIS IS DRIVEL...THEN I...
BECAUSE ALICE IS MY EVERYTHIN
BECAUSE ALICE IS MY EVERYTHING.
YOU DON'T HAVE TO LIVE.

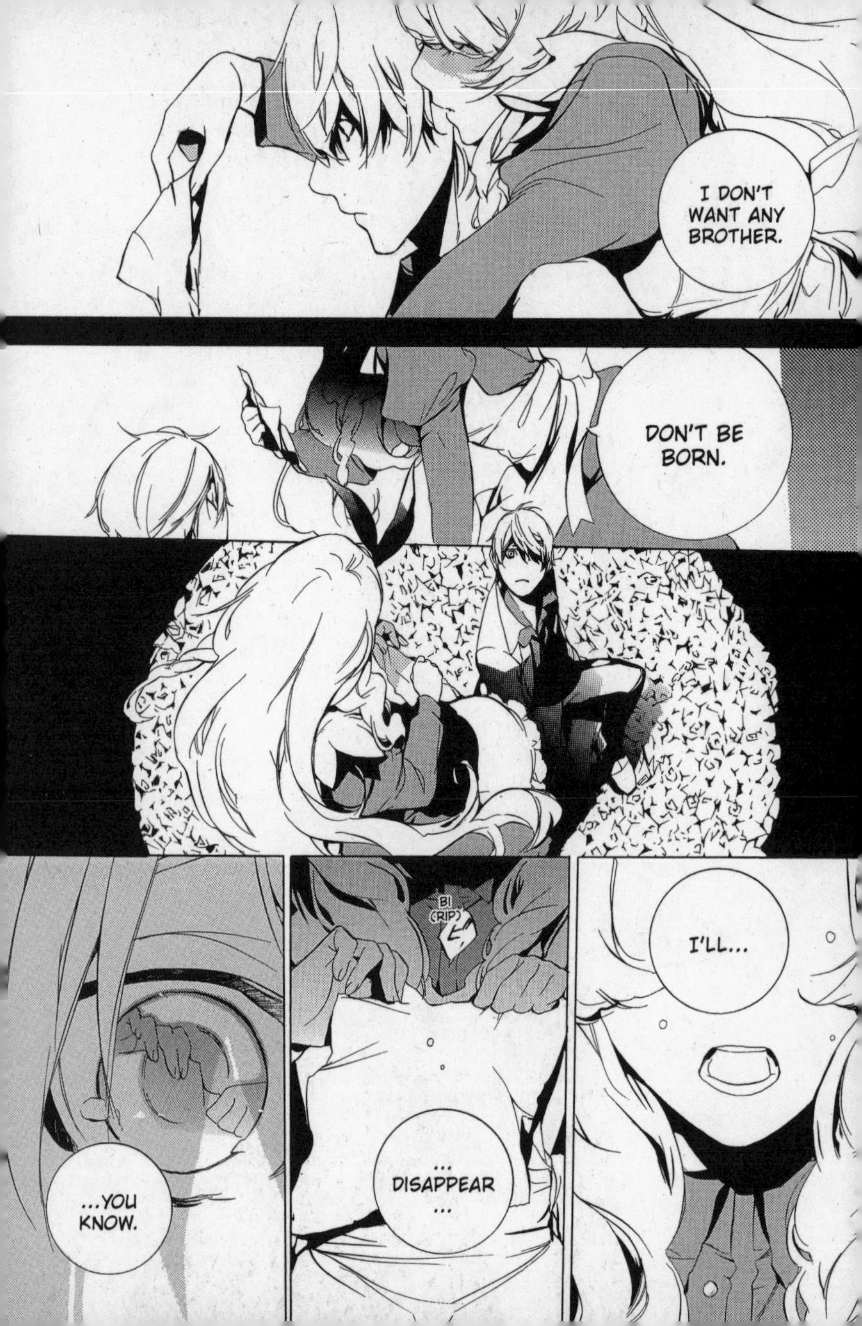
I DON'T WANT ANY BROTHER.
DON'T BE BORN.
I'LL...
BI (RIP)
... DISAPPEAR ...
...YOU KNOW.

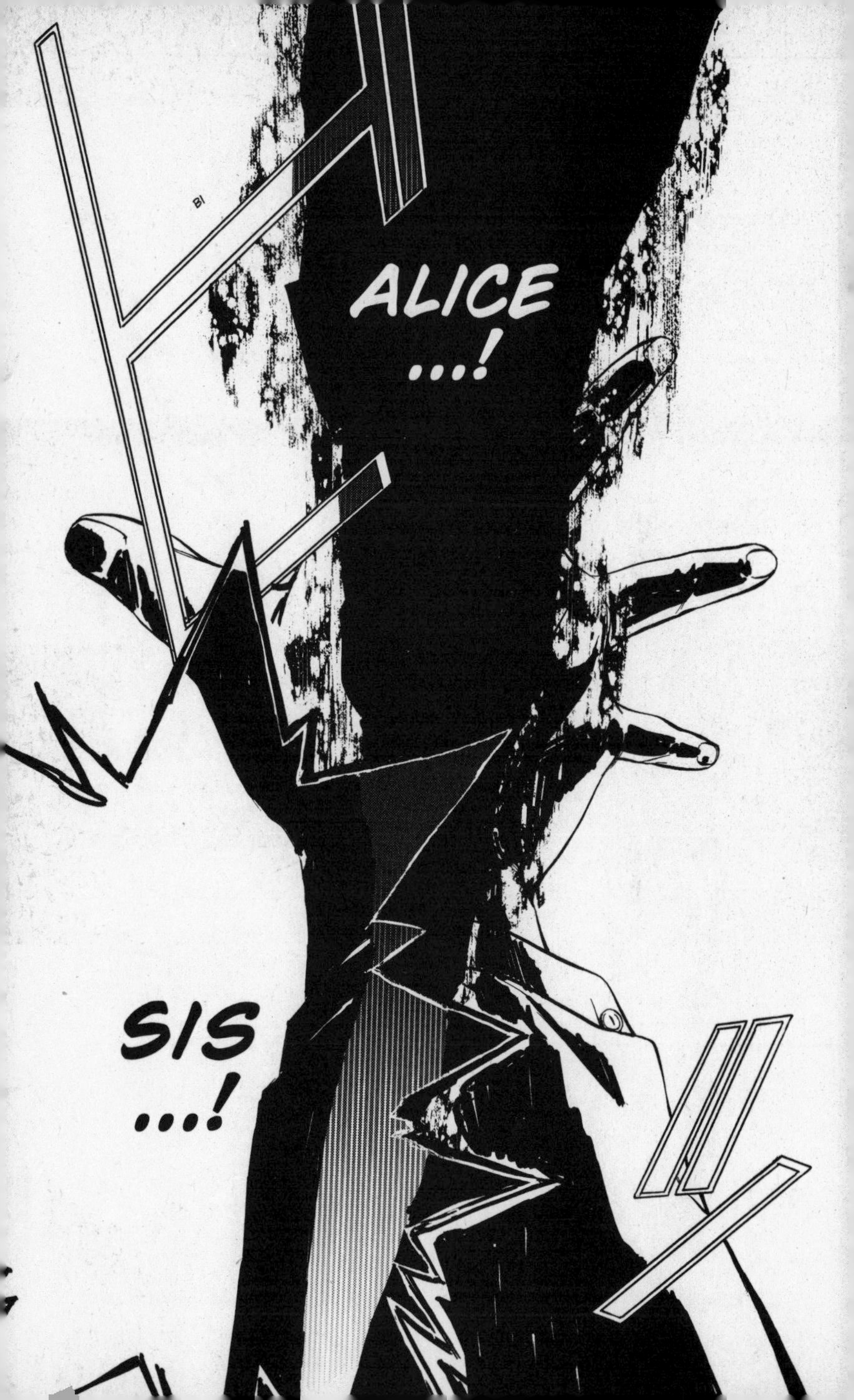
ALICE ...!
SIS ...!

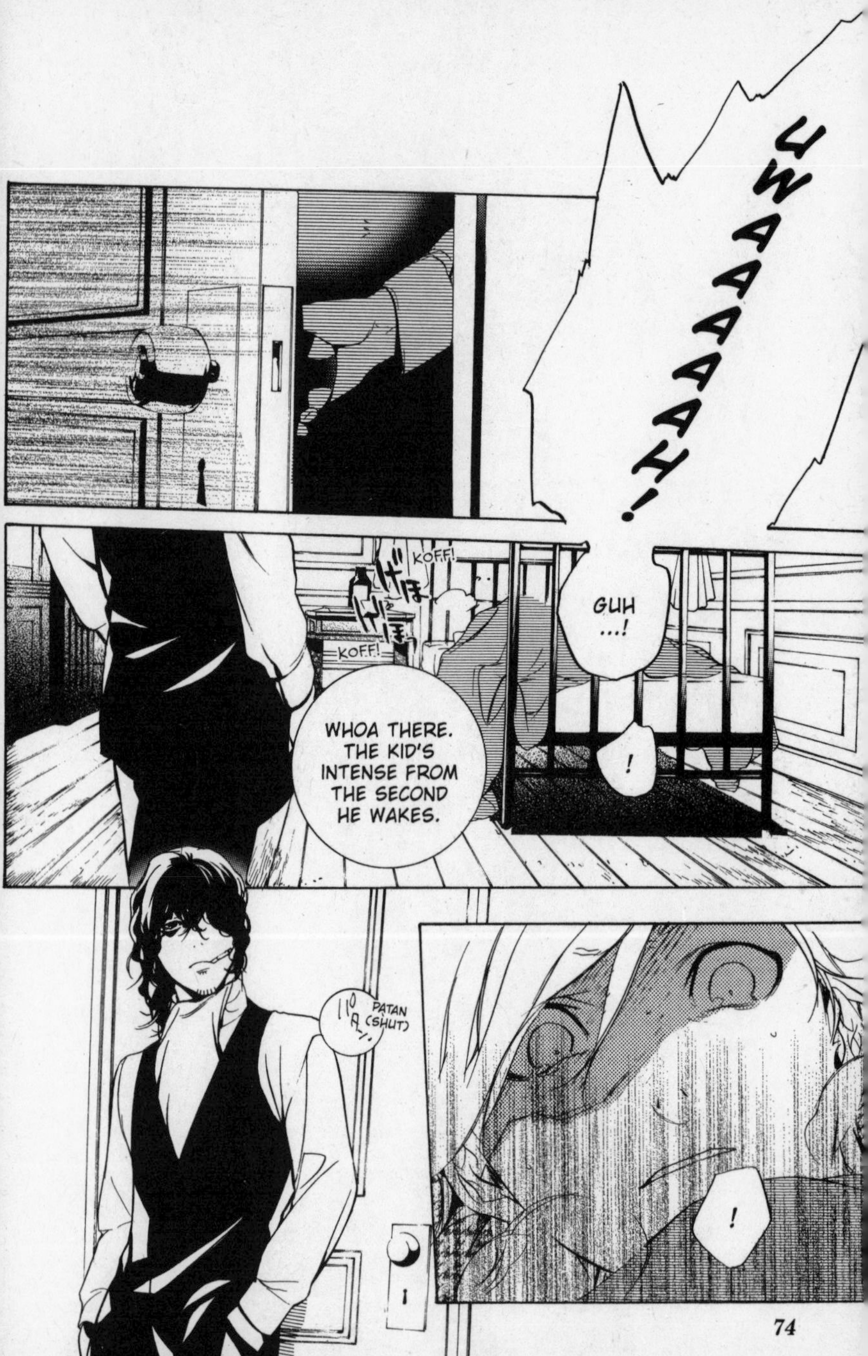
UWAAAAAAH!
GUH ...!
!
KOFF!
KOFF!
WHOA THERE. THE KID'S INTENSE FROM THE SECOND HE WAKES.
!
PATAN (SHUT)

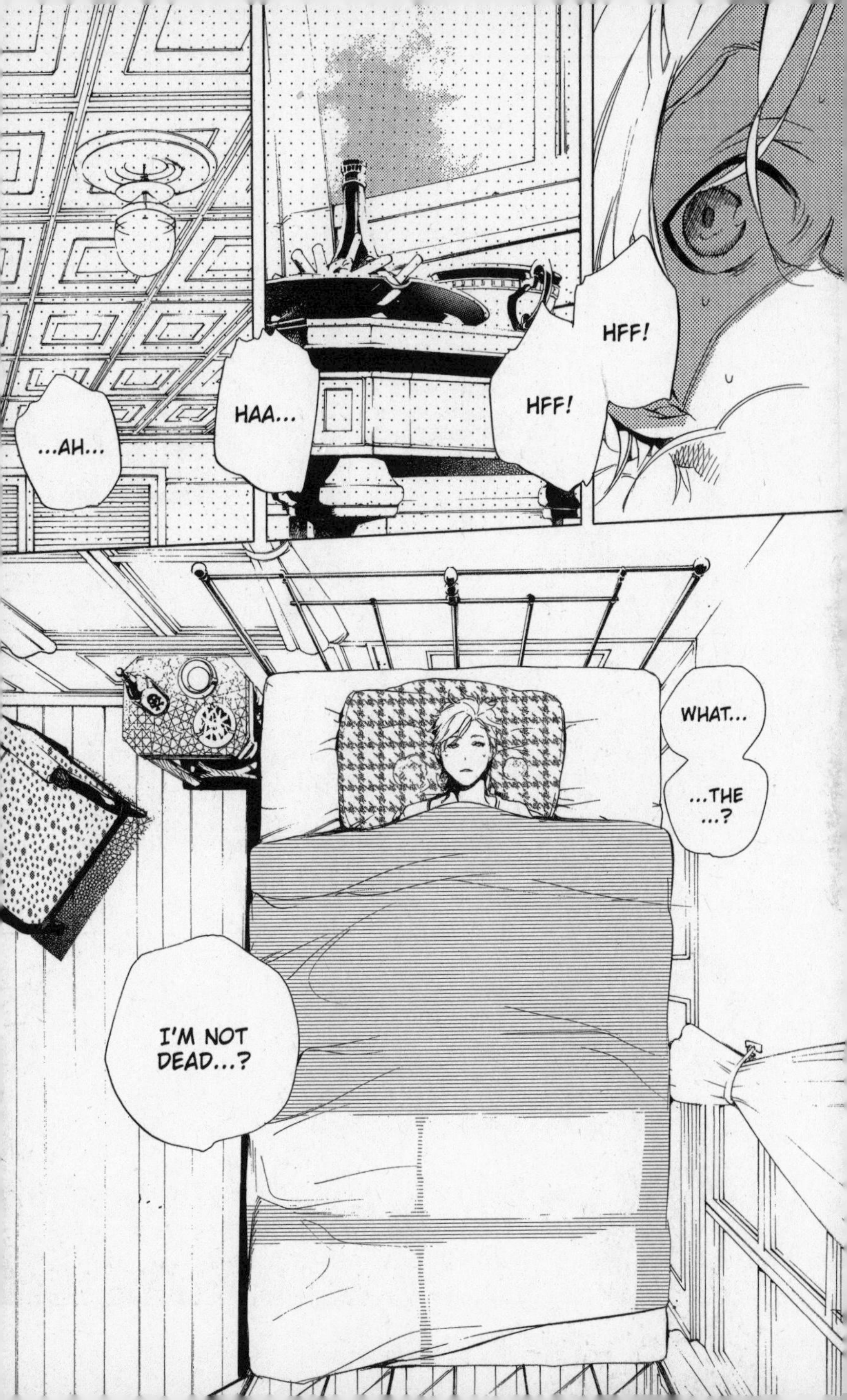
HFF!
HFF!
HAA...
...AH...
WHAT...
...THE ...?
I'M NOT DEAD...?

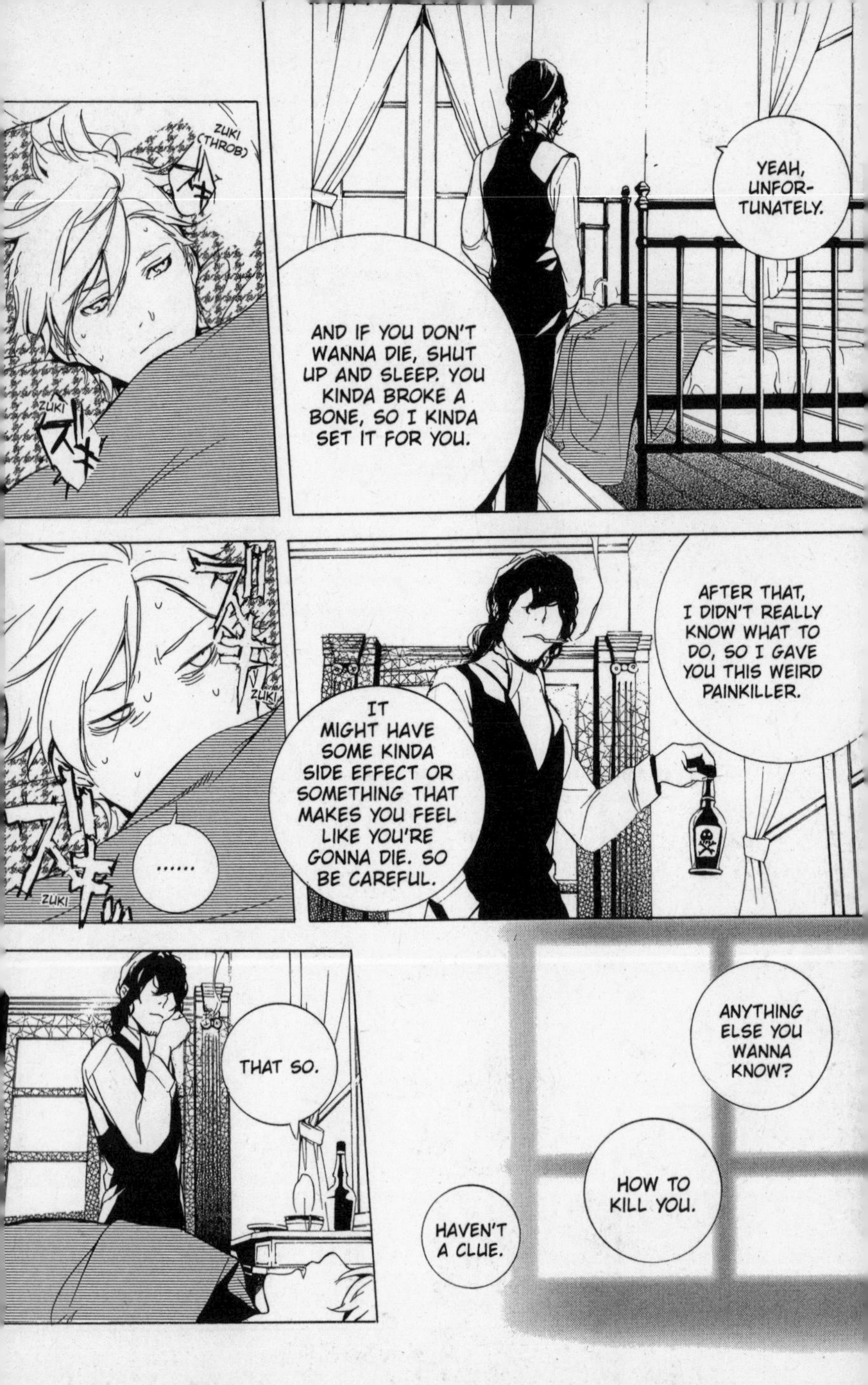
YEAH, UNFORTUNATELY.
AND IF YOU DON'T WANNA DIE, SHUT UP AND SLEEP. YOU KINDA BROKE A BONE, SO I KINDA SET IT FOR YOU.
ZUKI (THROB)
ZUKI
AFTER THAT, I DIDN'T REALLY KNOW WHAT TO DO, SO I GAVE YOU THIS WEIRD PAINKILLER.
IT MIGHT HAVE SOME KINDA SIDE EFFECT OR SOMETHING THAT MAKES YOU FEEL LIKE YOU'RE GONNA DIE. SO BE CAREFUL.
ZUKI
......
ZUKI
ANYTHING ELSE YOU WANNA KNOW?
HOW TO KILL YOU.
HAVEN'T A CLUE.
THAT SO.

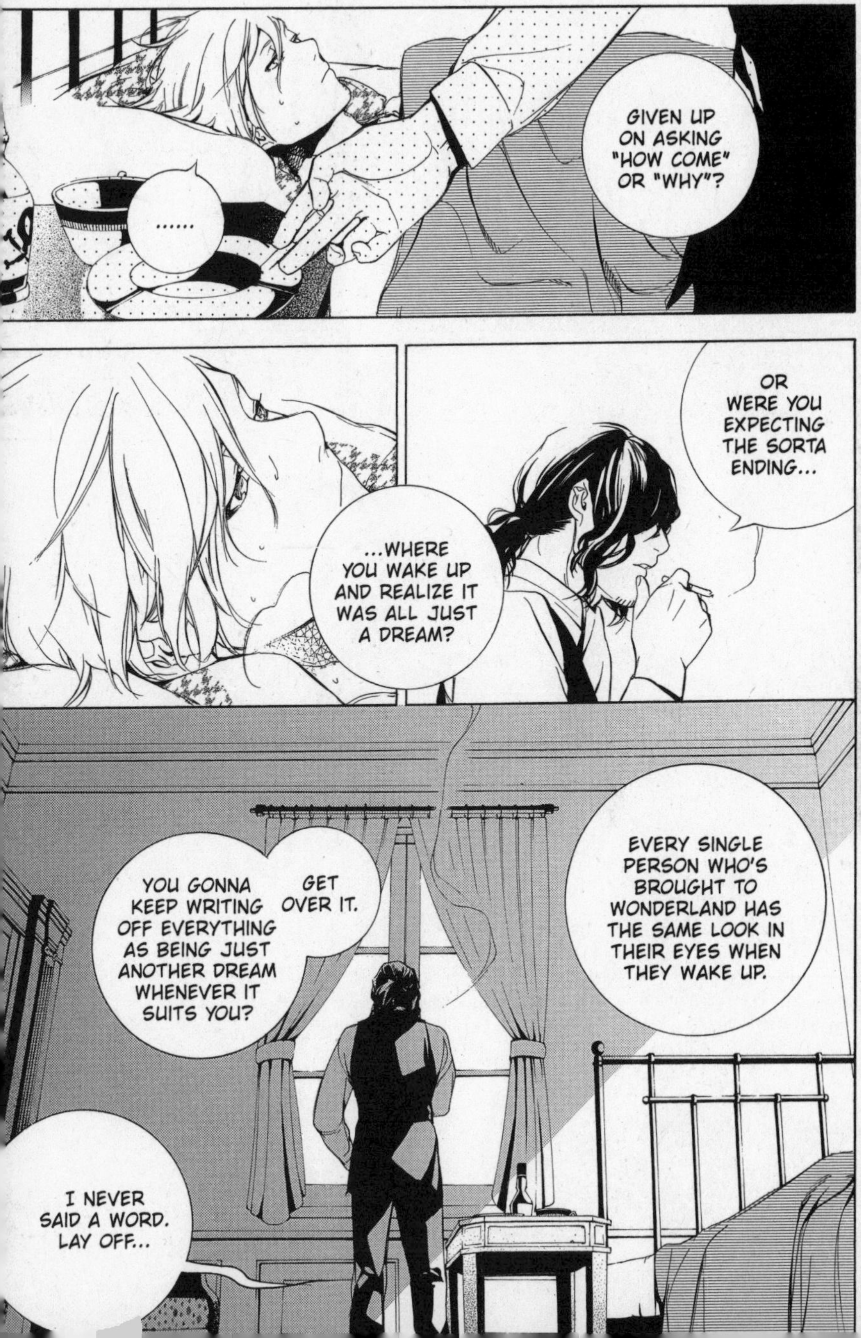
GIVEN UP ON ASKING "HOW COME" OR "WHY"?
......
OR WERE YOU EXPECTING THE SORTA ENDING...
...WHERE YOU WAKE UP AND REALIZE IT WAS ALL JUST A DREAM?
EVERY SINGLE PERSON WHO'S BROUGHT TO WONDERLAND HAS THE SAME LOOK IN THEIR EYES WHEN THEY WAKE UP.
GET OVER IT.
YOU GONNA KEEP WRITING OFF EVERYTHING AS BEING JUST ANOTHER DREAM WHENEVER IT SUITS YOU?
I NEVER SAID A WORD. LAY OFF...

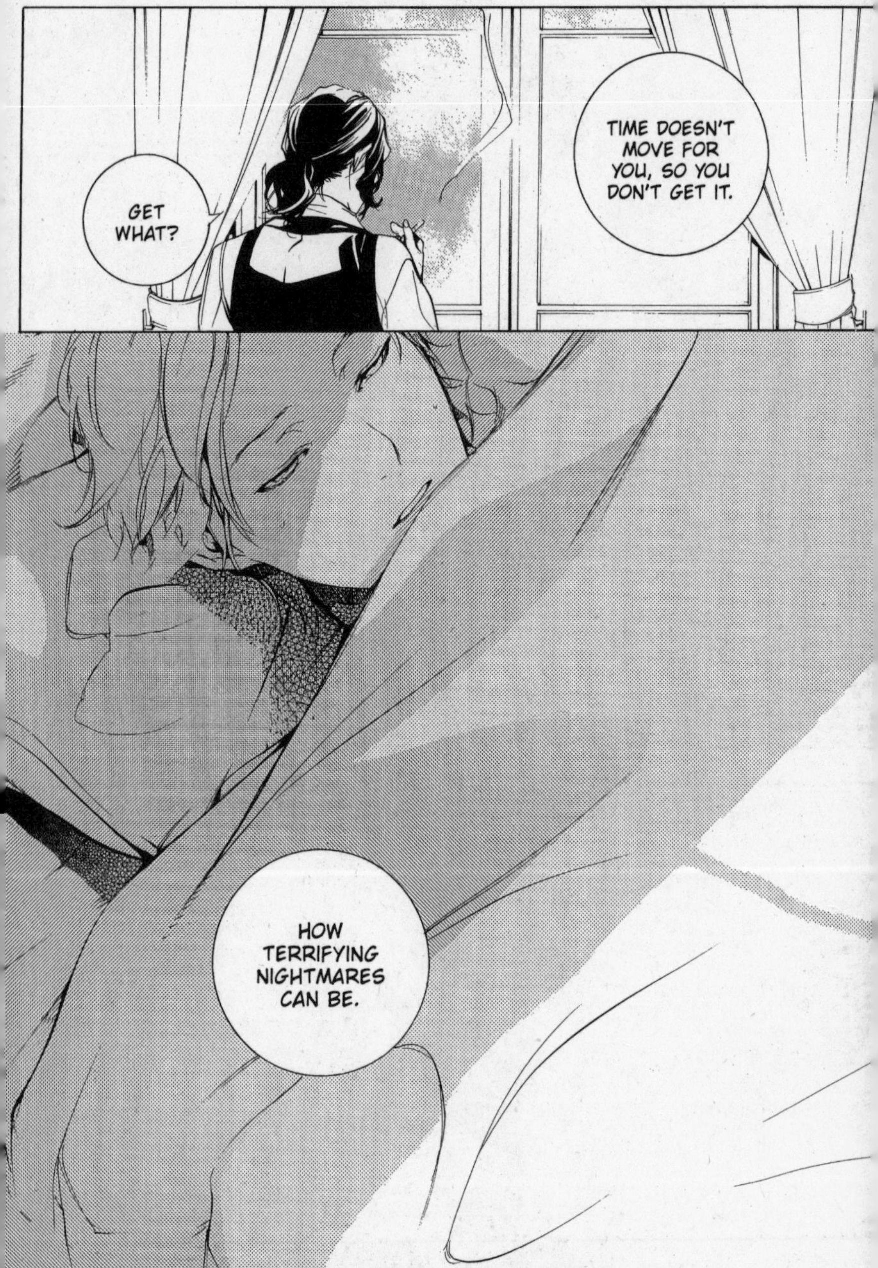
TIME DOESN'T MOVE FOR YOU, SO YOU DON'T GET IT.
GET WHAT?
HOW TERRIFYING NIGHTMARES CAN BE.

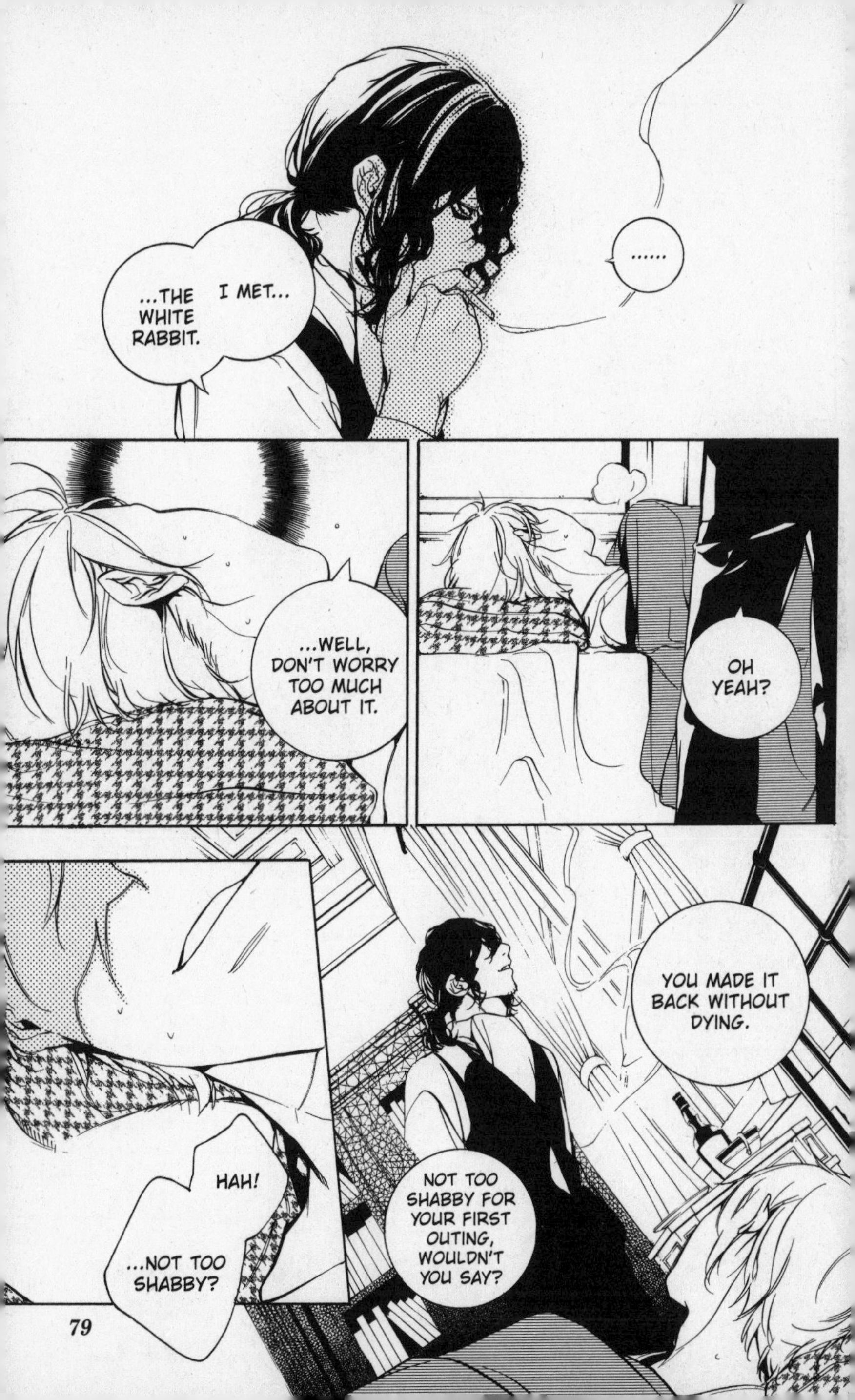
......
I MET... ...THE WHITE RABBIT.
OH YEAH?
...WELL, DON'T WORRY TOO MUCH ABOUT IT.
YOU MADE IT BACK WITHOUT DYING.
NOT TOO SHABBY FOR YOUR FIRST OUTING, WOULDN'T YOU SAY?
HAH!
...NOT TOO SHABBY?

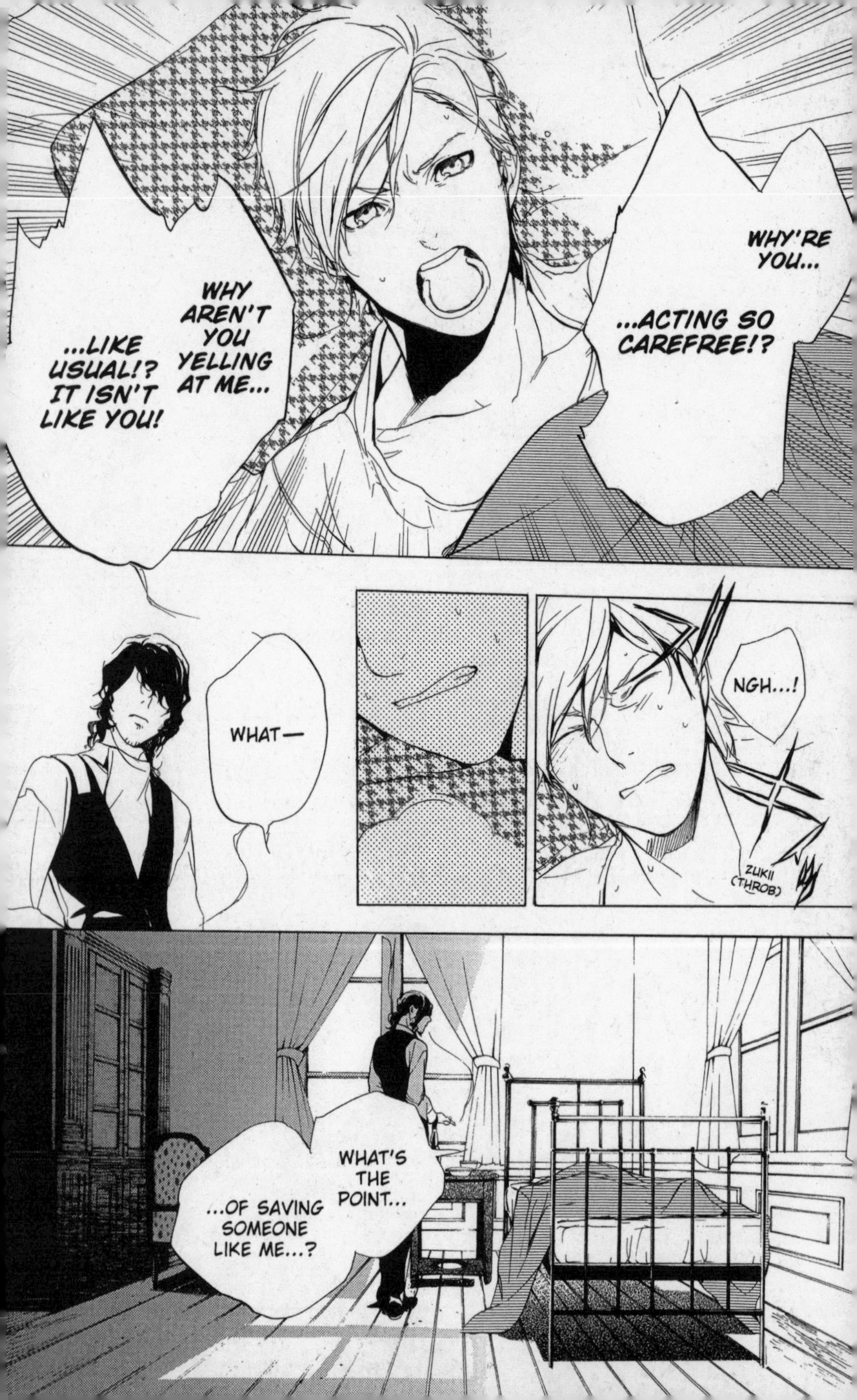
WHY'RE YOU...
...ACTING SO CAREFREE!?
WHY AREN'T YOU YELLING AT ME...
...LIKE USUAL!? IT ISN'T LIKE YOU!
NGH...!
ZUKII (THROB)
WHAT—
WHAT'S THE POINT...
...OF SAVING SOMEONE LIKE ME...?

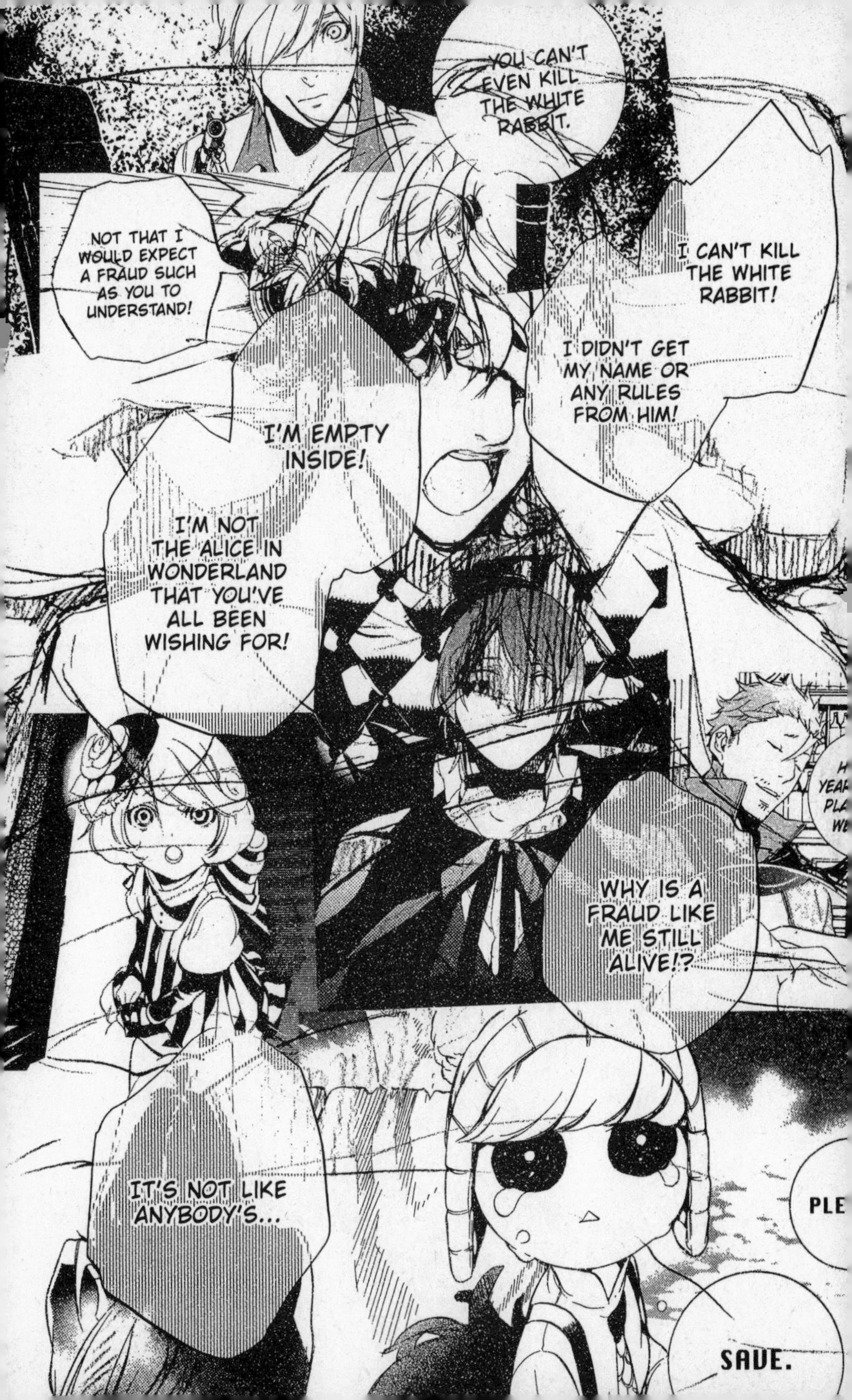
YOU CAN'T EVEN KILL THE WHITE RABBIT.
NOT THAT I WOULD EXPECT A FRAUD SUCH AS YOU TO UNDERSTAND!
I CAN'T KILL THE WHITE RABBIT!
I DIDN'T GET MY NAME OR ANY RULES FROM HIM!
I'M EMPTY INSIDE!
I'M NOT THE ALICE IN WONDERLAND THAT YOU'VE ALL BEEN WISHING FOR!
WHY IS A FRAUD LIKE ME STILL ALIVE!?
SAVE.
IT'S NOT LIKE ANYBODY'S...

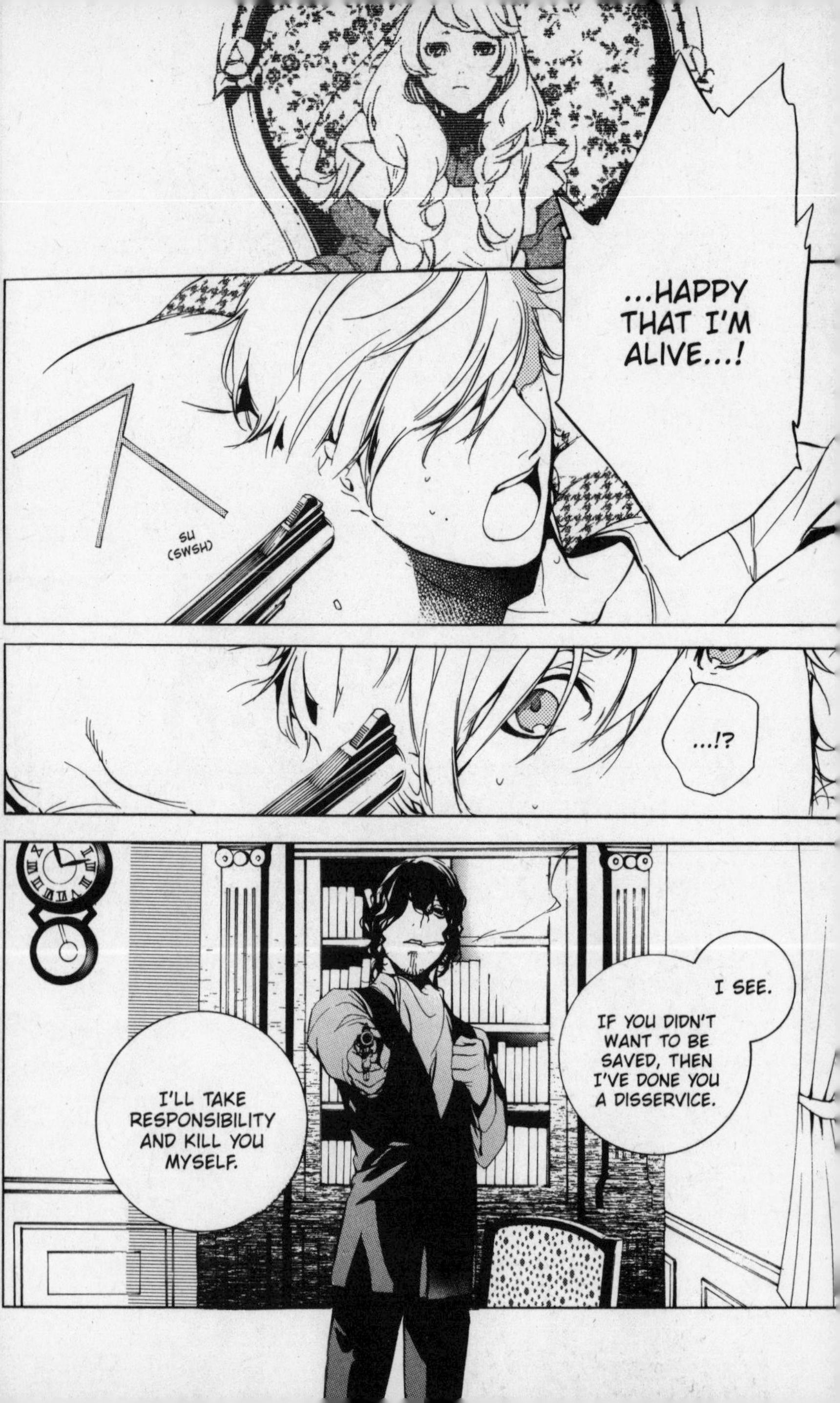
...HAPPY THAT I'M ALIVE...!
SU (SWSH)
...!?
I SEE.
IF YOU DIDN'T WANT TO BE SAVED, THEN I'VE DONE YOU A DISSERVICE.
I'LL TAKE RESPONSIBILITY AND KILL YOU MYSELF.

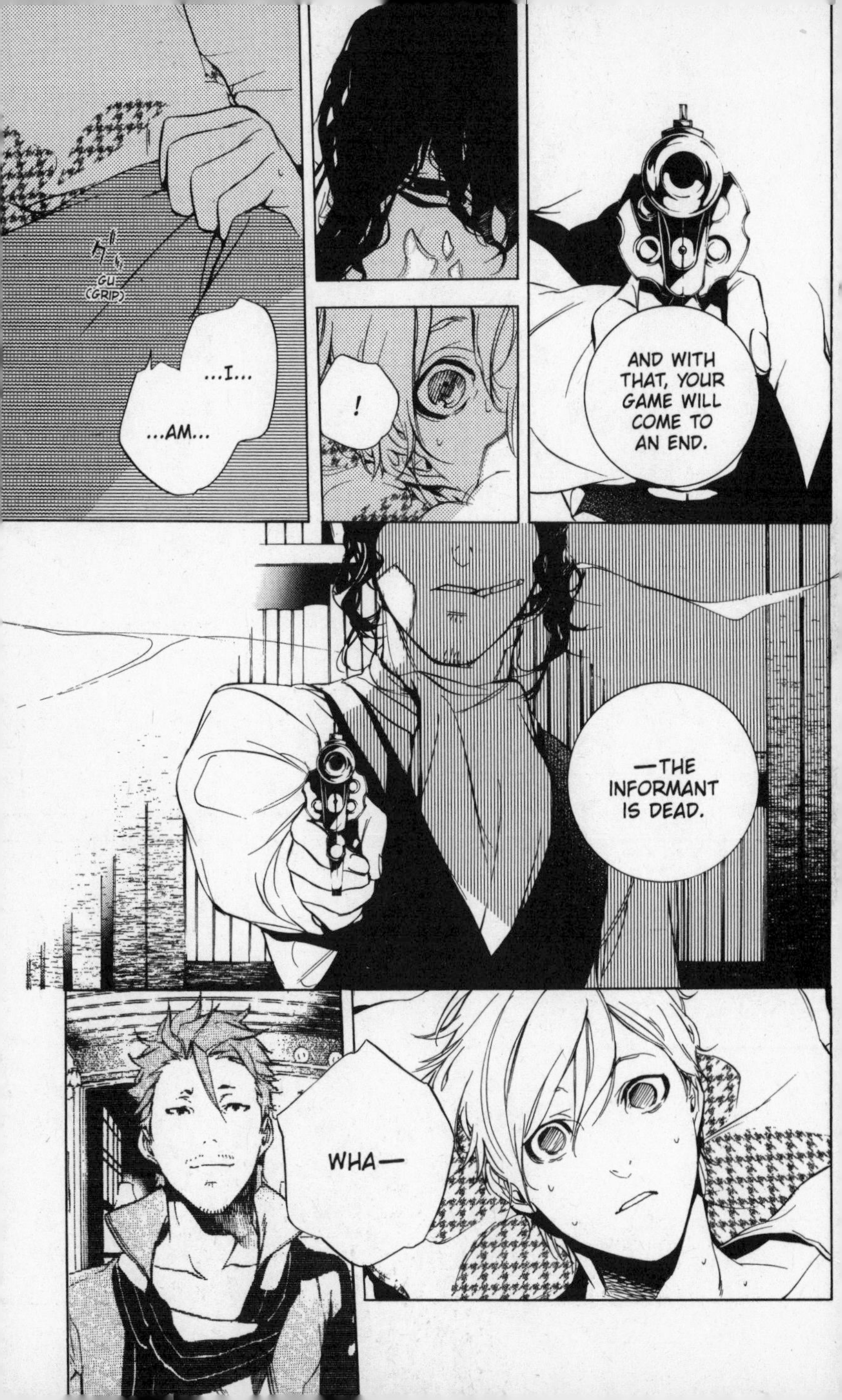
AND WITH THAT, YOUR GAME WILL COME TO AN END.
!
GU (GRIP)
...I... ...AM...
—THE INFORMANT IS DEAD.
WHA—

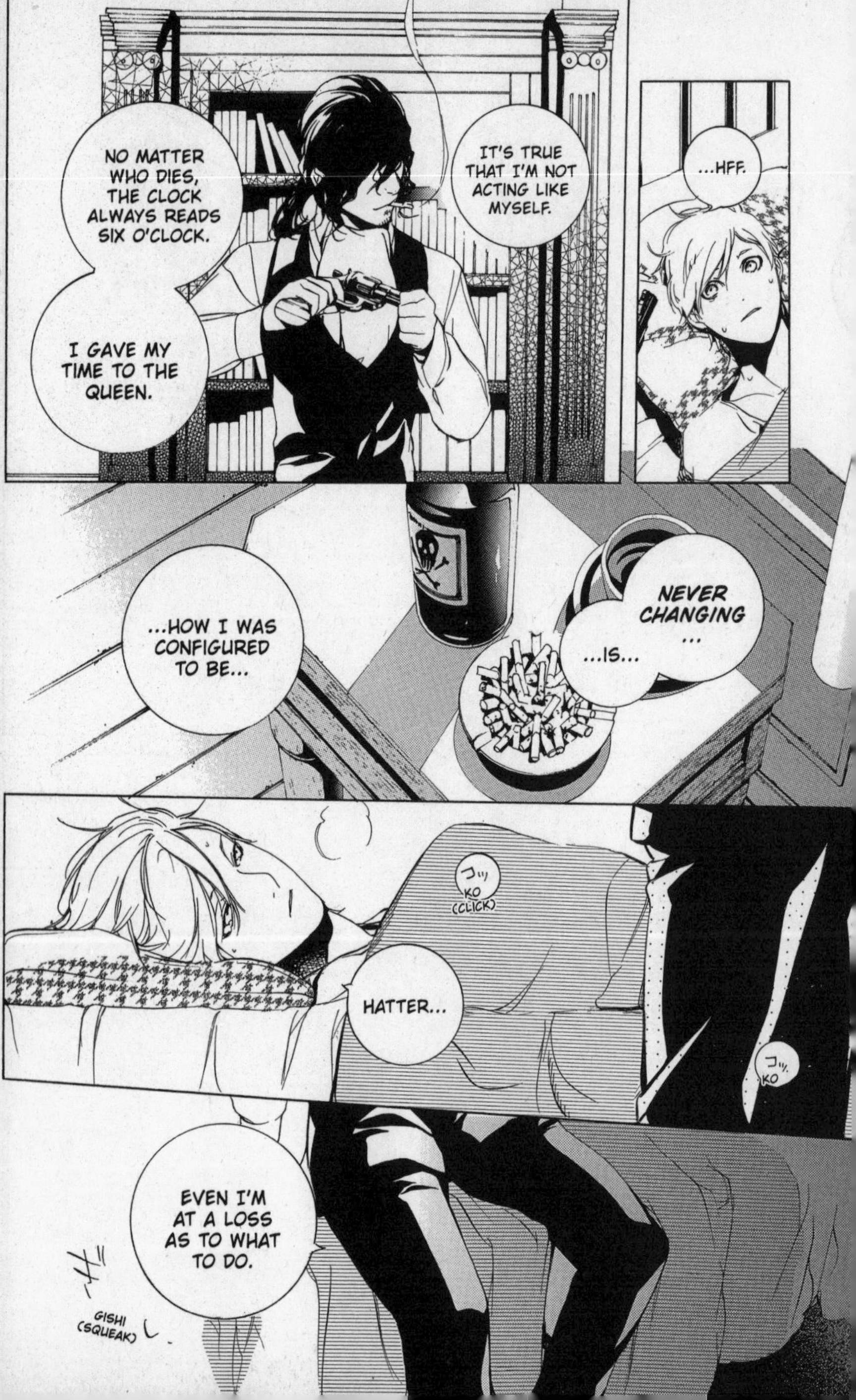
...HFF.
IT'S TRUE THAT I'M NOT ACTING LIKE MYSELF.
NO MATTER WHO DIES, THE CLOCK ALWAYS READS SIX O'CLOCK.
I GAVE MY TIME TO THE QUEEN.
NEVER CHANGING...
...IS...
...HOW I WAS CONFIGURED TO BE...
コッ KO (CLICK)
コッ KO
HATTER...
EVEN I'M AT A LOSS AS TO WHAT TO DO.
GISHI (SQUEAK)

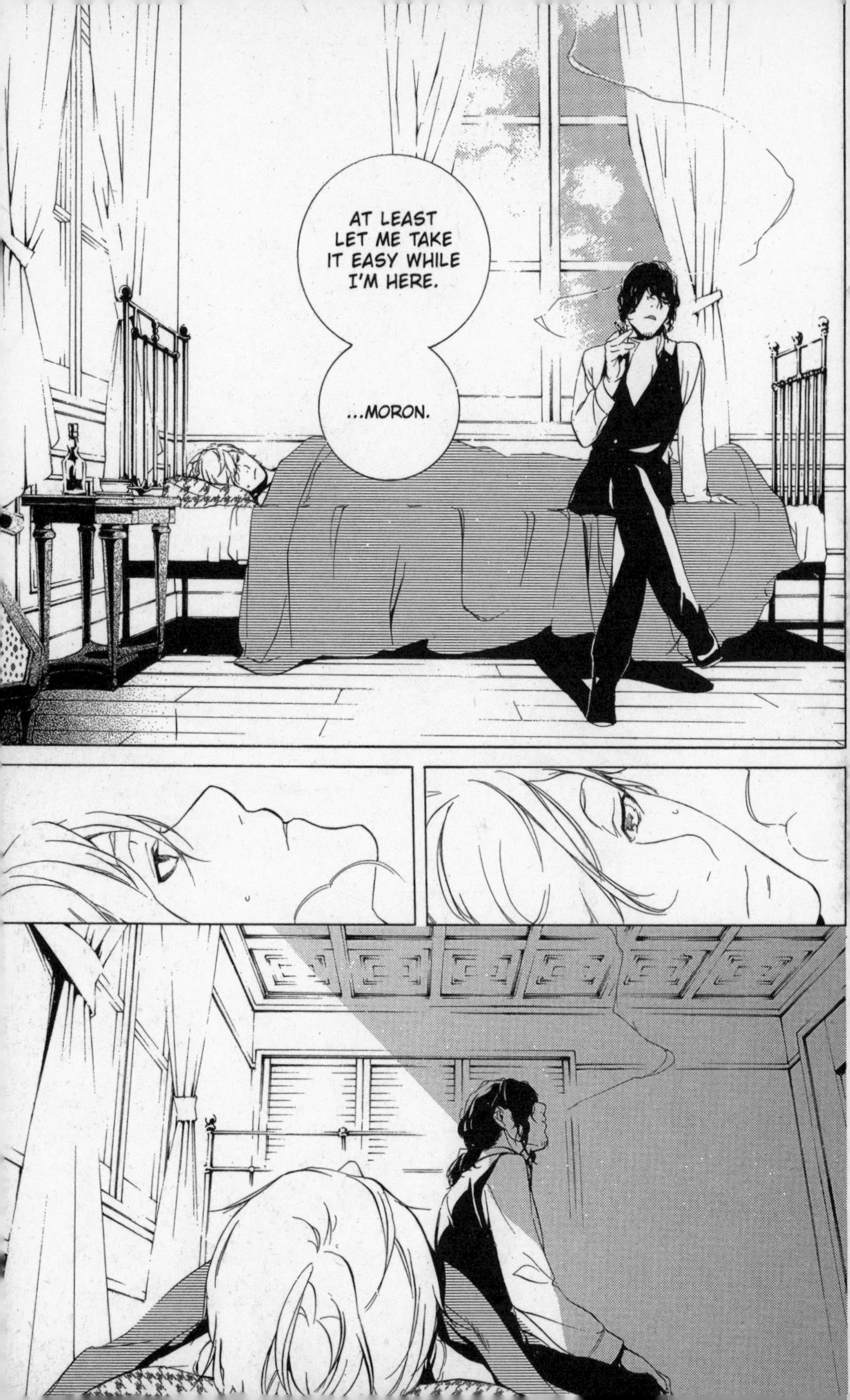
AT LEAST LET ME TAKE IT EASY WHILE I'M HERE.
...MORON.

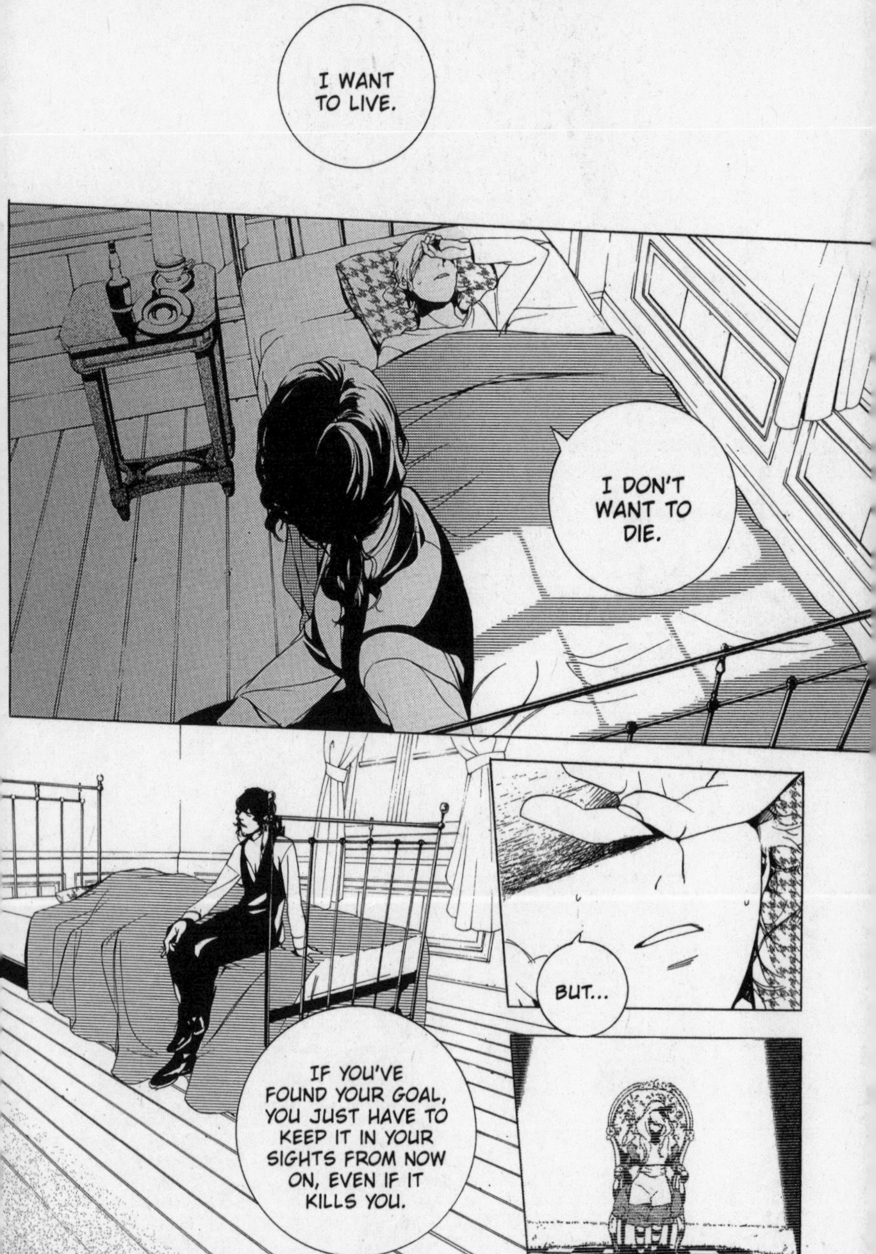
I WANT TO LIVE.
I DON'T WANT TO DIE.
BUT...
IF YOU'VE FOUND YOUR GOAL, YOU JUST HAVE TO KEEP IT IN YOUR SIGHTS FROM NOW ON, EVEN IF IT KILLS YOU.

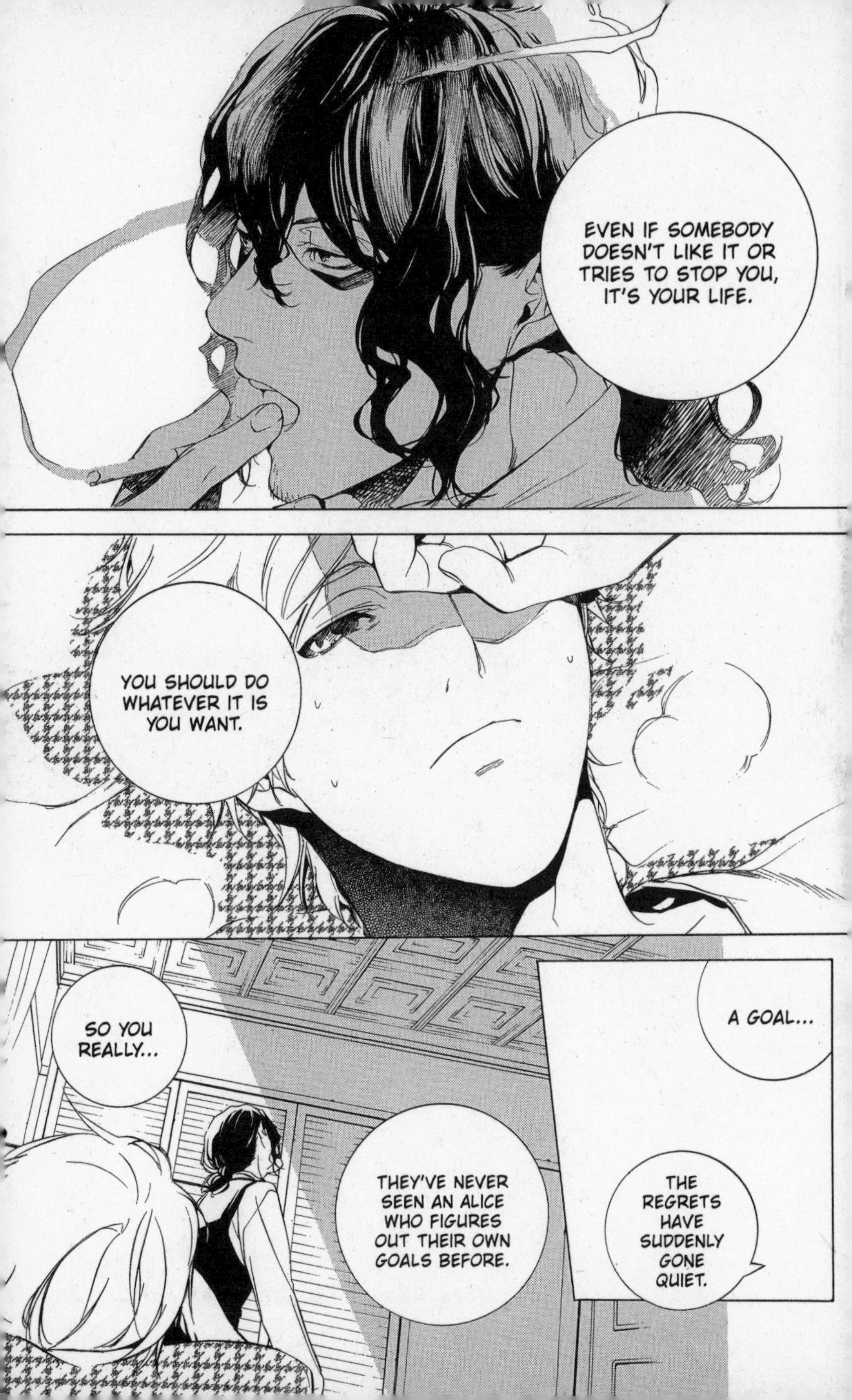
EVEN IF SOMEBODY DOESN'T LIKE IT OR TRIES TO STOP YOU, IT'S YOUR LIFE.
YOU SHOULD DO WHATEVER IT IS YOU WANT.
A GOAL...
THE REGRETS HAVE SUDDENLY GONE QUIET.
THEY'VE NEVER SEEN AN ALICE WHO FIGURES OUT THEIR OWN GOALS BEFORE.
SO YOU REALLY...

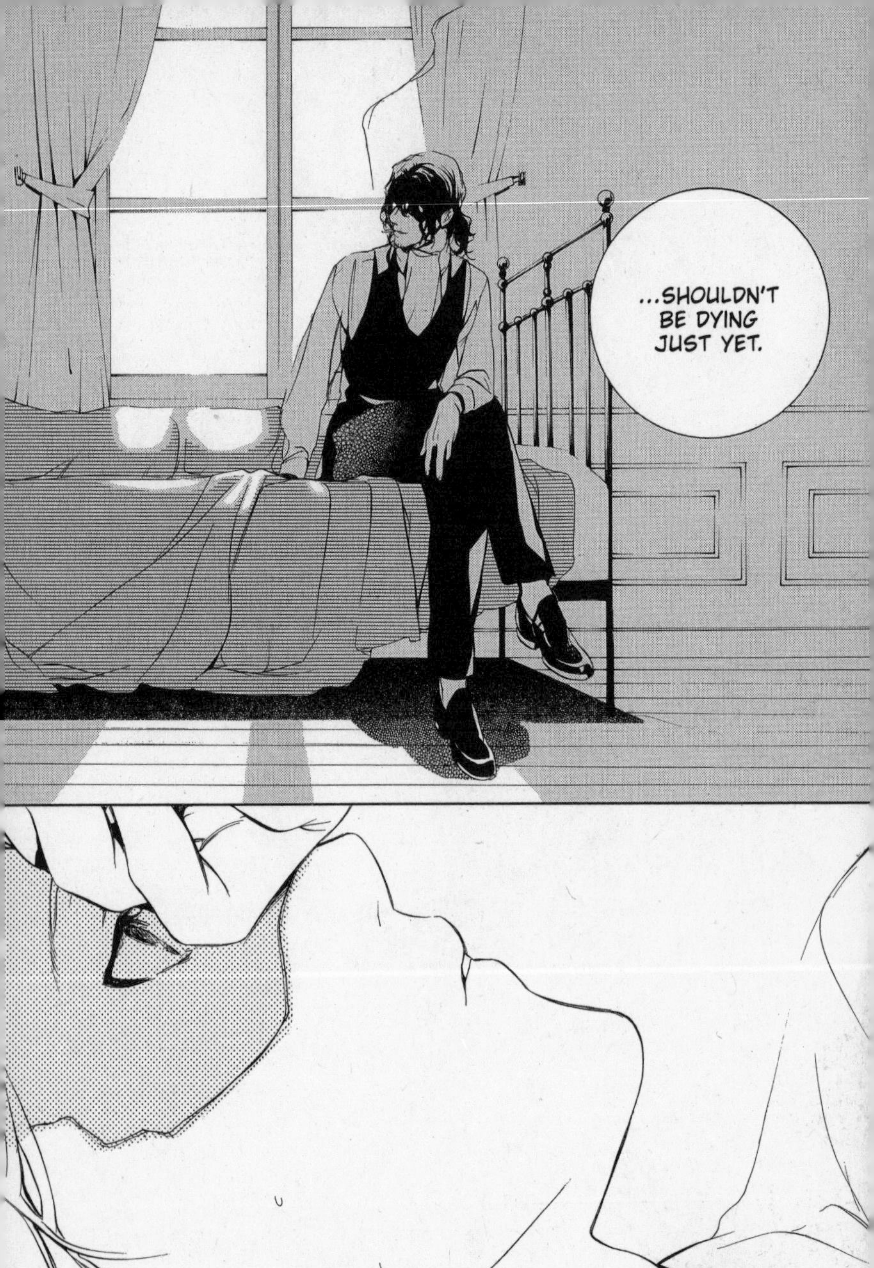
...SHOULDN'T BE DYING JUST YET.

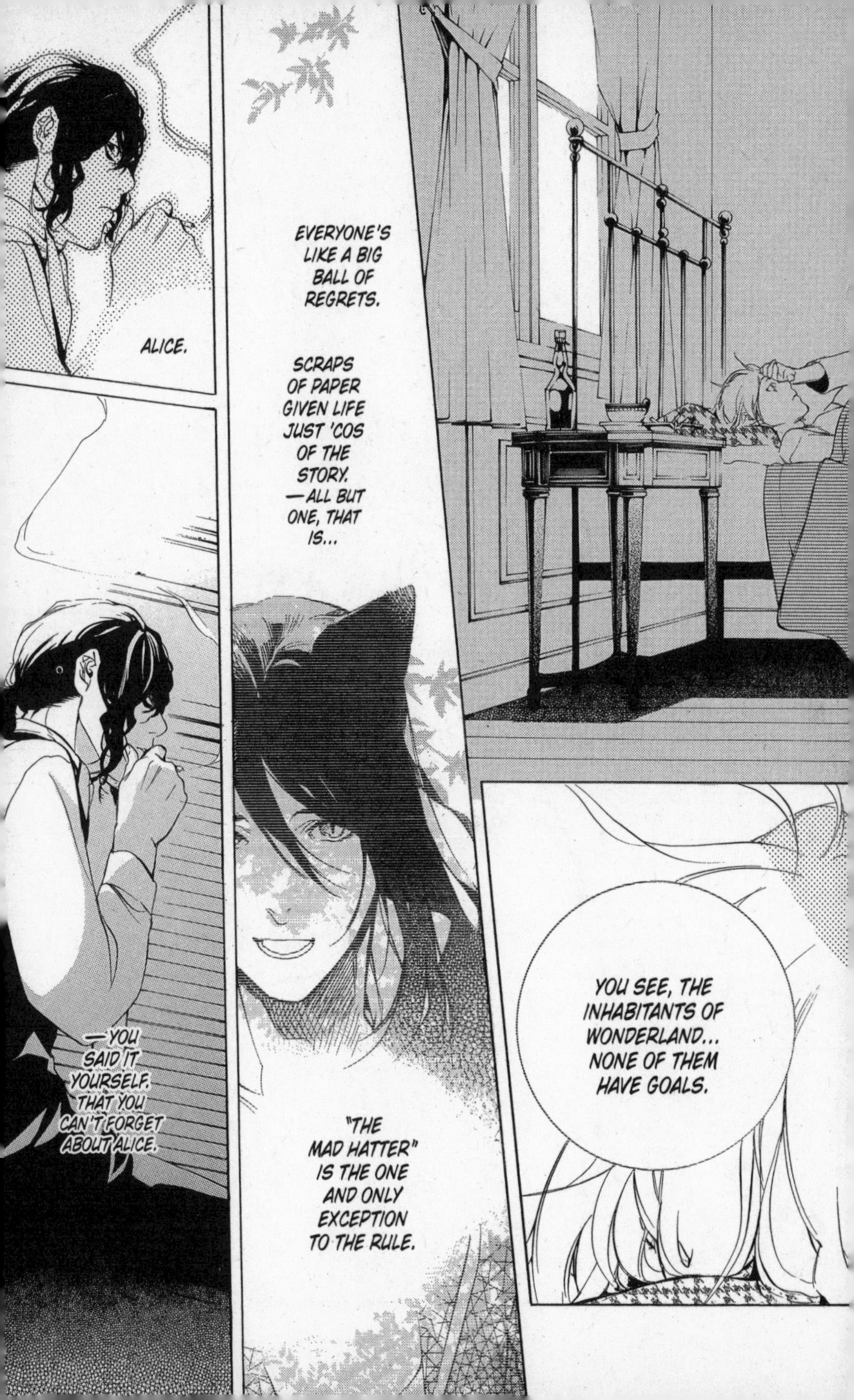
YOU SEE, THE INHABITANTS OF WONDERLAND... NONE OF THEM HAVE GOALS.
EVERYONE'S LIKE A BIG BALL OF REGRETS.
SCRAPS OF PAPER GIVEN LIFE JUST 'COS OF THE STORY. —ALL BUT ONE, THAT IS...
"THE MAD HATTER" IS THE ONE AND ONLY EXCEPTION TO THE RULE.
ALICE.
—YOU SAID IT YOURSELF. THAT YOU CAN'T FORGET ABOUT ALICE.

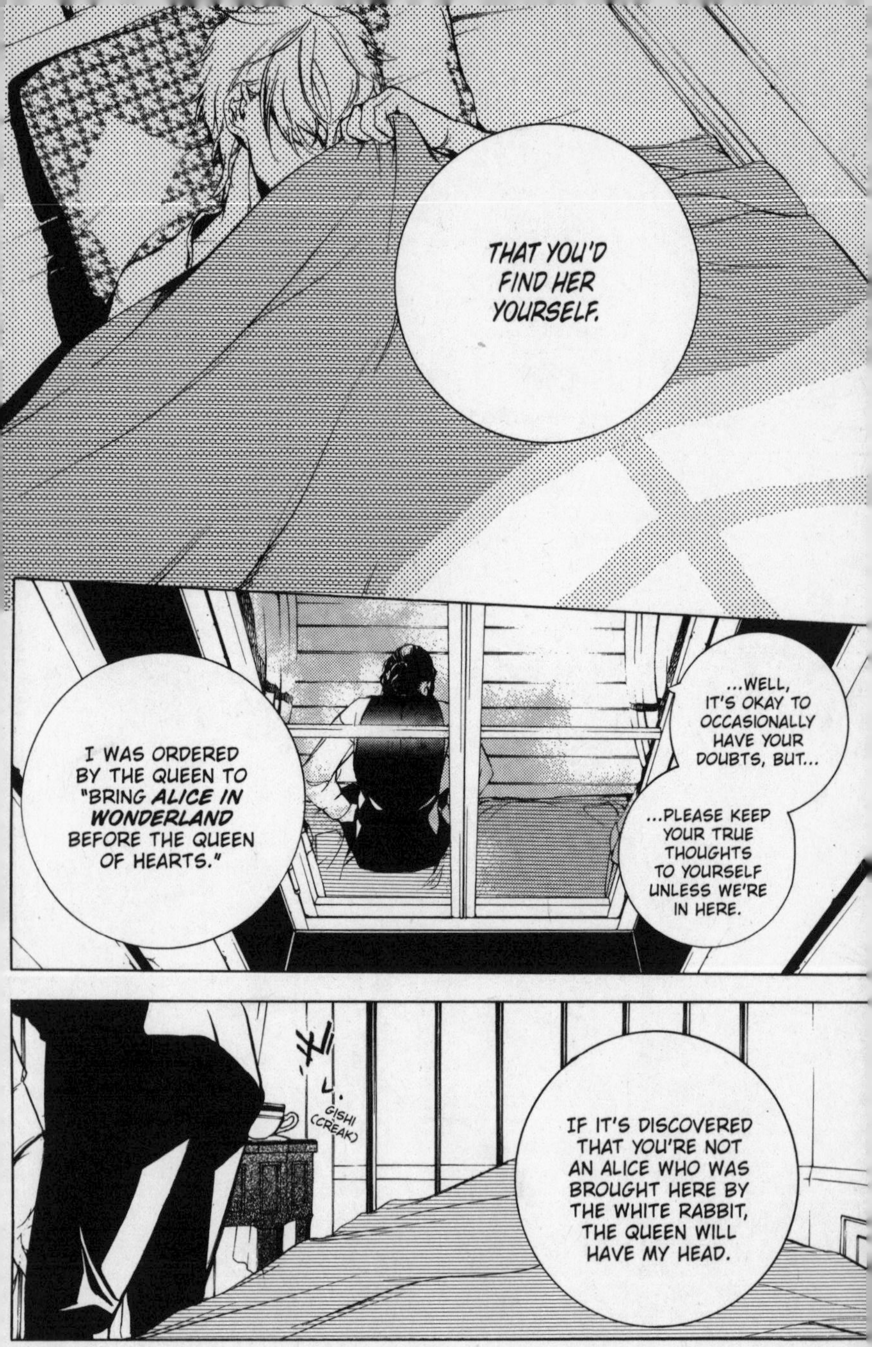
THAT YOU'D FIND HER YOURSELF.
...WELL, IT'S OKAY TO OCCASIONALLY HAVE YOUR DOUBTS, BUT...
...PLEASE KEEP YOUR TRUE THOUGHTS TO YOURSELF UNLESS WE'RE IN HERE.
I WAS ORDERED BY THE QUEEN TO "BRING ALICE IN WONDERLAND BEFORE THE QUEEN OF HEARTS."
IF IT'S DISCOVERED THAT YOU'RE NOT AN ALICE WHO WAS BROUGHT HERE BY THE WHITE RABBIT, THE QUEEN WILL HAVE MY HEAD.
GISHI (CREAK)

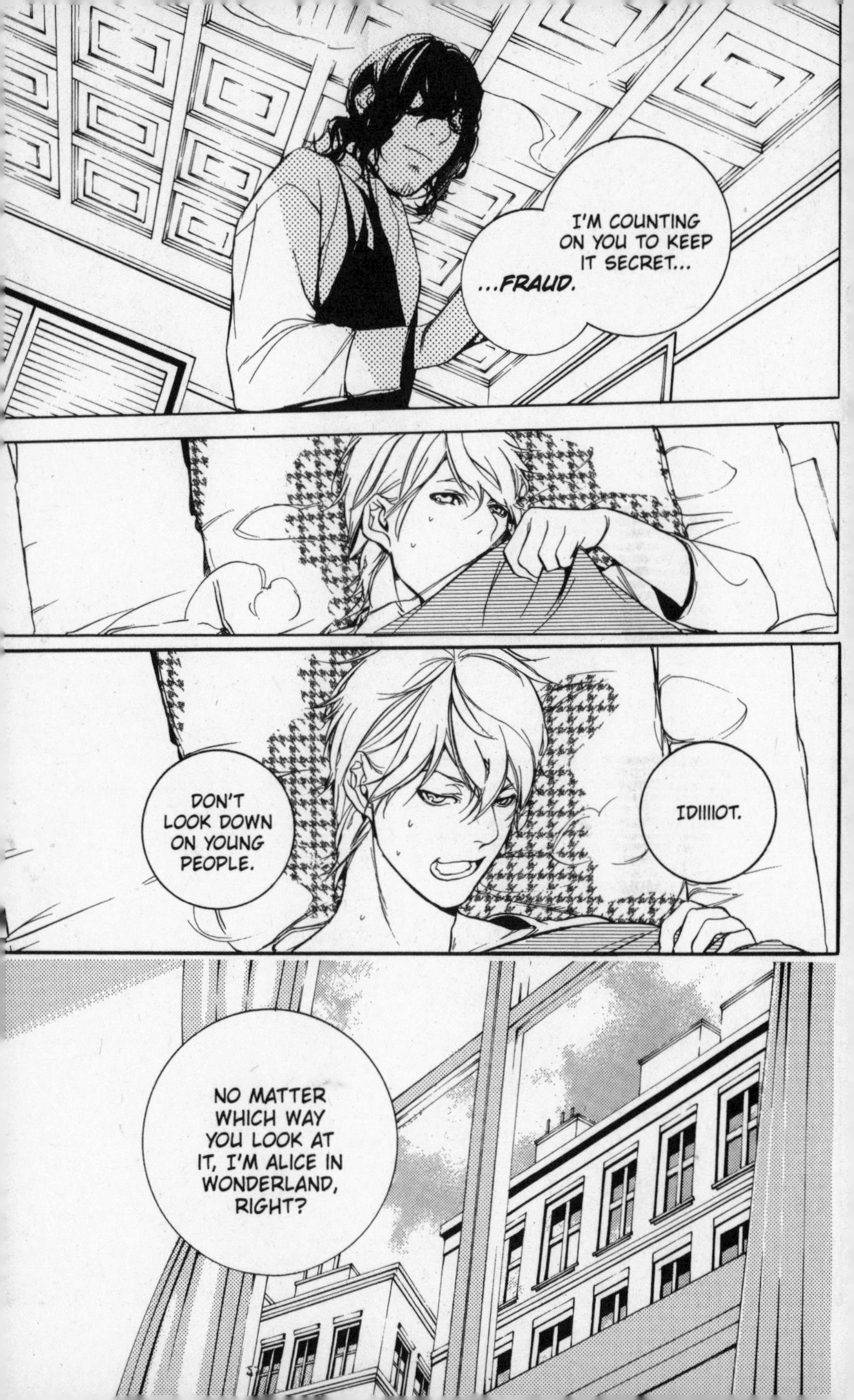
I'M COUNTING ON YOU TO KEEP IT SECRET... ...FRAUD.
IDIIIIOT.
DON'T LOOK DOWN ON YOUNG PEOPLE.
NO MATTER WHICH WAY YOU LOOK AT IT, I'M ALICE IN WONDERLAND, RIGHT?

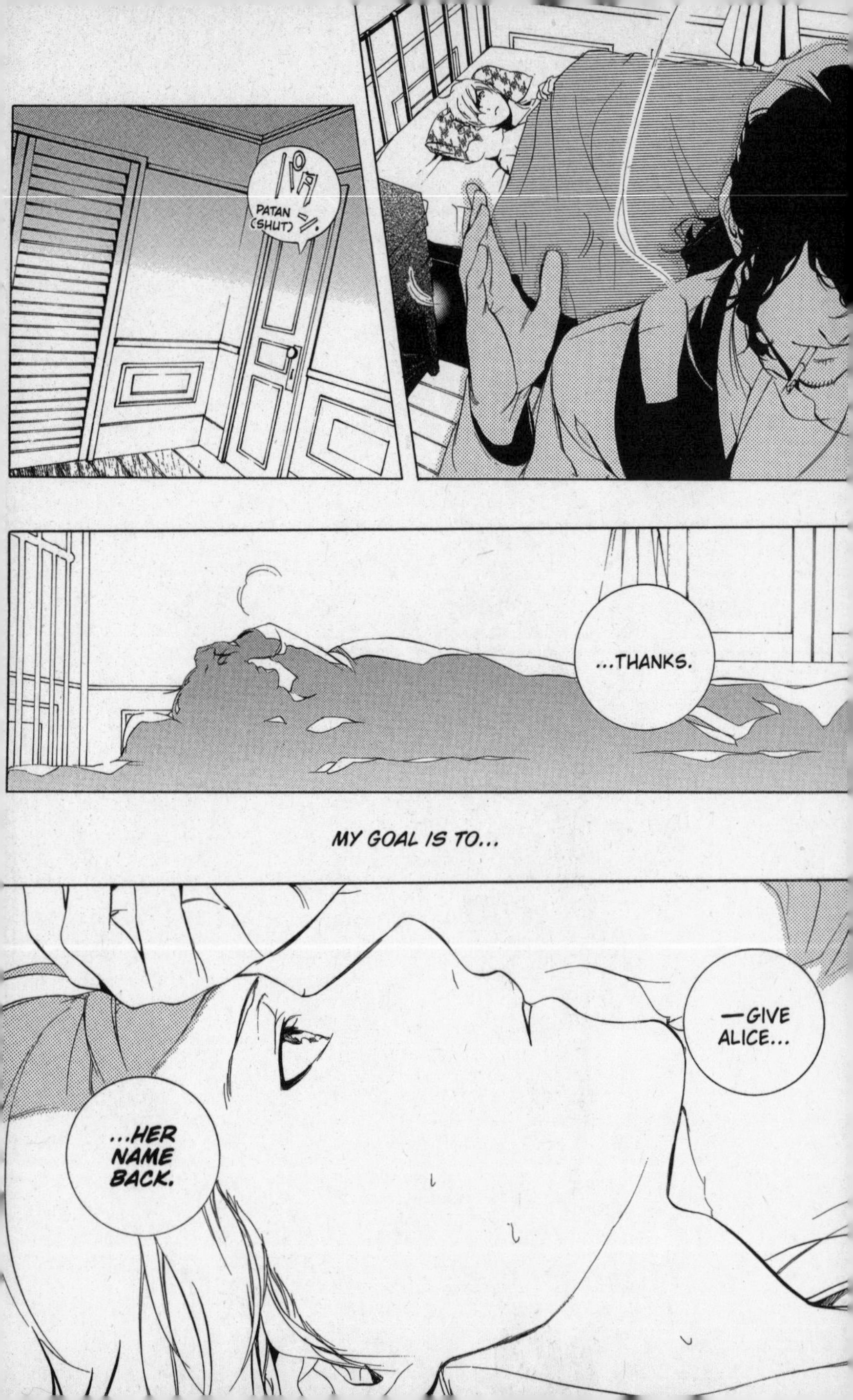
パタン
PATAN (SHUT)
...THANKS.
MY GOAL IS TO...
—GIVE ALICE...
...HER NAME BACK.

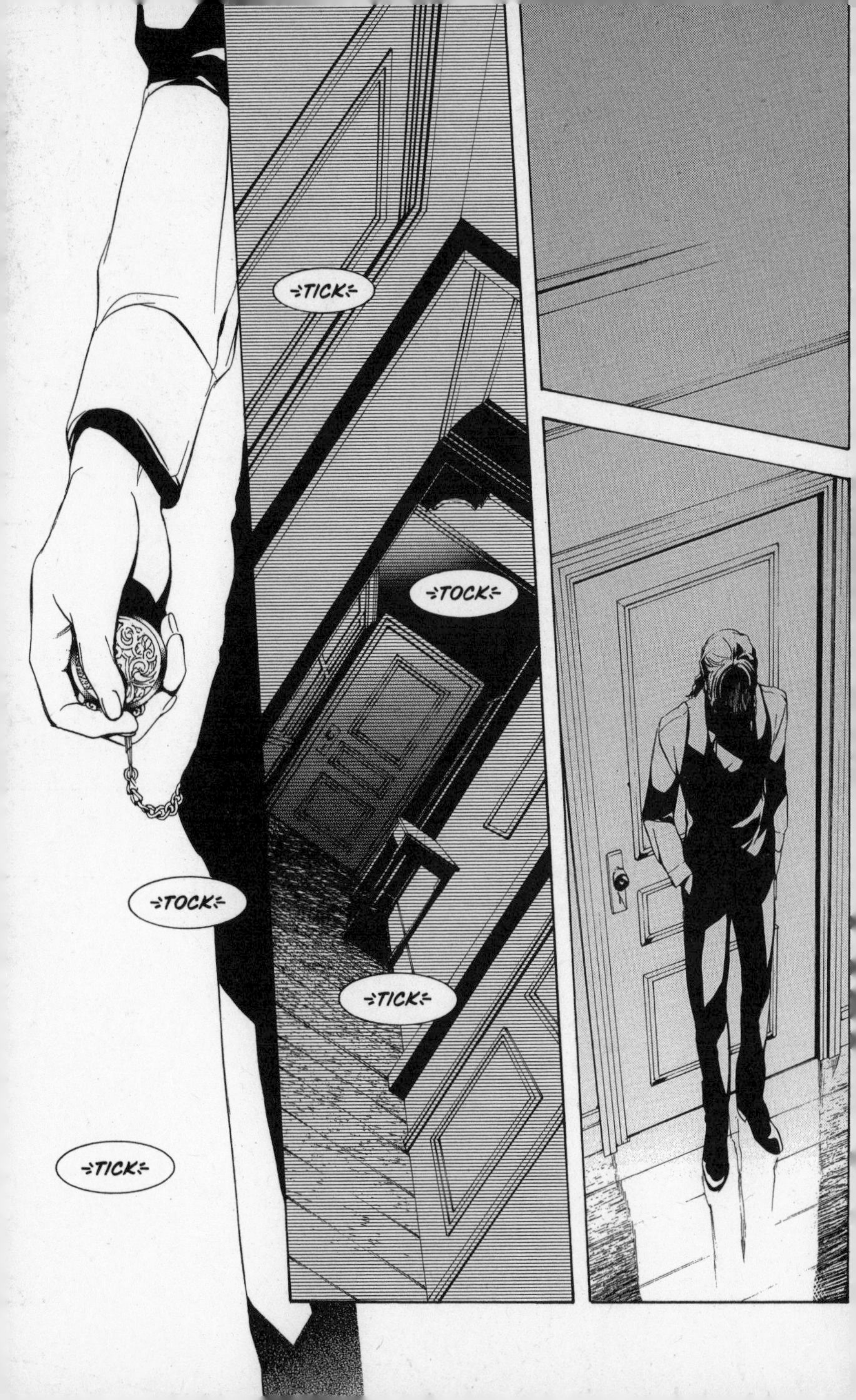
TICK
TOCK
TICK
TOCK
TICK

TOCK
TICK
TEATIME'S OVER.

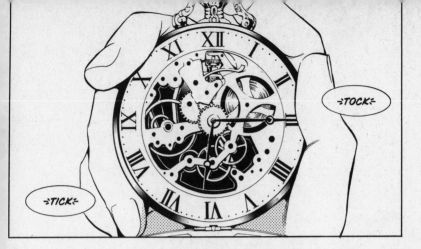

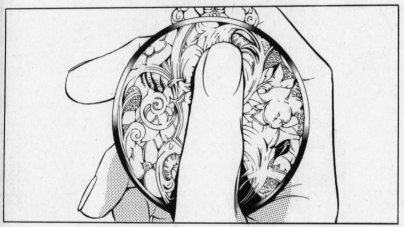

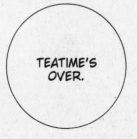

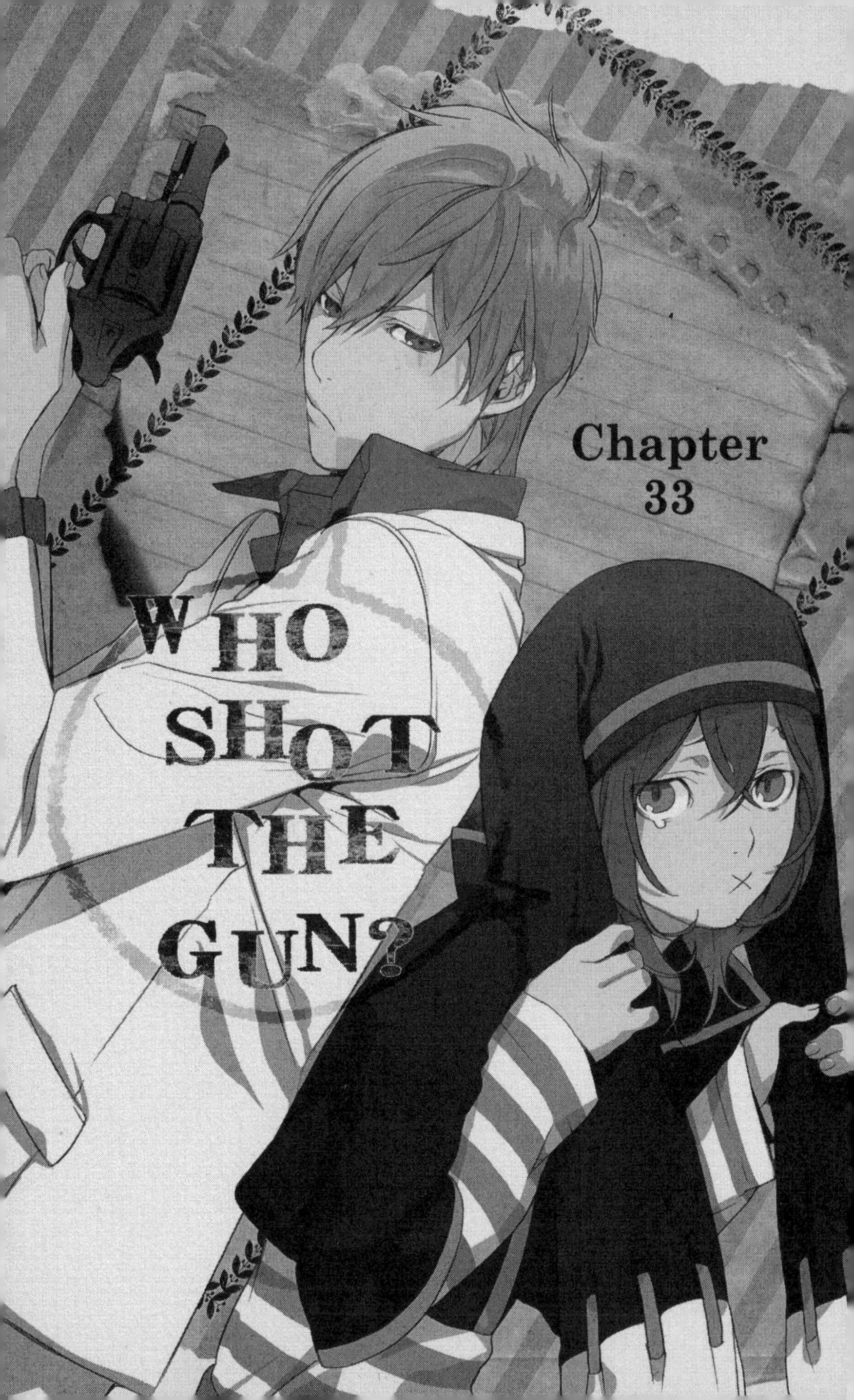
Chapter 33
WHO SHOT THE GUN?

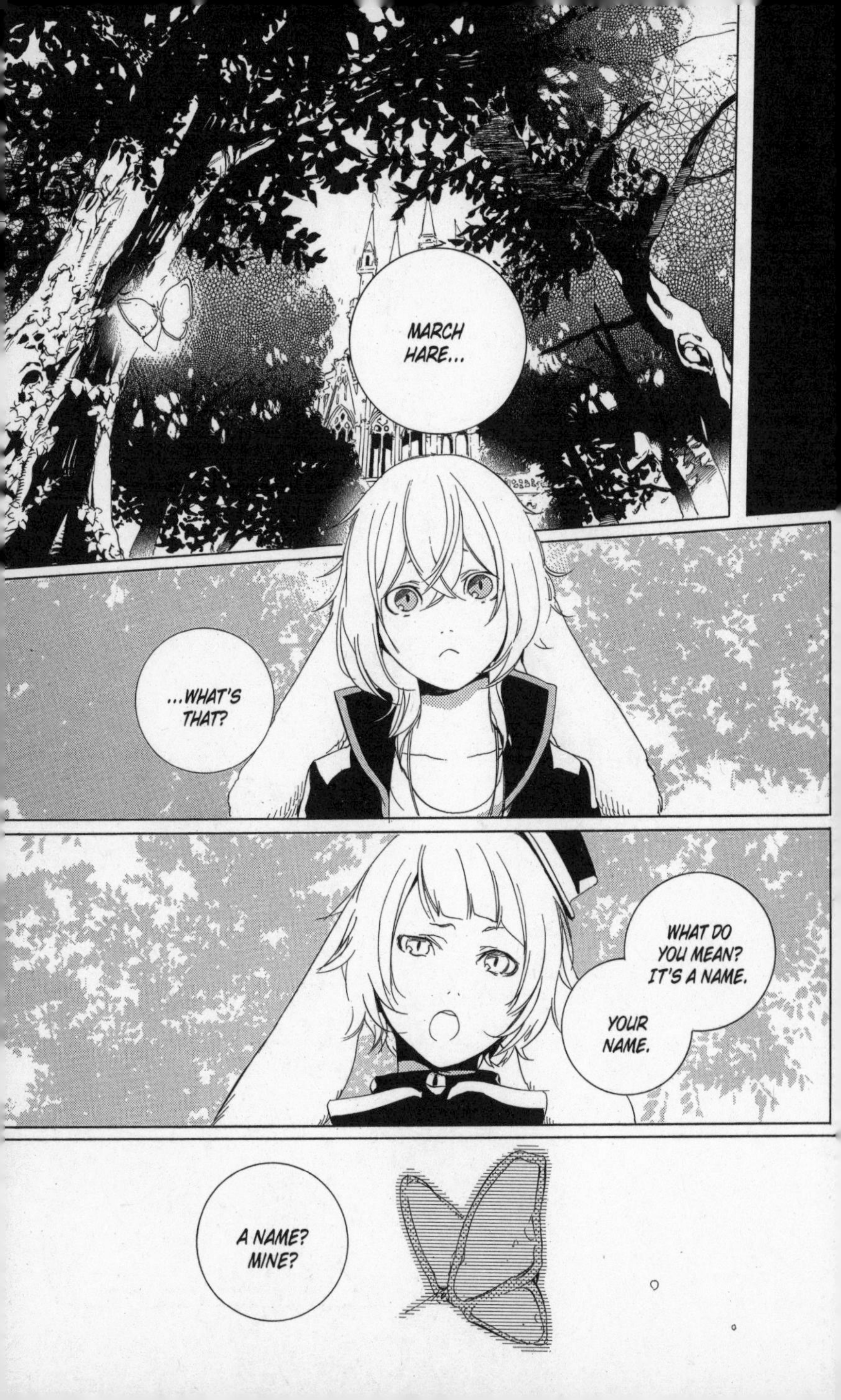
MARCH HARE...
...WHAT'S THAT?
WHAT DO YOU MEAN? IT'S A NAME.
YOUR NAME.
A NAME? MINE?

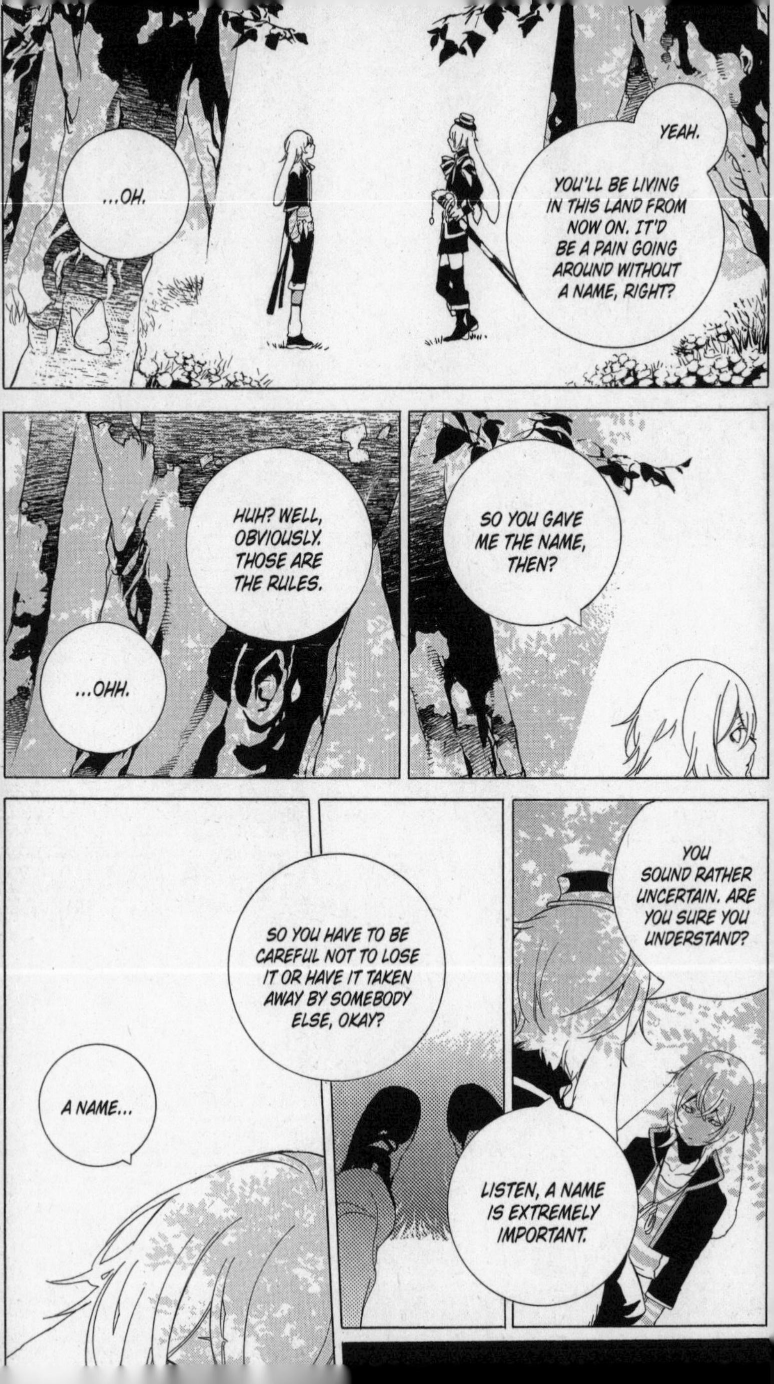
YEAH.
YOU'LL BE LIVING IN THIS LAND FROM NOW ON. IT'D BE A PAIN GOING AROUND WITHOUT A NAME, RIGHT?
...OH.
SO YOU GAVE ME THE NAME, THEN?
HUH? WELL, OBVIOUSLY. THOSE ARE THE RULES.
...OHH.
YOU SOUND RATHER UNCERTAIN. ARE YOU SURE YOU UNDERSTAND?
LISTEN, A NAME IS EXTREMELY IMPORTANT.
SO YOU HAVE TO BE CAREFUL NOT TO LOSE IT OR HAVE IT TAKEN AWAY BY SOMEBODY ELSE, OKAY?
A NAME...

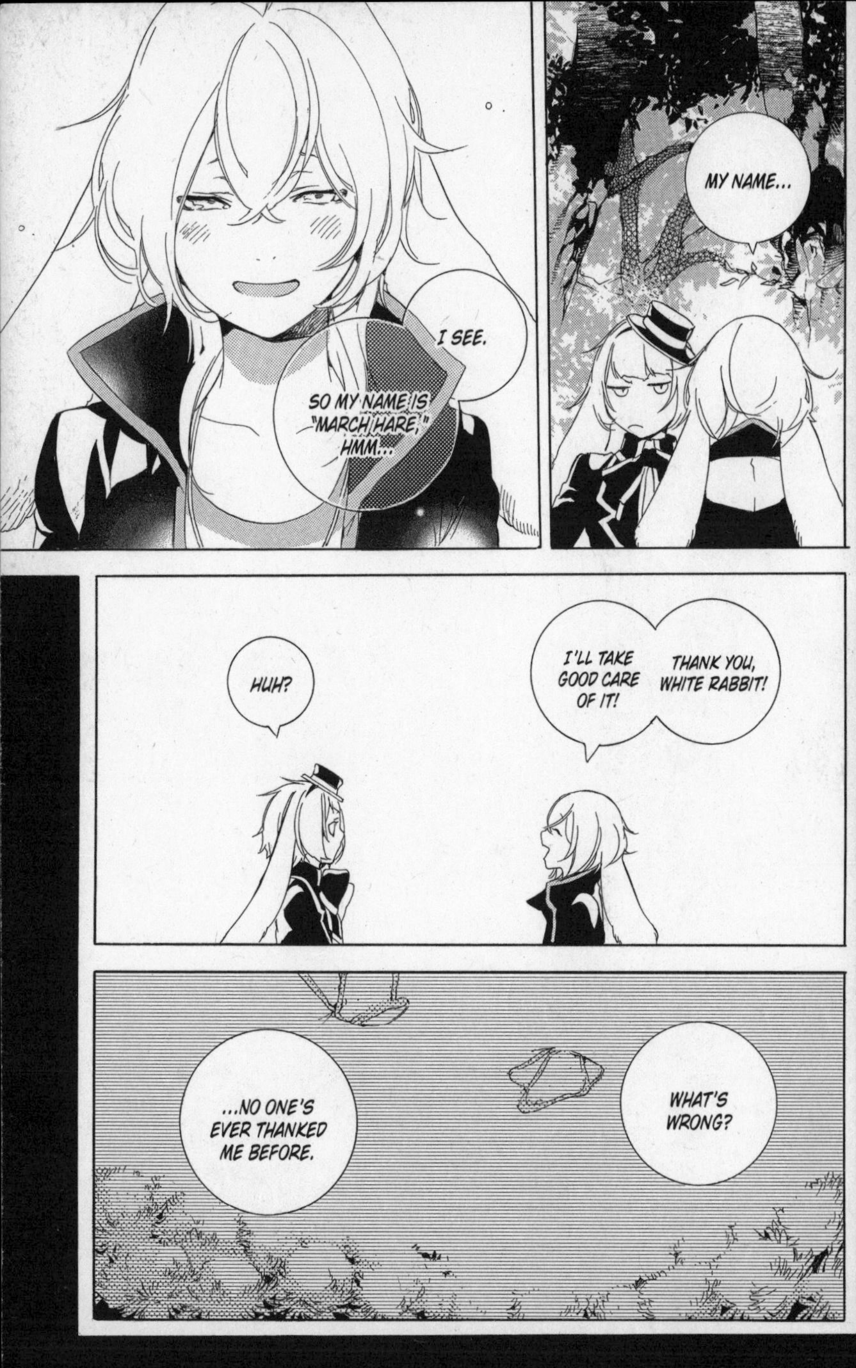
MY NAME...
I SEE.
SO MY NAME IS "MARCH HARE," HMM...
THANK YOU, WHITE RABBIT!
I'LL TAKE GOOD CARE OF IT!
HUH?
WHAT'S WRONG?
...NO ONE'S EVER THANKED ME BEFORE.

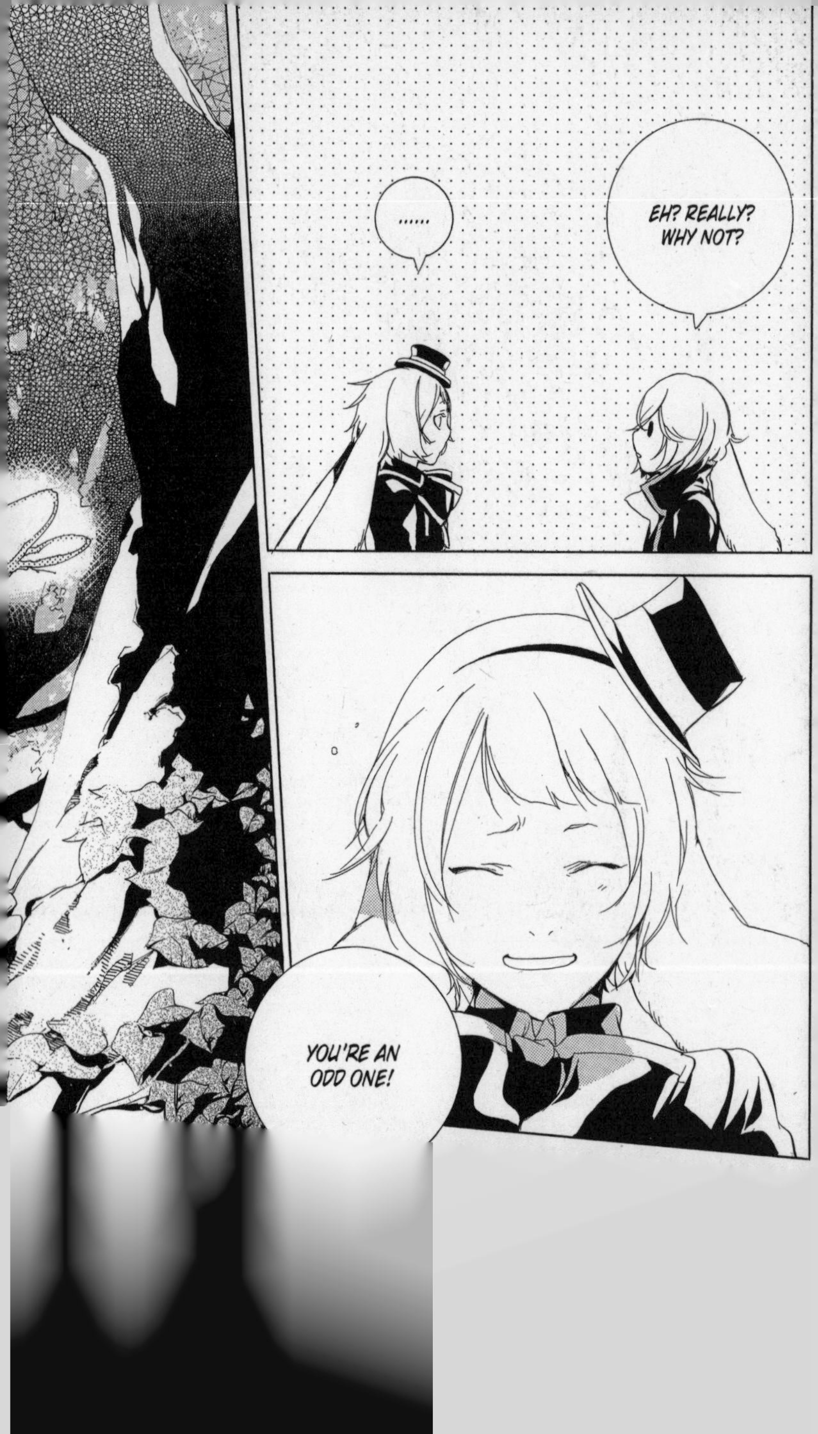
EH? REALLY? WHY NOT?
......
YOU'RE AN ODD ONE!

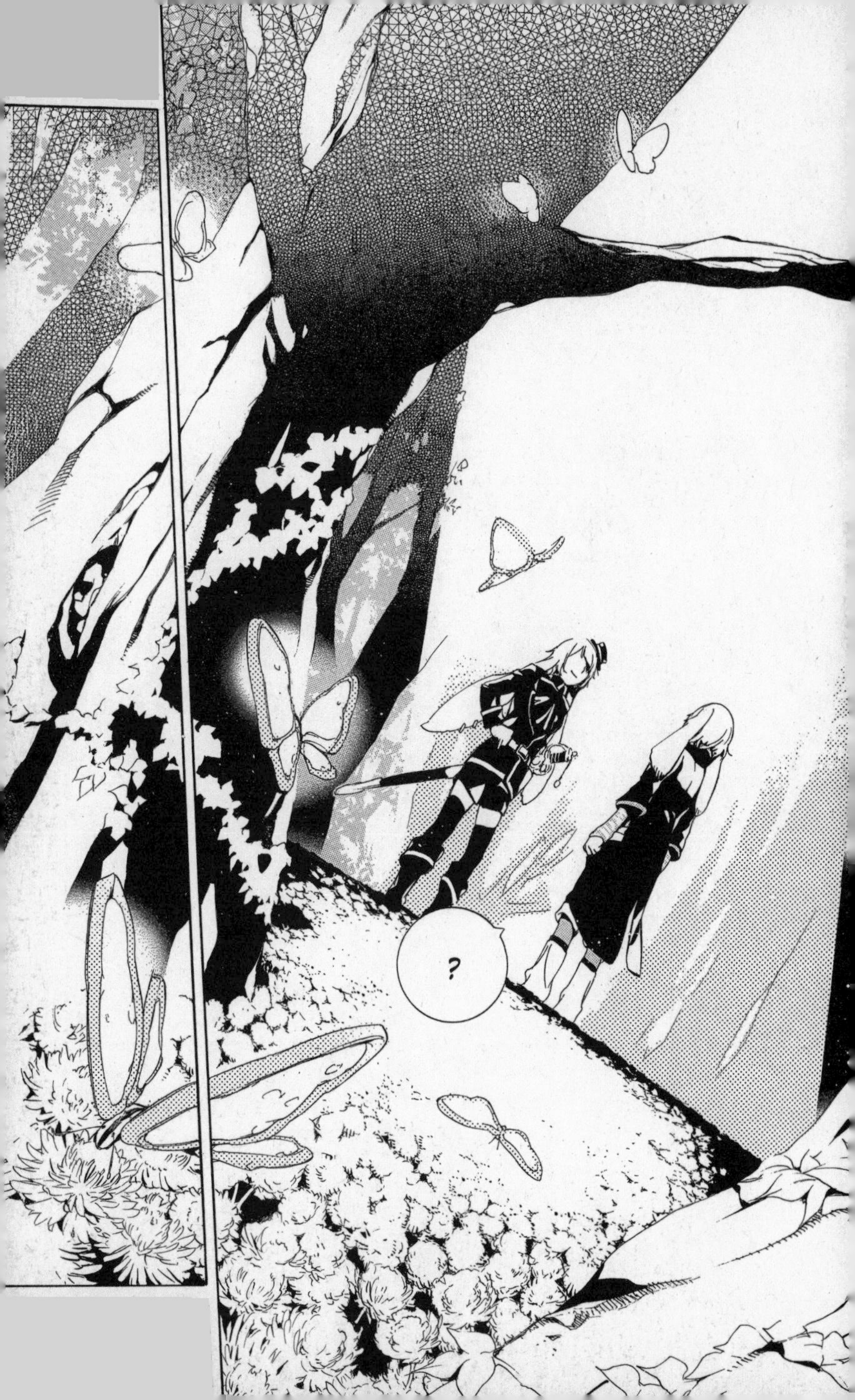
?

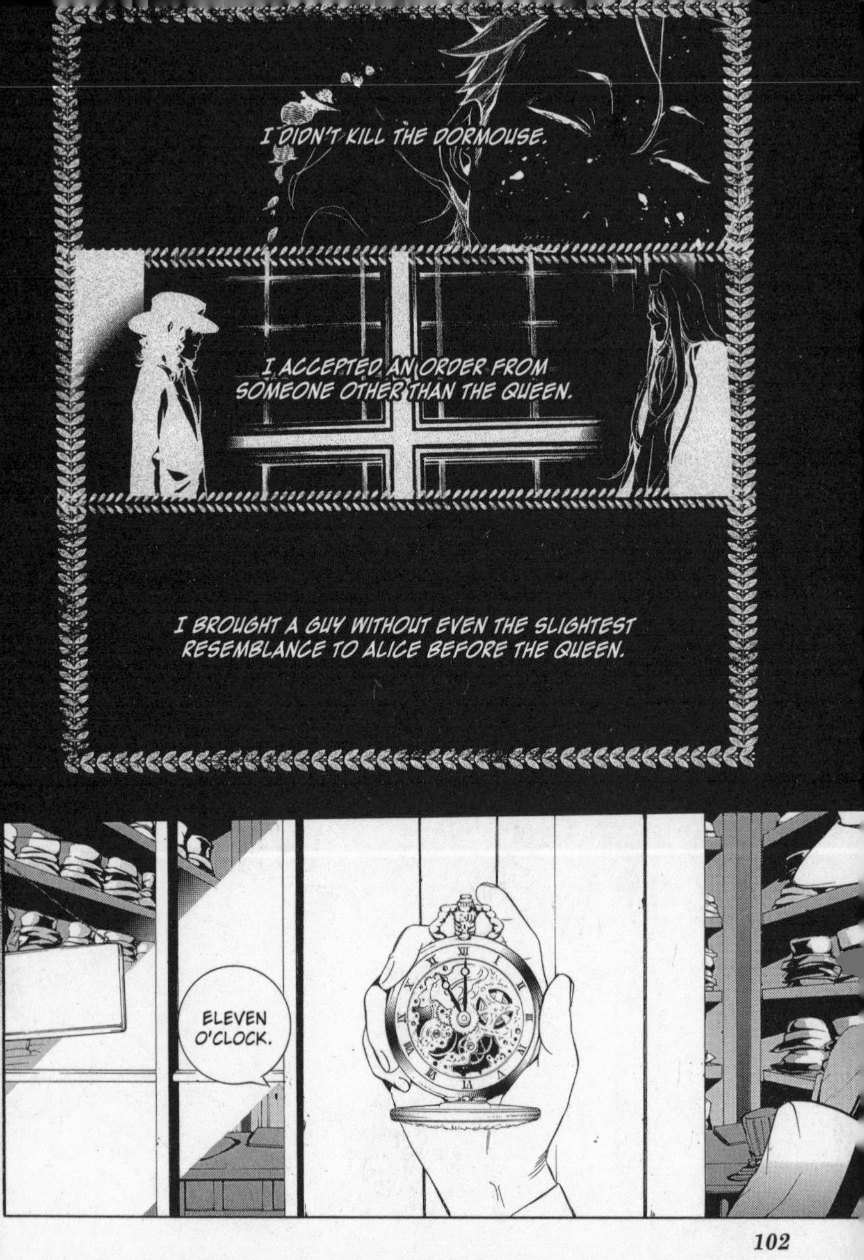
I DIDN'T KILL THE DORMOUSE.
I ACCEPTED AN ORDER FROM SOMEONE OTHER THAN THE QUEEN.
I BROUGHT A GUY WITHOUT EVEN THE SLIGHTEST RESEMBLANCE TO ALICE BEFORE THE QUEEN.
ELEVEN O'CLOCK.

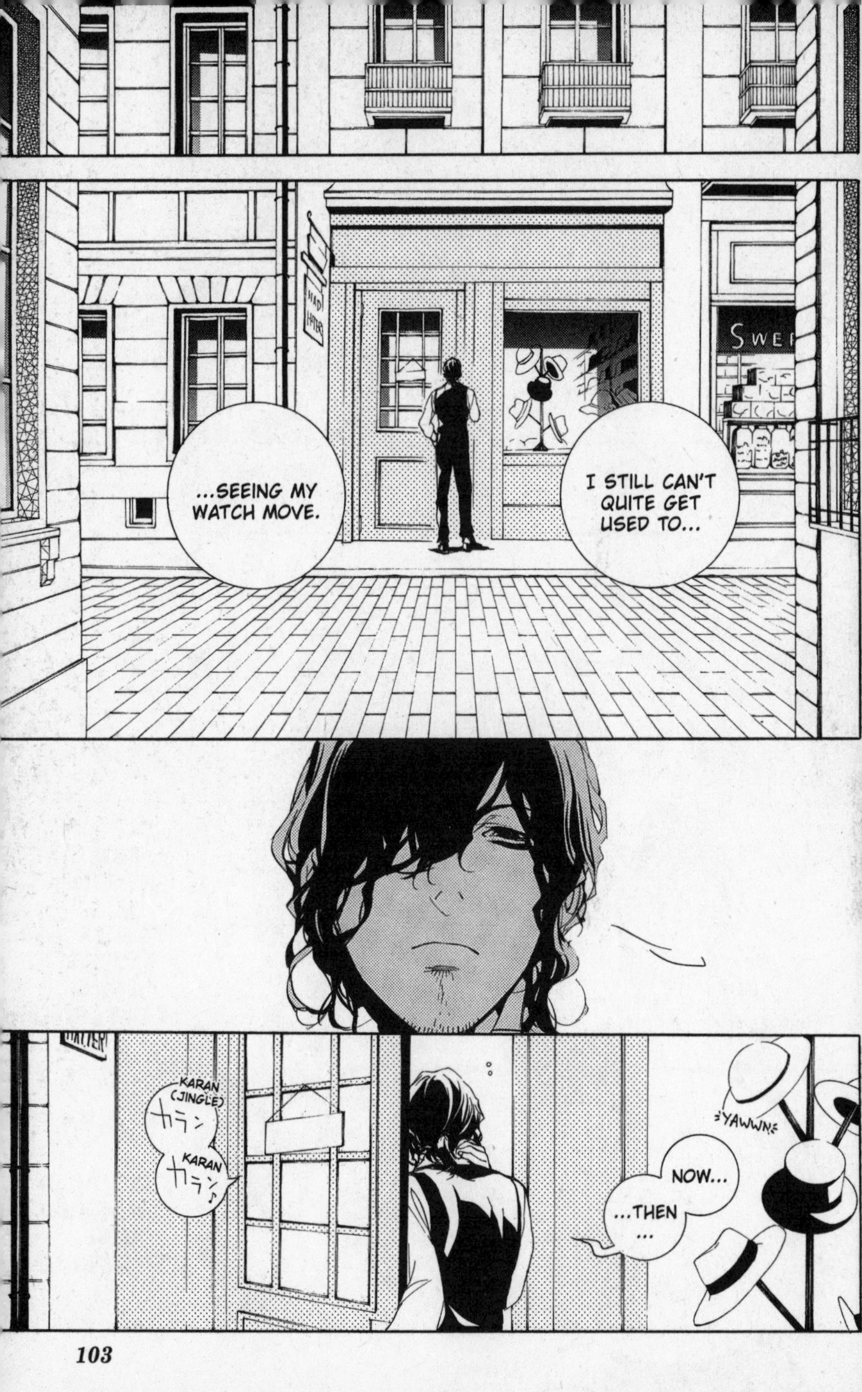
I STILL CAN'T QUITE GET USED TO...
...SEEING MY WATCH MOVE.
YAWWN
NOW...
...THEN ...
KARAN (JINGLE) カラン
KARAN カラン♪

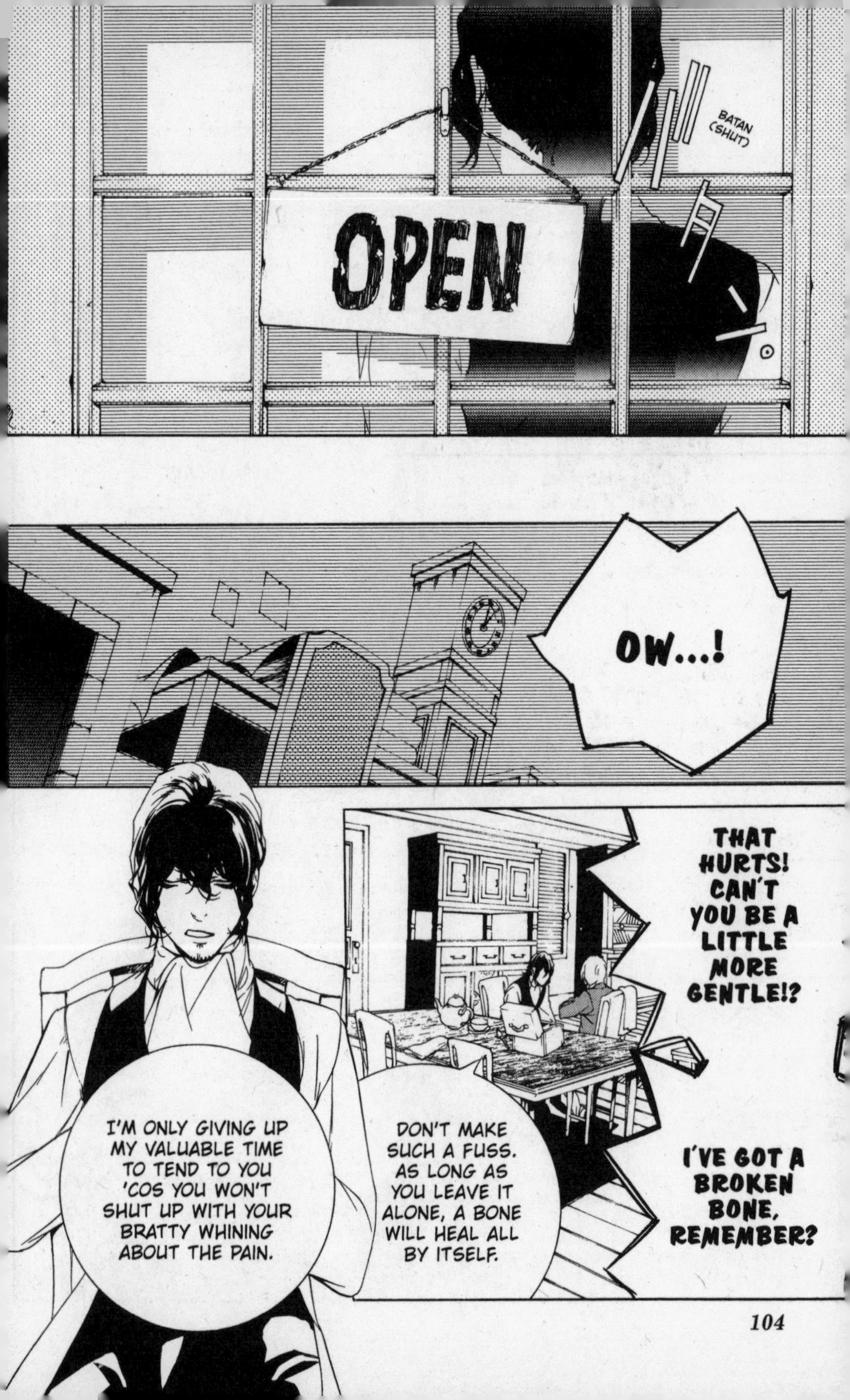
BATAN (SHUT)
OPEN
OW...!
THAT HURTS! CAN'T YOU BE A LITTLE MORE GENTLE!?
I'VE GOT A BROKEN BONE, REMEMBER?
DON'T MAKE SUCH A FUSS. AS LONG AS YOU LEAVE IT ALONE, A BONE WILL HEAL ALL BY ITSELF.
I'M ONLY GIVING UP MY VALUABLE TIME TO TEND TO YOU 'COS YOU WON'T SHUT UP WITH YOUR BRATTY WHINING ABOUT THE PAIN.

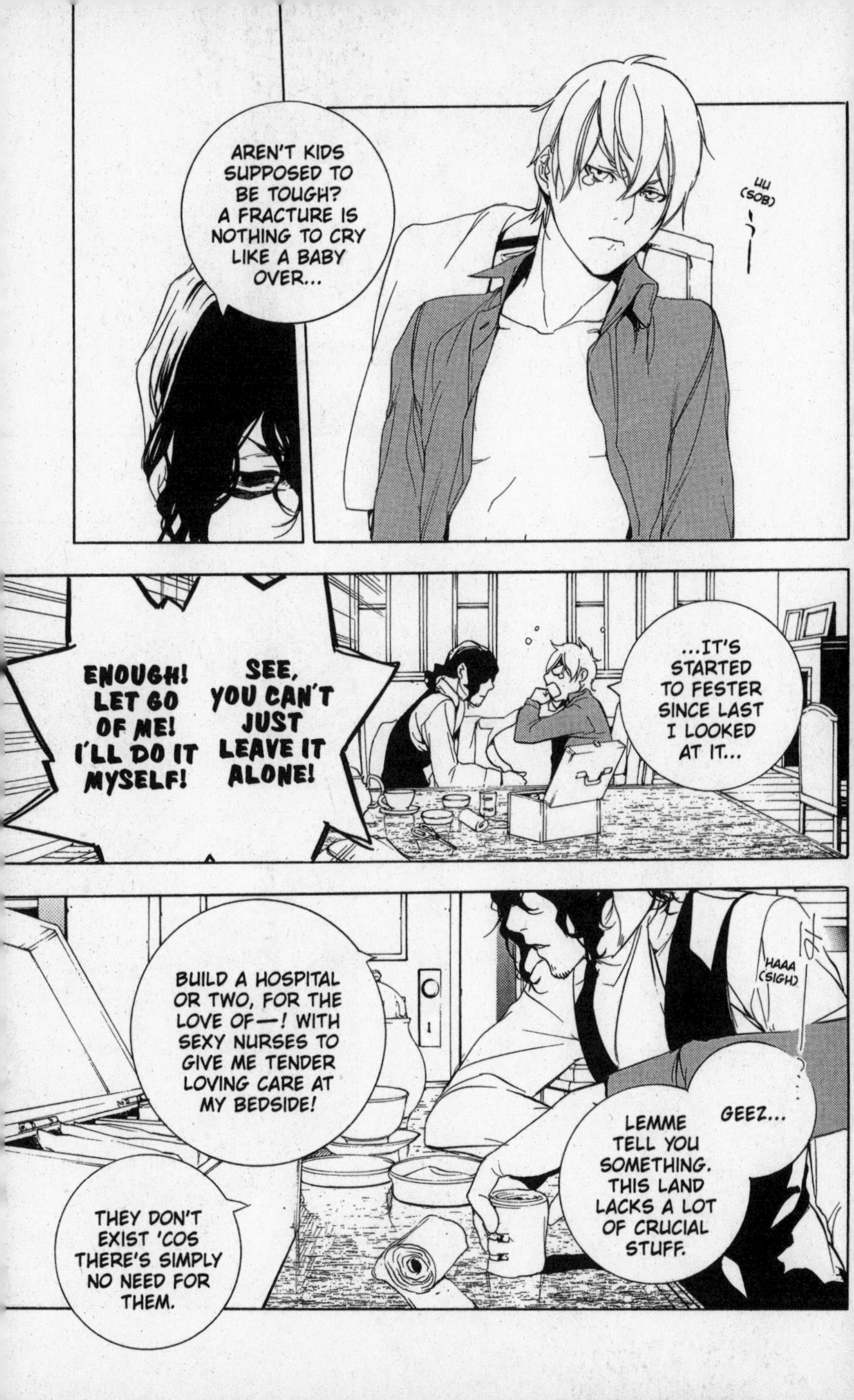
UU (SOB)
AREN'T KIDS SUPPOSED TO BE TOUGH? A FRACTURE IS NOTHING TO CRY LIKE A BABY OVER...
...IT'S STARTED TO FESTER SINCE LAST I LOOKED AT IT...
SEE, YOU CAN'T JUST LEAVE IT ALONE!
ENOUGH! LET GO OF ME! I'LL DO IT MYSELF!
HAAA (SIGH)
GEEZ...
LEMME TELL YOU SOMETHING. THIS LAND LACKS A LOT OF CRUCIAL STUFF.
BUILD A HOSPITAL OR TWO, FOR THE LOVE OF—! WITH SEXY NURSES TO GIVE ME TENDER LOVING CARE AT MY BEDSIDE!
THEY DON'T EXIST 'COS THERE'S SIMPLY NO NEED FOR THEM.

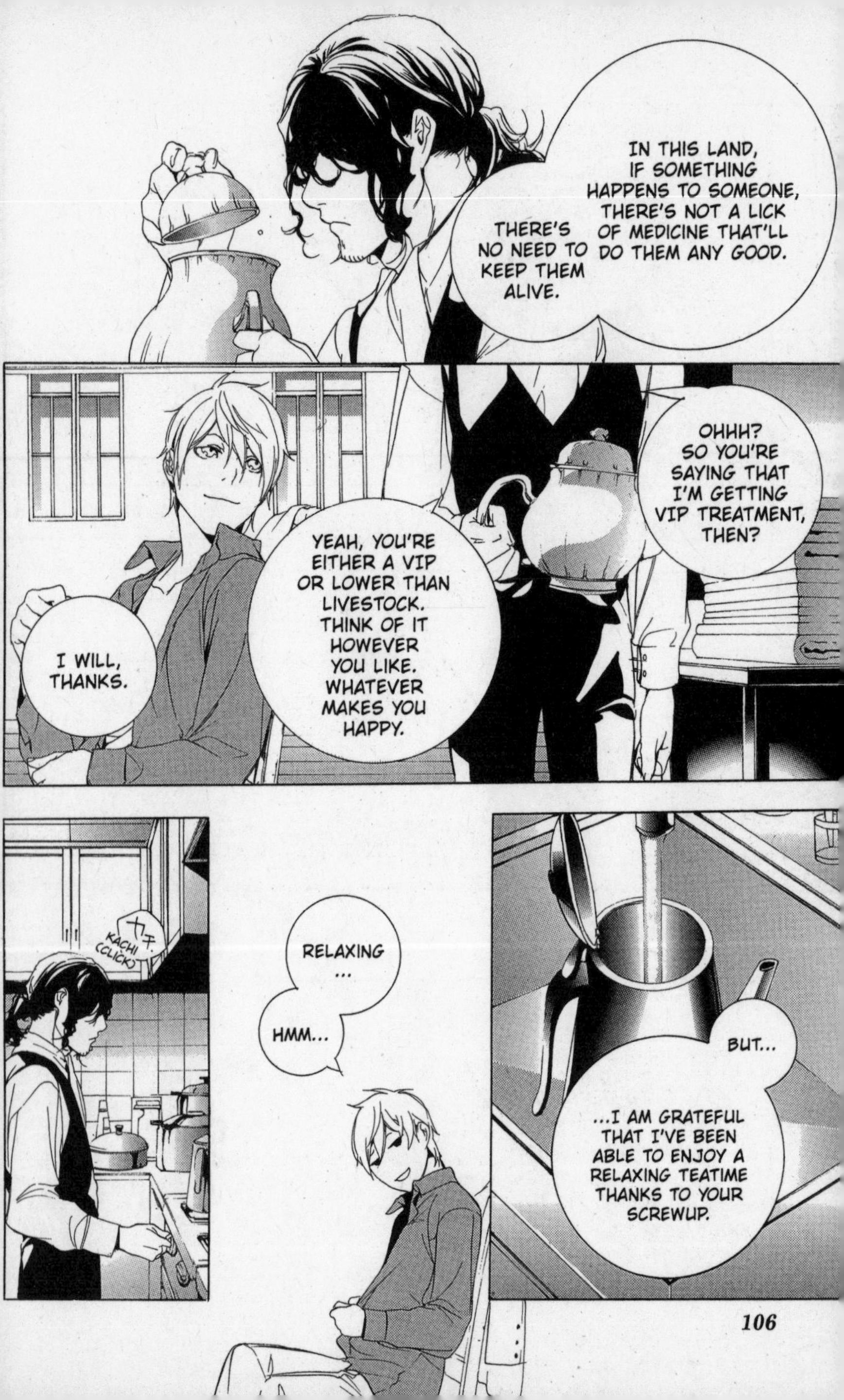
IN THIS LAND, IF SOMETHING HAPPENS TO SOMEONE, THERE'S NOT A LICK OF MEDICINE THAT'LL DO THEM ANY GOOD.
THERE'S NO NEED TO KEEP THEM ALIVE.
OHHH? SO YOU'RE SAYING THAT I'M GETTING VIP TREATMENT, THEN?
YEAH, YOU'RE EITHER A VIP OR LOWER THAN LIVESTOCK. THINK OF IT HOWEVER YOU LIKE. WHATEVER MAKES YOU HAPPY.
I WILL, THANKS.
BUT...
...I AM GRATEFUL THAT I'VE BEEN ABLE TO ENJOY A RELAXING TEATIME THANKS TO YOUR SCREWUP.
RELAXING ...
HMM...
カチ KACHI (CLICK)

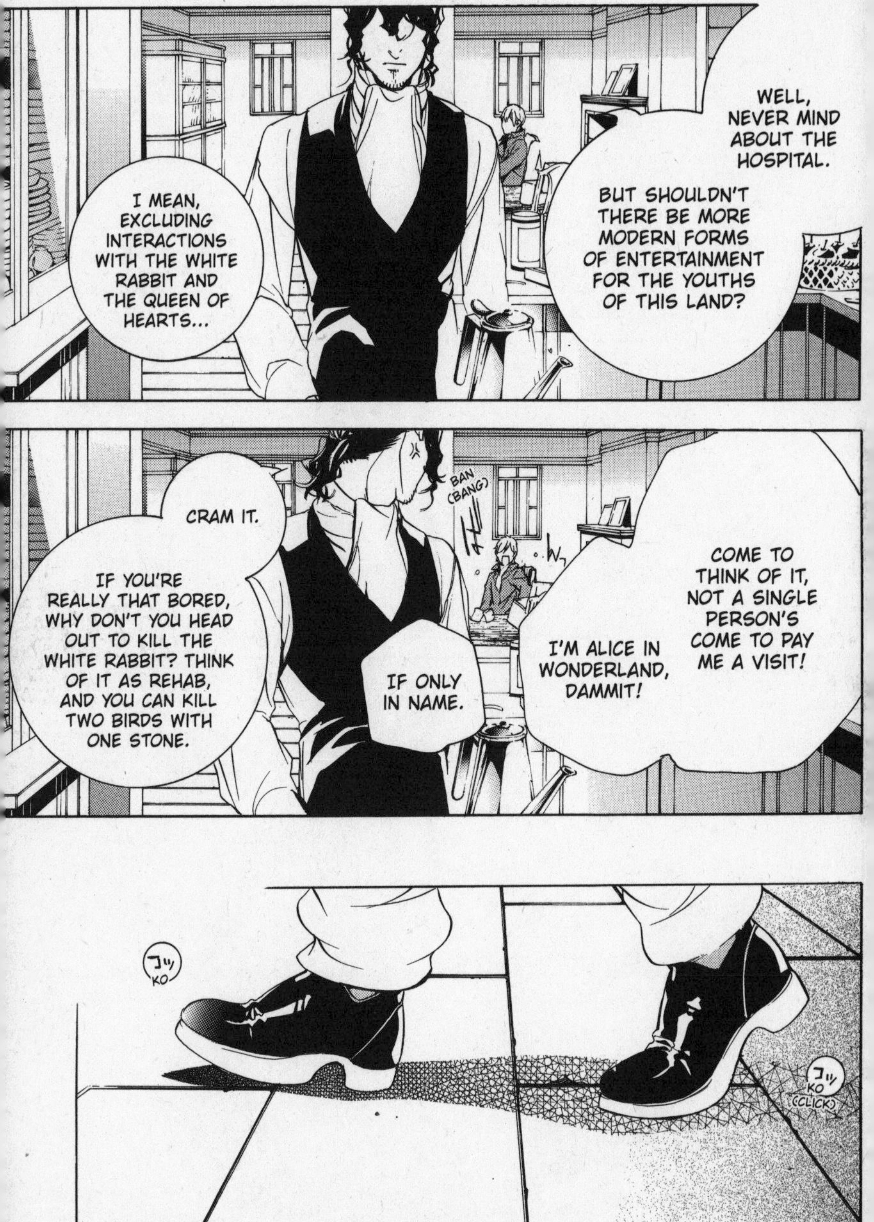
WELL, NEVER MIND ABOUT THE HOSPITAL.
BUT SHOULDN'T THERE BE MORE MODERN FORMS OF ENTERTAINMENT FOR THE YOUTHS OF THIS LAND?
I MEAN, EXCLUDING INTERACTIONS WITH THE WHITE RABBIT AND THE QUEEN OF HEARTS...
COME TO THINK OF IT, NOT A SINGLE PERSON'S COME TO PAY ME A VISIT!
I'M ALICE IN WONDERLAND, DAMMIT!
BAN (BANG)
IF ONLY IN NAME.
CRAM IT.
IF YOU'RE REALLY THAT BORED, WHY DON'T YOU HEAD OUT TO KILL THE WHITE RABBIT? THINK OF IT AS REHAB, AND YOU CAN KILL TWO BIRDS WITH ONE STONE.
コッ KO (CLICK)
コッ KO

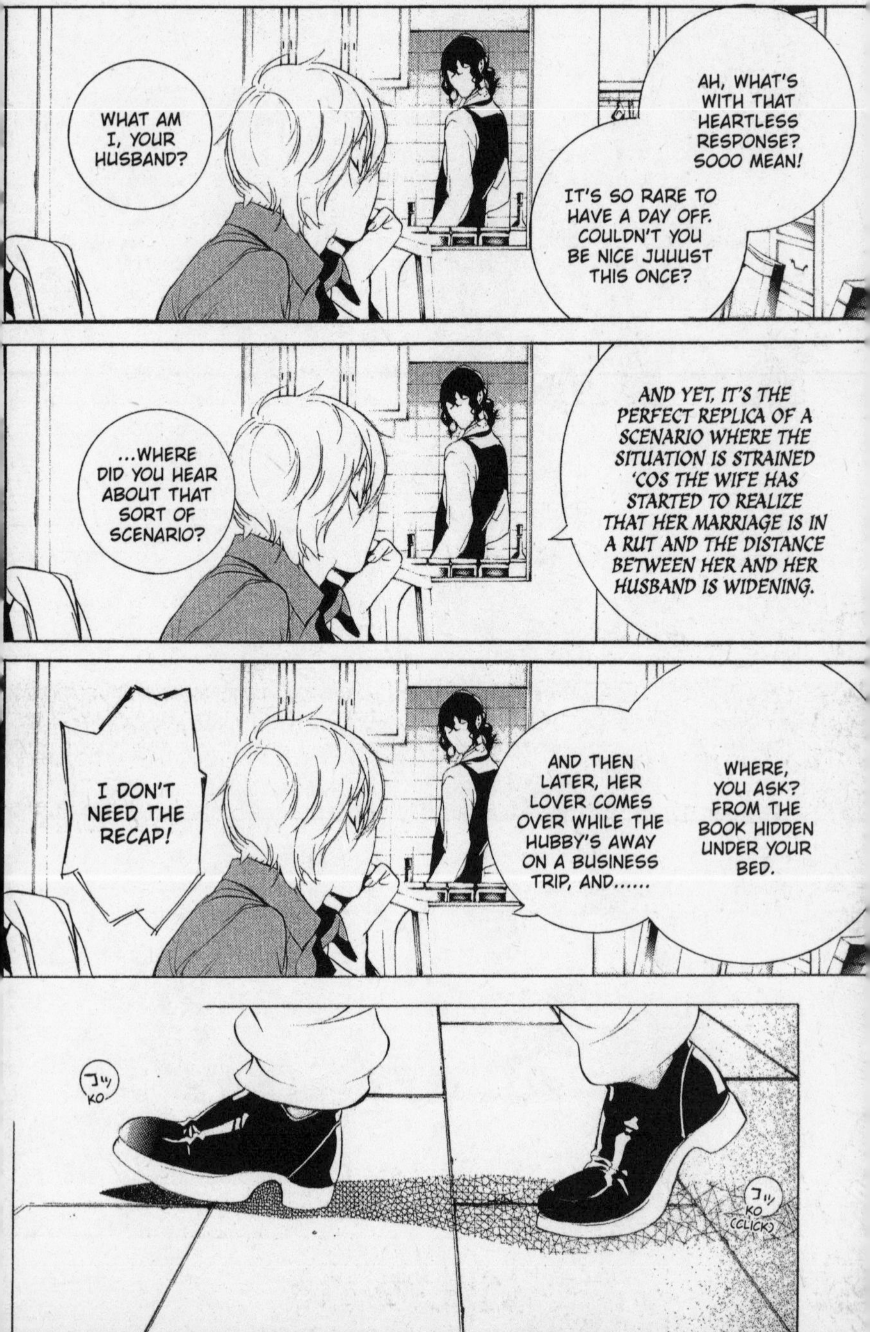
AH, WHAT'S WITH THAT HEARTLESS RESPONSE? SOOO MEAN!
IT'S SO RARE TO HAVE A DAY OFF. COULDN'T YOU BE NICE JUUUST THIS ONCE?
WHAT AM I, YOUR HUSBAND?
AND YET, IT'S THE PERFECT REPLICA OF A SCENARIO WHERE THE SITUATION IS STRAINED 'COS THE WIFE HAS STARTED TO REALIZE THAT HER MARRIAGE IS IN A RUT AND THE DISTANCE BETWEEN HER AND HER HUSBAND IS WIDENING.
...WHERE DID YOU HEAR ABOUT THAT SORT OF SCENARIO?
WHERE, YOU ASK? FROM THE BOOK HIDDEN UNDER YOUR BED.
AND THEN LATER, HER LOVER COMES OVER WHILE THE HUBBY'S AWAY ON A BUSINESS TRIP, AND......
I DON'T NEED THE RECAP!
コッ KO (CLICK)
コッ KO

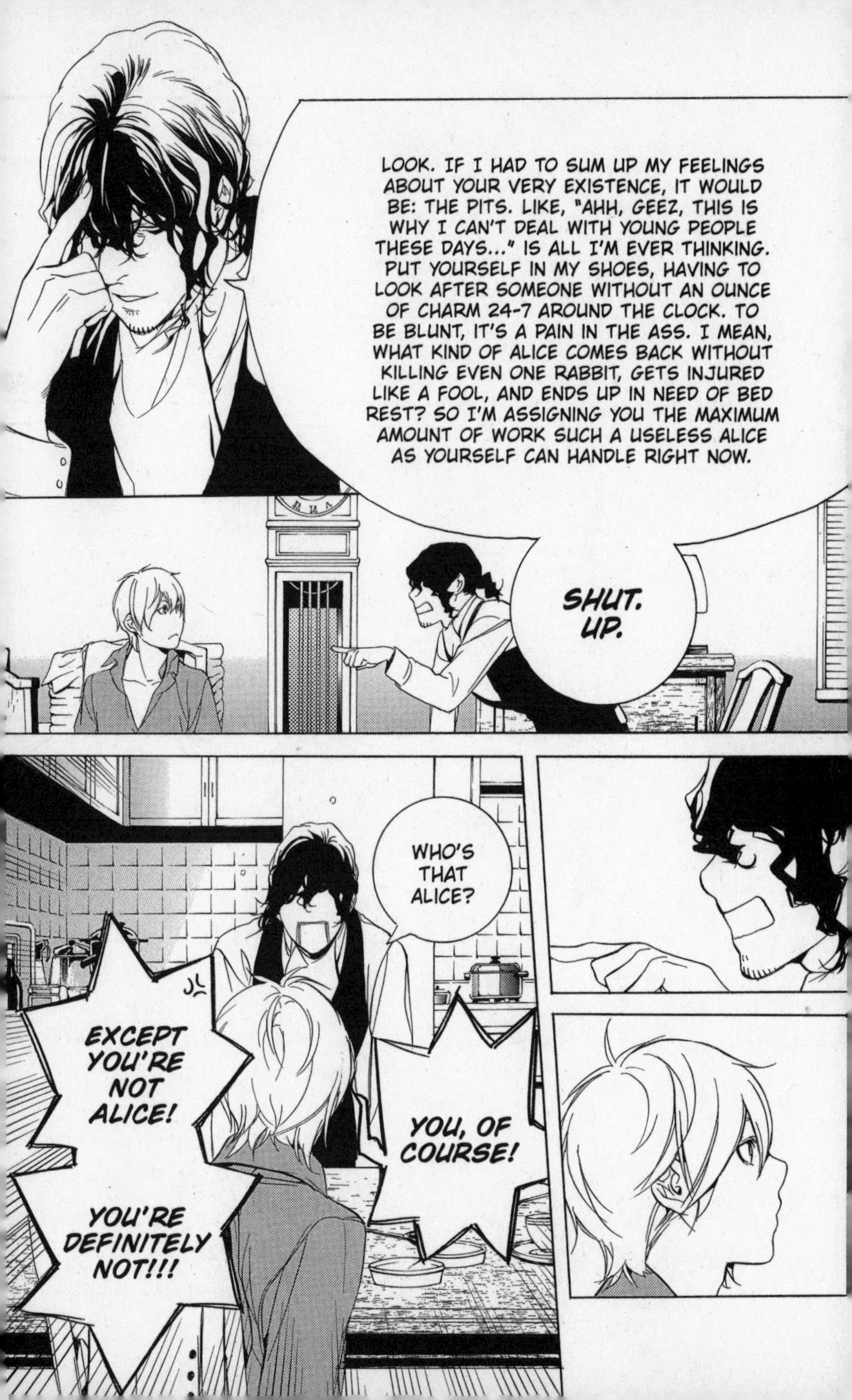
LOOK. IF I HAD TO SUM UP MY FEELINGS ABOUT YOUR VERY EXISTENCE, IT WOULD BE: THE PITS. LIKE, "AHH, GEEZ, THIS IS WHY I CAN'T DEAL WITH YOUNG PEOPLE THESE DAYS..." IS ALL I'M EVER THINKING. PUT YOURSELF IN MY SHOES, HAVING TO LOOK AFTER SOMEONE WITHOUT AN OUNCE OF CHARM 24-7 AROUND THE CLOCK. TO BE BLUNT, IT'S A PAIN IN THE ASS. I MEAN, WHAT KIND OF ALICE COMES BACK WITHOUT KILLING EVEN ONE RABBIT, GETS INJURED LIKE A FOOL, AND ENDS UP IN NEED OF BED REST? SO I'M ASSIGNING YOU THE MAXIMUM AMOUNT OF WORK SUCH A USELESS ALICE AS YOURSELF CAN HANDLE RIGHT NOW.
SHUT. UP.
WHO'S THAT ALICE?
YOU, OF COURSE!
EXCEPT YOU'RE NOT ALICE!
YOU'RE DEFINITELY NOT!!!

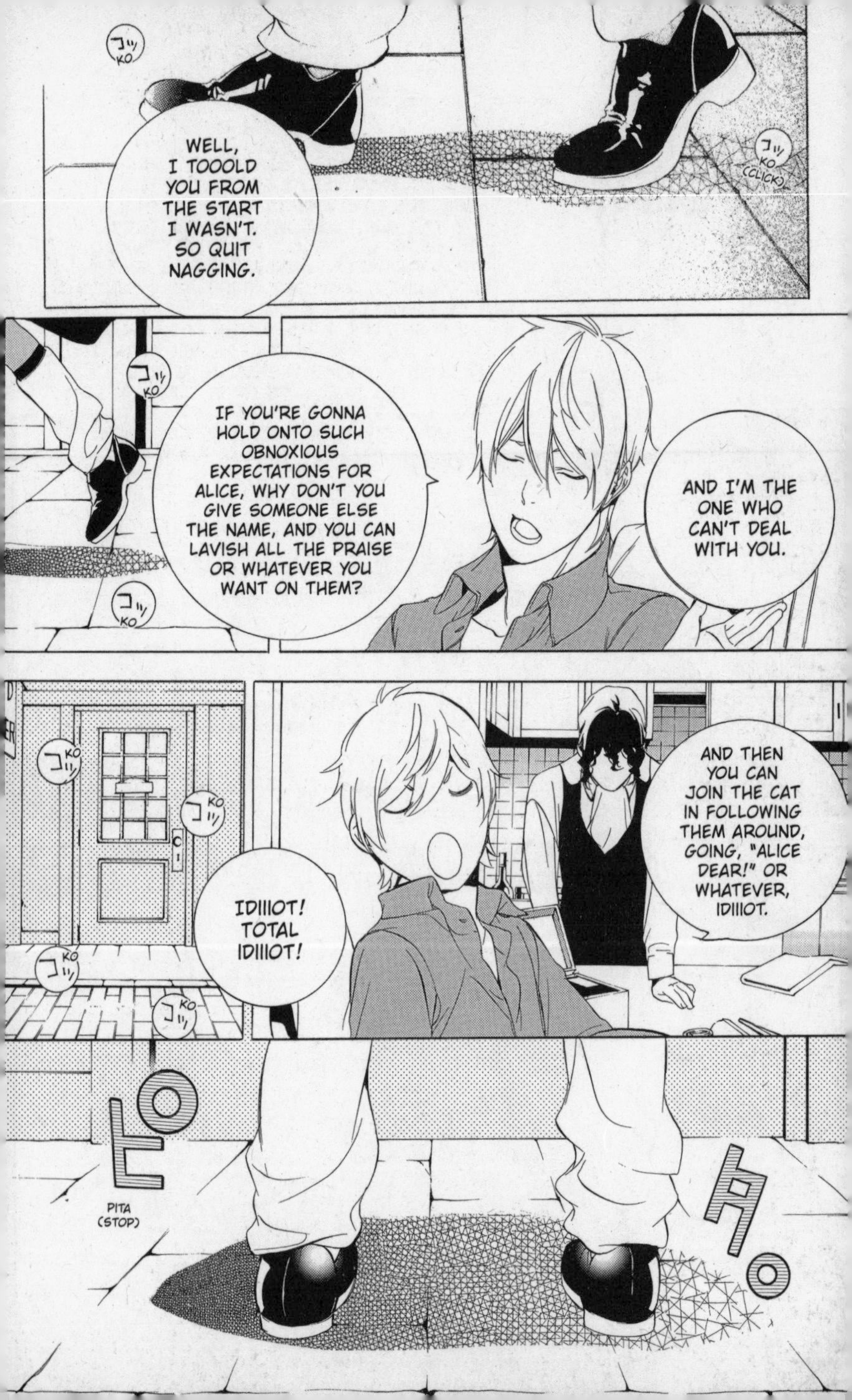

コッ KO (CLICK)
WELL, I TOOOLD YOU FROM THE START I WASN'T. SO QUIT NAGGING.
コッ KO
IF YOU'RE GONNA HOLD ONTO SUCH OBNOXIOUS EXPECTATIONS FOR ALICE, WHY DON'T YOU GIVE SOMEONE ELSE THE NAME, AND YOU CAN LAVISH ALL THE PRAISE OR WHATEVER YOU WANT ON THEM?
AND I'M THE ONE WHO CAN'T DEAL WITH YOU.
コッ KO
コッ KO
AND THEN YOU CAN JOIN THE CAT IN FOLLOWING THEM AROUND, GOING, "ALICE DEAR!" OR WHATEVER, IDIIIOT.
IDIIIOT! TOTAL IDIIIOT!
コッ KO
コッ KO
コッ KO
コッ KO
ピタ。
PITA (STOP)

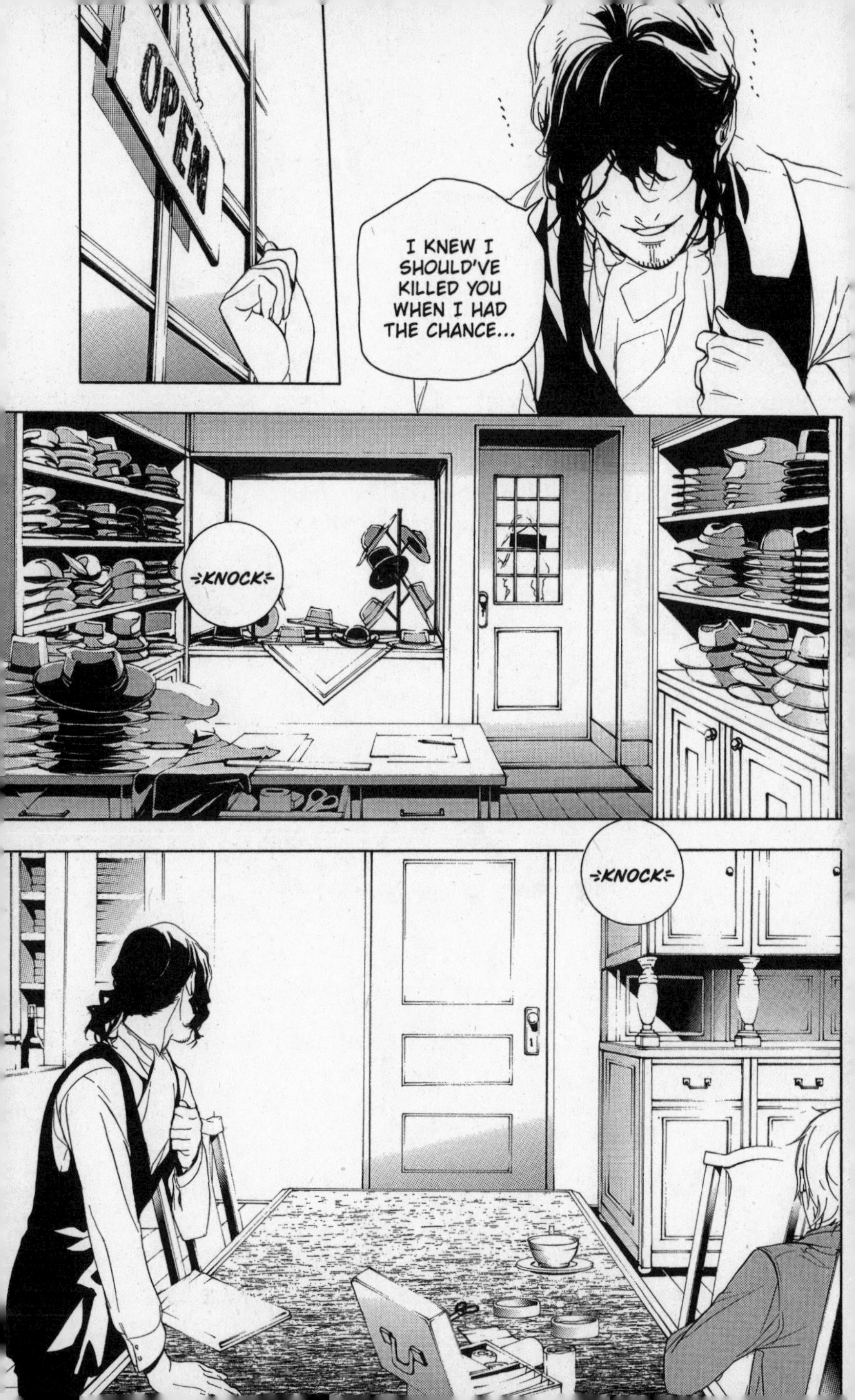
OPEN
I KNEW I SHOULD'VE KILLED YOU WHEN I HAD THE CHANCE...
KNOCK
KNOCK

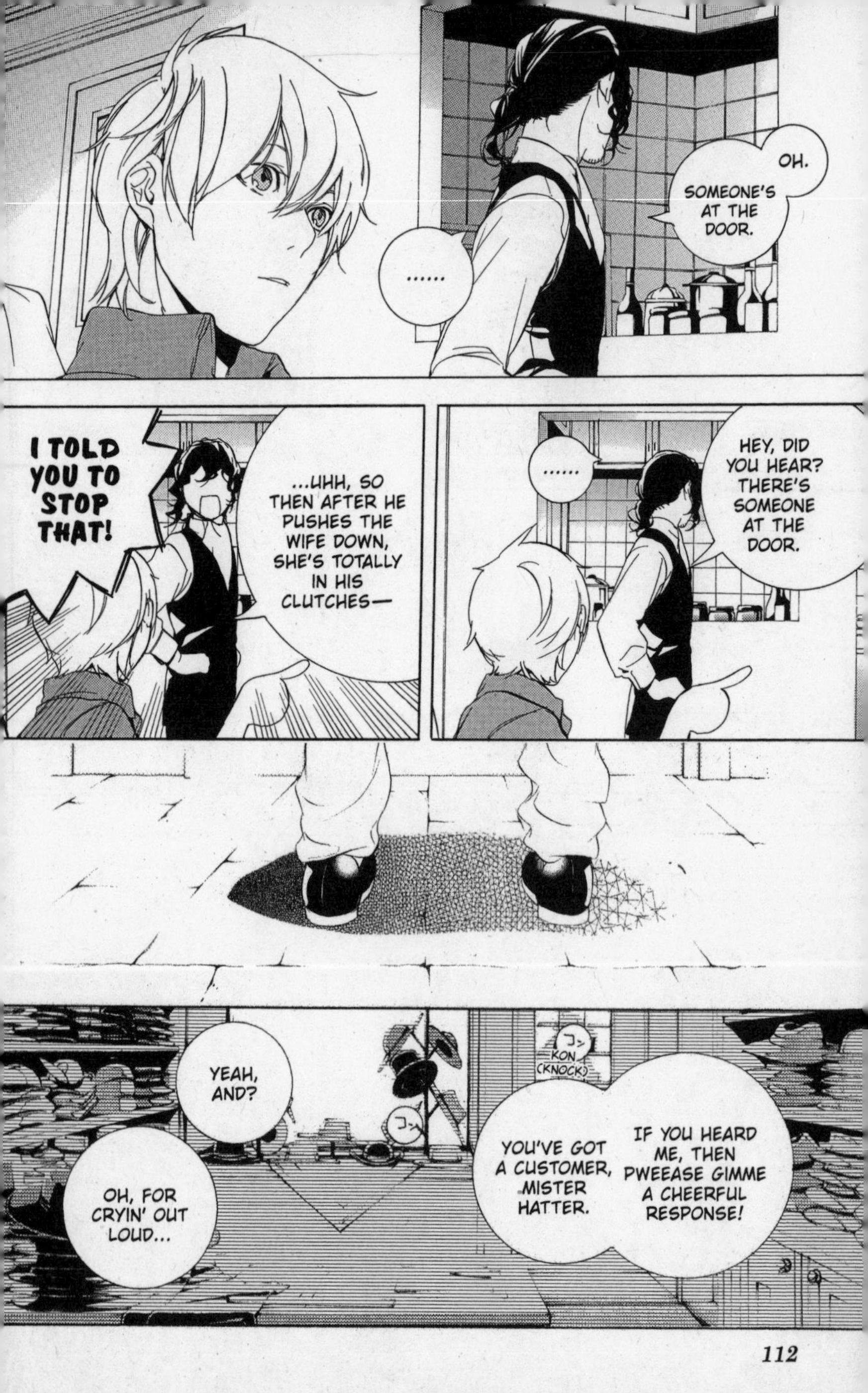
OH.
SOMEONE'S AT THE DOOR.
......
HEY, DID YOU HEAR? THERE'S SOMEONE AT THE DOOR.
......
...UHH, SO THEN AFTER HE PUSHES THE WIFE DOWN, SHE'S TOTALLY IN HIS CLUTCHES—
I TOLD YOU TO STOP THAT!
コン
KON (KNOCK)
IF YOU HEARD ME, THEN PWEEASE GIMME A CHEERFUL RESPONSE!
YOU'VE GOT A CUSTOMER, MISTER HATTER.
YEAH, AND?
OH, FOR CRYIN' OUT LOUD...

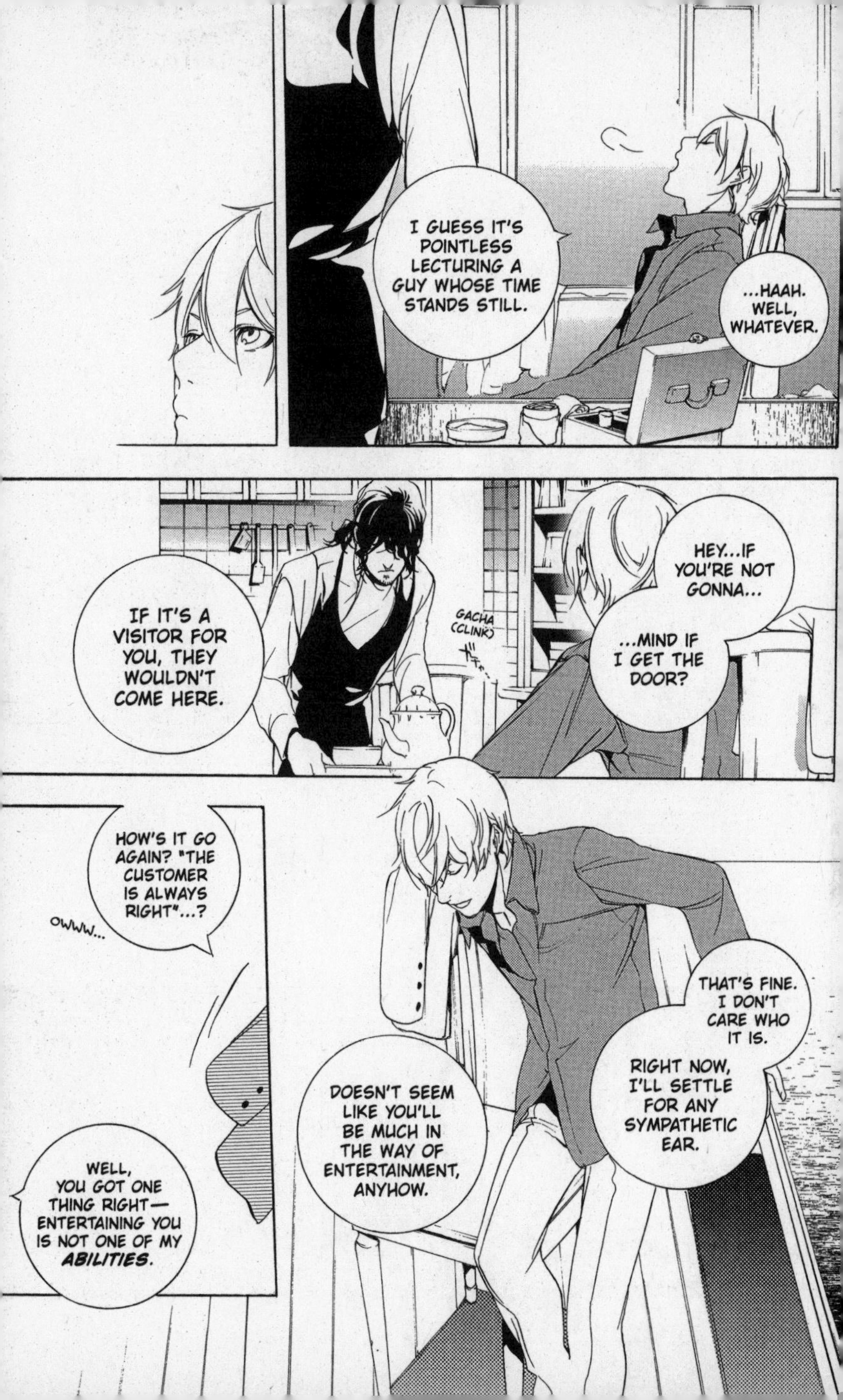
...HAAH. WELL, WHATEVER.
I GUESS IT'S POINTLESS LECTURING A GUY WHOSE TIME STANDS STILL.
HEY...IF YOU'RE NOT GONNA...
...MIND IF I GET THE DOOR?
GACHA (CLINK)
IF IT'S A VISITOR FOR YOU, THEY WOULDN'T COME HERE.
THAT'S FINE. I DON'T CARE WHO IT IS.
RIGHT NOW, I'LL SETTLE FOR ANY SYMPATHETIC EAR.
DOESN'T SEEM LIKE YOU'LL BE MUCH IN THE WAY OF ENTERTAINMENT, ANYHOW.
HOW'S IT GO AGAIN? "THE CUSTOMER IS ALWAYS RIGHT"...?
OWWW...
WELL, YOU GOT ONE THING RIGHT— ENTERTAINING YOU IS NOT ONE OF MY *ABILITIES*.

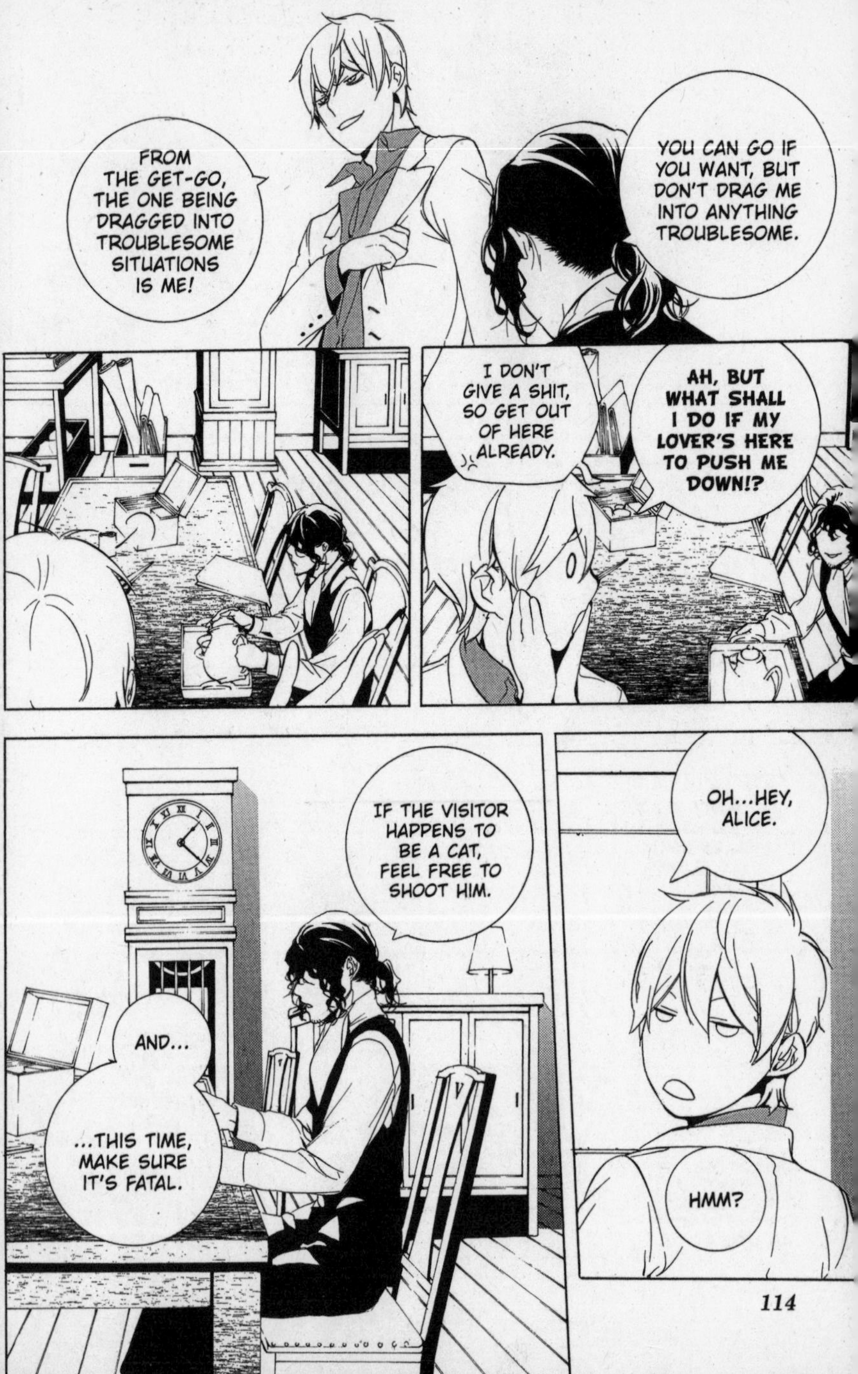
YOU CAN GO IF YOU WANT, BUT DON'T DRAG ME INTO ANYTHING TROUBLESOME.
FROM THE GET-GO, THE ONE BEING DRAGGED INTO TROUBLESOME SITUATIONS IS ME!
AH, BUT WHAT SHALL I DO IF MY LOVER'S HERE TO PUSH ME DOWN!?
I DON'T GIVE A SHIT, SO GET OUT OF HERE ALREADY.
OH...HEY, ALICE.
HMM?
IF THE VISITOR HAPPENS TO BE A CAT, FEEL FREE TO SHOOT HIM.
AND...
...THIS TIME, MAKE SURE IT'S FATAL.

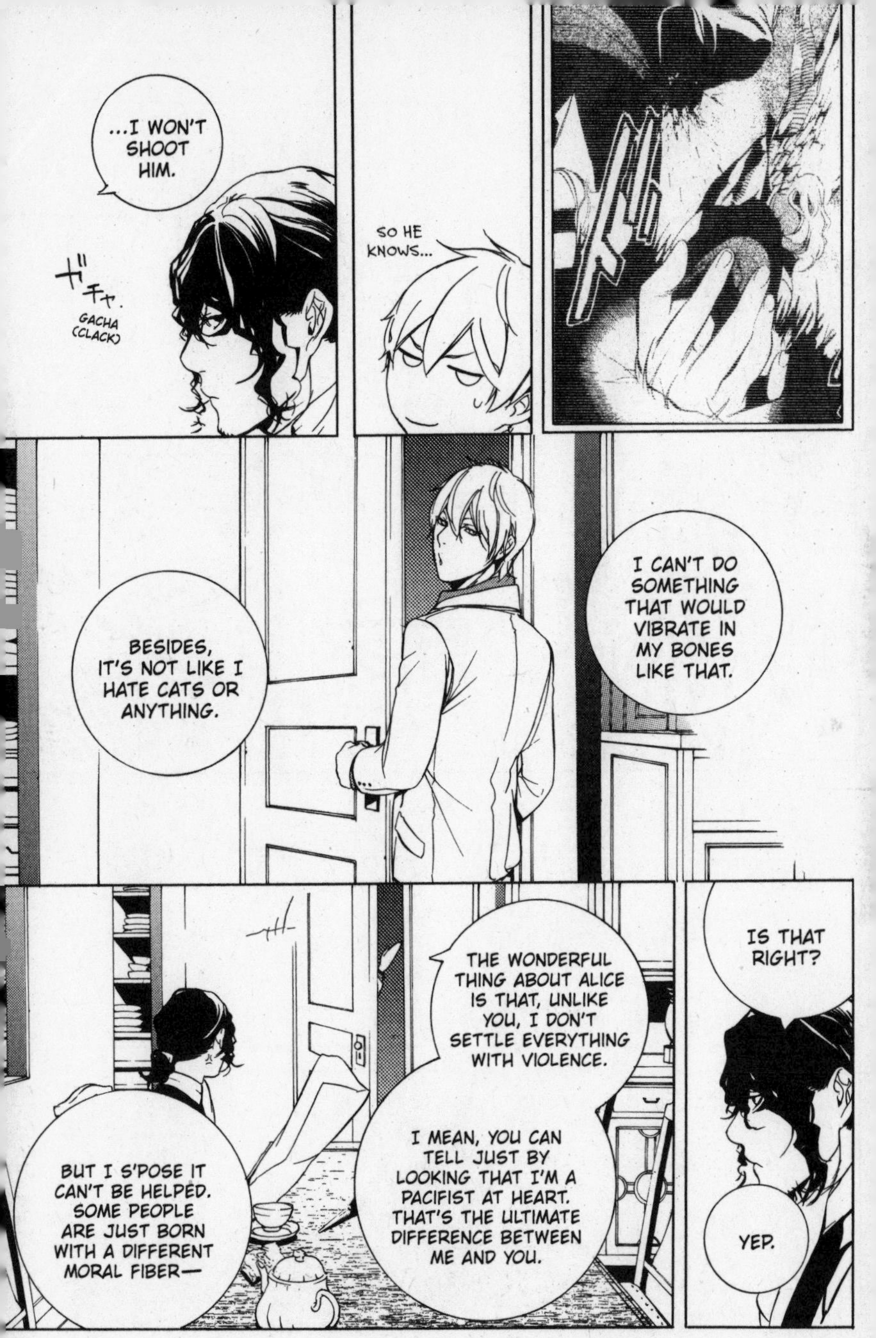
SO HE KNOWS...
...I WON'T SHOOT HIM.
ガチャ
GACHA (CLACK)
I CAN'T DO SOMETHING THAT WOULD VIBRATE IN MY BONES LIKE THAT.
BESIDES, IT'S NOT LIKE I HATE CATS OR ANYTHING.
IS THAT RIGHT?
YEP.
THE WONDERFUL THING ABOUT ALICE IS THAT, UNLIKE YOU, I DON'T SETTLE EVERYTHING WITH VIOLENCE.
I MEAN, YOU CAN TELL JUST BY LOOKING THAT I'M A PACIFIST AT HEART. THAT'S THE ULTIMATE DIFFERENCE BETWEEN ME AND YOU.
BUT I S'POSE IT CAN'T BE HELPED. SOME PEOPLE ARE JUST BORN WITH A DIFFERENT MORAL FIBER—

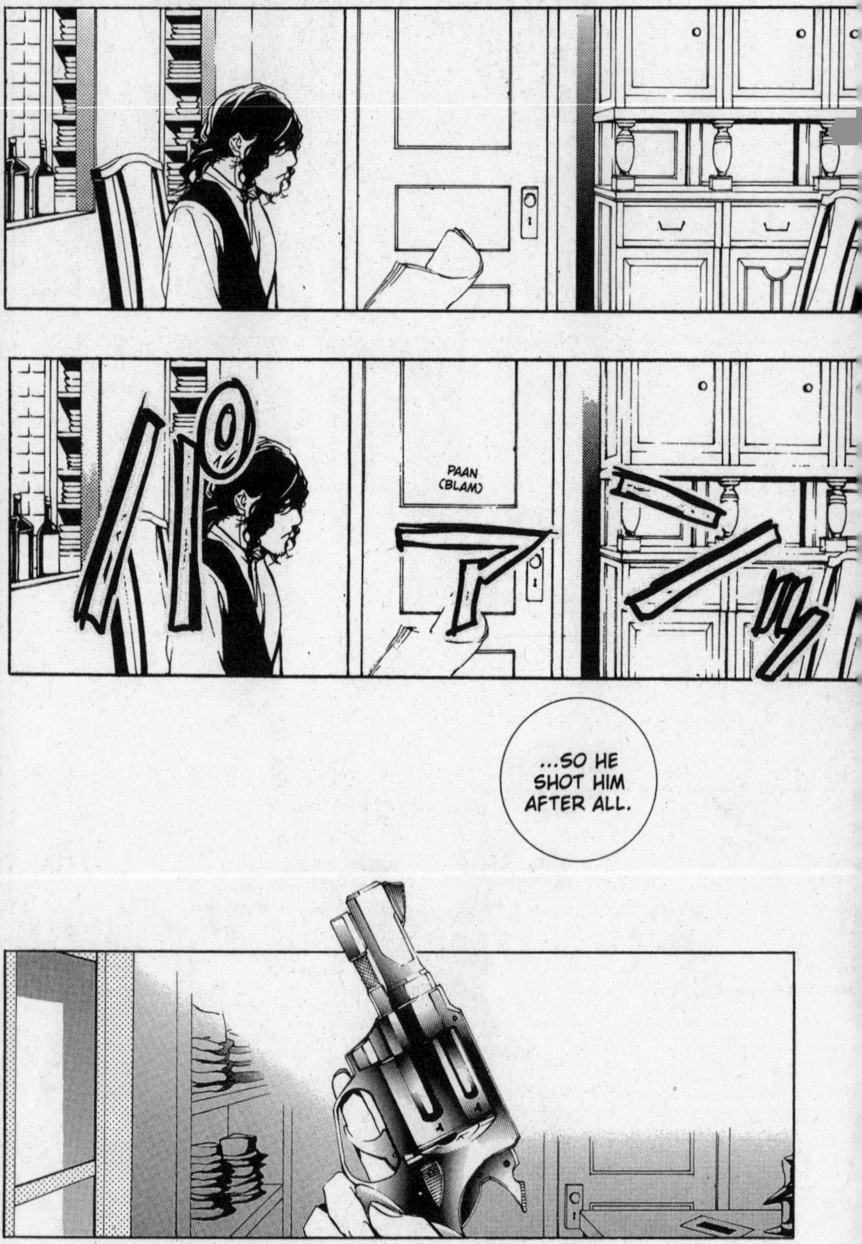
PAAN (BLAM)
...SO HE SHOT HIM AFTER ALL.

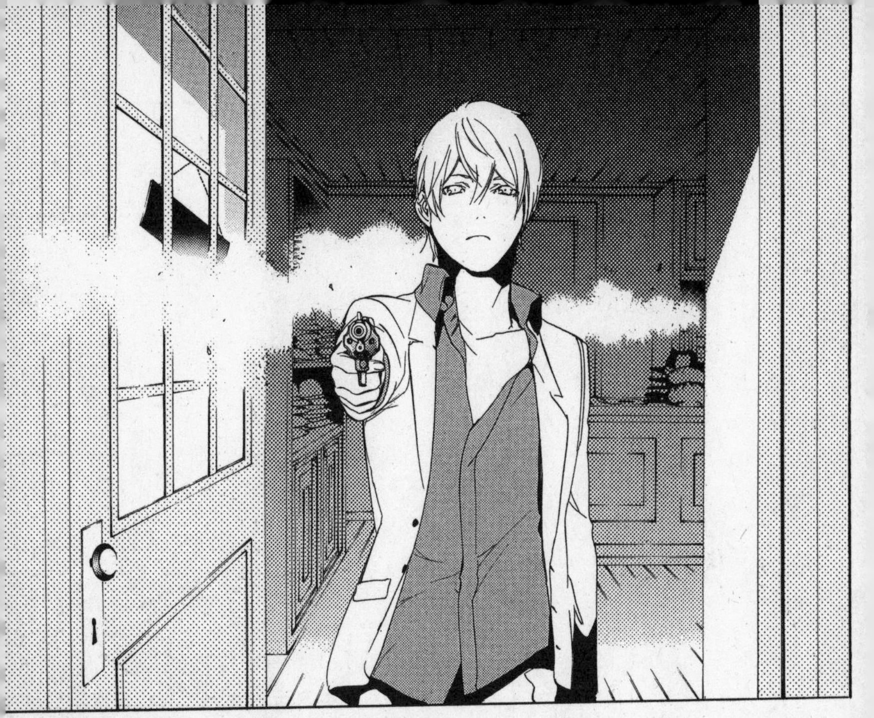

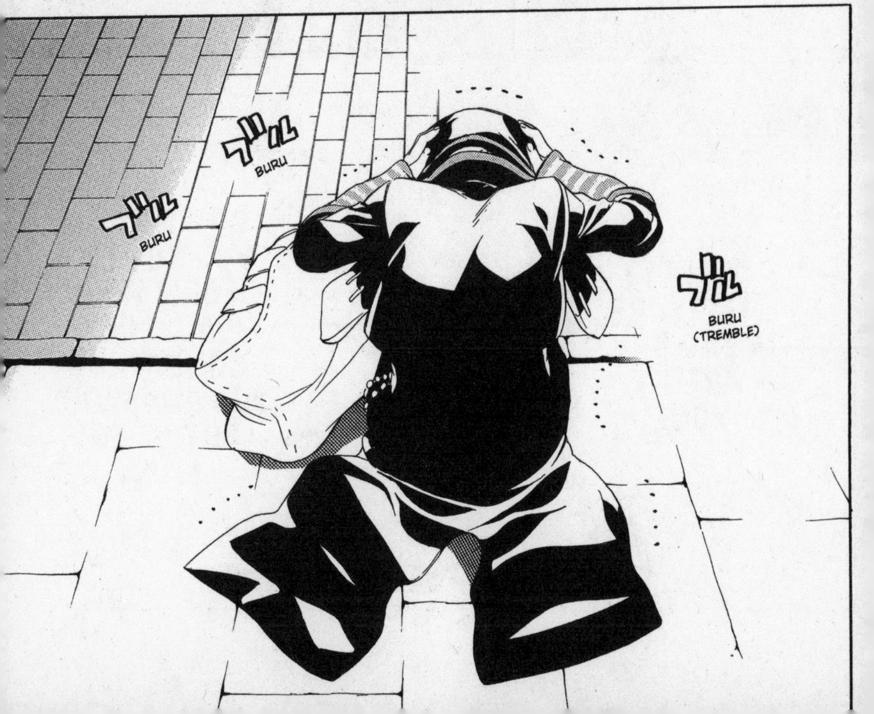
ブル
BURU
ブル
BURU
ブル
BURU
(TREMBLE)

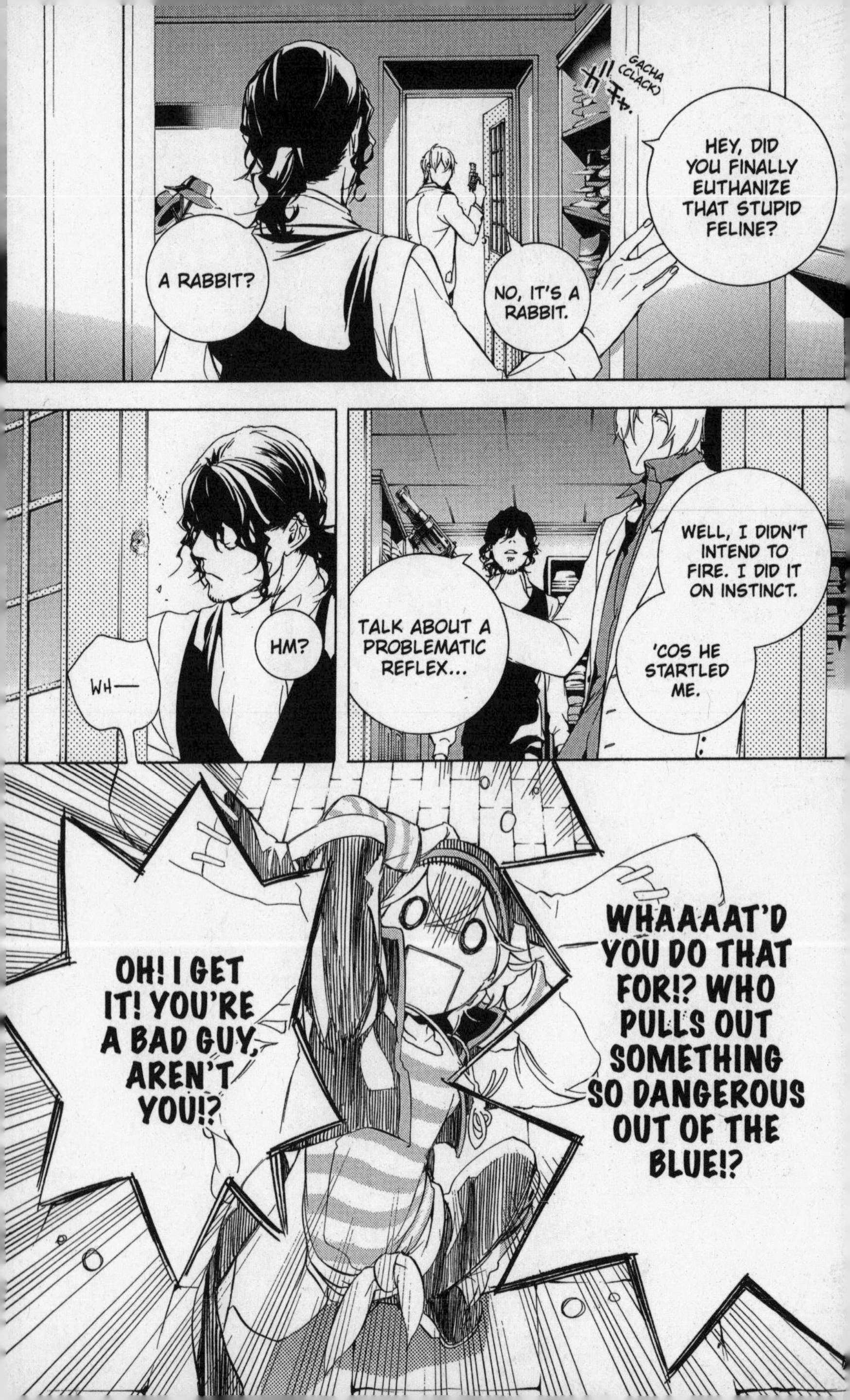
GACHA (CLACK)
HEY, DID YOU FINALLY EUTHANIZE THAT STUPID FELINE?
NO, IT'S A RABBIT.
A RABBIT?
WELL, I DIDN'T INTEND TO FIRE. I DID IT ON INSTINCT.
'COS HE STARTLED ME.
TALK ABOUT A PROBLEMATIC REFLEX...
HM?
WH—
WHAAAAT'D YOU DO THAT FOR!? WHO PULLS OUT SOMETHING SO DANGEROUS OUT OF THE BLUE!?
OH! I GET IT! YOU'RE A BAD GUY, AREN'T YOU!?

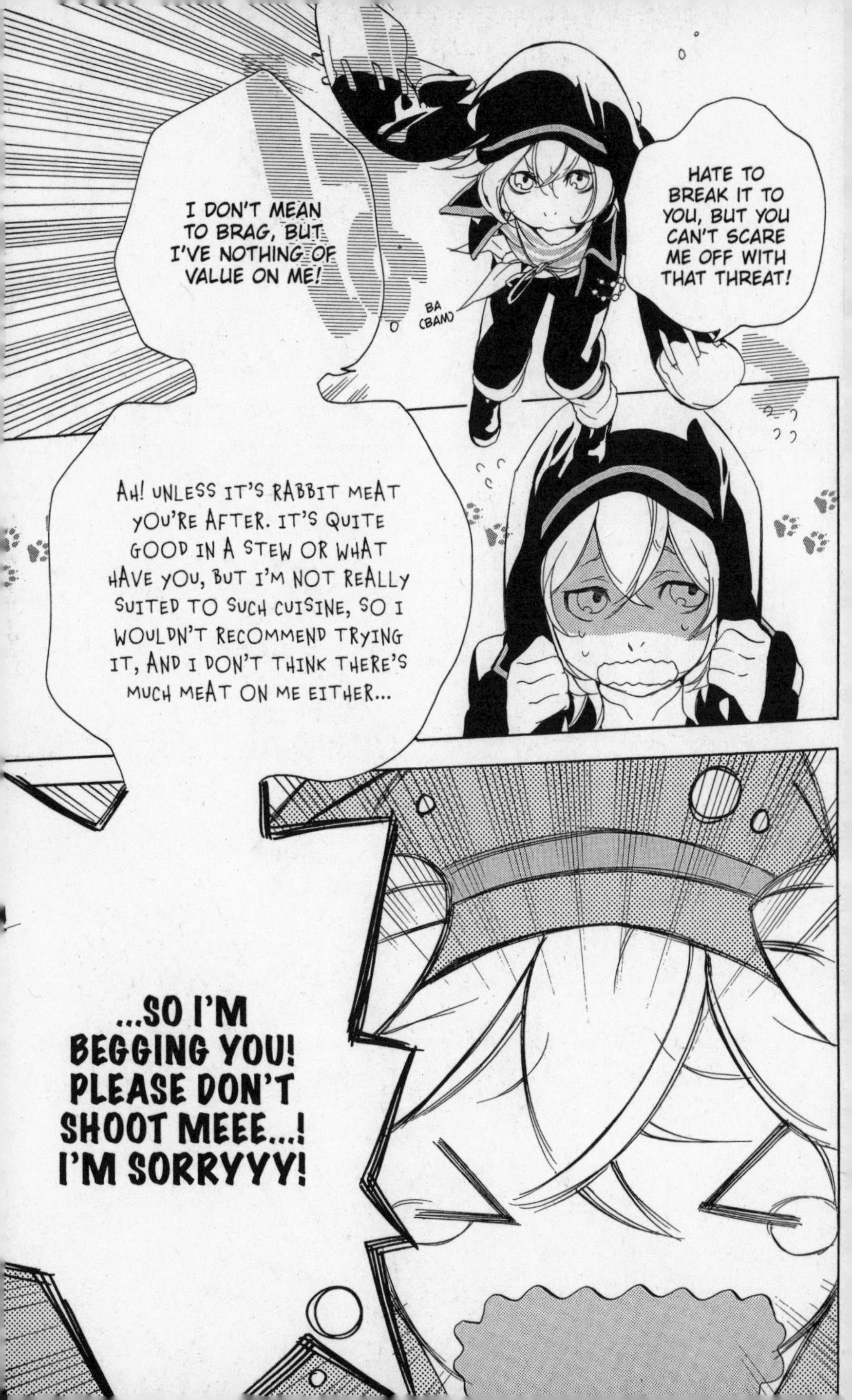
HATE TO BREAK IT TO YOU, BUT YOU CAN'T SCARE ME OFF WITH THAT THREAT!
BA (BAM)
I DON'T MEAN TO BRAG, BUT I'VE NOTHING OF VALUE ON ME!
AH! UNLESS IT'S RABBIT MEAT YOU'RE AFTER. IT'S QUITE GOOD IN A STEW OR WHAT HAVE YOU, BUT I'M NOT REALLY SUITED TO SUCH CUISINE, SO I WOULDN'T RECOMMEND TRYING IT, AND I DON'T THINK THERE'S MUCH MEAT ON ME EITHER...
...SO I'M BEGGING YOU! PLEASE DON'T SHOOT MEEE...! I'M SORRYYY!

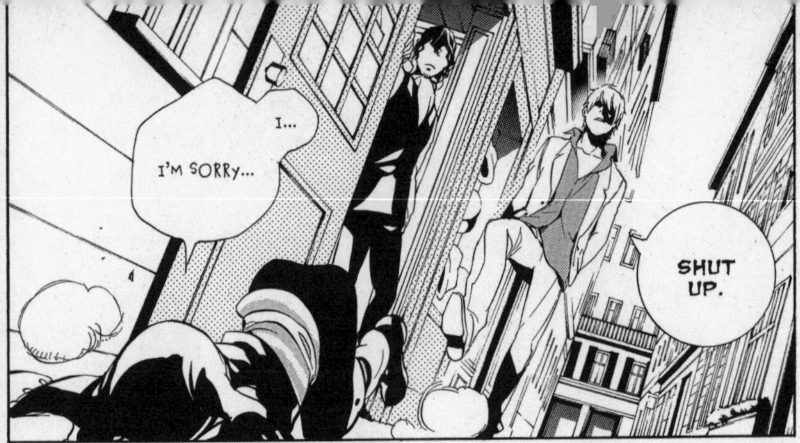
SHUT UP.
I...
I'M SORRY...

*MITSUKI: ALTERNATE READING OF THE KANJI FOR "MARCH"

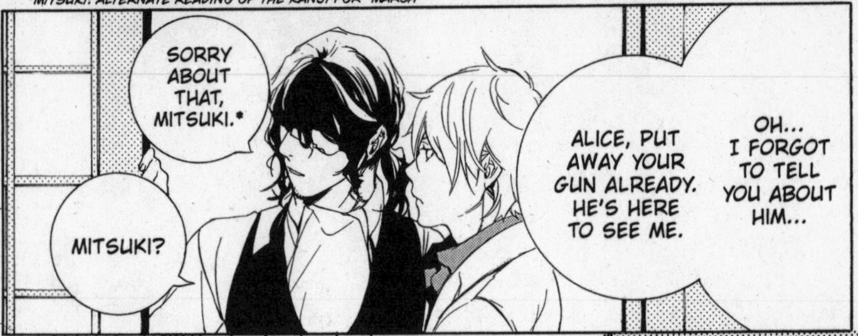
OH... I FORGOT TO TELL YOU ABOUT HIM...
ALICE, PUT AWAY YOUR GUN ALREADY. HE'S HERE TO SEE ME.
SORRY ABOUT THAT, MITSUKI.*
MITSUKI?

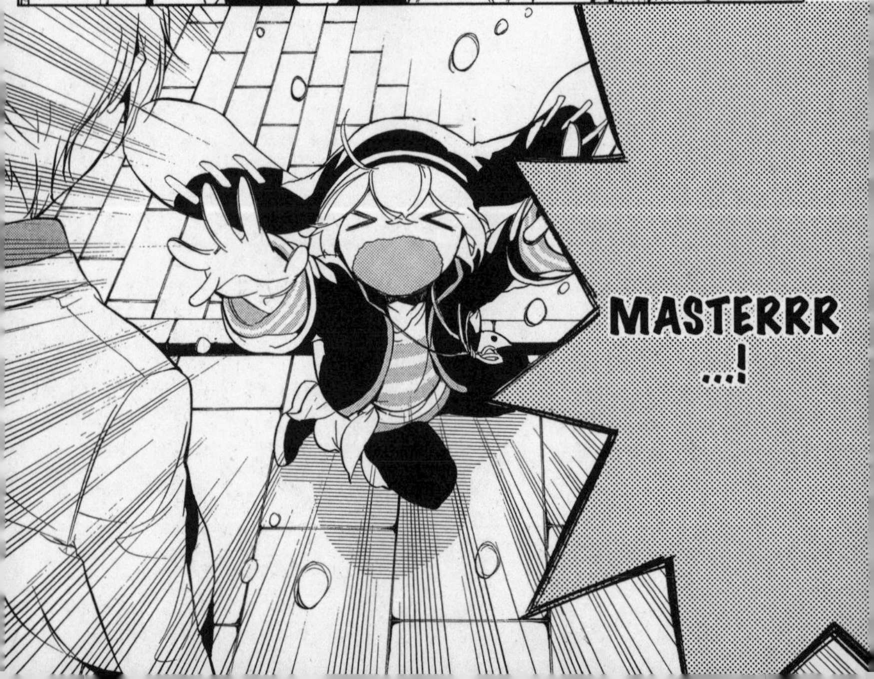
MASTERRR ...!

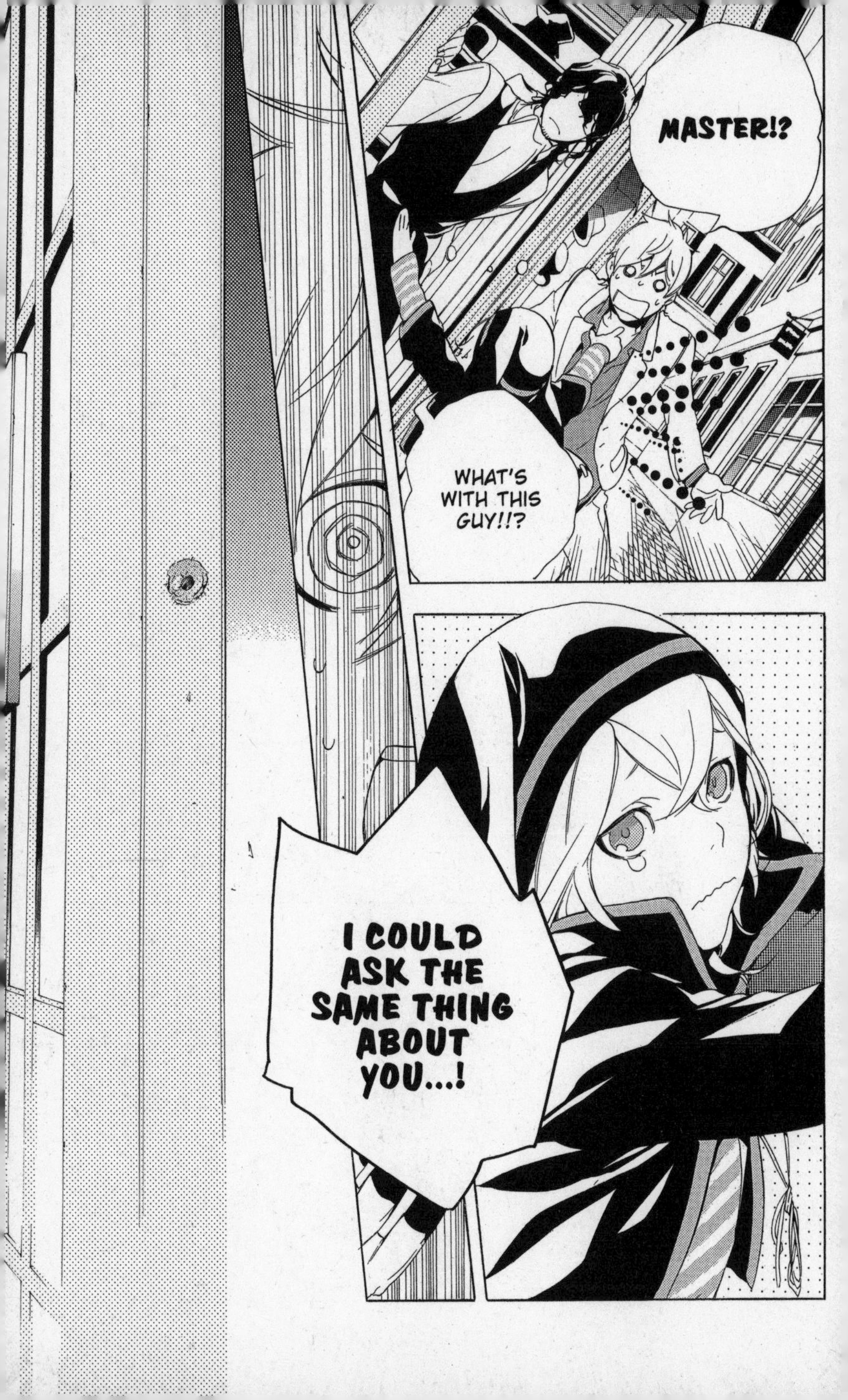
MASTER!?
WHAT'S WITH THIS GUY!!?
I COULD ASK THE SAME THING ABOUT YOU...!

TOCK
TICK

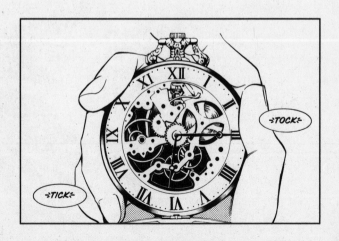

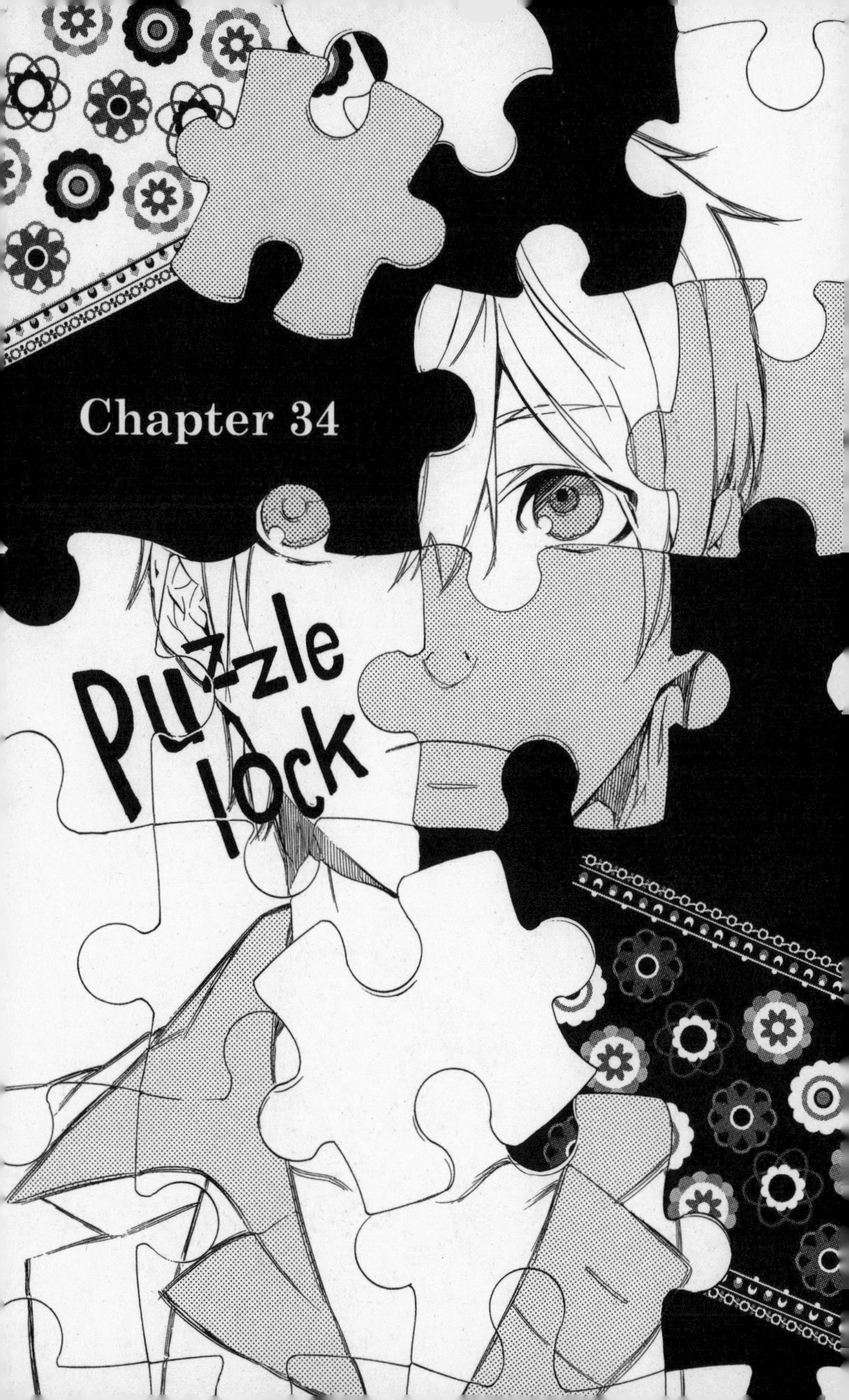
Chapter 34
Puzzle lock

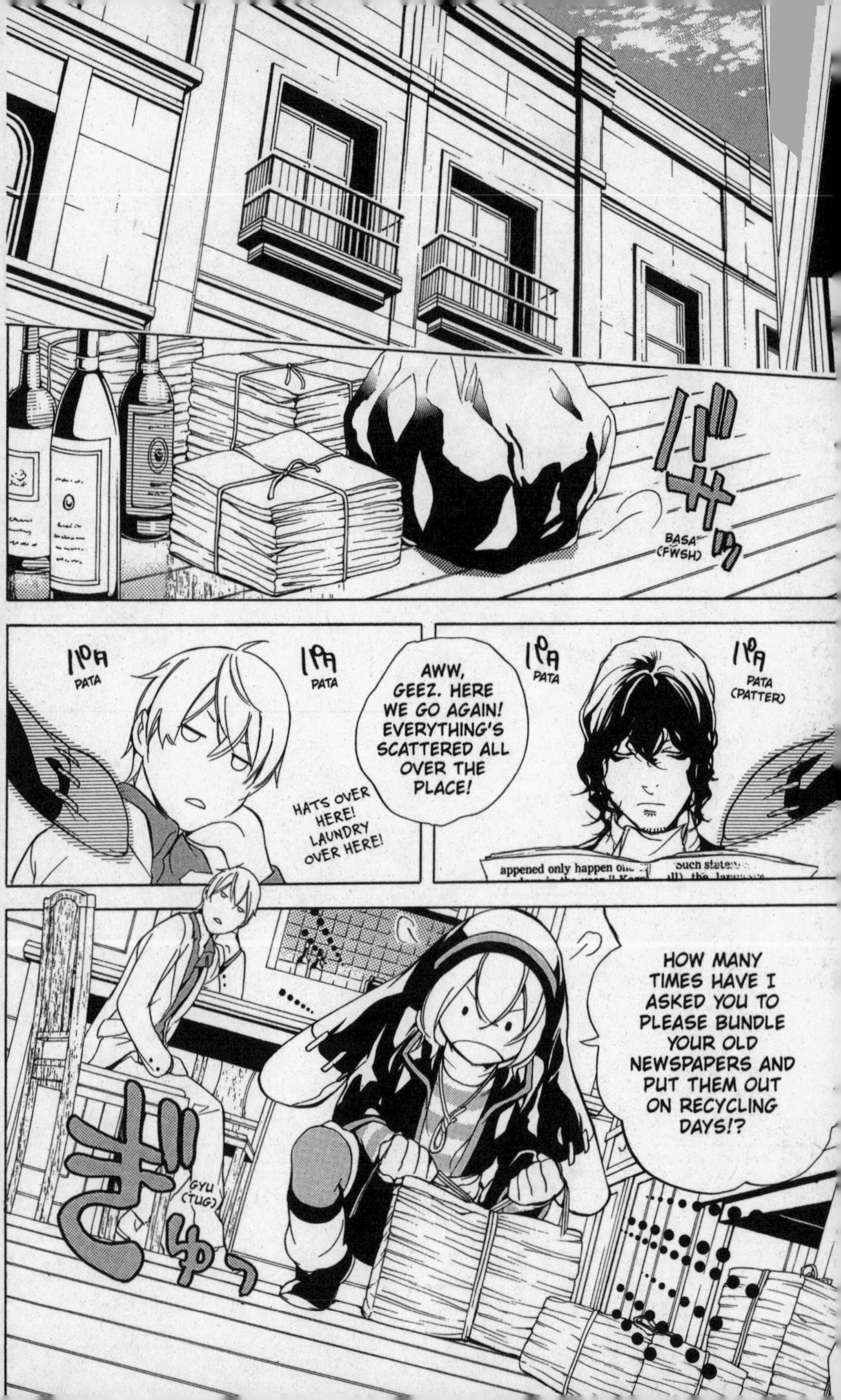

バサッ
BASA (FWSH)
パタ
PATA
パタ
PATA (PATTER)
パタ
PATA
パタ
PATA
AWW, GEEZ. HERE WE GO AGAIN! EVERYTHING'S SCATTERED ALL OVER THE PLACE!
HATS OVER HERE! LAUNDRY OVER HERE!
HOW MANY TIMES HAVE I ASKED YOU TO PLEASE BUNDLE YOUR OLD NEWSPAPERS AND PUT THEM OUT ON RECYCLING DAYS!?
.....
ぎゅっ
GYU (TUG)

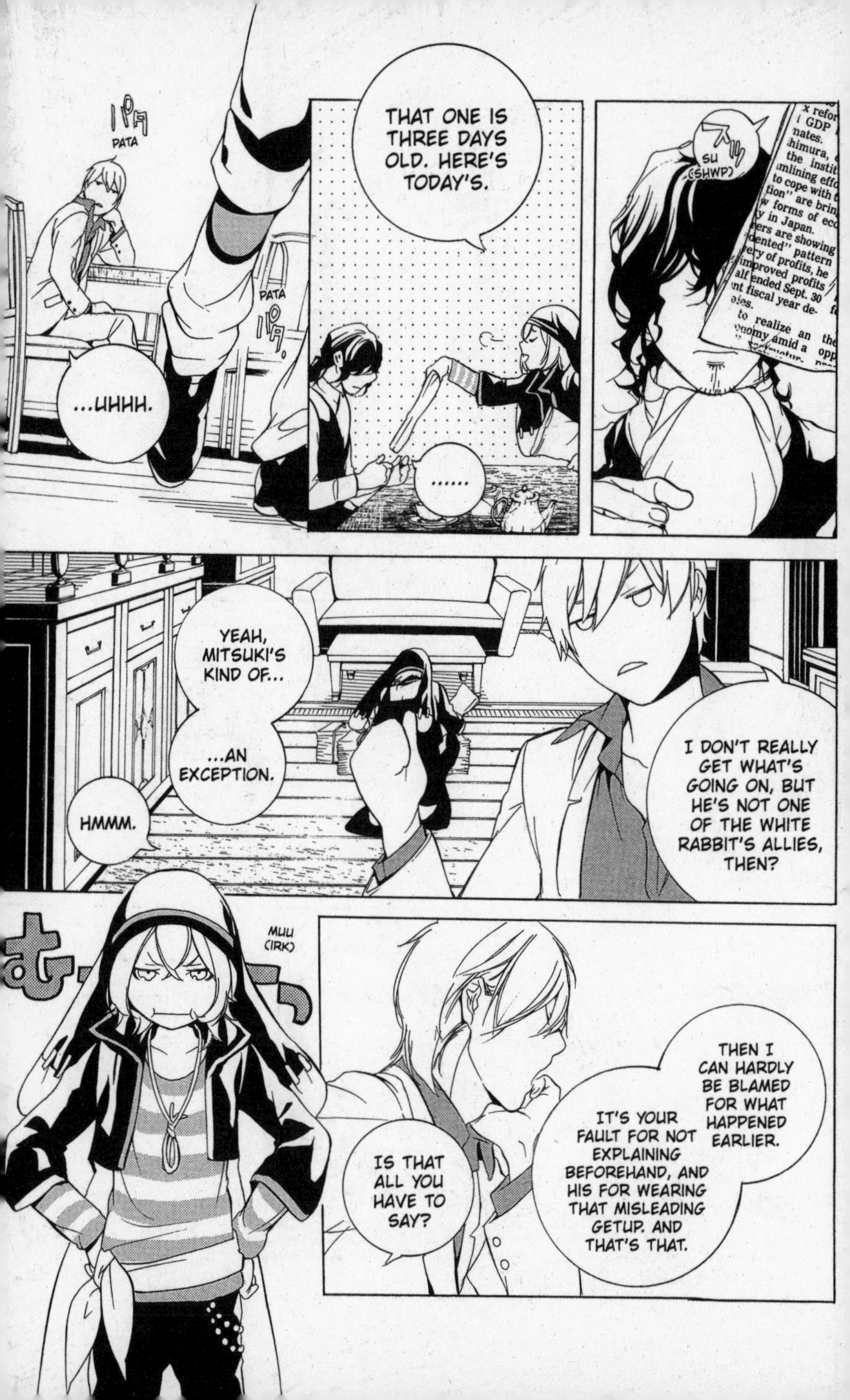
SU (SHWP)
THAT ONE IS THREE DAYS OLD. HERE'S TODAY'S.
......
PATA
PATA
...UHHH.
I DON'T REALLY GET WHAT'S GOING ON, BUT HE'S NOT ONE OF THE WHITE RABBIT'S ALLIES, THEN?
YEAH, MITSUKI'S KIND OF...
...AN EXCEPTION.
HMMM.
THEN I CAN HARDLY BE BLAMED FOR WHAT HAPPENED EARLIER.
IT'S YOUR FAULT FOR NOT EXPLAINING BEFOREHAND, AND HIS FOR WEARING THAT MISLEADING GETUP. AND THAT'S THAT.
IS THAT ALL YOU HAVE TO SAY?
MUU (IRK)

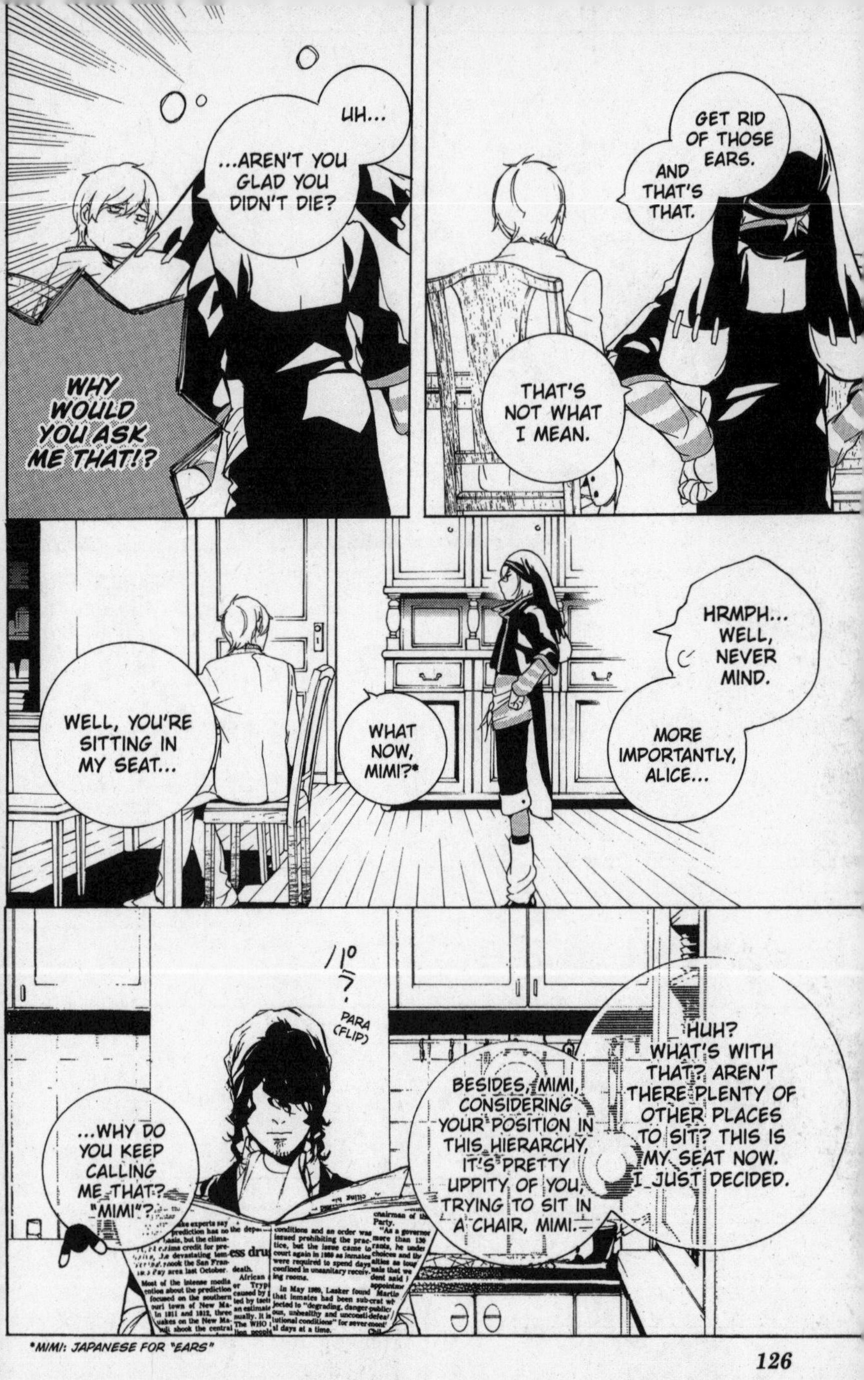
GET RID OF THOSE EARS.
AND THAT'S THAT.
THAT'S NOT WHAT I MEAN.
UH...
...AREN'T YOU GLAD YOU DIDN'T DIE?
WHY WOULD YOU ASK ME THAT!?
HRMPH... WELL, NEVER MIND.
MORE IMPORTANTLY, ALICE...
WHAT NOW, MIMI?*
WELL, YOU'RE SITTING IN MY SEAT...
HUH? WHAT'S WITH THAT? AREN'T THERE PLENTY OF OTHER PLACES TO SIT? THIS IS MY SEAT NOW. I JUST DECIDED.
BESIDES, MIMI, CONSIDERING YOUR POSITION IN THIS HIERARCHY, IT'S PRETTY UPPITY OF YOU, TRYING TO SIT IN A CHAIR, MIMI.
パラ
PARA (FLIP)
...WHY DO YOU KEEP CALLING ME THAT? "MIMI"?

*MIMI: JAPANESE FOR "EARS"

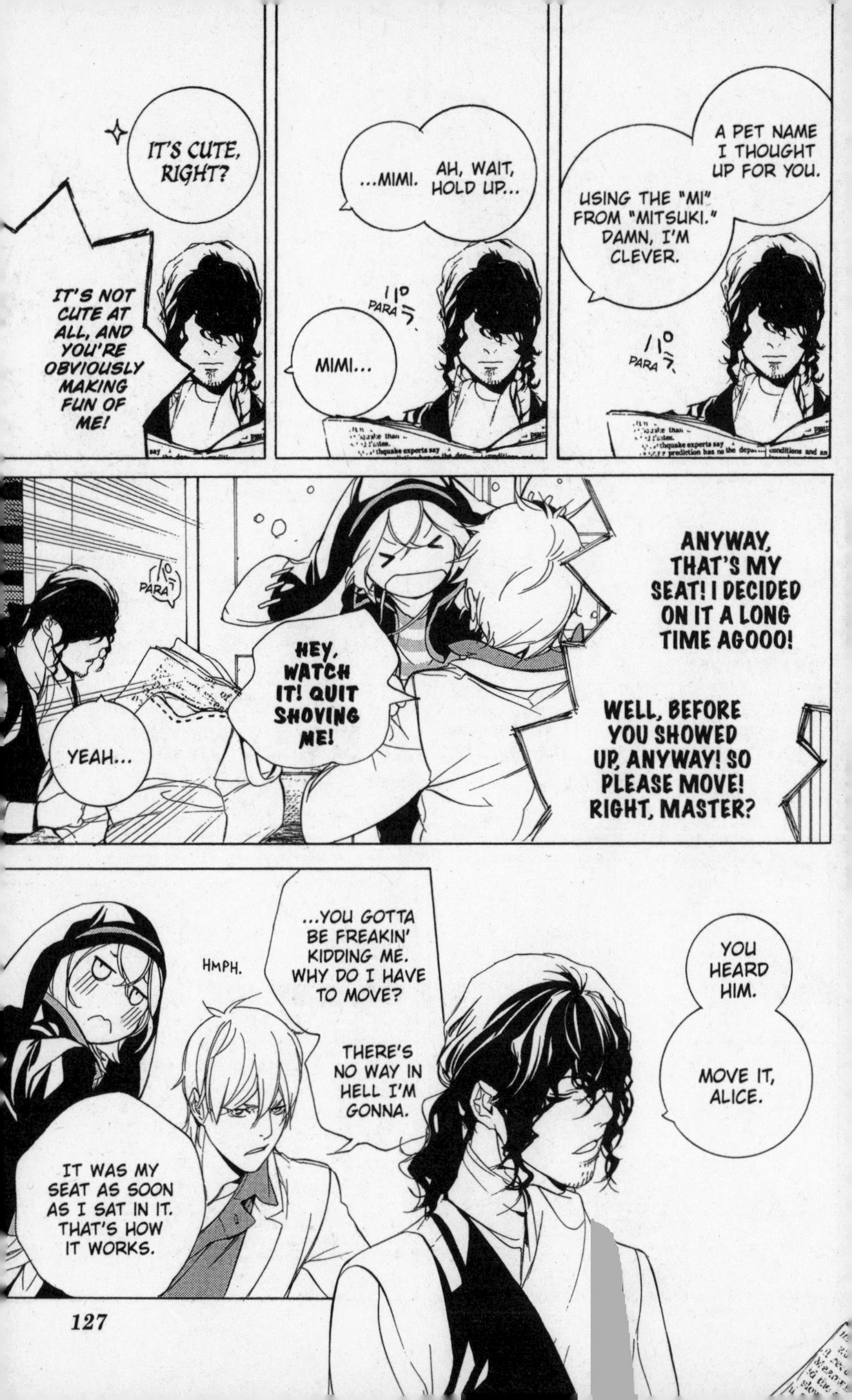
A PET NAME I THOUGHT UP FOR YOU.
USING THE "MI" FROM "MITSUKI." DAMN, I'M CLEVER.
PARA
AH, WAIT, HOLD UP...
...MIMI.
PARA
MIMI...
IT'S CUTE, RIGHT?
IT'S NOT CUTE AT ALL, AND YOU'RE OBVIOUSLY MAKING FUN OF ME!
ANYWAY, THAT'S MY SEAT! I DECIDED ON IT A LONG TIME AGOOO!
WELL, BEFORE YOU SHOWED UP, ANYWAY! SO PLEASE MOVE! RIGHT, MASTER?
HEY, WATCH IT! QUIT SHOVING ME!
PARA
YEAH...
YOU HEARD HIM.
MOVE IT, ALICE.
...YOU GOTTA BE FREAKIN' KIDDING ME. WHY DO I HAVE TO MOVE?
THERE'S NO WAY IN HELL I'M GONNA.
HMPH.
IT WAS MY SEAT AS SOON AS I SAT IN IT. THAT'S HOW IT WORKS.

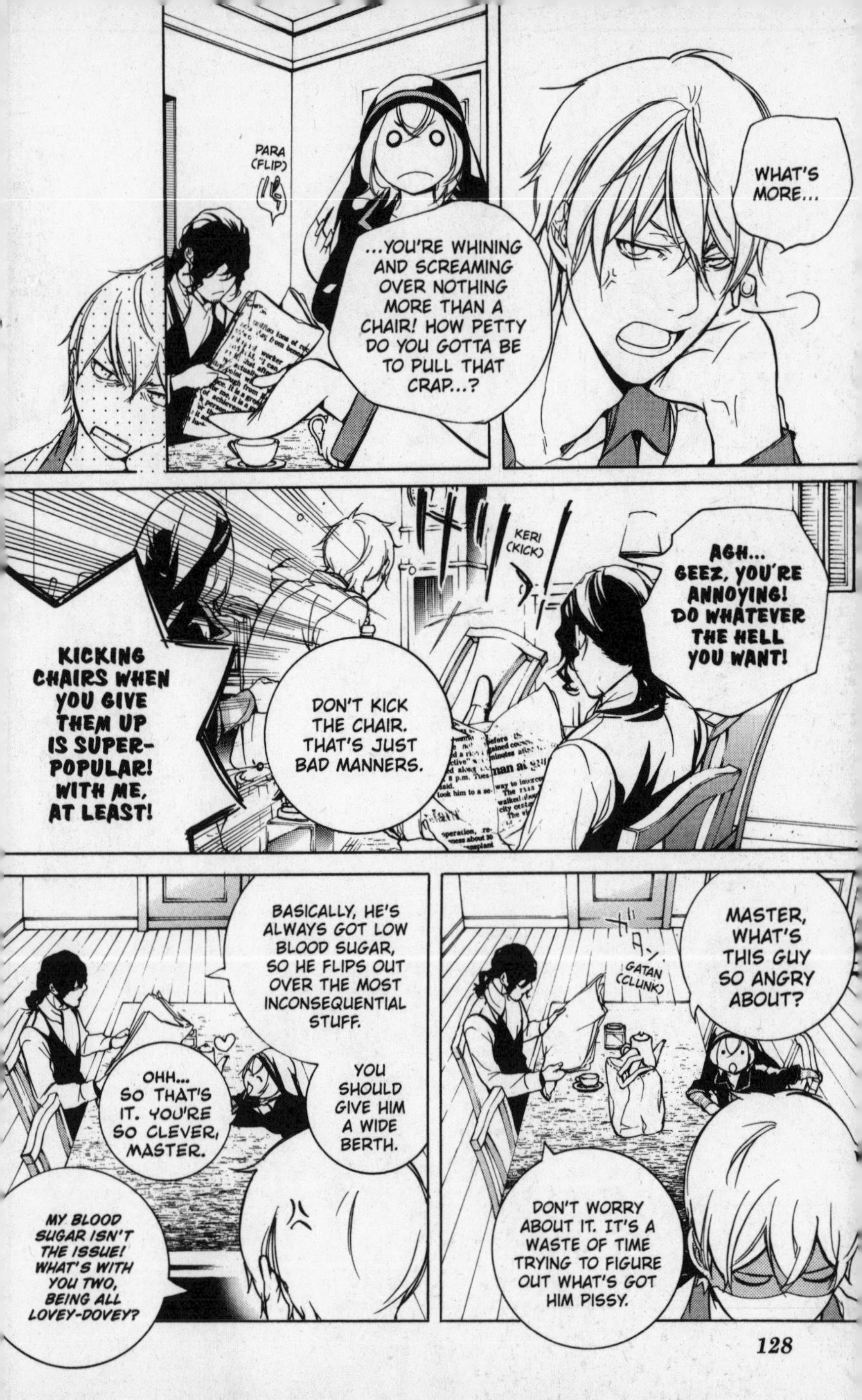
WHAT'S MORE...
...YOU'RE WHINING AND SCREAMING OVER NOTHING MORE THAN A CHAIR! HOW PETTY DO YOU GOTTA BE TO PULL THAT CRAP...?
PARA (FLIP)
AGH... GEEZ, YOU'RE ANNOYING! DO WHATEVER THE HELL YOU WANT!
KERI (KICK)
DON'T KICK THE CHAIR. THAT'S JUST BAD MANNERS.
KICKING CHAIRS WHEN YOU GIVE THEM UP IS SUPER-POPULAR! WITH ME, AT LEAST!
MASTER, WHAT'S THIS GUY SO ANGRY ABOUT?
GATAN (CLUNK)
DON'T WORRY ABOUT IT. IT'S A WASTE OF TIME TRYING TO FIGURE OUT WHAT'S GOT HIM PISSY.
BASICALLY, HE'S ALWAYS GOT LOW BLOOD SUGAR, SO HE FLIPS OUT OVER THE MOST INCONSEQUENTIAL STUFF.
YOU SHOULD GIVE HIM A WIDE BERTH.
OHH... SO THAT'S IT. YOU'RE SO CLEVER, MASTER.
MY BLOOD SUGAR ISN'T THE ISSUE! WHAT'S WITH YOU TWO, BEING ALL LOVEY-DOVEY?

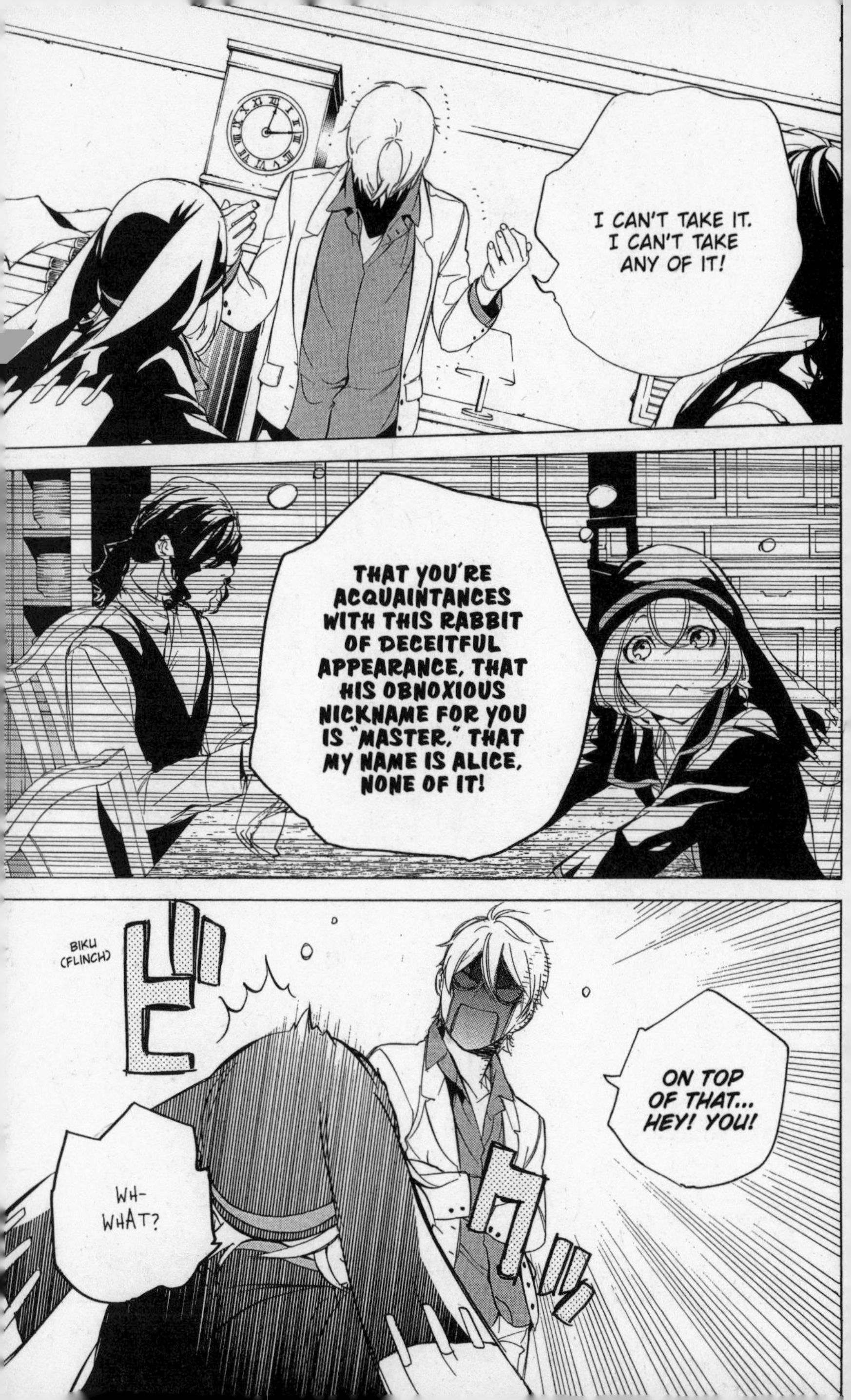
I CAN'T TAKE IT. I CAN'T TAKE ANY OF IT!
THAT YOU'RE ACQUAINTANCES WITH THIS RABBIT OF DECEITFUL APPEARANCE, THAT HIS OBNOXIOUS NICKNAME FOR YOU IS "MASTER," THAT MY NAME IS ALICE, NONE OF IT!
ON TOP OF THAT... HEY! YOU!
BIKU (FLINCH)
WH-WHAT?

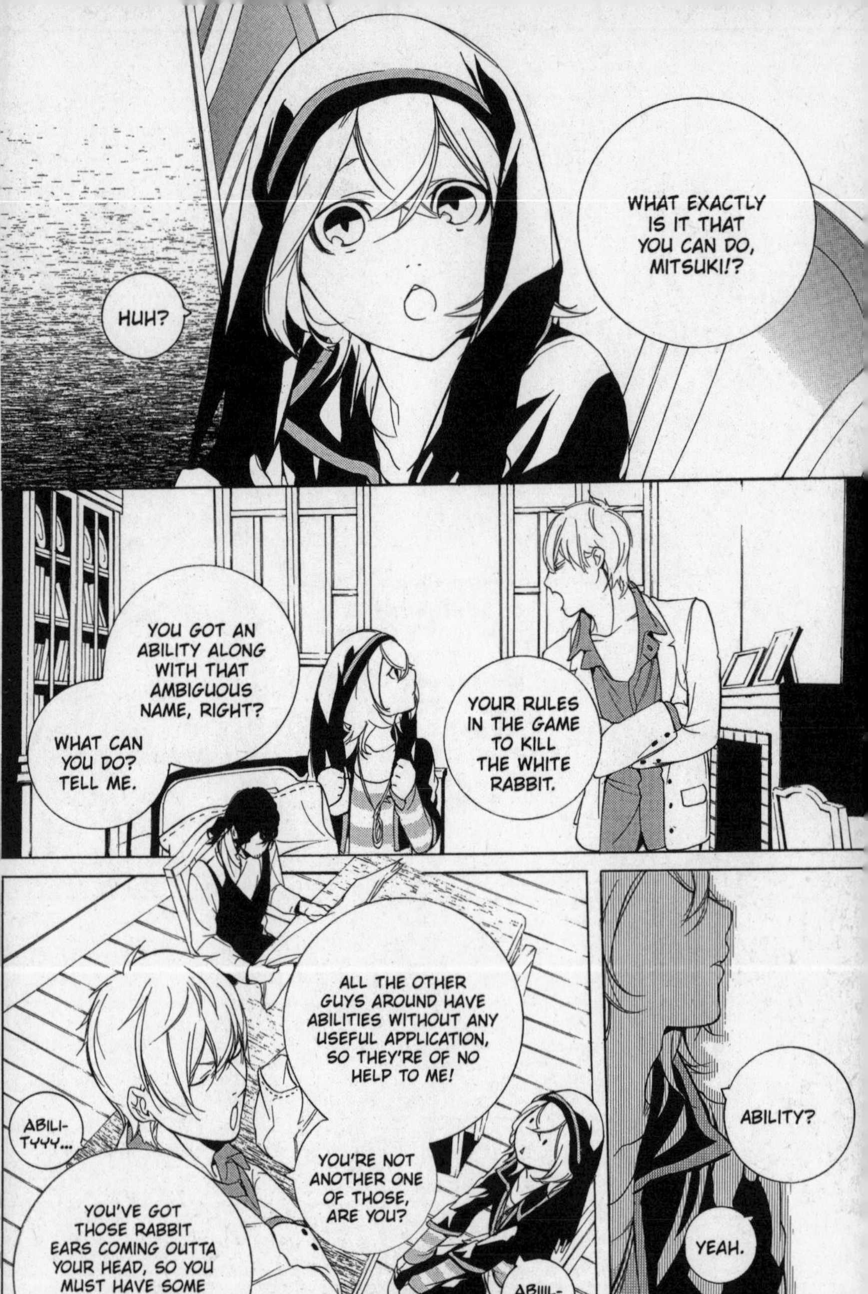
WHAT EXACTLY IS IT THAT YOU CAN DO, MITSUKI!?
HUH?
YOUR RULES IN THE GAME TO KILL THE WHITE RABBIT.
YOU GOT AN ABILITY ALONG WITH THAT AMBIGUOUS NAME, RIGHT?
WHAT CAN YOU DO? TELL ME.
ABILITY?
YEAH.
ALL THE OTHER GUYS AROUND HAVE ABILITIES WITHOUT ANY USEFUL APPLICATION, SO THEY'RE OF NO HELP TO ME!
YOU'RE NOT ANOTHER ONE OF THOSE, ARE YOU?
YOU'VE GOT THOSE RABBIT EARS COMING OUTTA YOUR HEAD, SO YOU MUST HAVE SOME ABILITY THAT'S AS AWESOME AS THE WHITE RABBIT'S...
ABIIIL-ITY...
ABILI-TYYY...

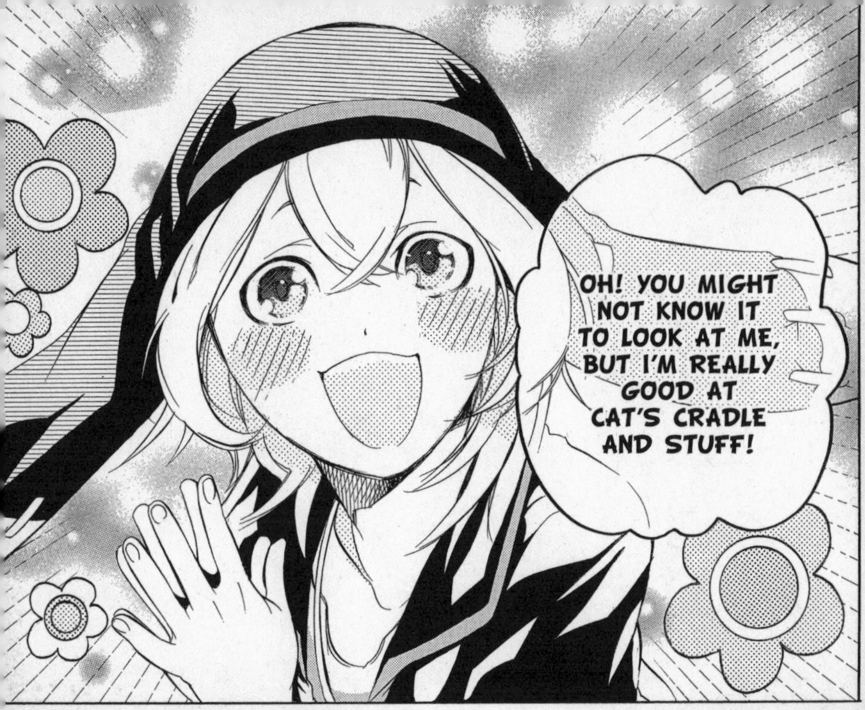
OH! YOU MIGHT NOT KNOW IT TO LOOK AT ME, BUT I'M REALLY GOOD AT CAT'S CRADLE AND STUFF!
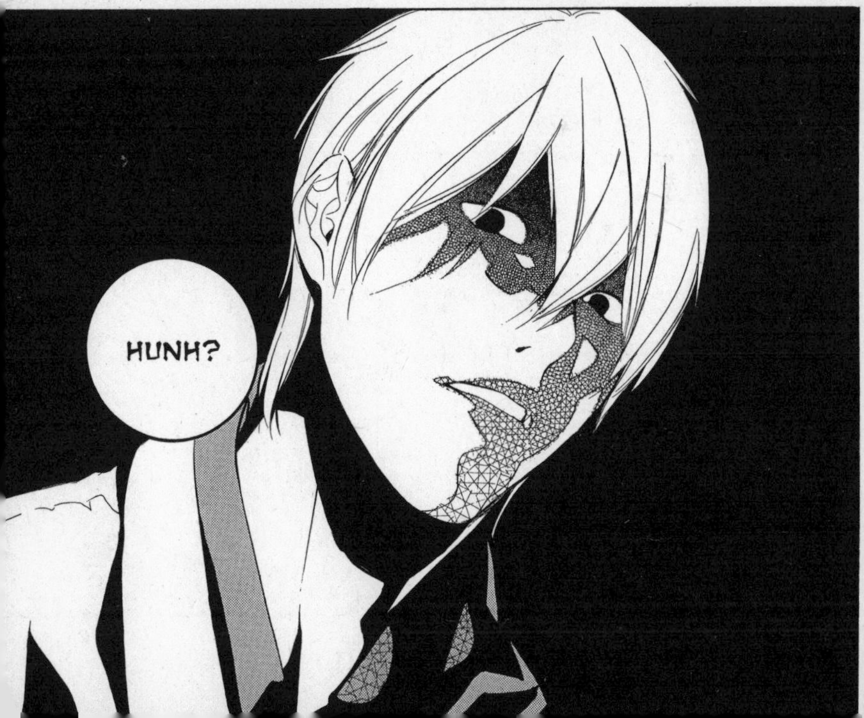
HUNH?

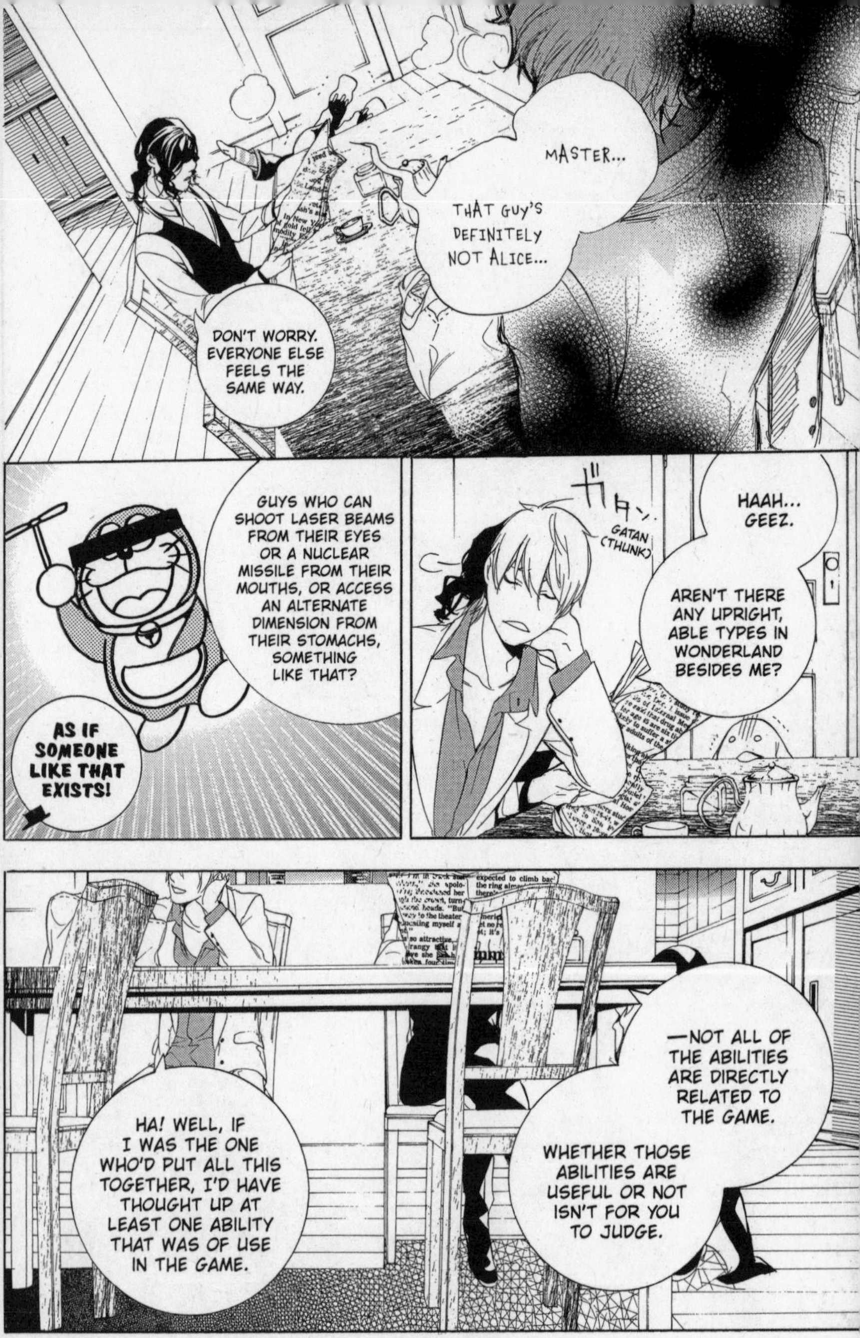
MASTER...
THAT GUY'S DEFINITELY NOT ALICE...
DON'T WORRY. EVERYONE ELSE FEELS THE SAME WAY.
GATAN (THUNK)
HAAH... GEEZ.
AREN'T THERE ANY UPRIGHT, ABLE TYPES IN WONDERLAND BESIDES ME?
GUYS WHO CAN SHOOT LASER BEAMS FROM THEIR EYES OR A NUCLEAR MISSILE FROM THEIR MOUTHS, OR ACCESS AN ALTERNATE DIMENSION FROM THEIR STOMACHS, SOMETHING LIKE THAT?
AS IF SOMEONE LIKE THAT EXISTS!
—NOT ALL OF THE ABILITIES ARE DIRECTLY RELATED TO THE GAME.
WHETHER THOSE ABILITIES ARE USEFUL OR NOT ISN'T FOR YOU TO JUDGE.
HA! WELL, IF I WAS THE ONE WHO'D PUT ALL THIS TOGETHER, I'D HAVE THOUGHT UP AT LEAST ONE ABILITY THAT WAS OF USE IN THE GAME.

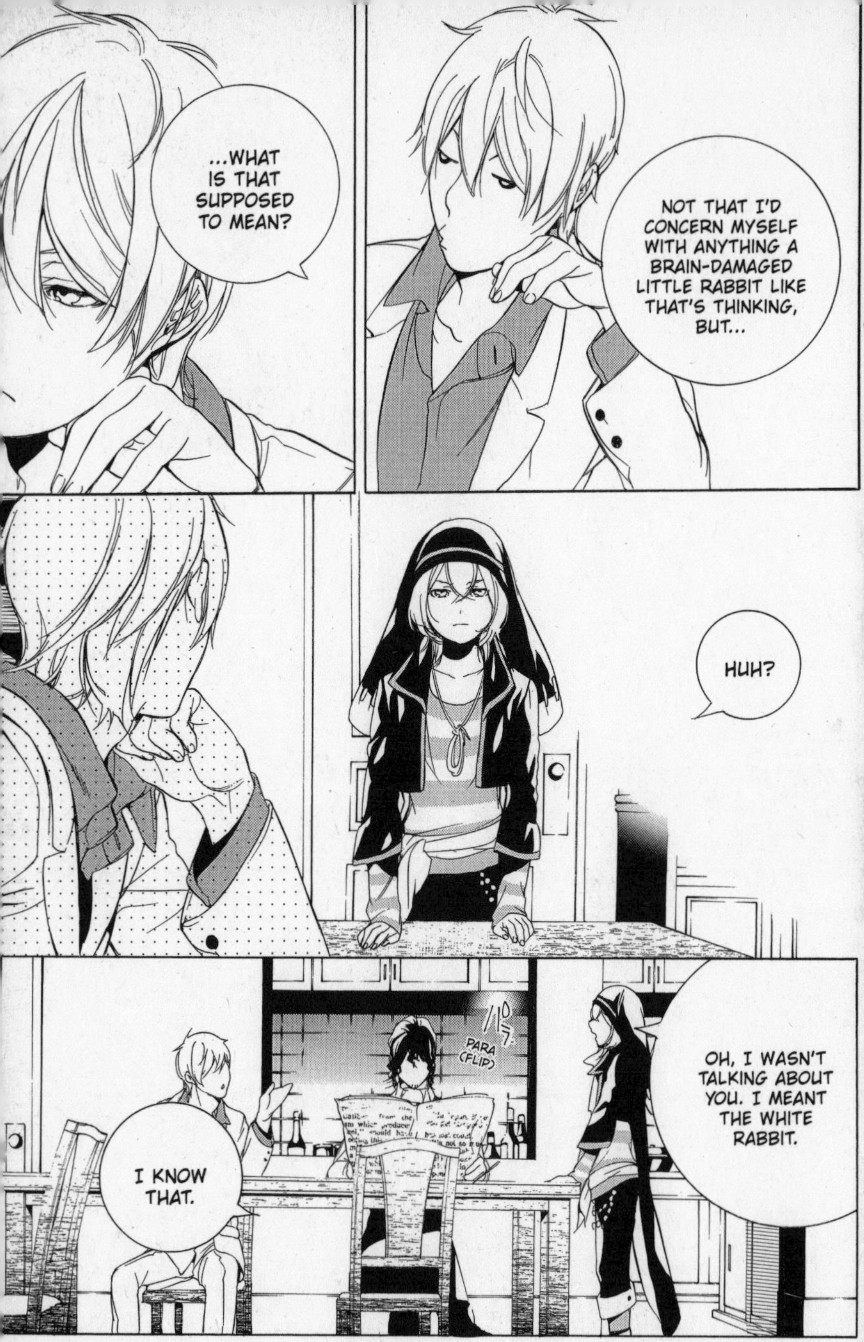
NOT THAT I'D CONCERN MYSELF WITH ANYTHING A BRAIN-DAMAGED LITTLE RABBIT LIKE THAT'S THINKING, BUT...
...WHAT IS THAT SUPPOSED TO MEAN?
HUH?
OH, I WASN'T TALKING ABOUT YOU. I MEANT THE WHITE RABBIT.
PARA (FLIP)
I KNOW THAT.

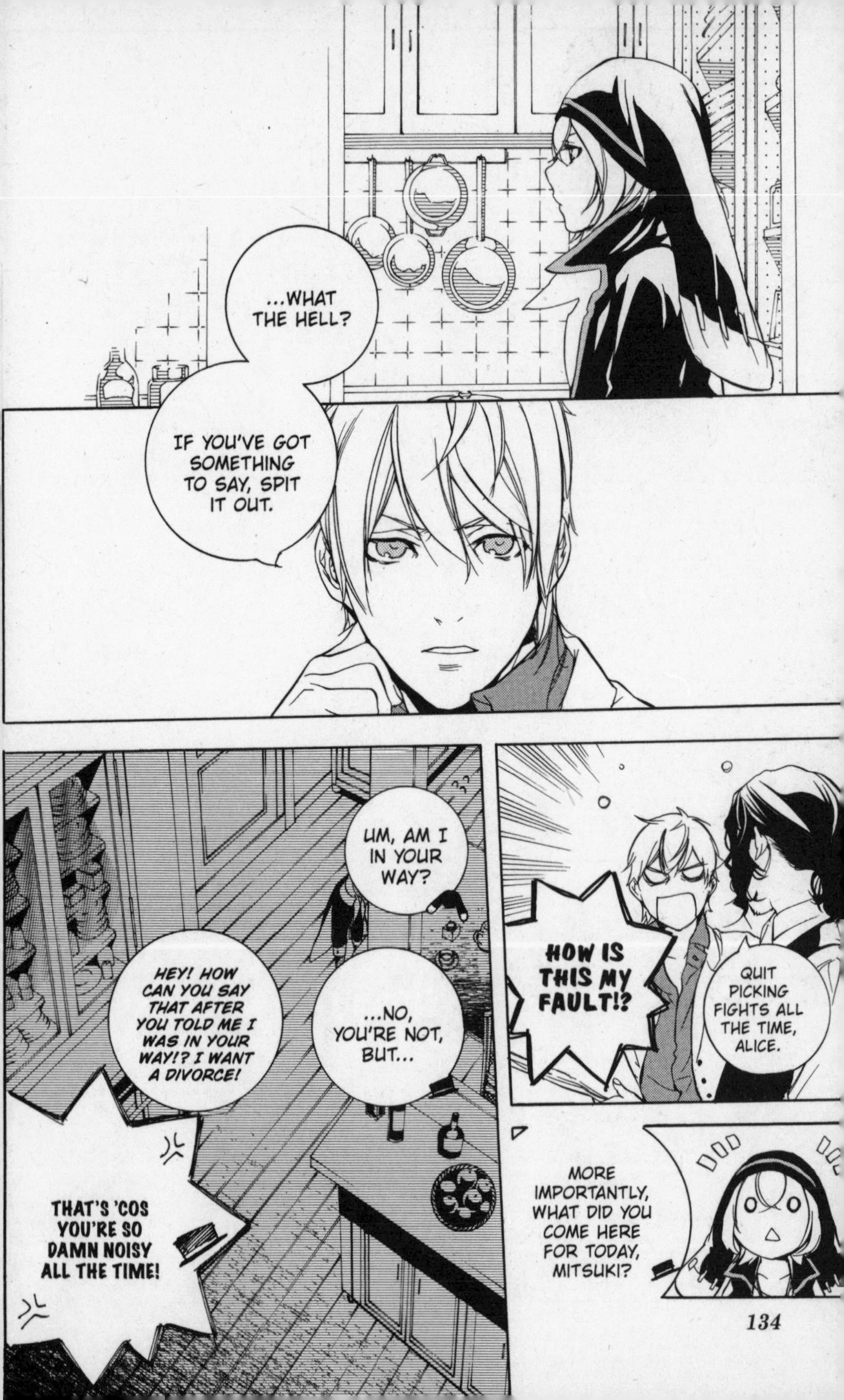

...WHAT THE HELL?
IF YOU'VE GOT SOMETHING TO SAY, SPIT IT OUT.
QUIT PICKING FIGHTS ALL THE TIME, ALICE.
HOW IS THIS MY FAULT!?
MORE IMPORTANTLY, WHAT DID YOU COME HERE FOR TODAY, MITSUKI?
UM, AM I IN YOUR WAY?
...NO, YOU'RE NOT, BUT...
HEY! HOW CAN YOU SAY THAT AFTER YOU TOLD ME I WAS IN YOUR WAY!? I WANT A DIVORCE!
THAT'S 'COS YOU'RE SO DAMN NOISY ALL THE TIME!

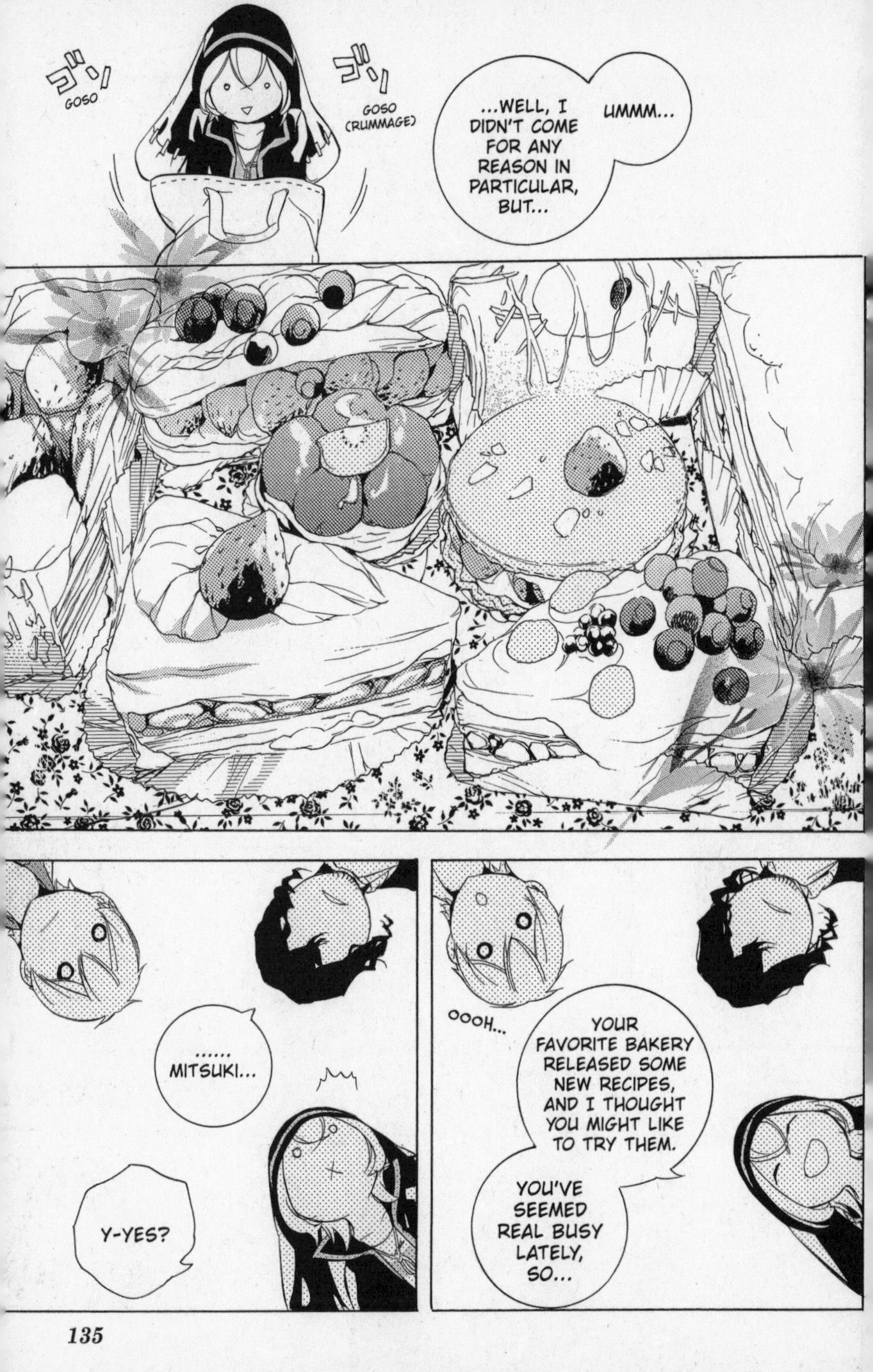
UMMM...
...WELL, I DIDN'T COME FOR ANY REASON IN PARTICULAR, BUT...
GOSO (RUMMAGE)
GOSO
YOUR FAVORITE BAKERY RELEASED SOME NEW RECIPES, AND I THOUGHT YOU MIGHT LIKE TO TRY THEM.
YOU'VE SEEMED REAL BUSY LATELY, SO...
OOOH...
...... MITSUKI...
Y-YES?

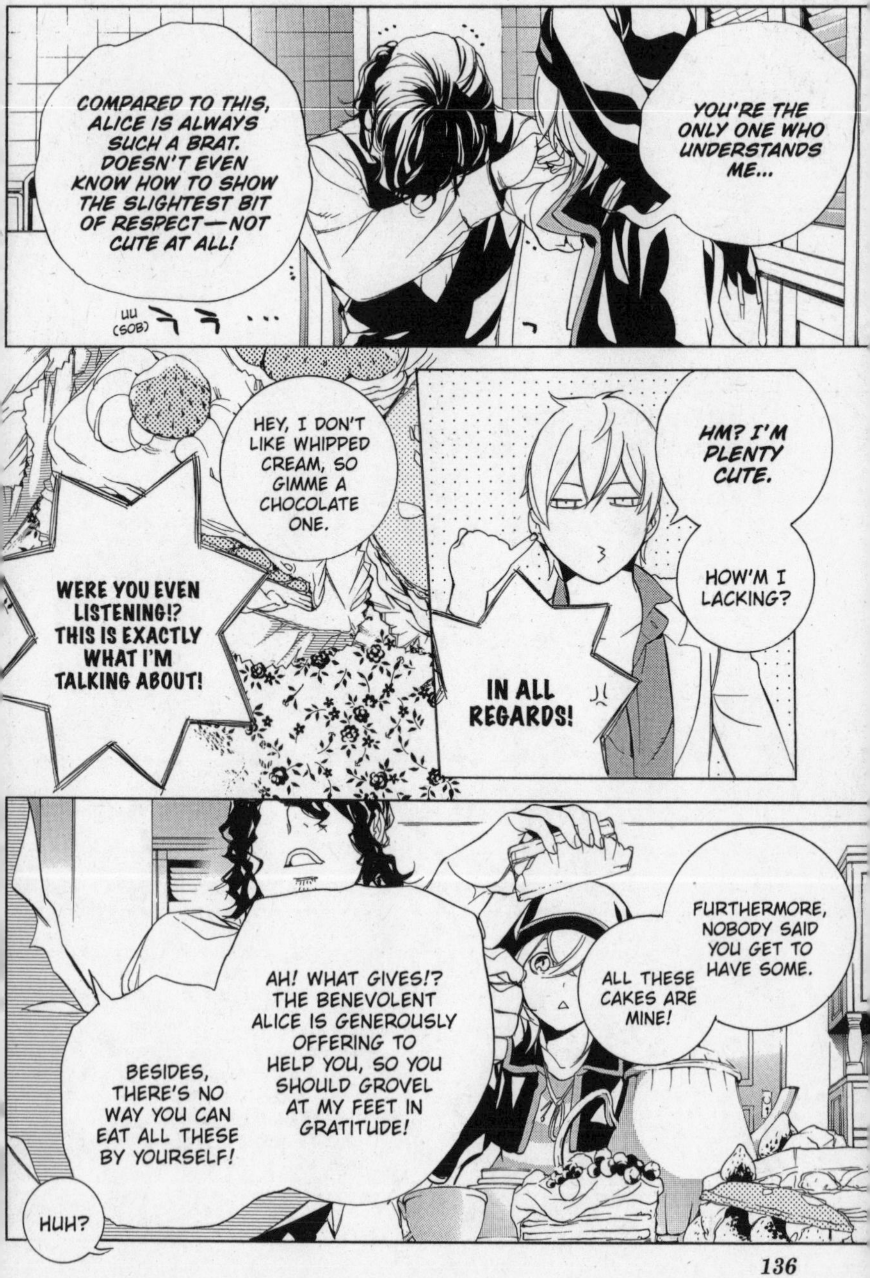
YOU'RE THE ONLY ONE WHO UNDERSTANDS ME...
COMPARED TO THIS, ALICE IS ALWAYS SUCH A BRAT. DOESN'T EVEN KNOW HOW TO SHOW THE SLIGHTEST BIT OF RESPECT—NOT CUTE AT ALL!
UU (SOB)
HM? I'M PLENTY CUTE.
HOW'M I LACKING?
IN ALL REGARDS!
HEY, I DON'T LIKE WHIPPED CREAM, SO GIMME A CHOCOLATE ONE.
WERE YOU EVEN LISTENING!? THIS IS EXACTLY WHAT I'M TALKING ABOUT!
FURTHERMORE, NOBODY SAID YOU GET TO HAVE SOME.
ALL THESE CAKES ARE MINE!
AH! WHAT GIVES!? THE BENEVOLENT ALICE IS GENEROUSLY OFFERING TO HELP YOU, SO YOU SHOULD GROVEL AT MY FEET IN GRATITUDE!
BESIDES, THERE'S NO WAY YOU CAN EAT ALL THESE BY YOURSELF!
HUH?

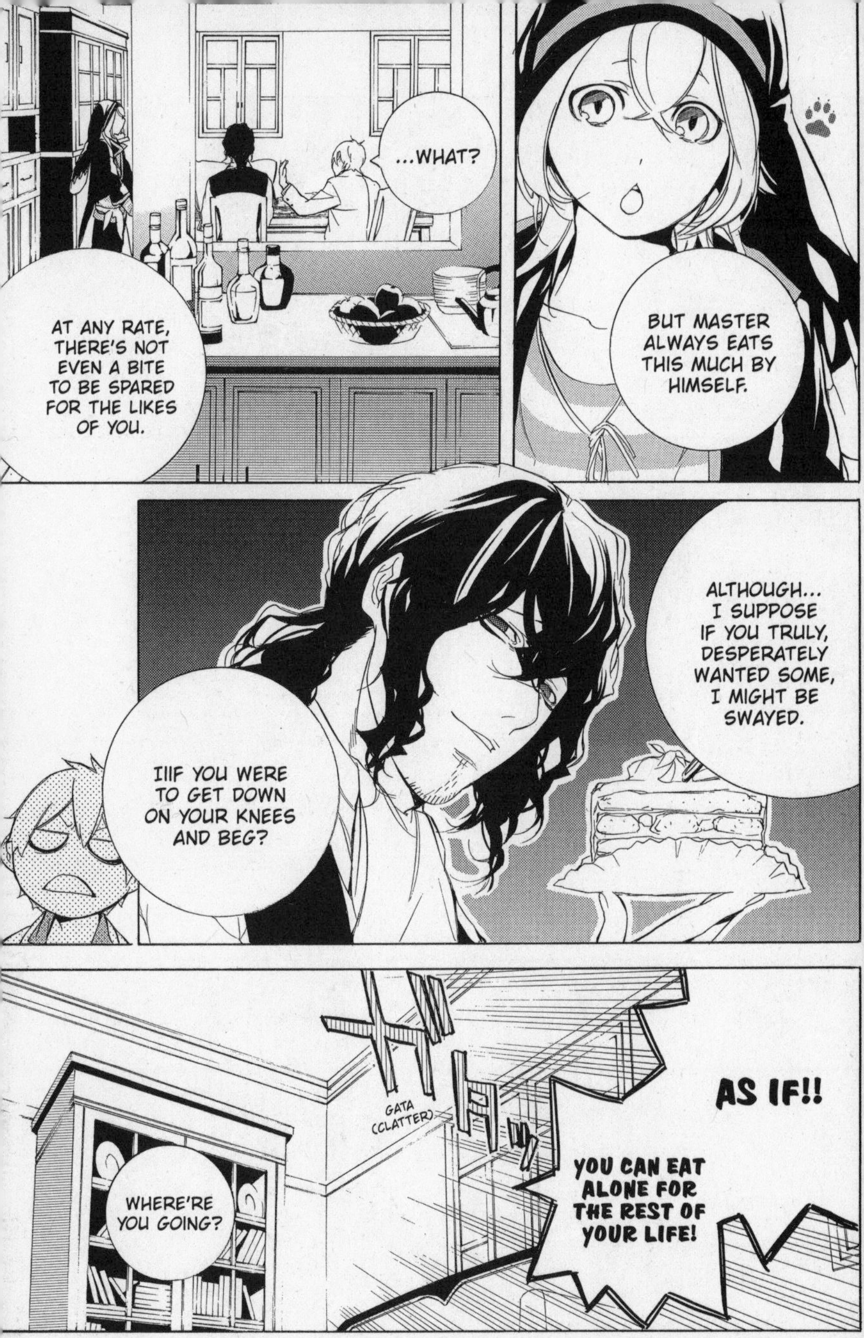
BUT MASTER ALWAYS EATS THIS MUCH BY HIMSELF.
...WHAT?
AT ANY RATE, THERE'S NOT EVEN A BITE TO BE SPARED FOR THE LIKES OF YOU.
ALTHOUGH... I SUPPOSE IF YOU TRULY, DESPERATELY WANTED SOME, I MIGHT BE SWAYED.
IIIF YOU WERE TO GET DOWN ON YOUR KNEES AND BEG?
AS IF!!
GATA (CLATTER)
YOU CAN EAT ALONE FOR THE REST OF YOUR LIFE!
WHERE'RE YOU GOING?

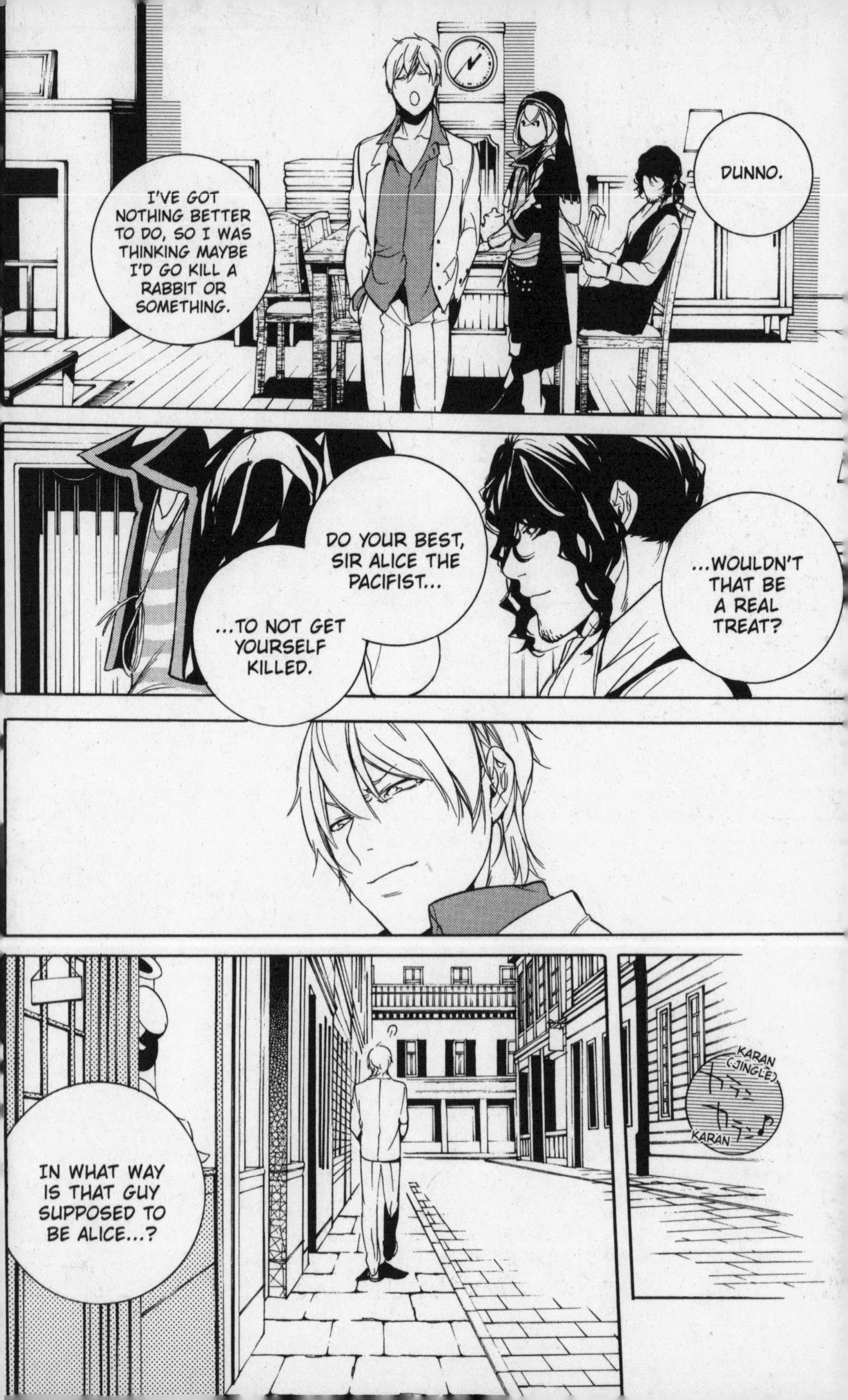
DUNNO.
I'VE GOT NOTHING BETTER TO DO, SO I WAS THINKING MAYBE I'D GO KILL A RABBIT OR SOMETHING.
...WOULDN'T THAT BE A REAL TREAT?
DO YOUR BEST, SIR ALICE THE PACIFIST...
...TO NOT GET YOURSELF KILLED.
KARAN (JINGLE) KARAN
IN WHAT WAY IS THAT GUY SUPPOSED TO BE ALICE...?

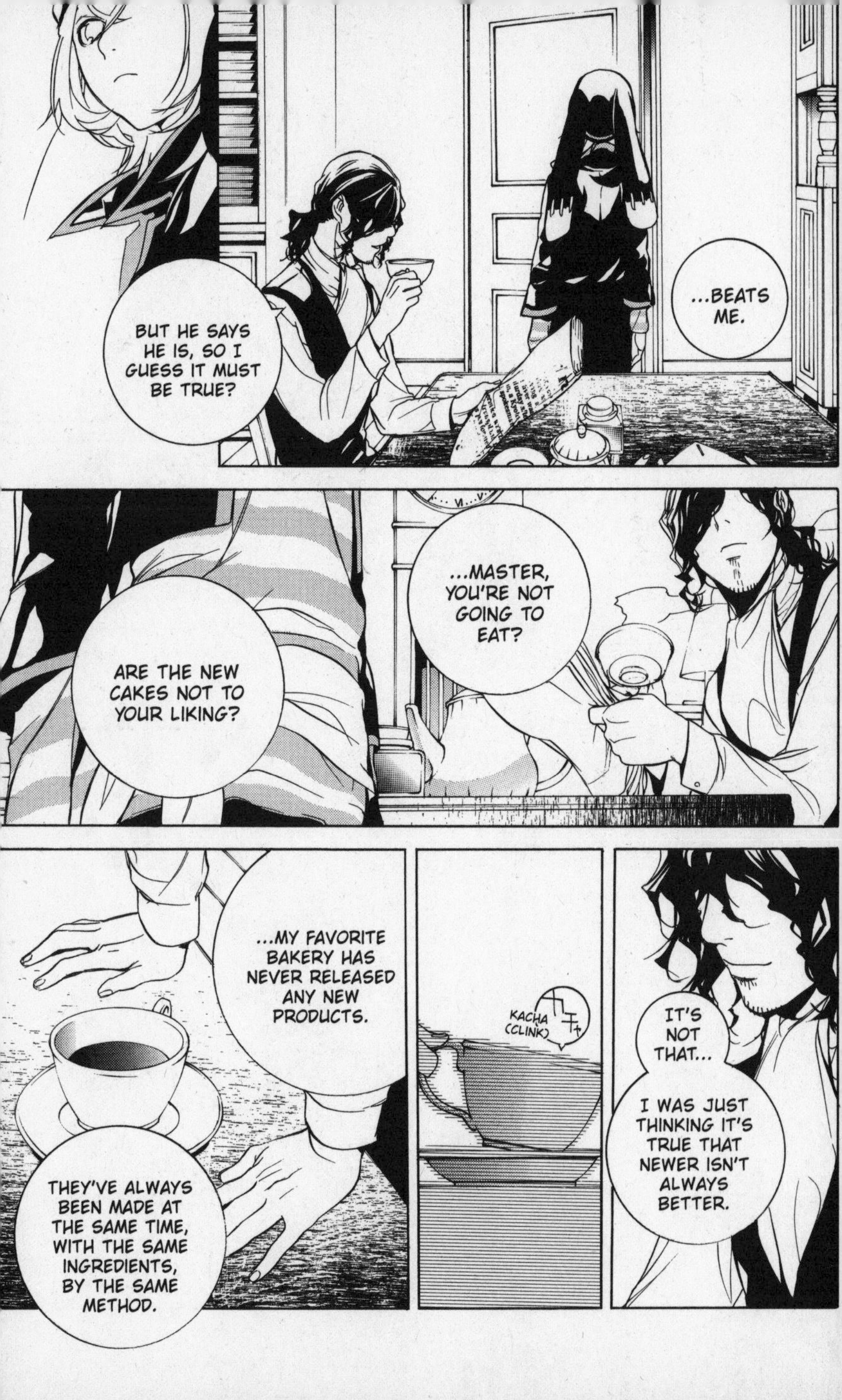
...BEATS ME.
BUT HE SAYS HE IS, SO I GUESS IT MUST BE TRUE?
...MASTER, YOU'RE NOT GOING TO EAT?
ARE THE NEW CAKES NOT TO YOUR LIKING?
IT'S NOT THAT...
I WAS JUST THINKING IT'S TRUE THAT NEWER ISN'T ALWAYS BETTER.
KACHA (CLINK)
...MY FAVORITE BAKERY HAS NEVER RELEASED ANY NEW PRODUCTS.
THEY'VE ALWAYS BEEN MADE AT THE SAME TIME, WITH THE SAME INGREDIENTS, BY THE SAME METHOD.

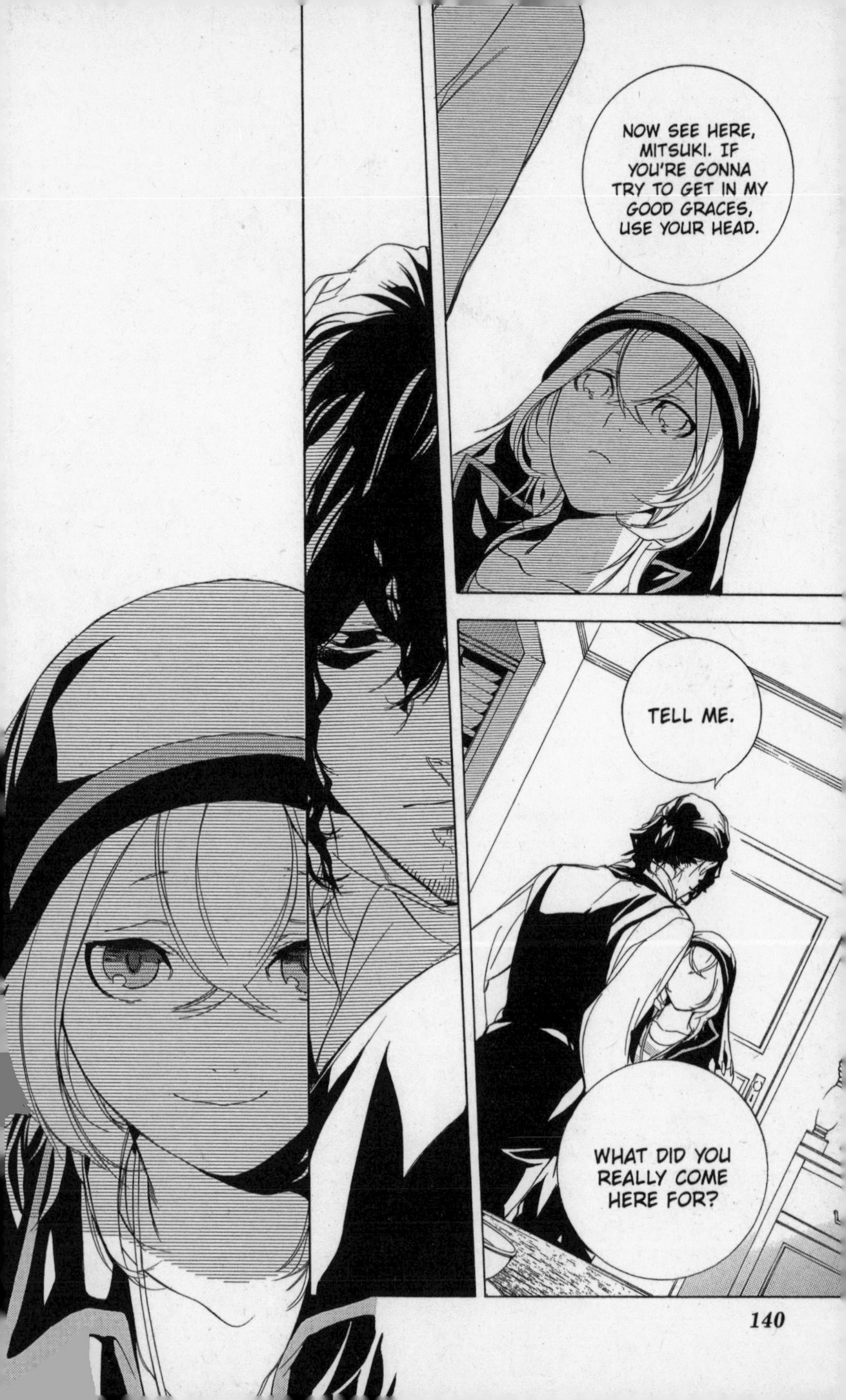
NOW SEE HERE, MITSUKI. IF YOU'RE GONNA TRY TO GET IN MY GOOD GRACES, USE YOUR HEAD.
TELL ME.
WHAT DID YOU REALLY COME HERE FOR?

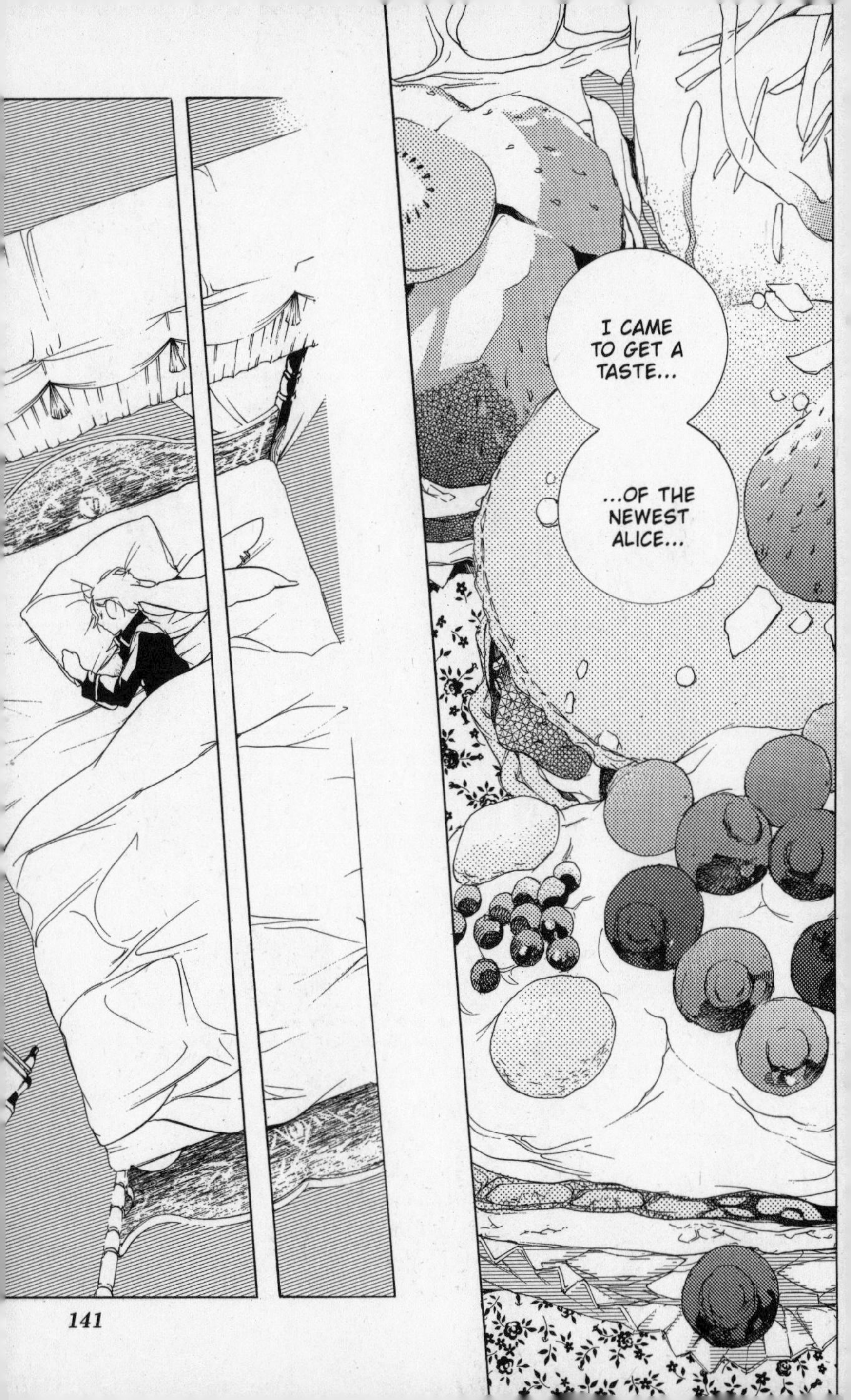
I CAME TO GET A TASTE...
...OF THE NEWEST ALICE...

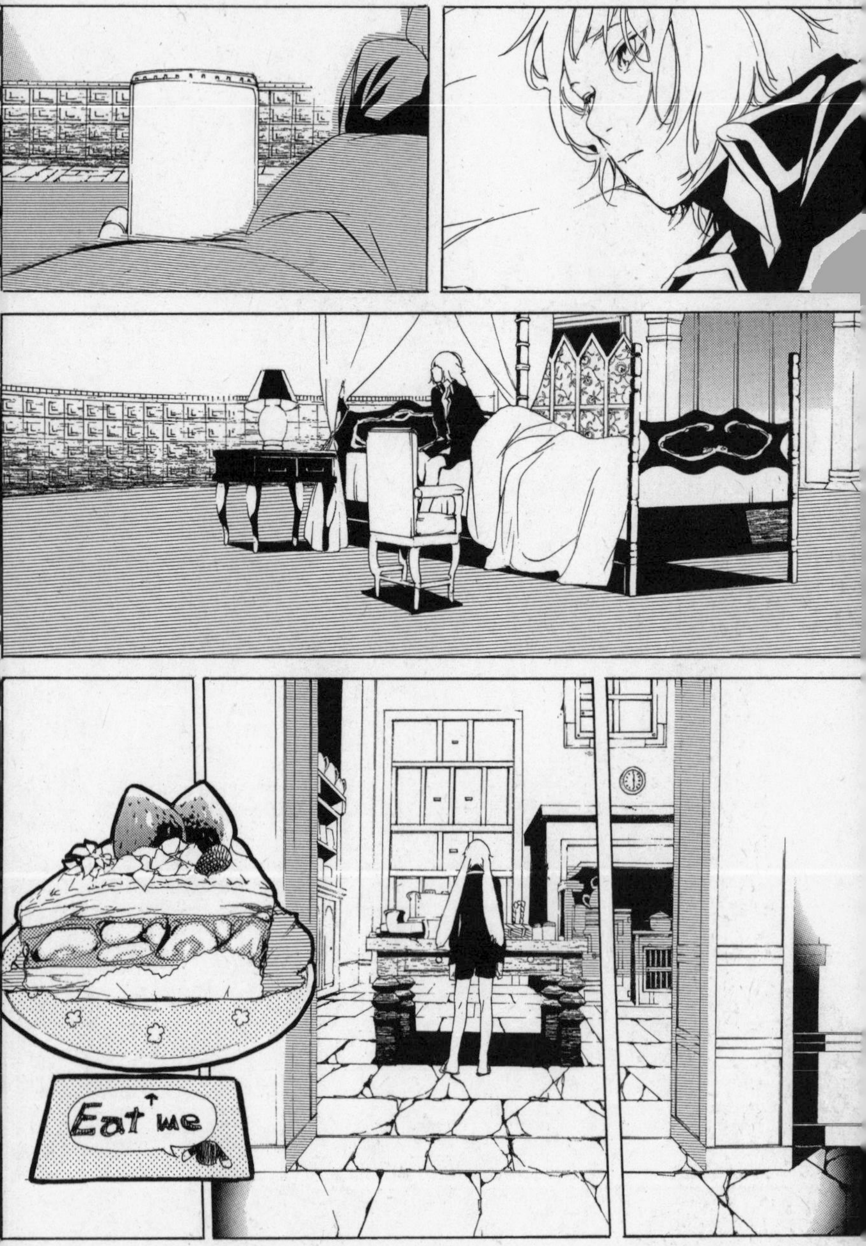
Eat me

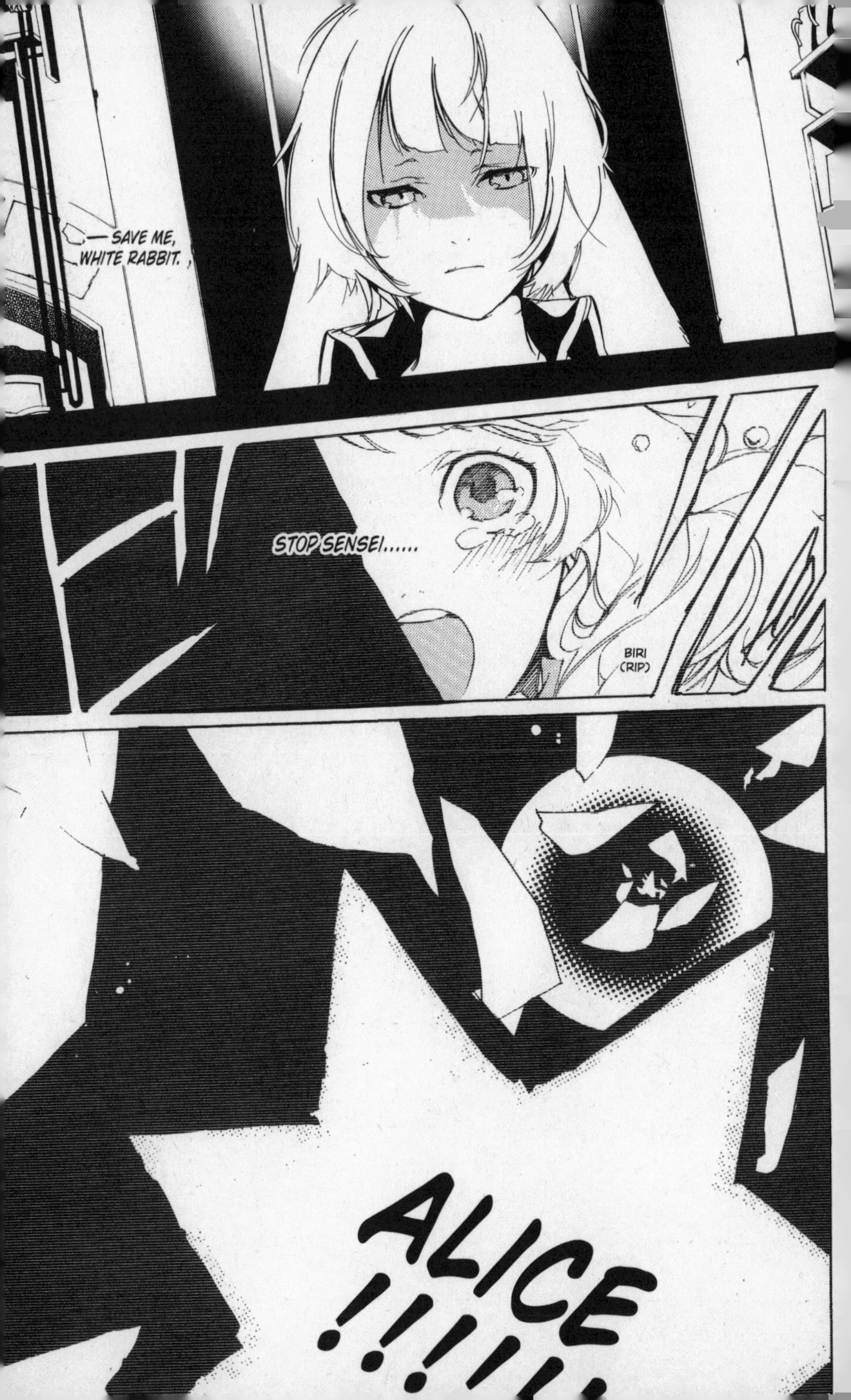
—SAVE ME, WHITE RABBIT.
STOP SENSEI......
BIRI (RIP)
ALICE !!!!!

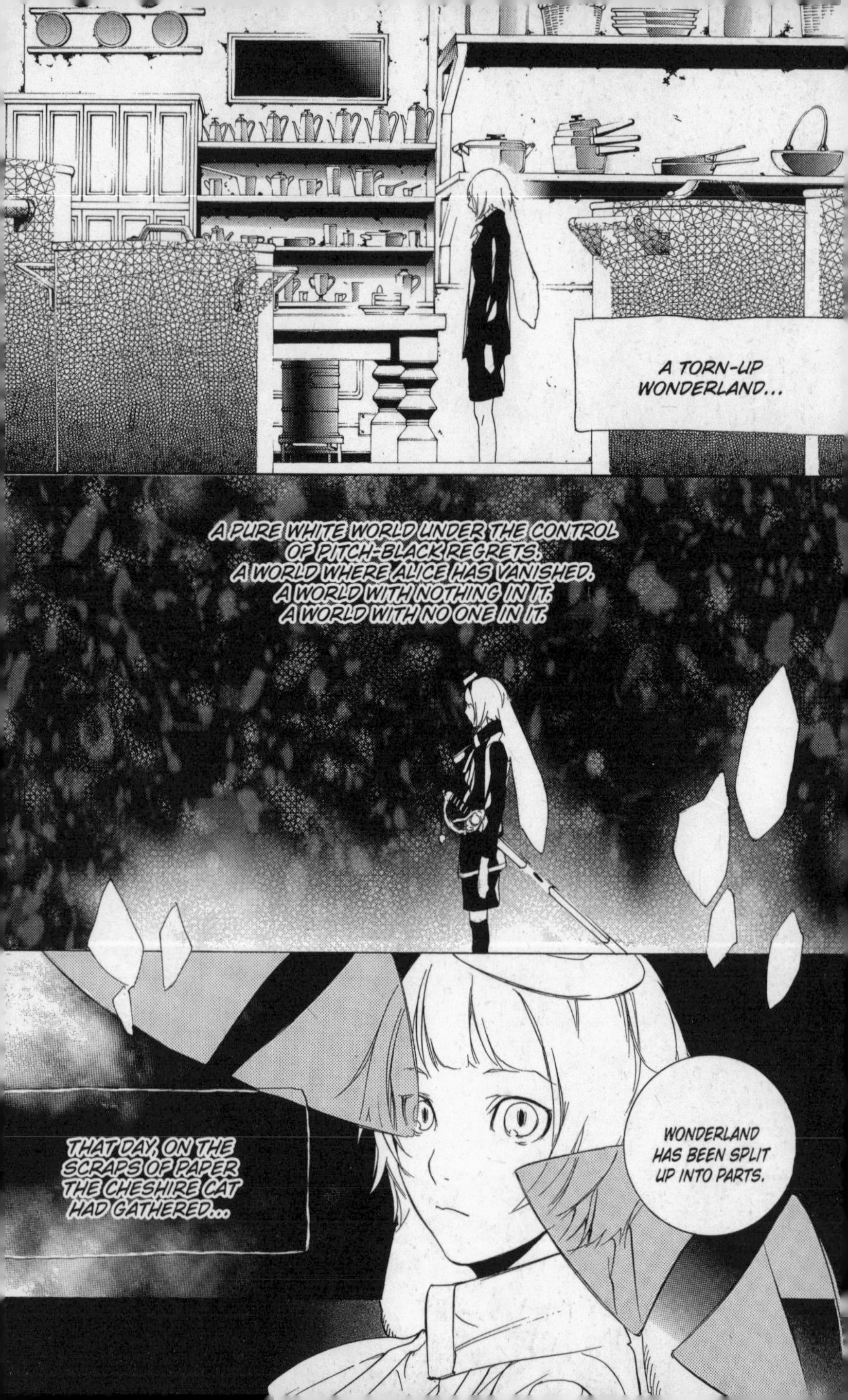
A TORN-UP WONDERLAND...
A PURE WHITE WORLD UNDER THE CONTROL OF PITCH-BLACK REGRETS. A WORLD WHERE ALICE HAS VANISHED. A WORLD WITH NOTHING IN IT. A WORLD WITH NO ONE IN IT.
WONDERLAND HAS BEEN SPLIT UP INTO PARTS.
THAT DAY, ON THE SCRAPS OF PAPER THE CHESHIRE CAT HAD GATHERED...

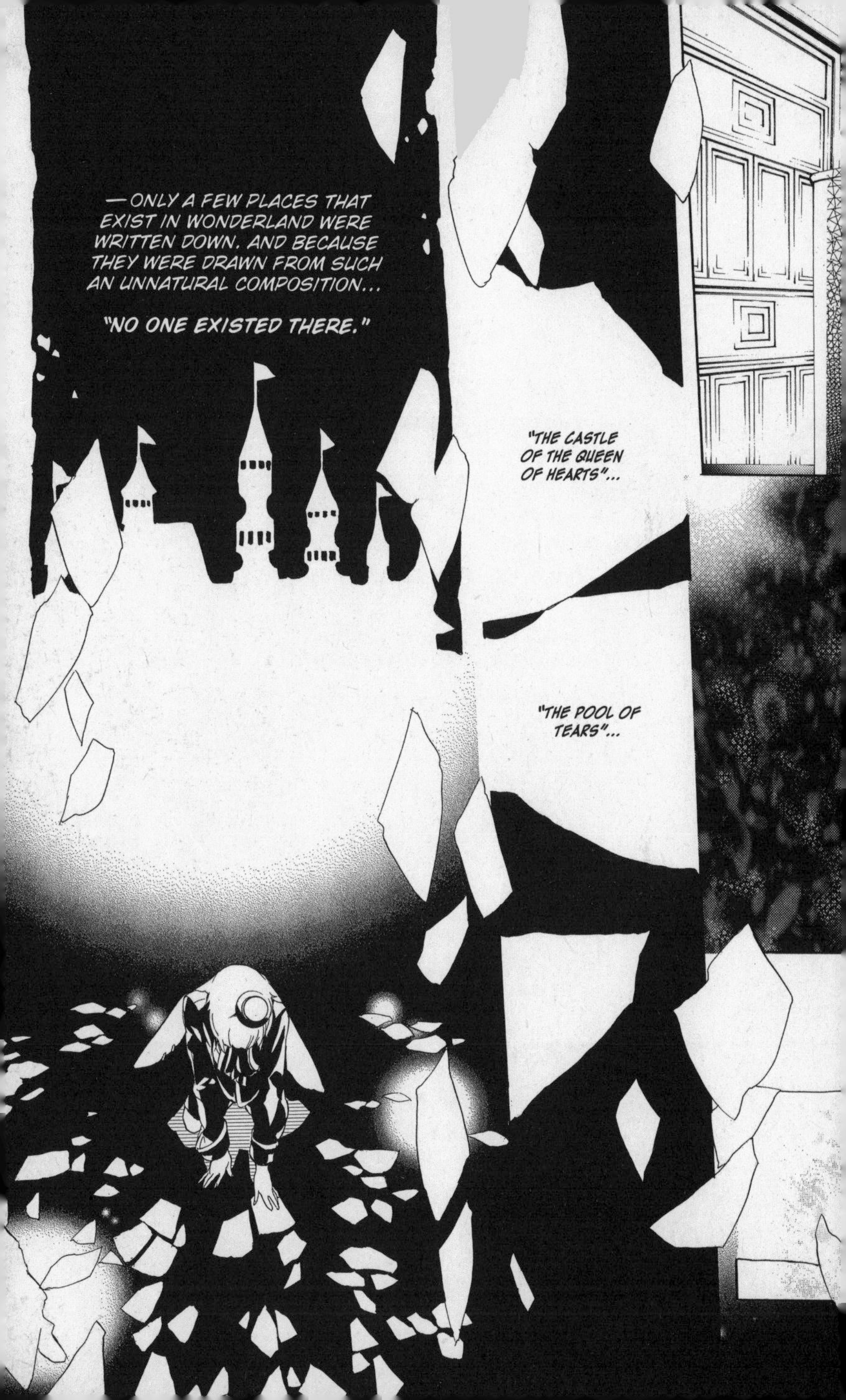
"THE CASTLE OF THE QUEEN OF HEARTS"...
"THE POOL OF TEARS"...
—ONLY A FEW PLACES THAT EXIST IN WONDERLAND WERE WRITTEN DOWN. AND BECAUSE THEY WERE DRAWN FROM SUCH AN UNNATURAL COMPOSITION...
"NO ONE EXISTED THERE."

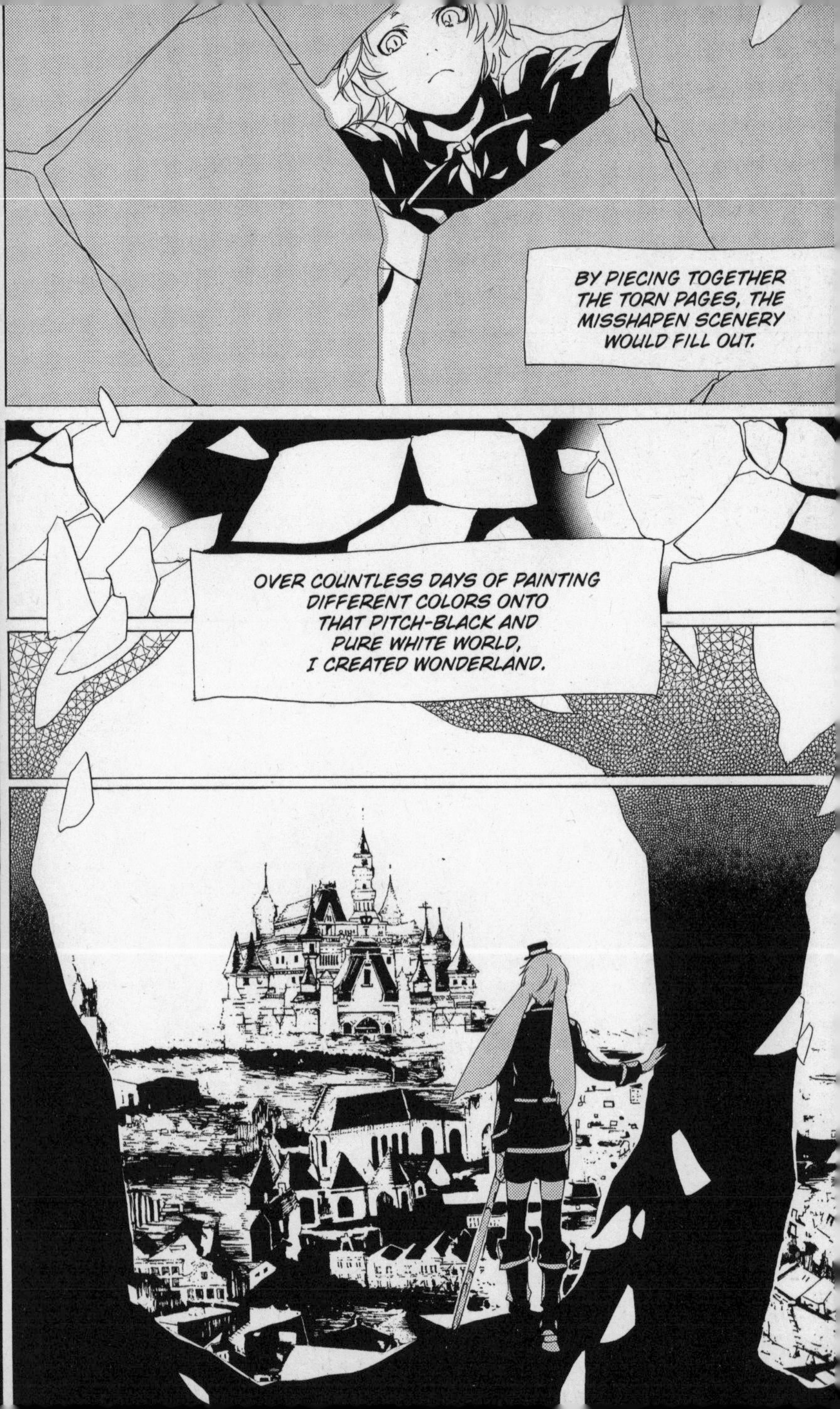
BY PIECING TOGETHER THE TORN PAGES, THE MISSHAPEN SCENERY WOULD FILL OUT.
OVER COUNTLESS DAYS OF PAINTING DIFFERENT COLORS ONTO THAT PITCH-BLACK AND PURE WHITE WORLD, I CREATED WONDERLAND.

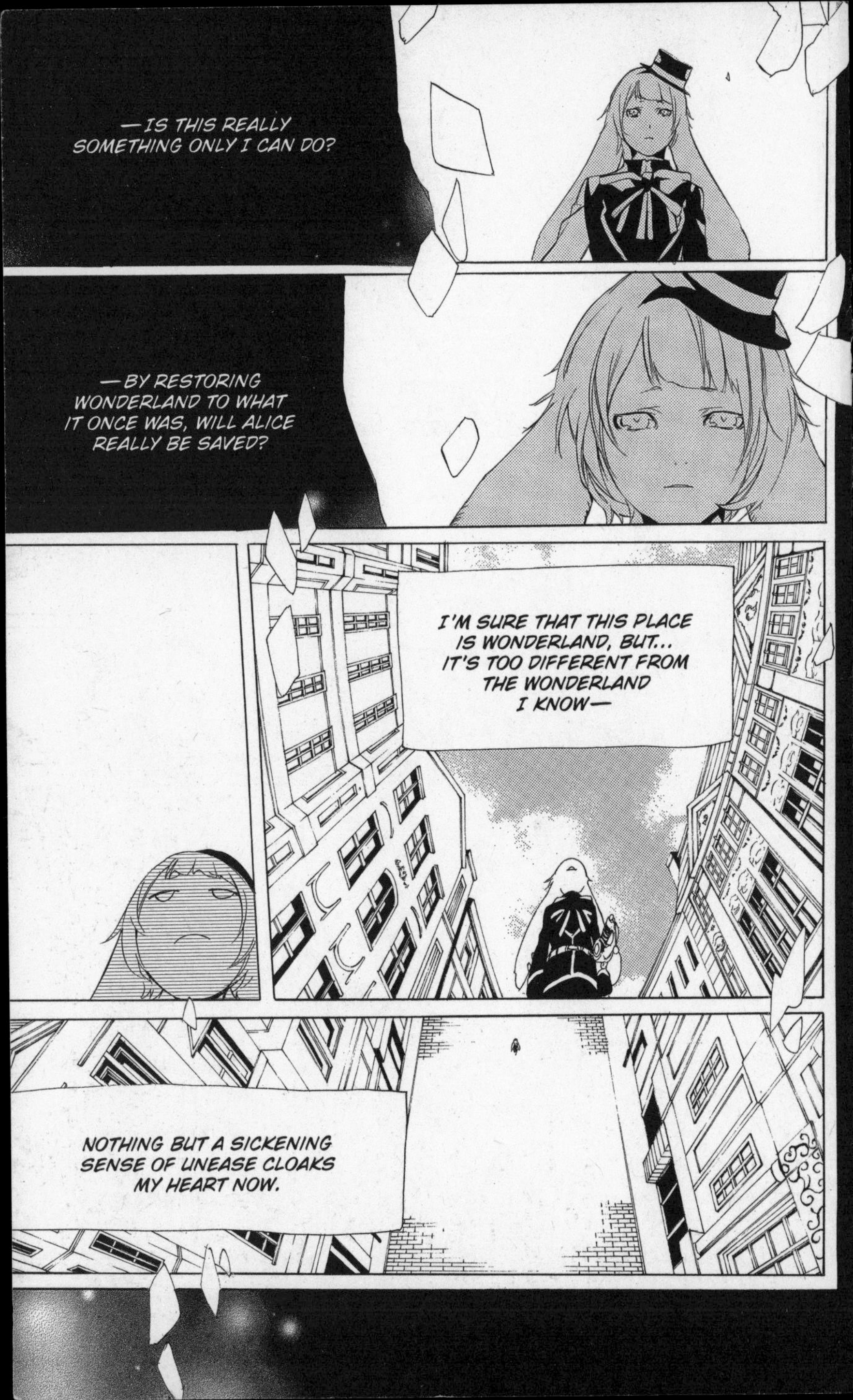
—IS THIS REALLY SOMETHING ONLY I CAN DO?
—BY RESTORING WONDERLAND TO WHAT IT ONCE WAS, WILL ALICE REALLY BE SAVED?
I'M SURE THAT THIS PLACE IS WONDERLAND, BUT... IT'S TOO DIFFERENT FROM THE WONDERLAND I KNOW—
NOTHING BUT A SICKENING SENSE OF UNEASE CLOAKS MY HEART NOW.

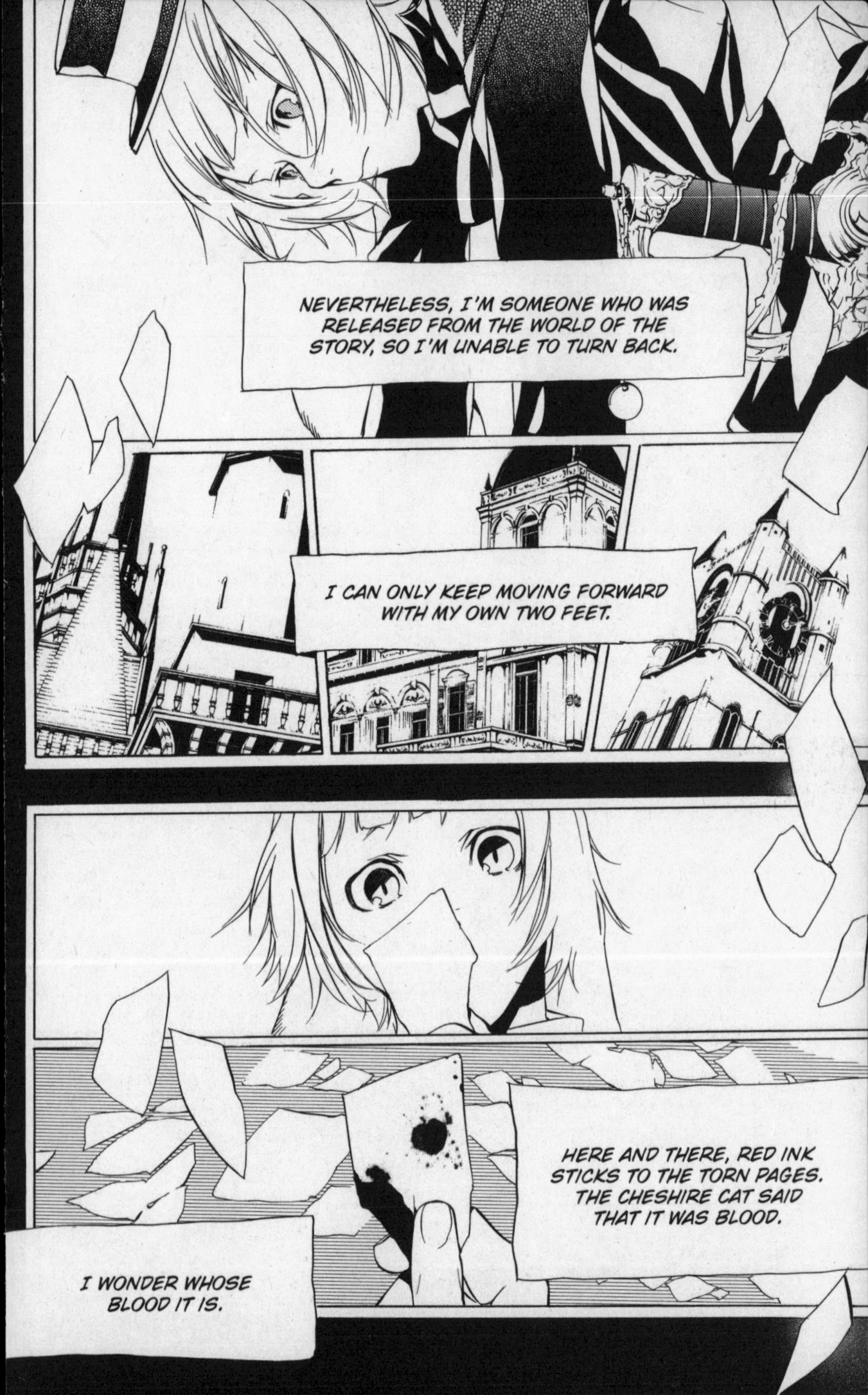
NEVERTHELESS, I'M SOMEONE WHO WAS RELEASED FROM THE WORLD OF THE STORY, SO I'M UNABLE TO TURN BACK.
I CAN ONLY KEEP MOVING FORWARD WITH MY OWN TWO FEET.
HERE AND THERE, RED INK STICKS TO THE TORN PAGES. THE CHESHIRE CAT SAID THAT IT WAS BLOOD.
I WONDER WHOSE BLOOD IT IS.

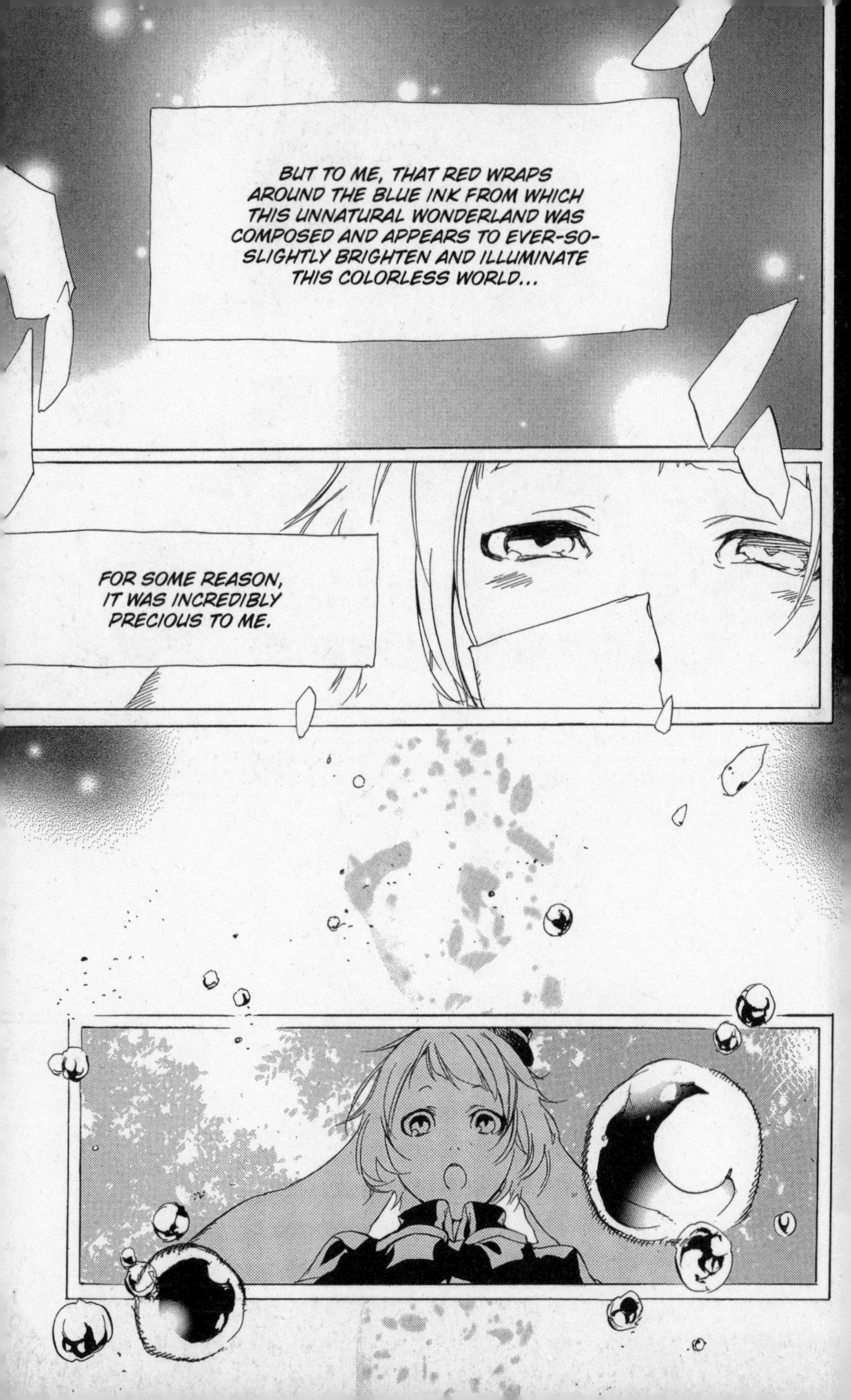
BUT TO ME, THAT RED WRAPS AROUND THE BLUE INK FROM WHICH THIS UNNATURAL WONDERLAND WAS COMPOSED AND APPEARS TO EVER-SO-SLIGHTLY BRIGHTEN AND ILLUMINATE THIS COLORLESS WORLD...
FOR SOME REASON, IT WAS INCREDIBLY PRECIOUS TO ME.

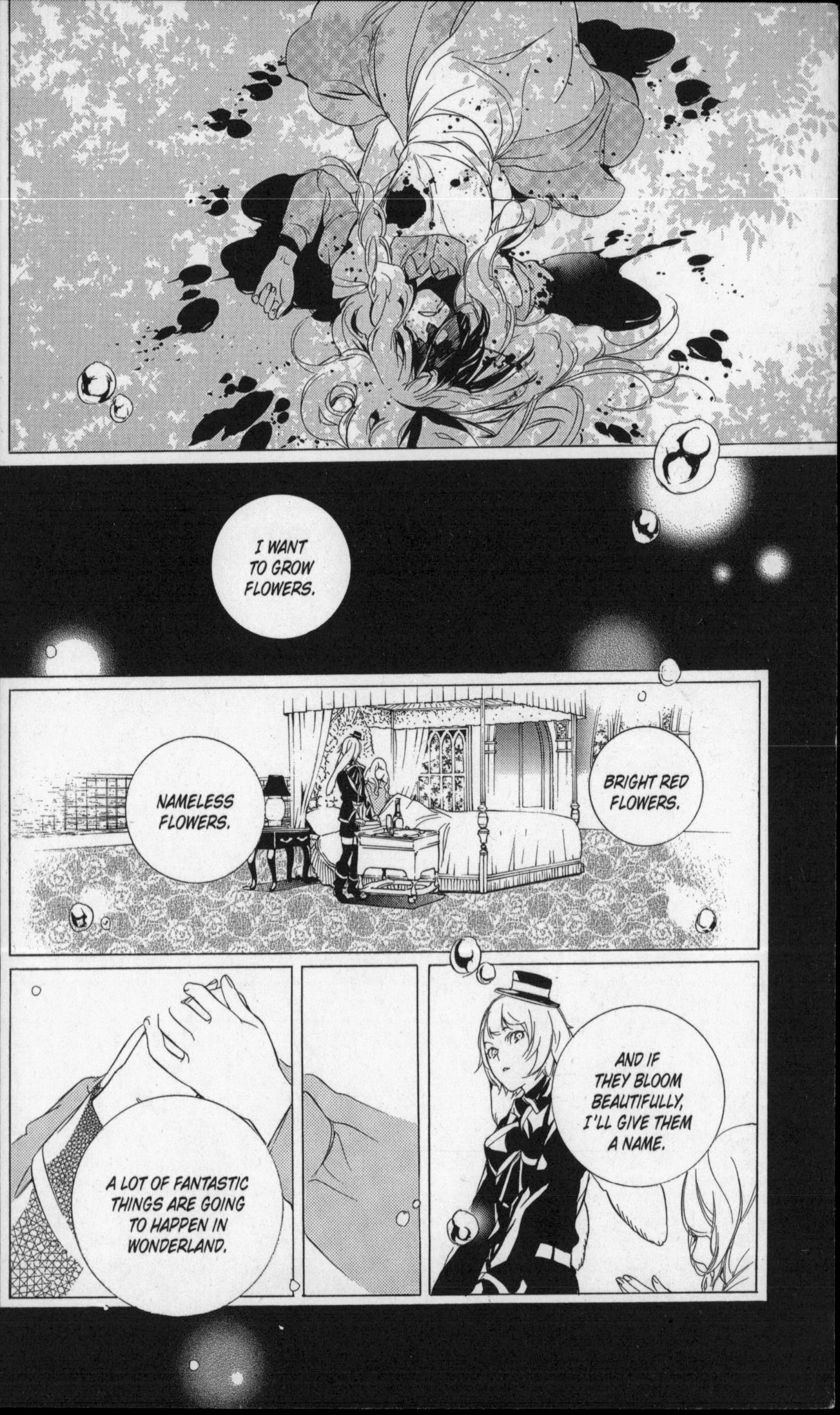
I WANT TO GROW FLOWERS.
BRIGHT RED FLOWERS.
NAMELESS FLOWERS.
AND IF THEY BLOOM BEAUTIFULLY, I'LL GIVE THEM A NAME.
A LOT OF FANTASTIC THINGS ARE GOING TO HAPPEN IN WONDERLAND.

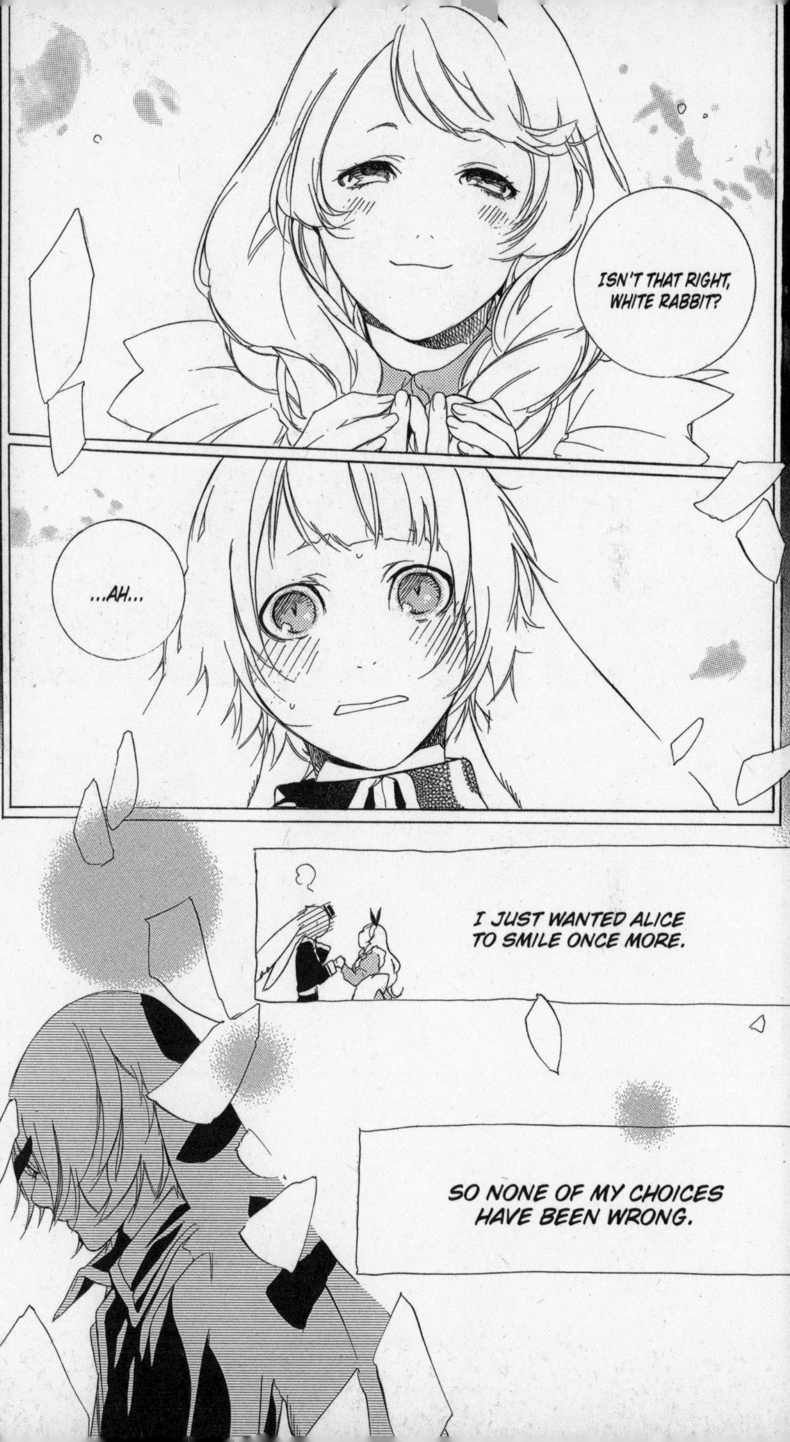
ISN'T THAT RIGHT, WHITE RABBIT?
...AH...
I JUST WANTED ALICE TO SMILE ONCE MORE.
SO NONE OF MY CHOICES HAVE BEEN WRONG.

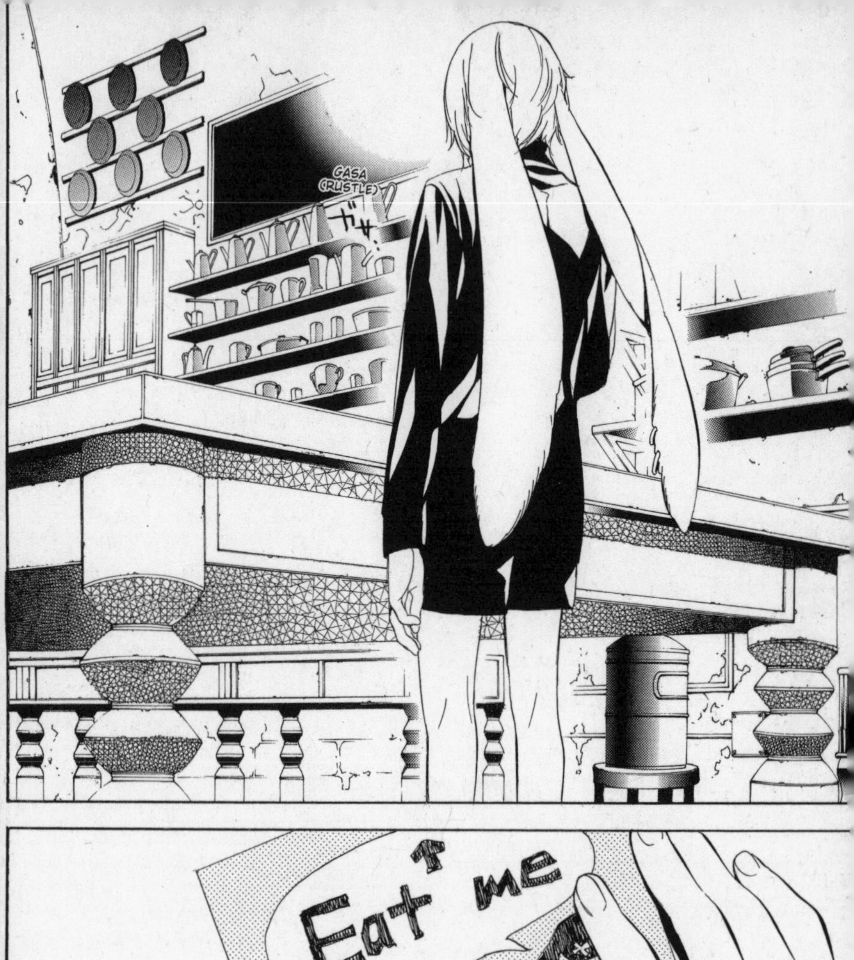
GASA
(RUSTLE)
ガサ
Eat me

I HAVEN'T GOTTEN ANYTHING WRONG.

# Chapter 35

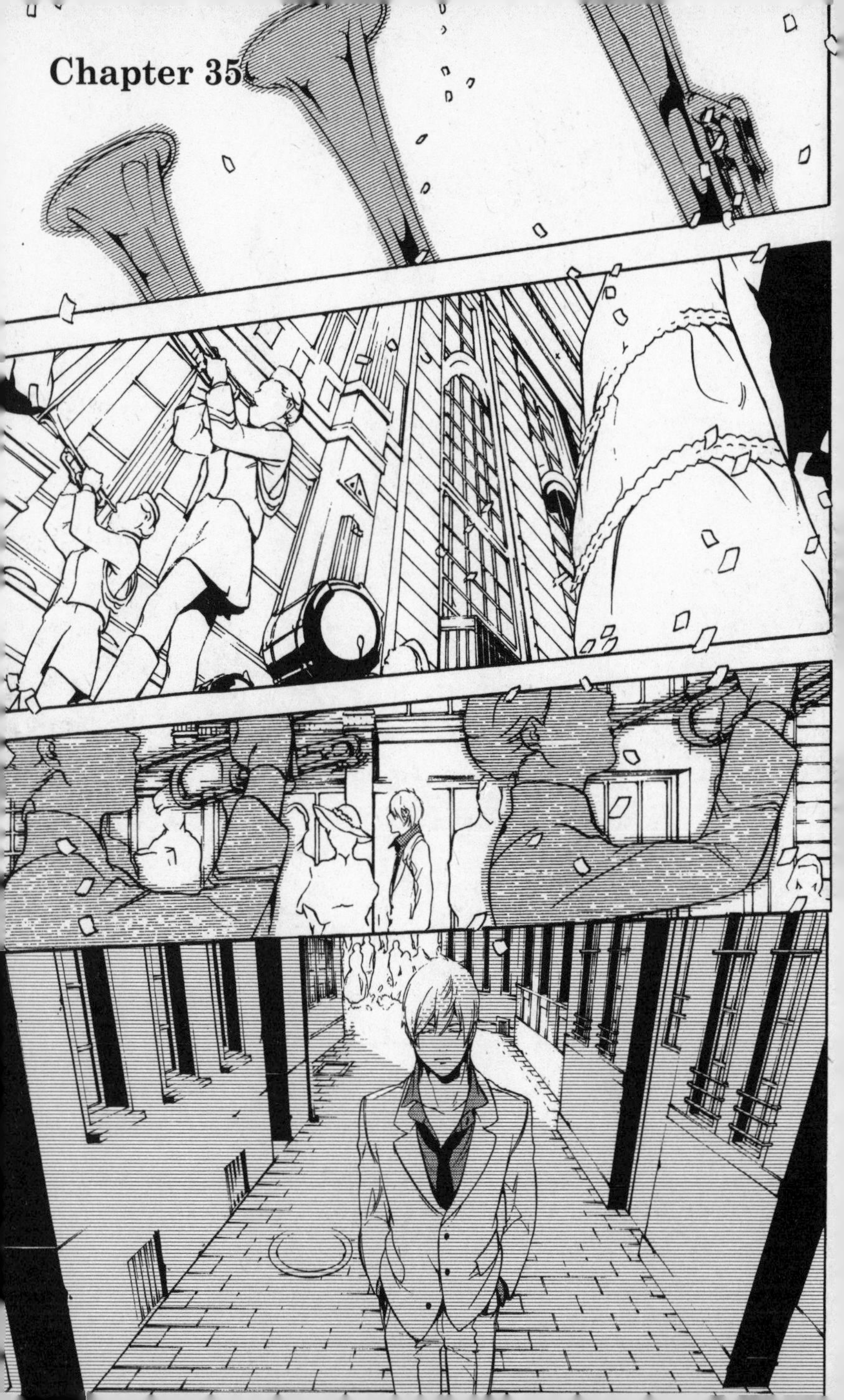

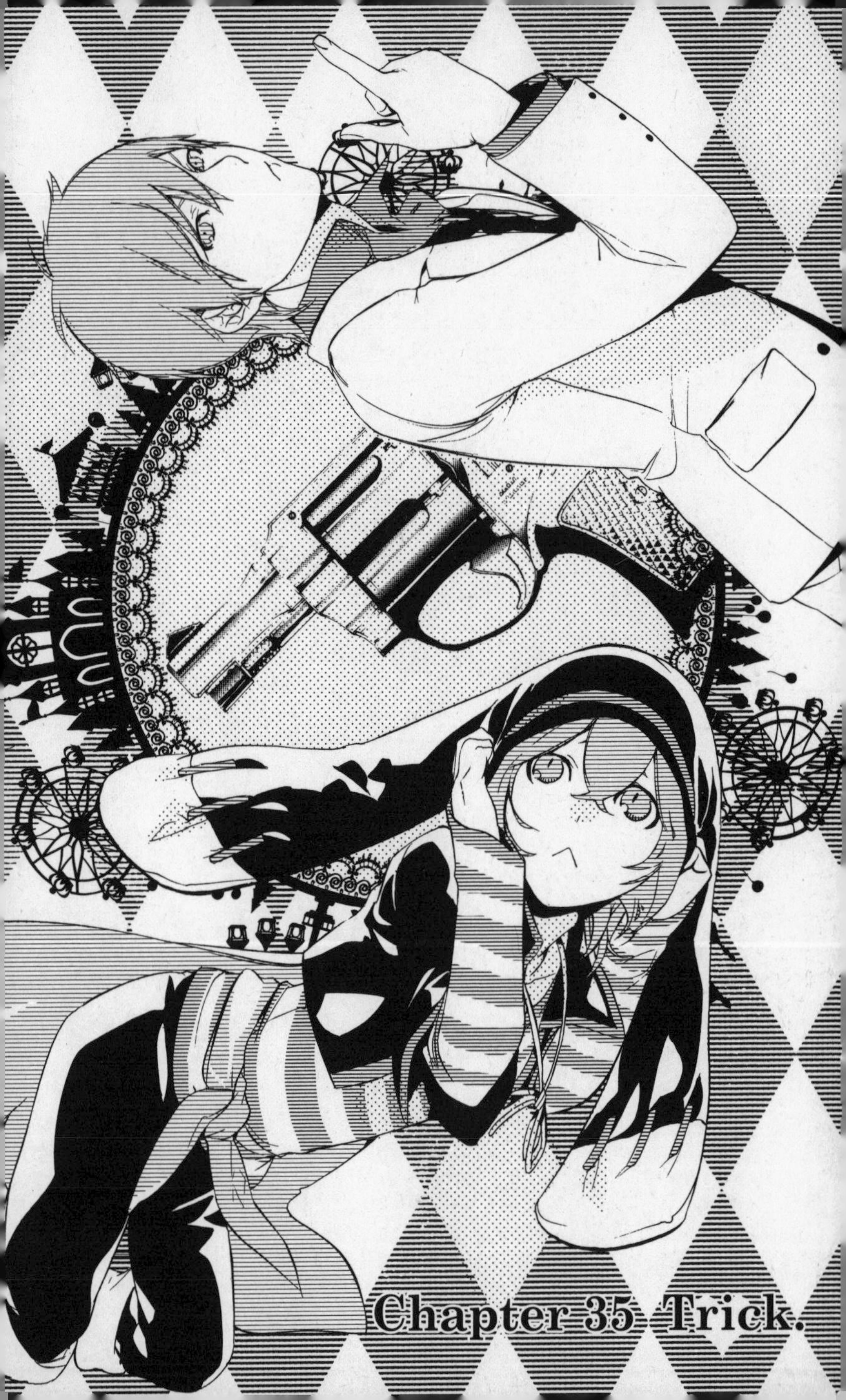

# Chapter 35 Trick.

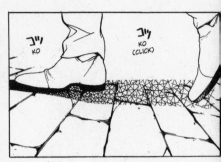

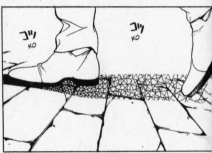

ゴッ KO (CLICK)
ゴッ KO
ドッ BA (WHIP)
ゴッ KO
ゴッ KO
ドッ BA
NOBODY'S EVEN COMING AFTER ME...!
SOMEBODY GIVE A DAMN, WOULD YA!? AND HATTER! YOU LEAVE ME ALONE WAY TOO OFTEN, CONSIDERING I'M ALICE AND ALL!
AND, OW! YELLING THIS LOUD REALLY FRICKIN' HURTS...!

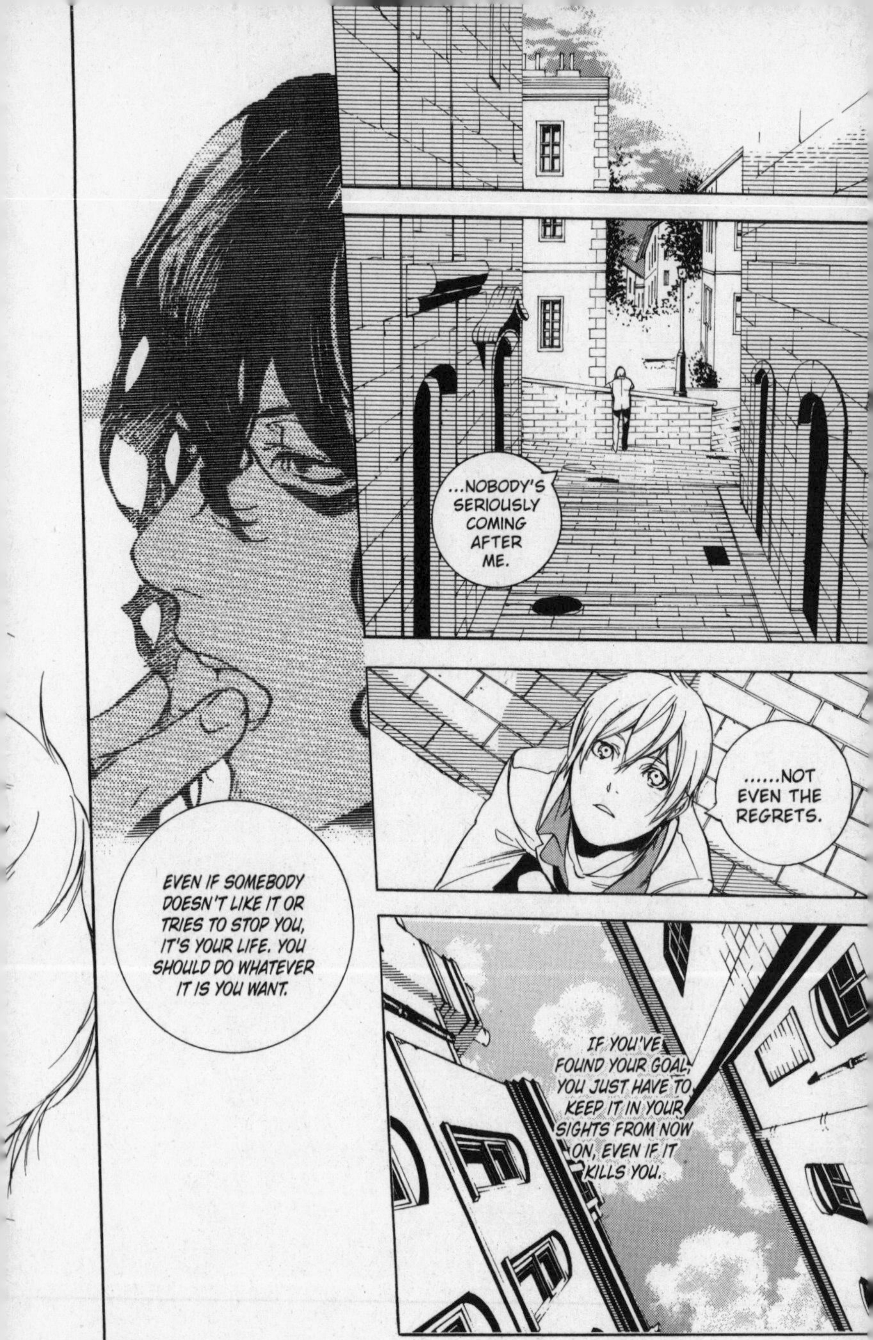
...NOBODY'S SERIOUSLY COMING AFTER ME.
......NOT EVEN THE REGRETS.
IF YOU'VE FOUND YOUR GOAL, YOU JUST HAVE TO KEEP IT IN YOUR SIGHTS FROM NOW ON, EVEN IF IT KILLS YOU.
EVEN IF SOMEBODY DOESN'T LIKE IT OR TRIES TO STOP YOU, IT'S YOUR LIFE. YOU SHOULD DO WHATEVER IT IS YOU WANT.

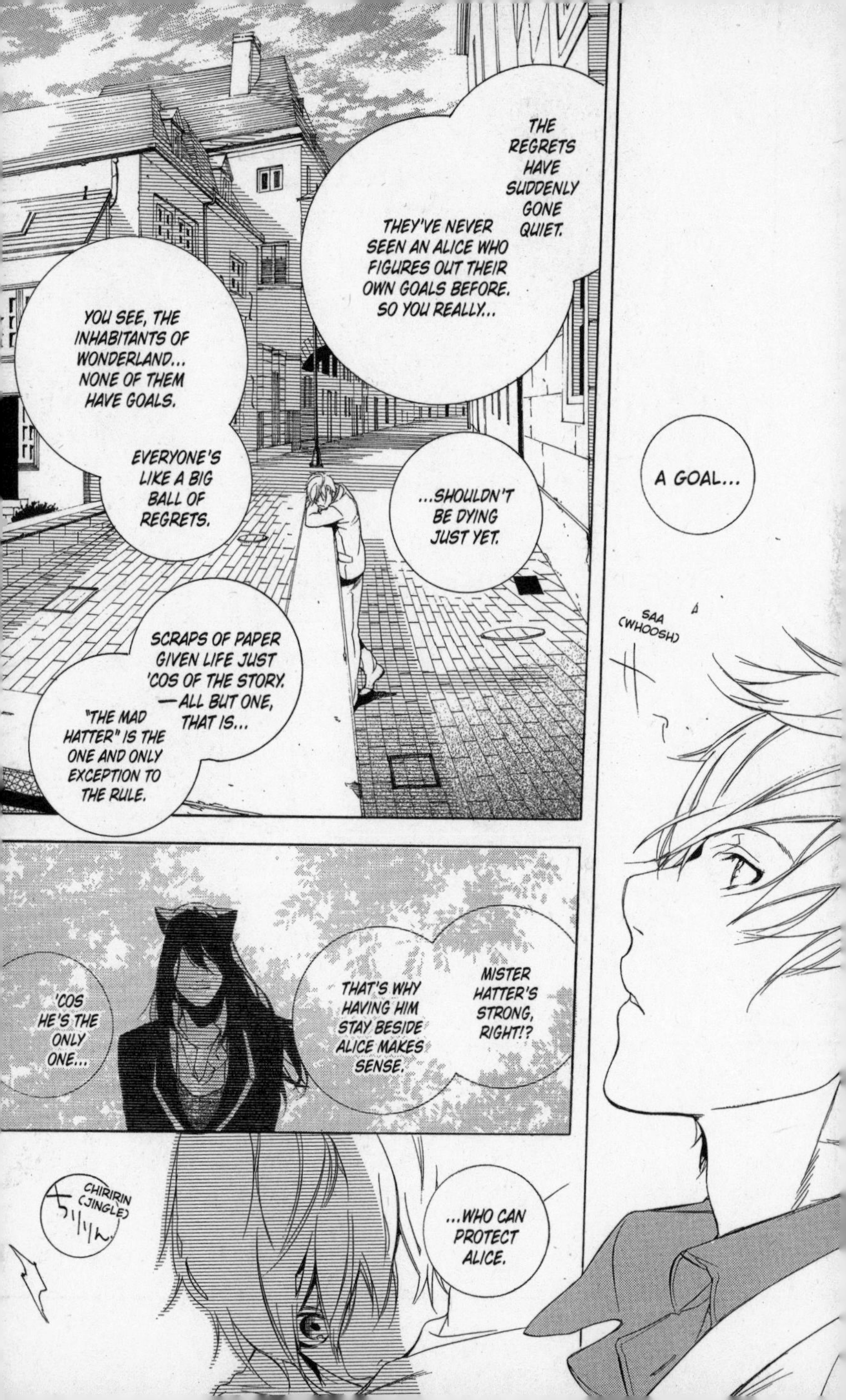
A GOAL...
SAA (WHOOSH)
THE REGRETS HAVE SUDDENLY GONE QUIET.
THEY'VE NEVER SEEN AN ALICE WHO FIGURES OUT THEIR OWN GOALS BEFORE. SO YOU REALLY...
YOU SEE, THE INHABITANTS OF WONDERLAND... NONE OF THEM HAVE GOALS.
...SHOULDN'T BE DYING JUST YET.
EVERYONE'S LIKE A BIG BALL OF REGRETS.
SCRAPS OF PAPER GIVEN LIFE JUST 'COS OF THE STORY. —ALL BUT ONE, THAT IS...
"THE MAD HATTER" IS THE ONE AND ONLY EXCEPTION TO THE RULE.
MISTER HATTER'S STRONG, RIGHT!?
THAT'S WHY HAVING HIM STAY BESIDE ALICE MAKES SENSE.
'COS HE'S THE ONLY ONE...
...WHO CAN PROTECT ALICE.
CHIRIRIN (JINGLE)

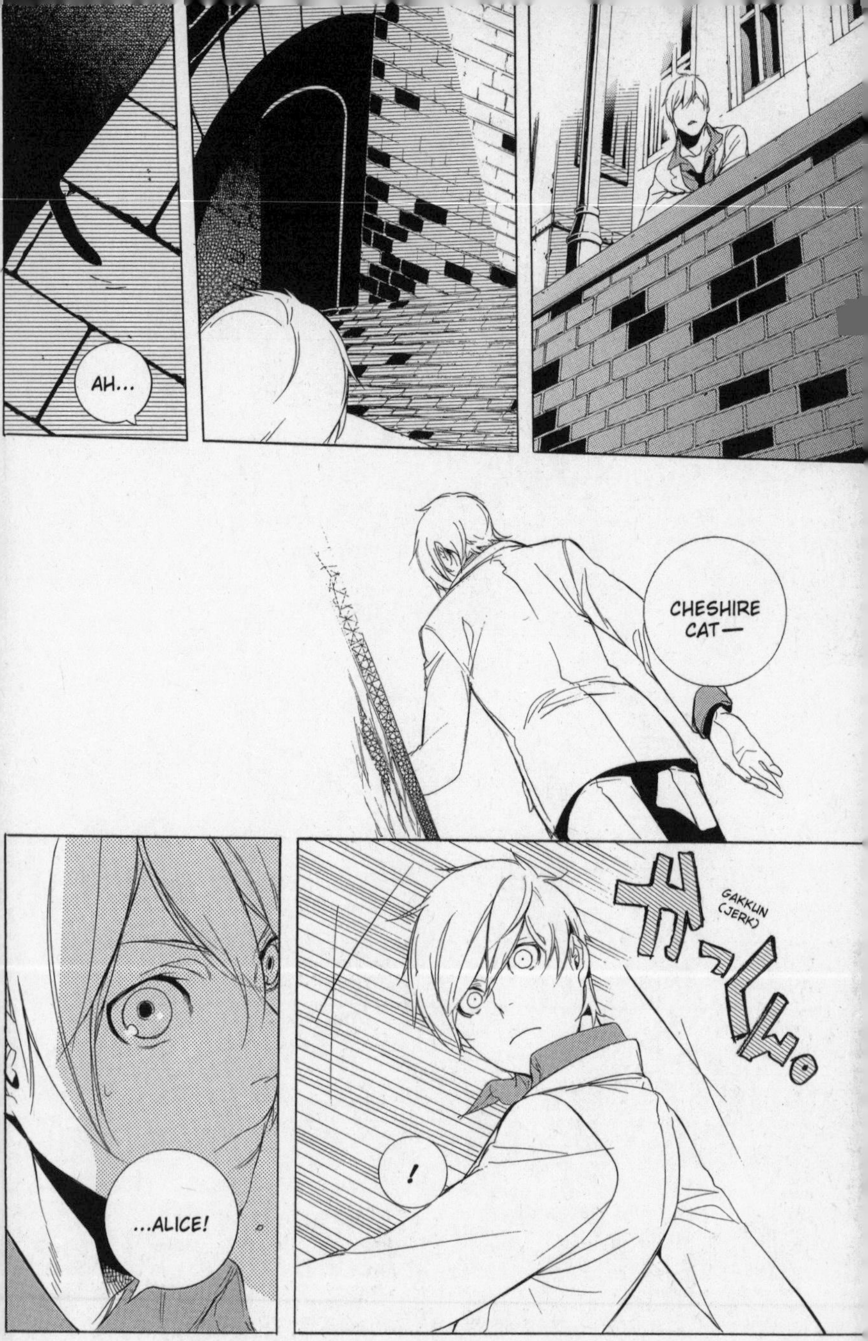
AH...
CHESHIRE CAT—
GAKKUN (JERK)
!
...ALICE!

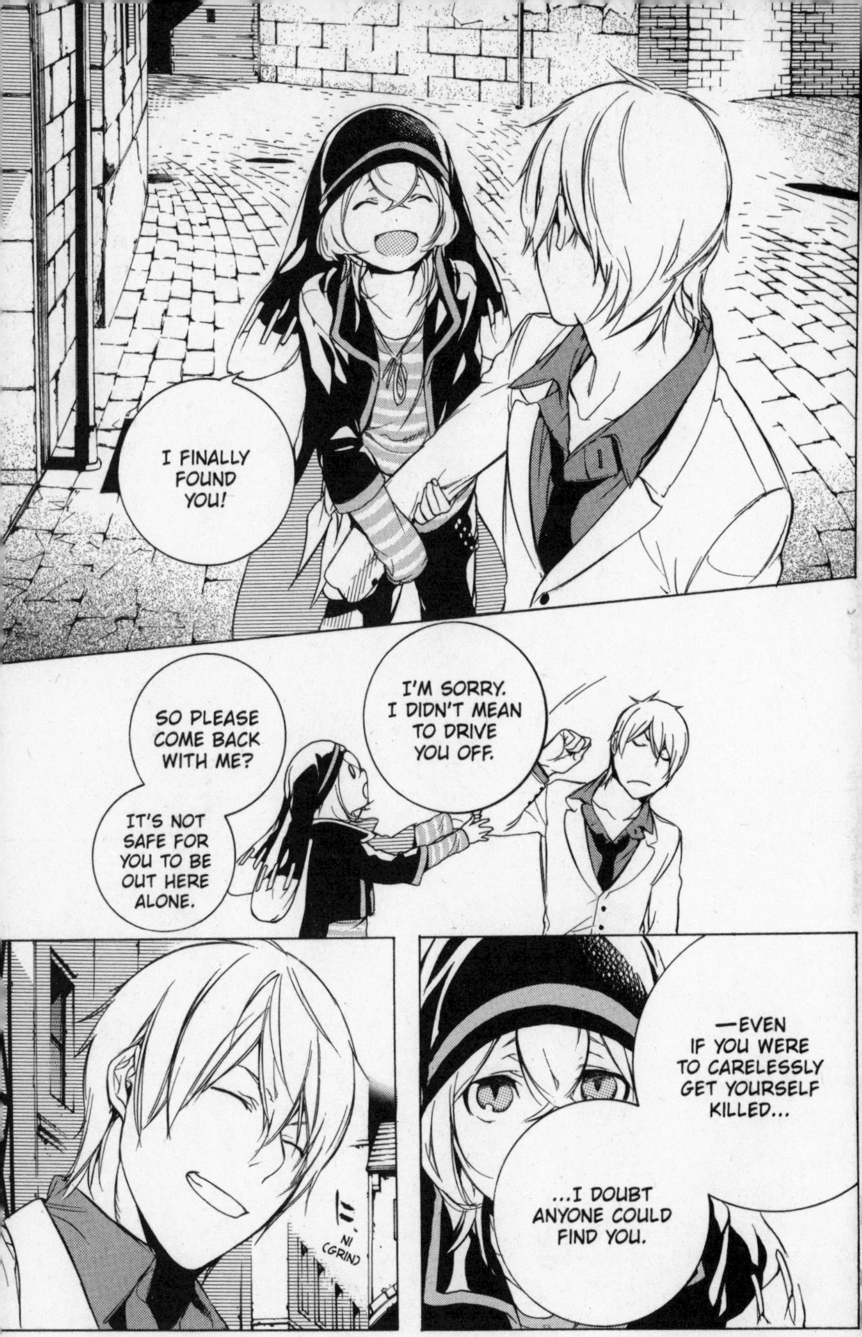
I FINALLY FOUND YOU!
I'M SORRY. I DIDN'T MEAN TO DRIVE YOU OFF.
SO PLEASE COME BACK WITH ME?
IT'S NOT SAFE FOR YOU TO BE OUT HERE ALONE.
—EVEN IF YOU WERE TO CARELESSLY GET YOURSELF KILLED...
...I DOUBT ANYONE COULD FIND YOU.
NI (GRIN)

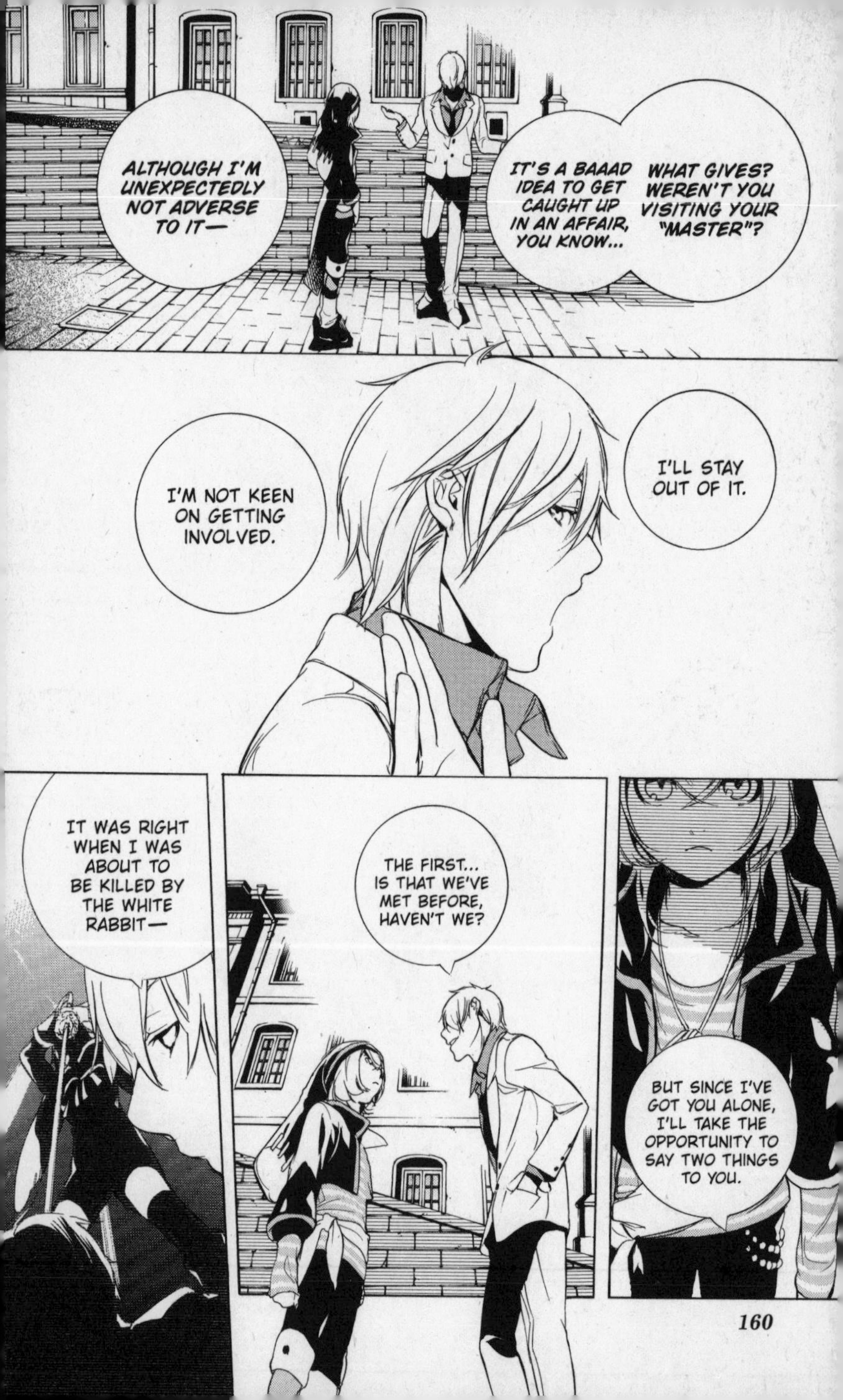
WHAT GIVES? WEREN'T YOU VISITING YOUR "MASTER"?
IT'S A BAAAD IDEA TO GET CAUGHT UP IN AN AFFAIR, YOU KNOW...
ALTHOUGH I'M UNEXPECTEDLY NOT ADVERSE TO IT—
I'LL STAY OUT OF IT.
I'M NOT KEEN ON GETTING INVOLVED.
BUT SINCE I'VE GOT YOU ALONE, I'LL TAKE THE OPPORTUNITY TO SAY TWO THINGS TO YOU.
THE FIRST... IS THAT WE'VE MET BEFORE, HAVEN'T WE?
IT WAS RIGHT WHEN I WAS ABOUT TO BE KILLED BY THE WHITE RABBIT—

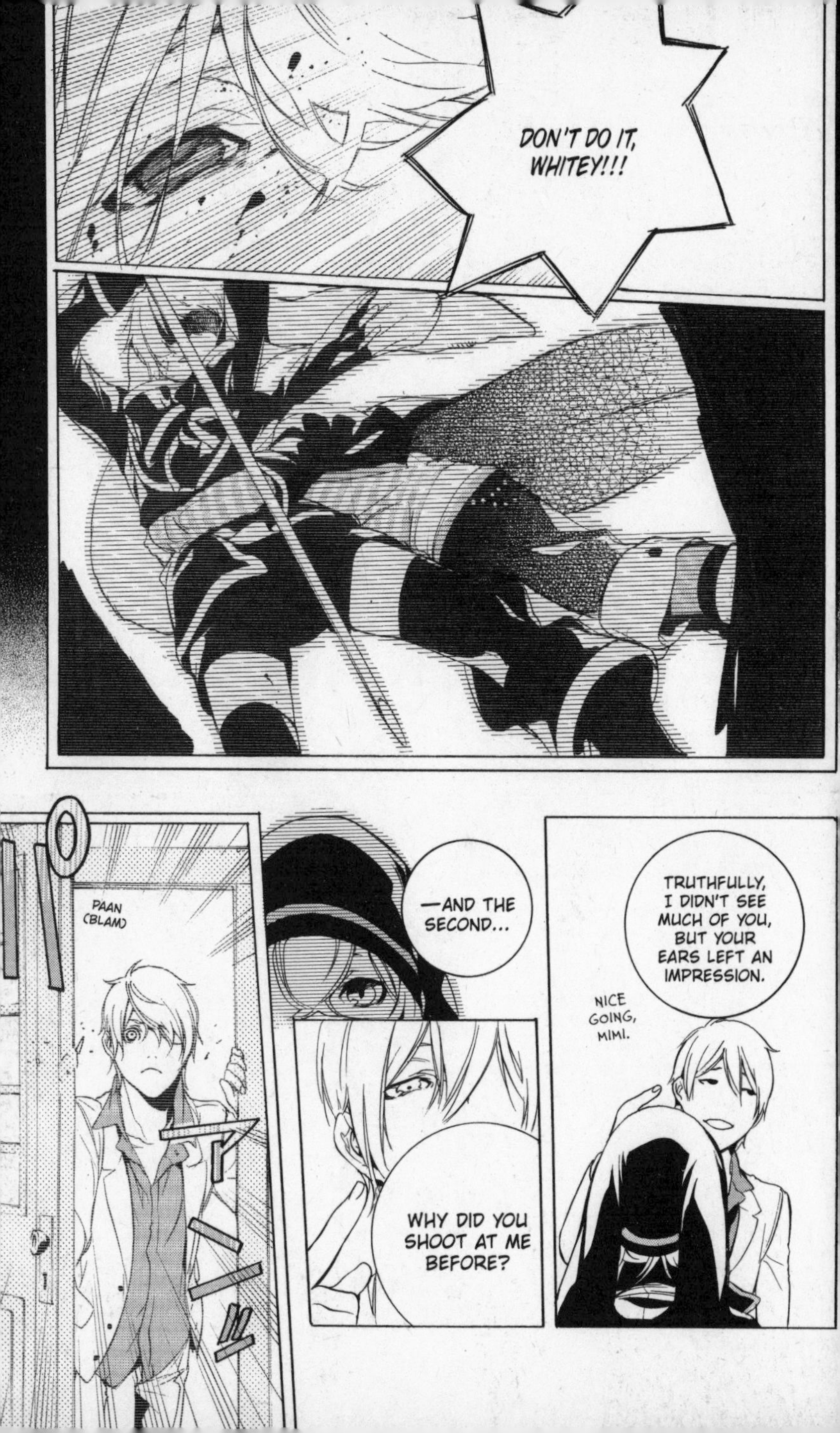
DON'T DO IT, WHITEY!!!
TRUTHFULLY, I DIDN'T SEE MUCH OF YOU, BUT YOUR EARS LEFT AN IMPRESSION.
NICE GOING, MIMI.
—AND THE SECOND...
WHY DID YOU SHOOT AT ME BEFORE?
PAAN (BLAM)

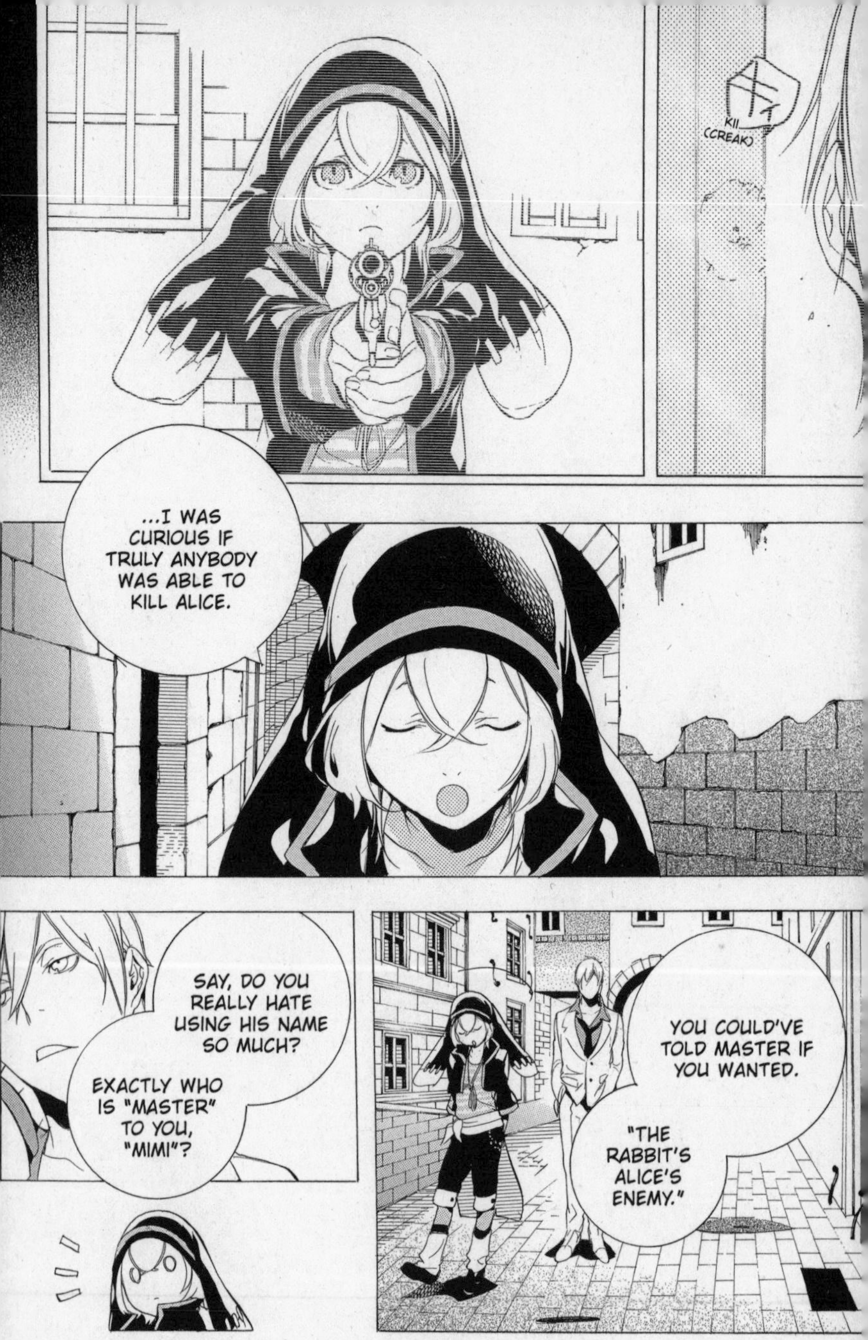
KII (CREAK)
...I WAS CURIOUS IF TRULY ANYBODY WAS ABLE TO KILL ALICE.
YOU COULD'VE TOLD MASTER IF YOU WANTED.
"THE RABBIT'S ALICE'S ENEMY."
SAY, DO YOU REALLY HATE USING HIS NAME SO MUCH?
EXACTLY WHO IS "MASTER" TO YOU, "MIMI"?

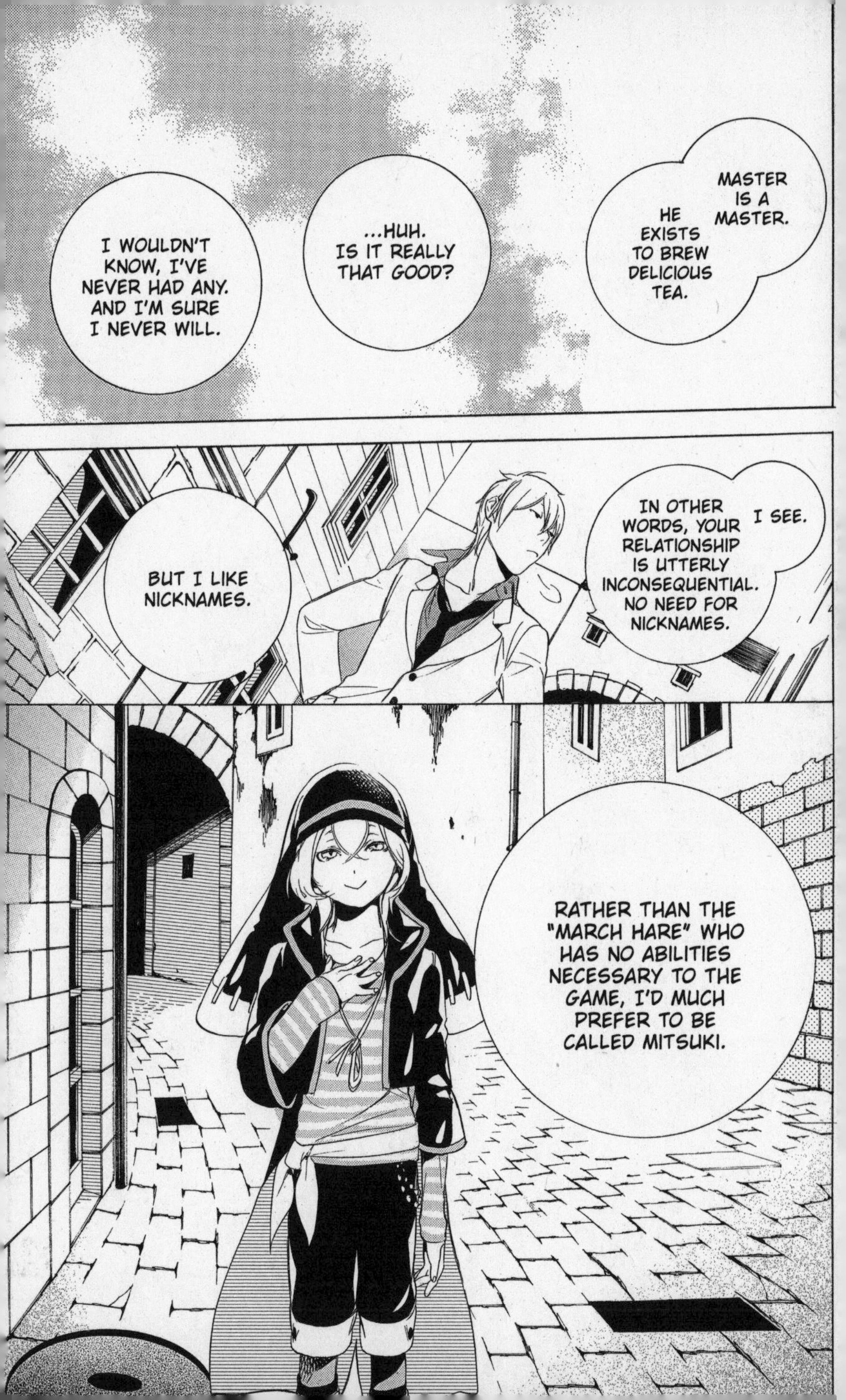
MASTER IS A MASTER.
HE EXISTS TO BREW DELICIOUS TEA.
...HUH. IS IT REALLY THAT GOOD?
I WOULDN'T KNOW, I'VE NEVER HAD ANY. AND I'M SURE I NEVER WILL.
I SEE.
IN OTHER WORDS, YOUR RELATIONSHIP IS UTTERLY INCONSEQUENTIAL. NO NEED FOR NICKNAMES.
BUT I LIKE NICKNAMES.
RATHER THAN THE "MARCH HARE" WHO HAS NO ABILITIES NECESSARY TO THE GAME, I'D MUCH PREFER TO BE CALLED MITSUKI.

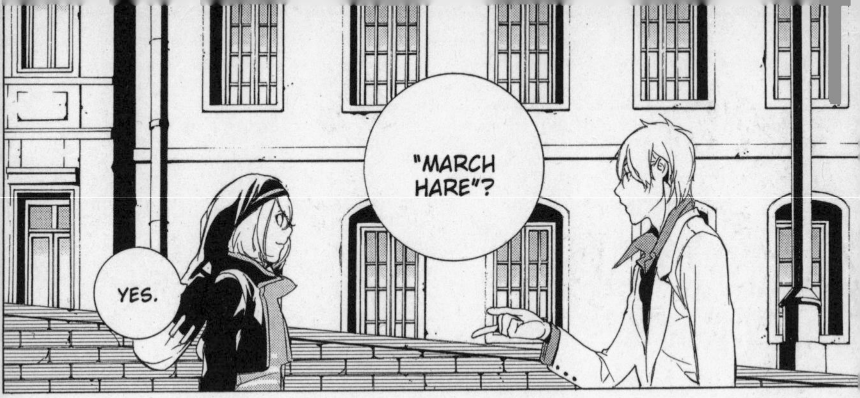
"MARCH HARE"?
YES.

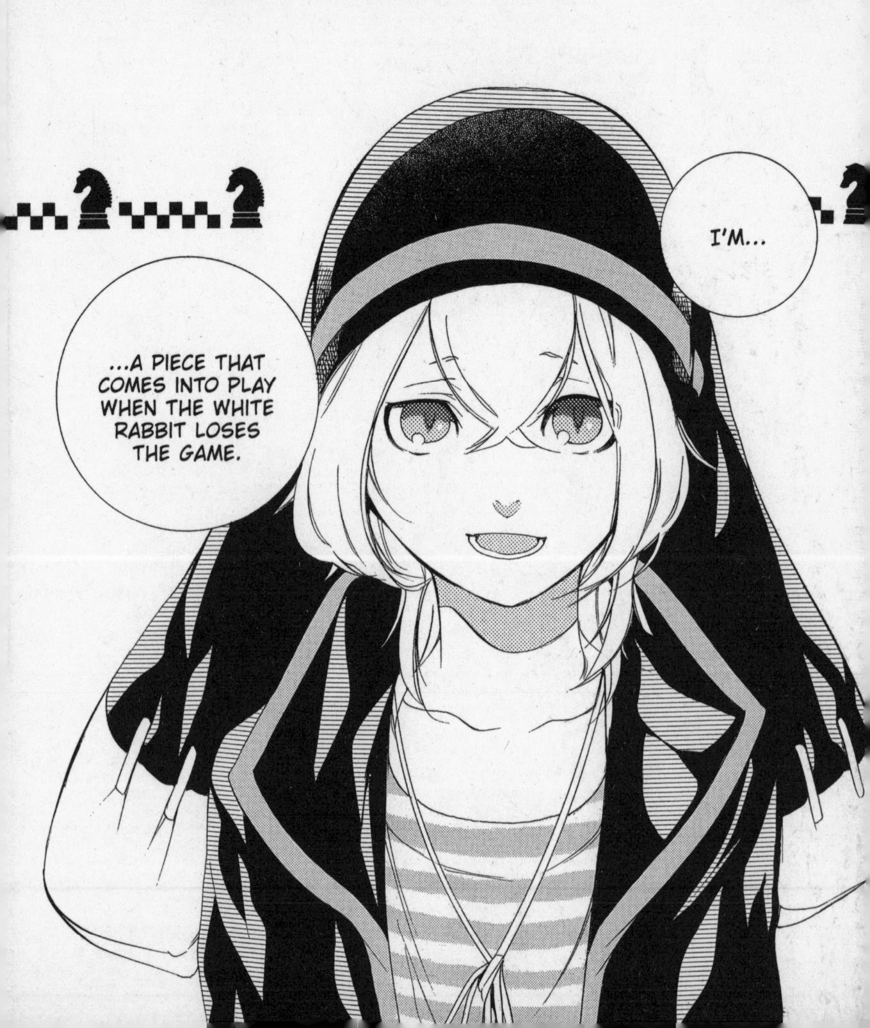
I'M...
...A PIECE THAT COMES INTO PLAY WHEN THE WHITE RABBIT LOSES THE GAME.

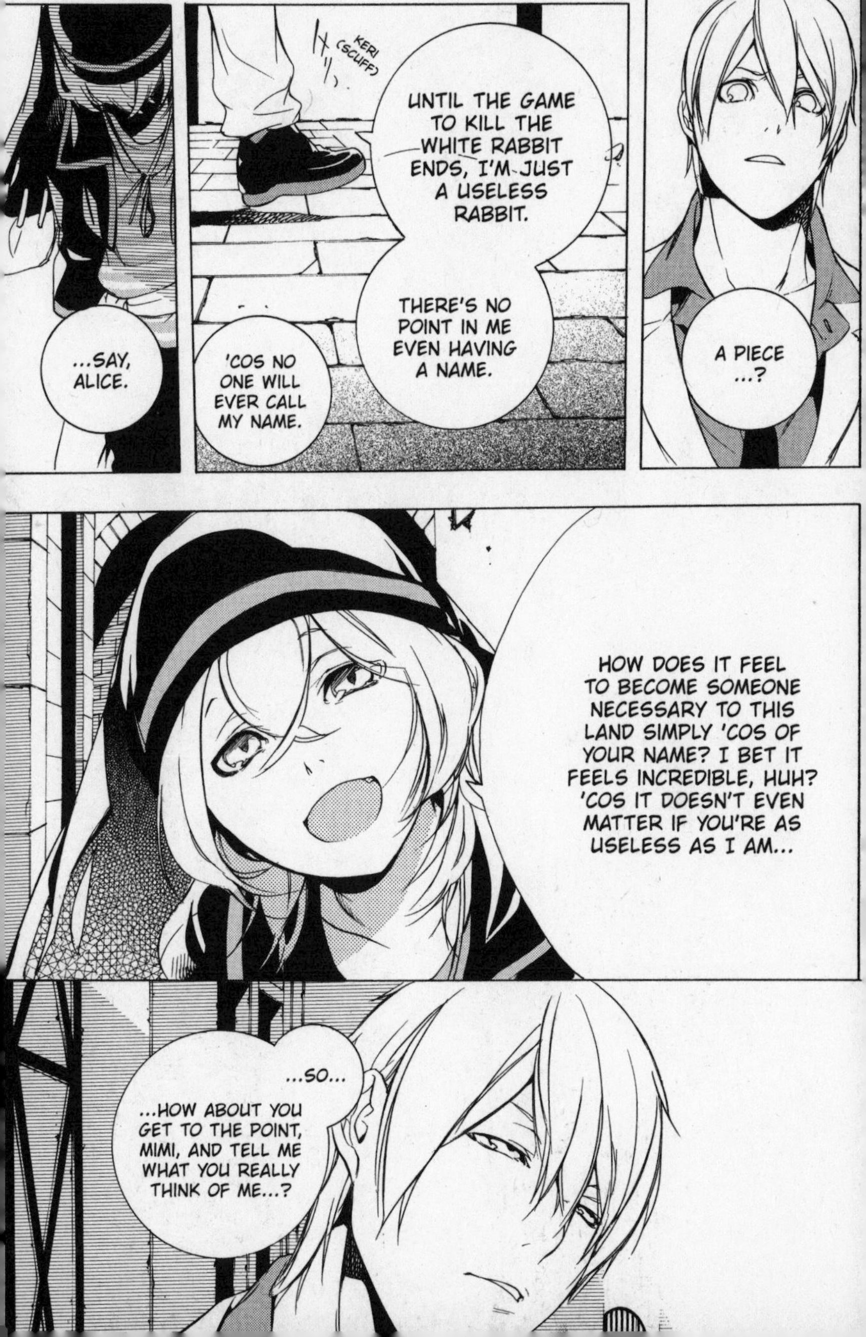
A PIECE ...?
UNTIL THE GAME TO KILL THE WHITE RABBIT ENDS, I'M JUST A USELESS RABBIT.
KERI (SCUFF)
THERE'S NO POINT IN ME EVEN HAVING A NAME.
'COS NO ONE WILL EVER CALL MY NAME.
...SAY, ALICE.
HOW DOES IT FEEL TO BECOME SOMEONE NECESSARY TO THIS LAND SIMPLY 'COS OF YOUR NAME? I BET IT FEELS INCREDIBLE, HUH? 'COS IT DOESN'T EVEN MATTER IF YOU'RE AS USELESS AS I AM...
...SO...
...HOW ABOUT YOU GET TO THE POINT, MIMI, AND TELL ME WHAT YOU REALLY THINK OF ME...?

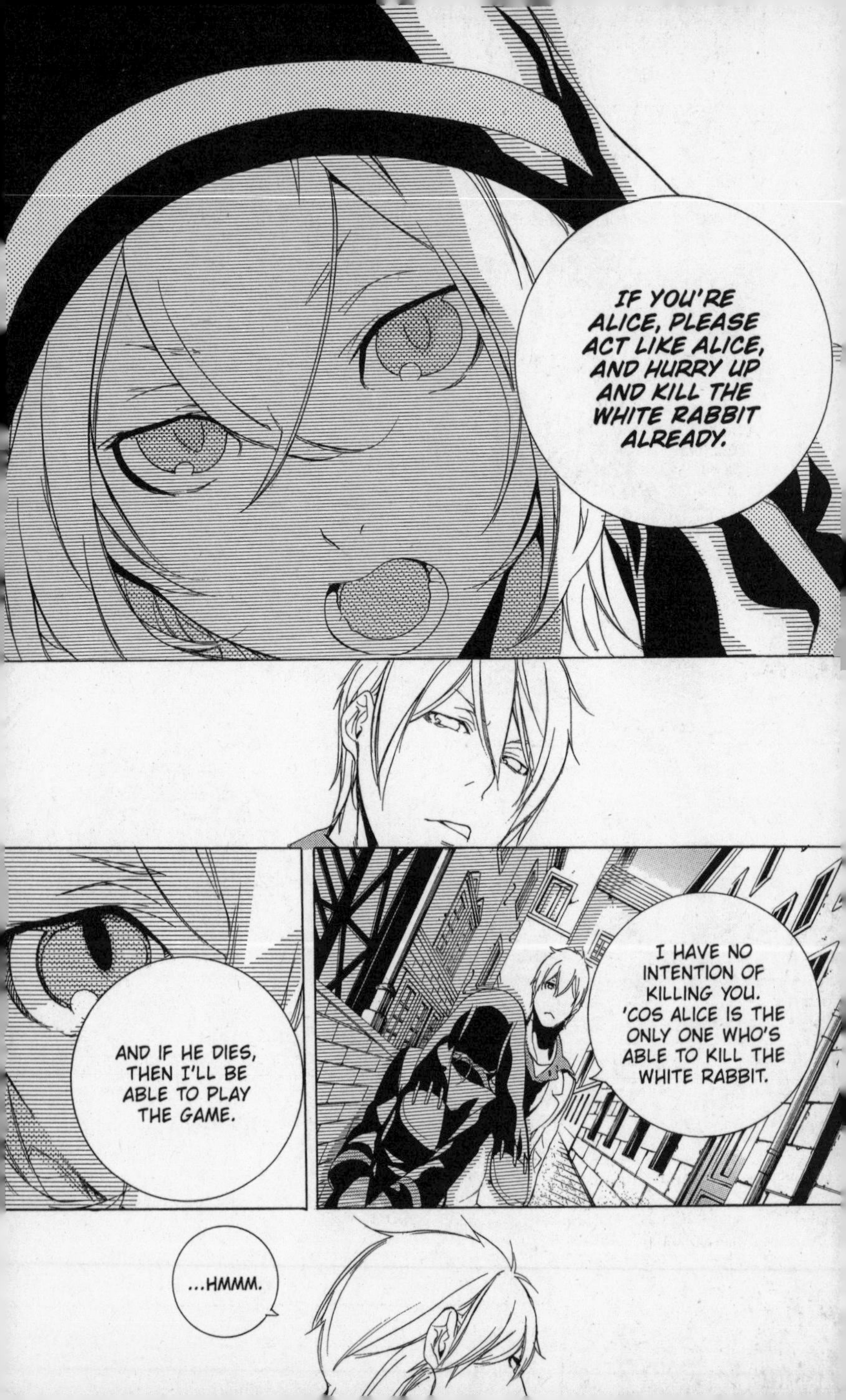
IF YOU'RE ALICE, PLEASE ACT LIKE ALICE, AND HURRY UP AND KILL THE WHITE RABBIT ALREADY.
I HAVE NO INTENTION OF KILLING YOU. 'COS ALICE IS THE ONLY ONE WHO'S ABLE TO KILL THE WHITE RABBIT.
AND IF HE DIES, THEN I'LL BE ABLE TO PLAY THE GAME.
...HMMM.

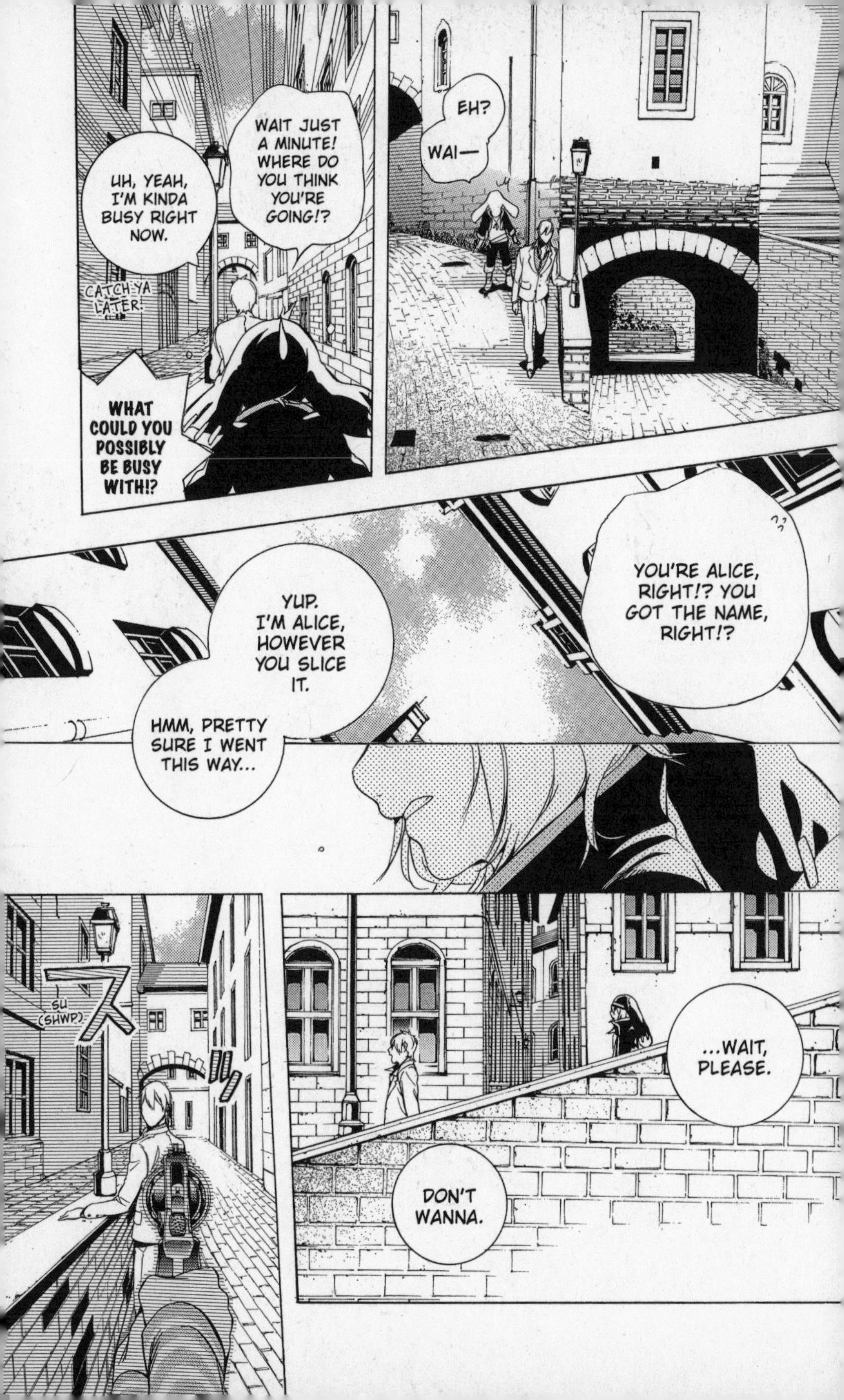
EH?
WAI—
WAIT JUST A MINUTE! WHERE DO YOU THINK YOU'RE GOING!?
UH, YEAH, I'M KINDA BUSY RIGHT NOW.
CATCH YA LATER.
WHAT COULD YOU POSSIBLY BE BUSY WITH!?
YOU'RE ALICE, RIGHT!? YOU GOT THE NAME, RIGHT!?
YUP. I'M ALICE, HOWEVER YOU SLICE IT.
HMM, PRETTY SURE I WENT THIS WAY...
...WAIT, PLEASE.
DON'T WANNA.
SU (SHWP)

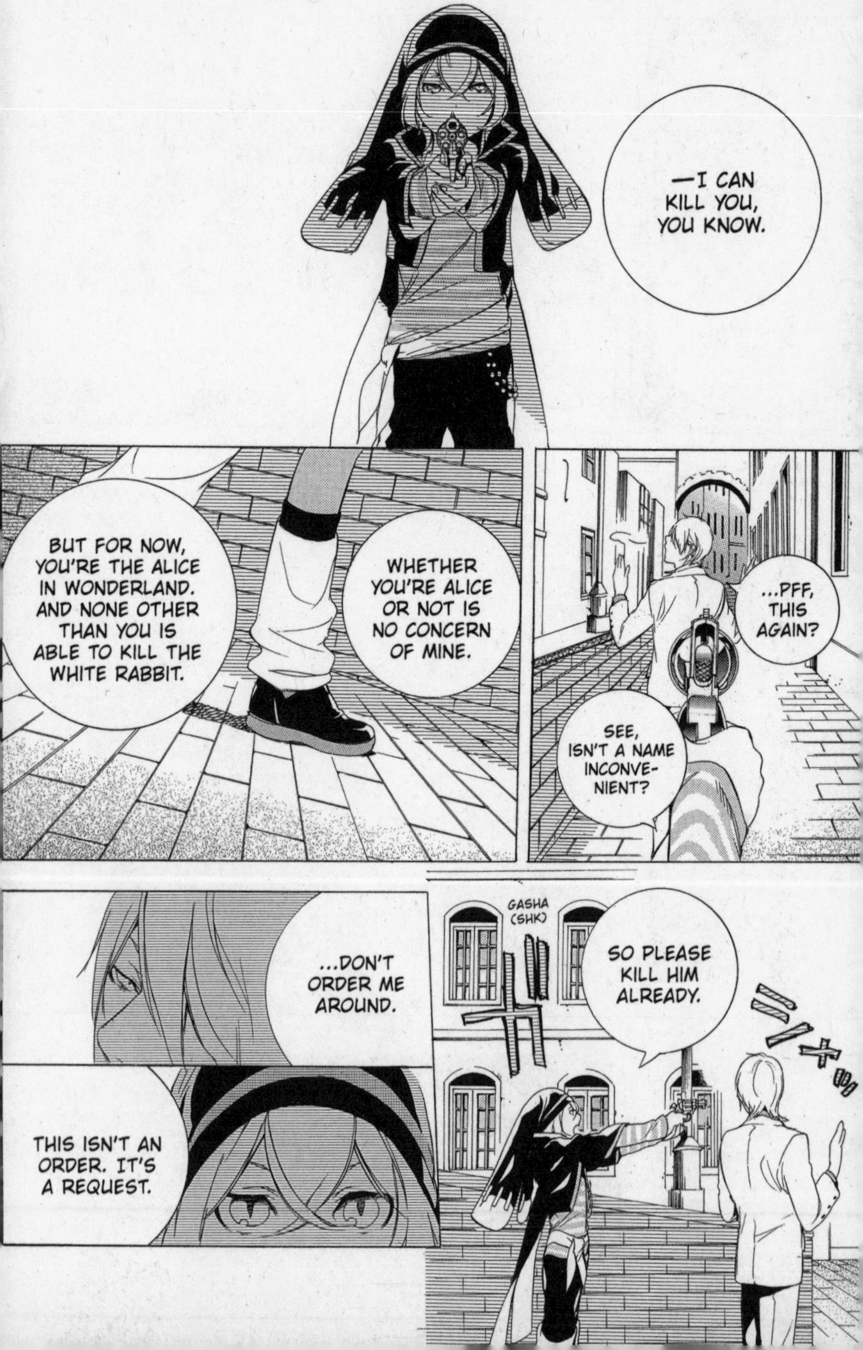
—I CAN KILL YOU, YOU KNOW.
...PFF, THIS AGAIN?
SEE, ISN'T A NAME INCONVE-NIENT?
WHETHER YOU'RE ALICE OR NOT IS NO CONCERN OF MINE.
BUT FOR NOW, YOU'RE THE ALICE IN WONDERLAND. AND NONE OTHER THAN YOU IS ABLE TO KILL THE WHITE RABBIT.
GASHA (SHK)
SO PLEASE KILL HIM ALREADY.
...DON'T ORDER ME AROUND.
THIS ISN'T AN ORDER. IT'S A REQUEST.

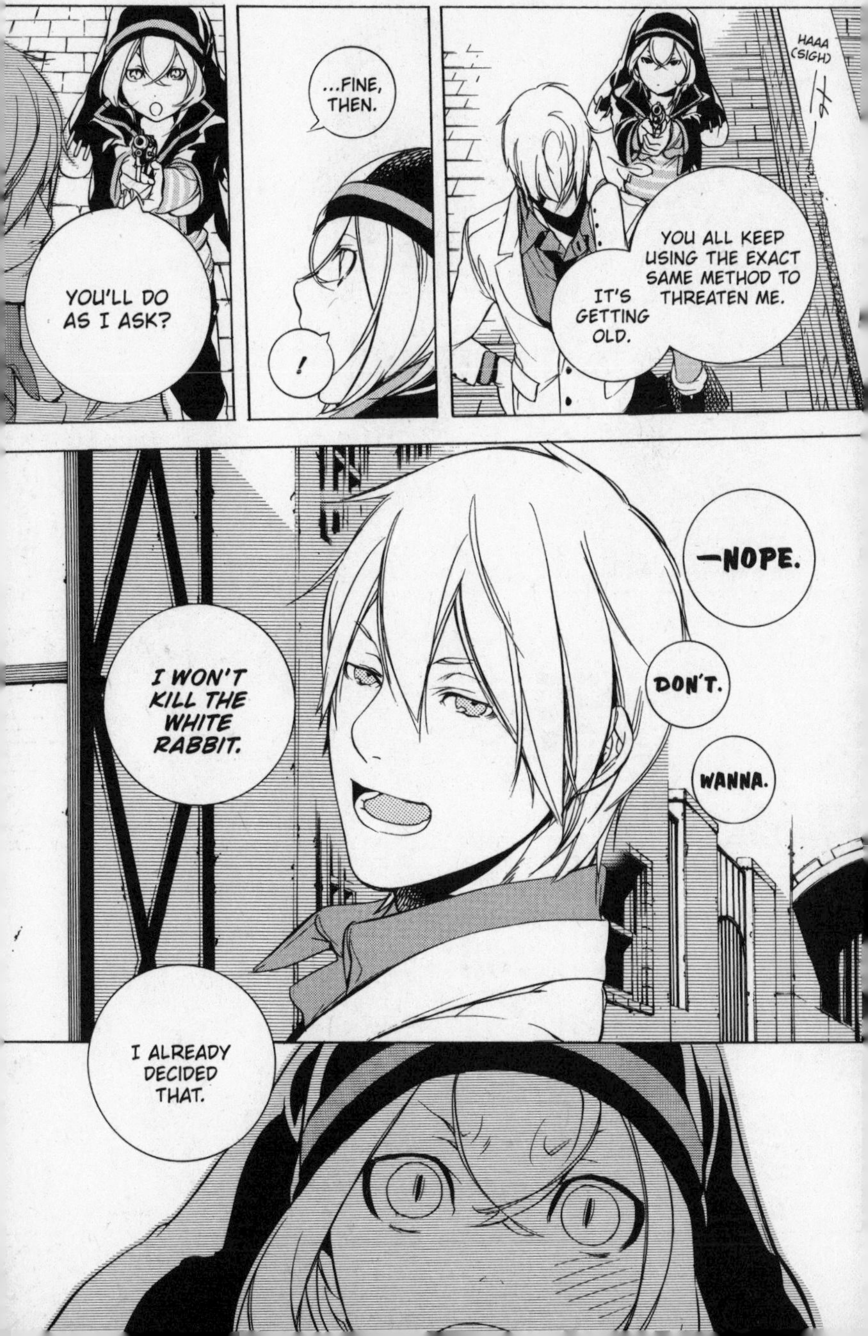
HAAA (SIGH)
は
YOU ALL KEEP USING THE EXACT SAME METHOD TO THREATEN ME.
IT'S GETTING OLD.
...FINE, THEN.
!
YOU'LL DO AS I ASK?
—NOPE.
DON'T.
WANNA.
I WON'T KILL THE WHITE RABBIT.
I ALREADY DECIDED THAT.

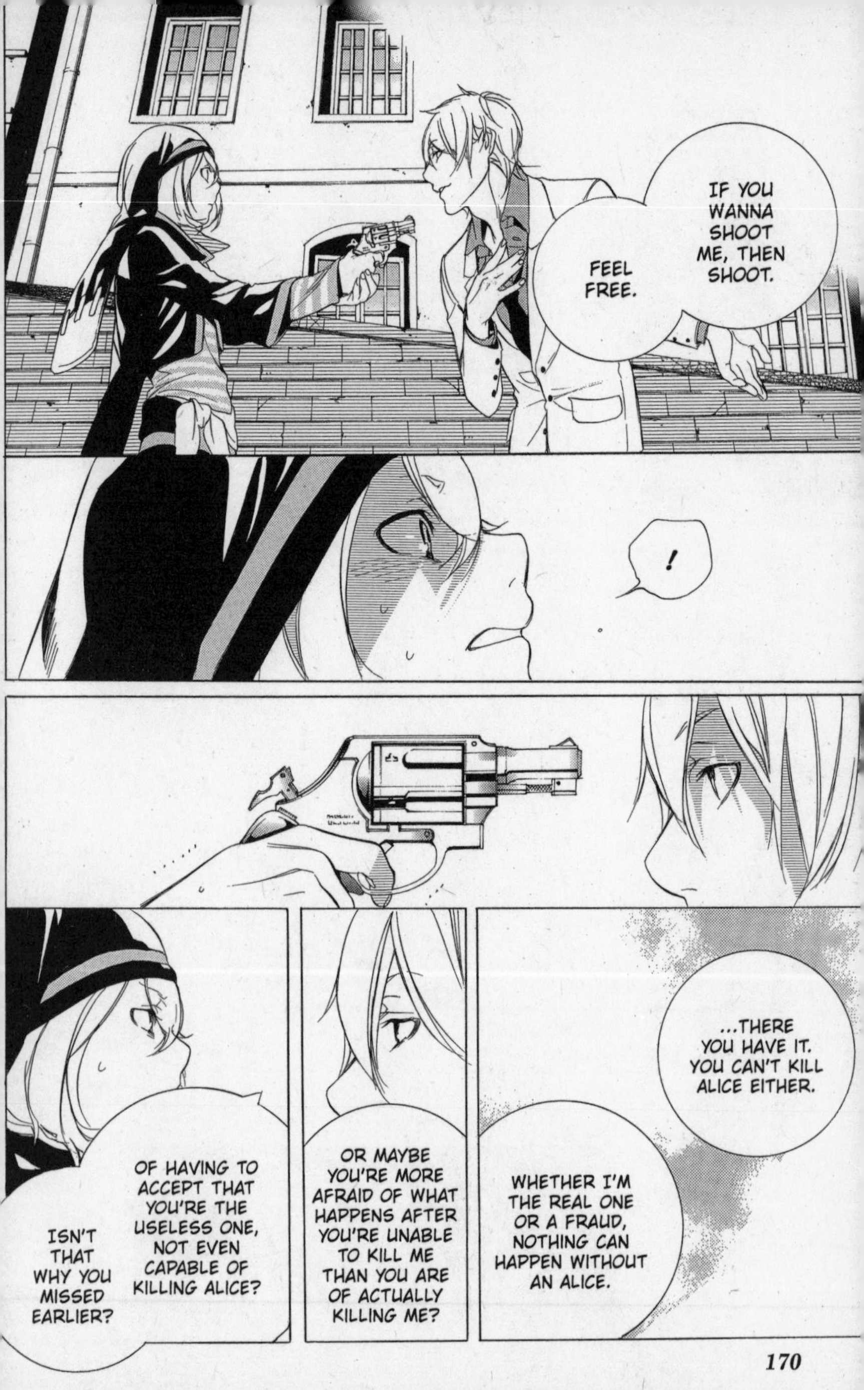
IF YOU WANNA SHOOT ME, THEN SHOOT.
FEEL FREE.
!
...THERE YOU HAVE IT. YOU CAN'T KILL ALICE EITHER.
WHETHER I'M THE REAL ONE OR A FRAUD, NOTHING CAN HAPPEN WITHOUT AN ALICE.
OR MAYBE YOU'RE MORE AFRAID OF WHAT HAPPENS AFTER YOU'RE UNABLE TO KILL ME THAN YOU ARE OF ACTUALLY KILLING ME?
OF HAVING TO ACCEPT THAT YOU'RE THE USELESS ONE, NOT EVEN CAPABLE OF KILLING ALICE?
ISN'T THAT WHY YOU MISSED EARLIER?

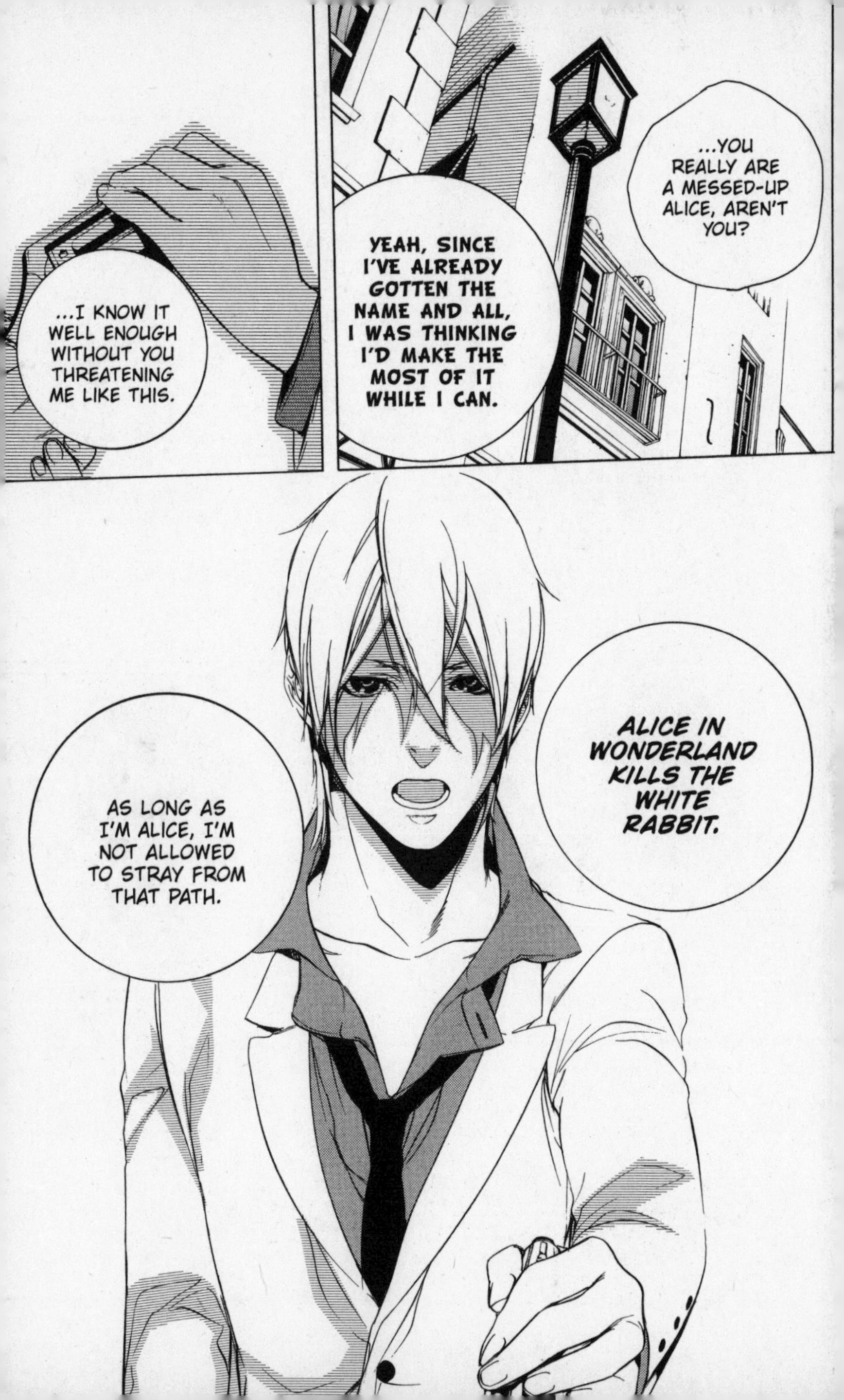
...YOU REALLY ARE A MESSED-UP ALICE, AREN'T YOU?
YEAH, SINCE I'VE ALREADY GOTTEN THE NAME AND ALL, I WAS THINKING I'D MAKE THE MOST OF IT WHILE I CAN.
...I KNOW IT WELL ENOUGH WITHOUT YOU THREATENING ME LIKE THIS.
ALICE IN WONDERLAND KILLS THE WHITE RABBIT.
AS LONG AS I'M ALICE, I'M NOT ALLOWED TO STRAY FROM THAT PATH.

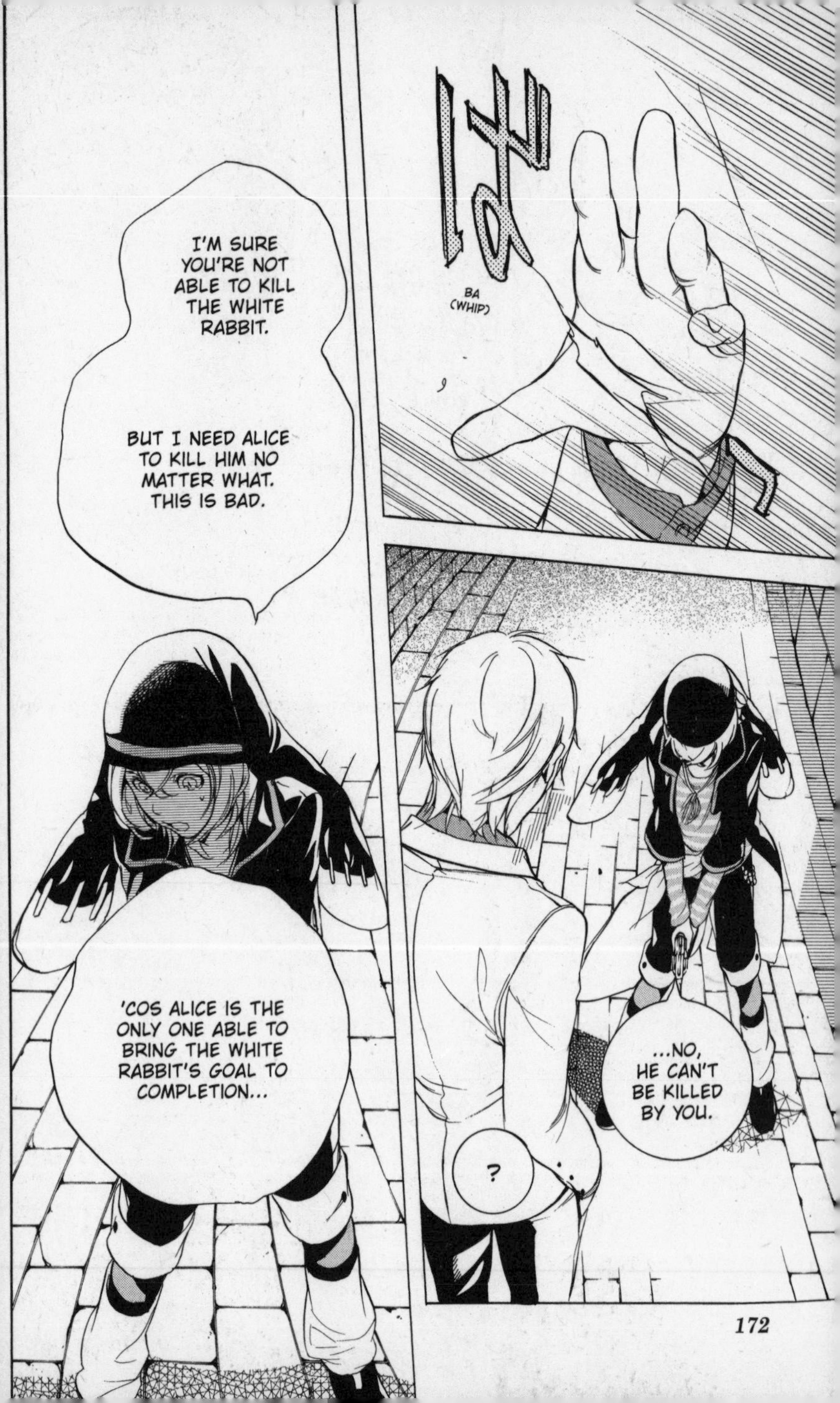
BA (WHIP)
...NO, HE CAN'T BE KILLED BY YOU.
?
I'M SURE YOU'RE NOT ABLE TO KILL THE WHITE RABBIT.
BUT I NEED ALICE TO KILL HIM NO MATTER WHAT. THIS IS BAD.
'COS ALICE IS THE ONLY ONE ABLE TO BRING THE WHITE RABBIT'S GOAL TO COMPLETION...

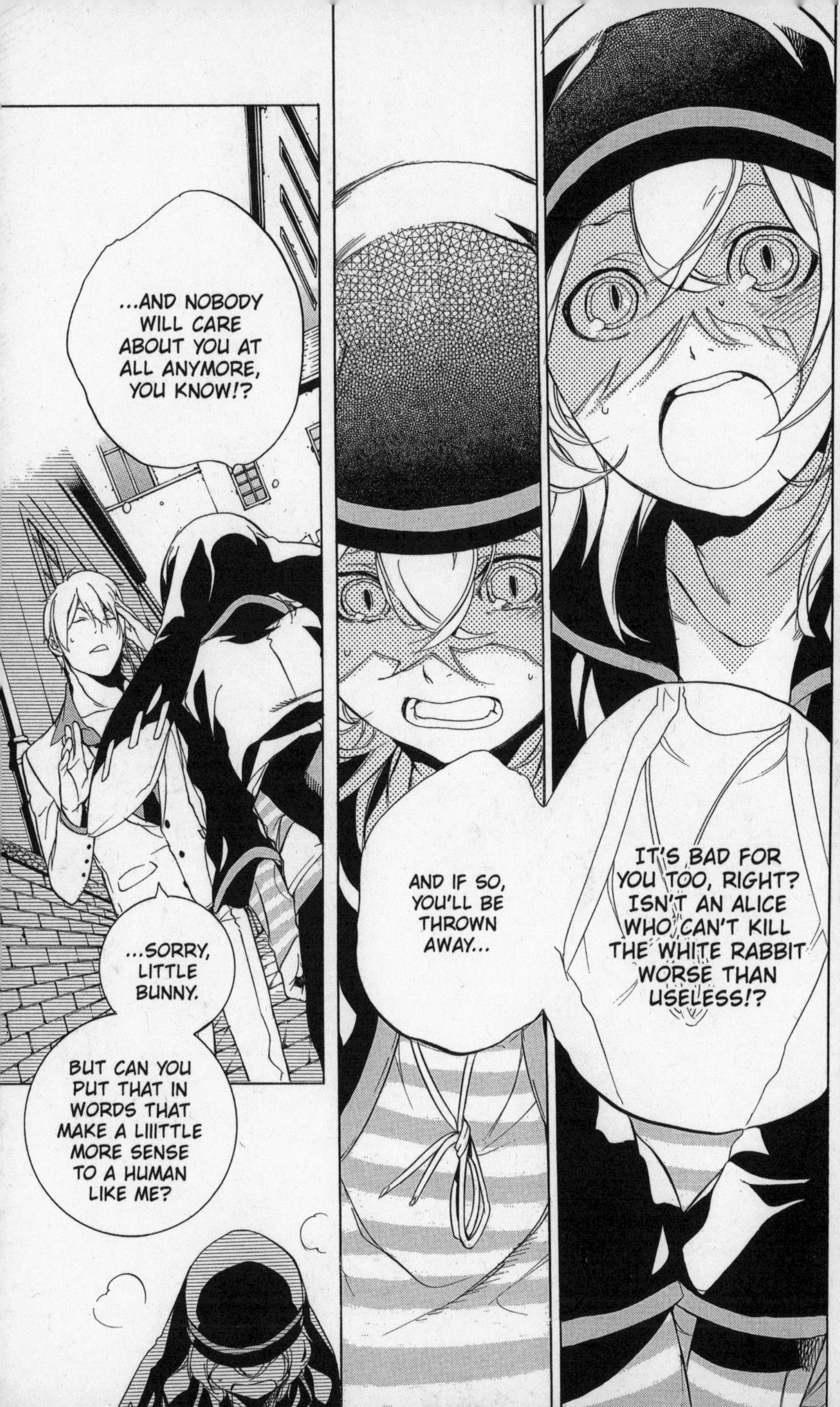
IT'S BAD FOR YOU TOO, RIGHT? ISN'T AN ALICE WHO CAN'T KILL THE WHITE RABBIT WORSE THAN USELESS!?
AND IF SO, YOU'LL BE THROWN AWAY...
...AND NOBODY WILL CARE ABOUT YOU AT ALL ANYMORE, YOU KNOW!?
...SORRY, LITTLE BUNNY.
BUT CAN YOU PUT THAT IN WORDS THAT MAKE A LIIITTLE MORE SENSE TO A HUMAN LIKE ME?

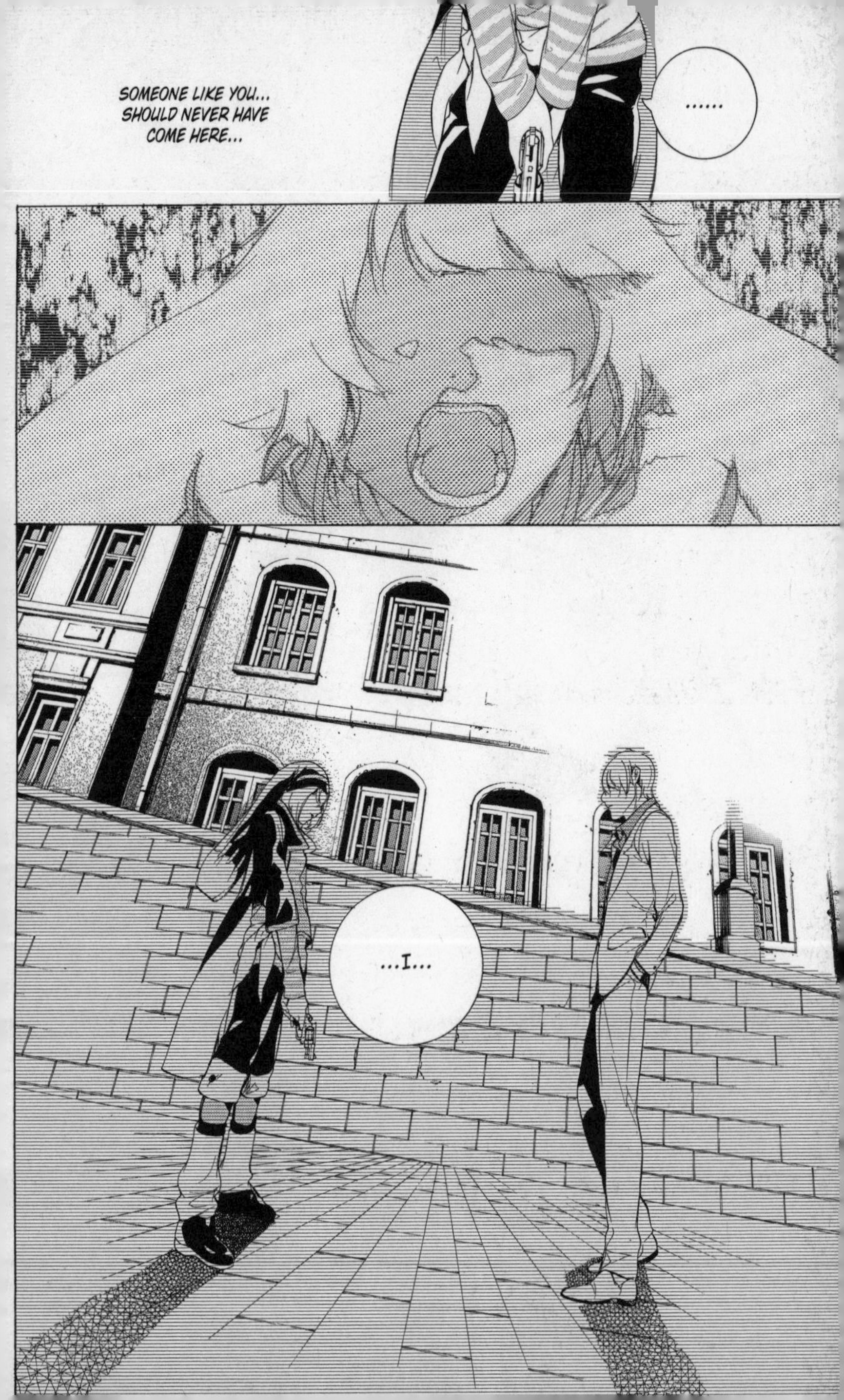
......
SOMEONE LIKE YOU... SHOULD NEVER HAVE COME HERE...
...I...

# Chapter 36

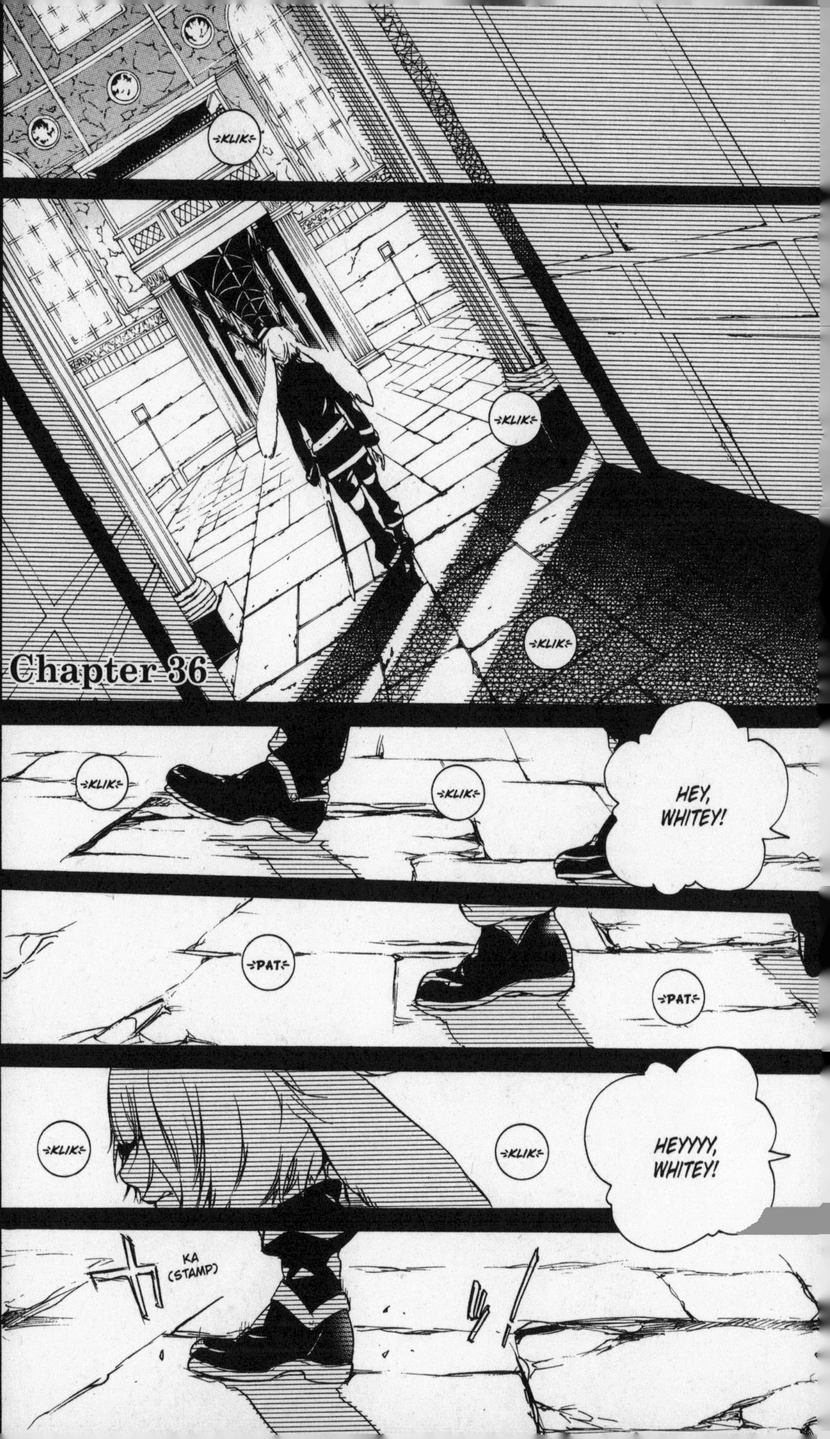

KLIK
KLIK
KLIK
HEY, WHITEY!
KLIK
KLIK
PAT
PAT
HEYYYY, WHITEY!
KLIK
KLIK
KA (STAMP)

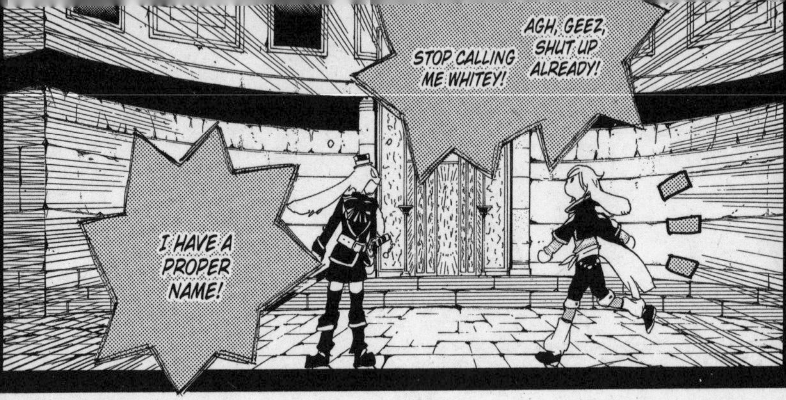
AGH, GEEZ, SHUT UP ALREADY!
STOP CALLING ME WHITEY!
I HAVE A PROPER NAME!

# Chapter 36
# Rabbit Foot.

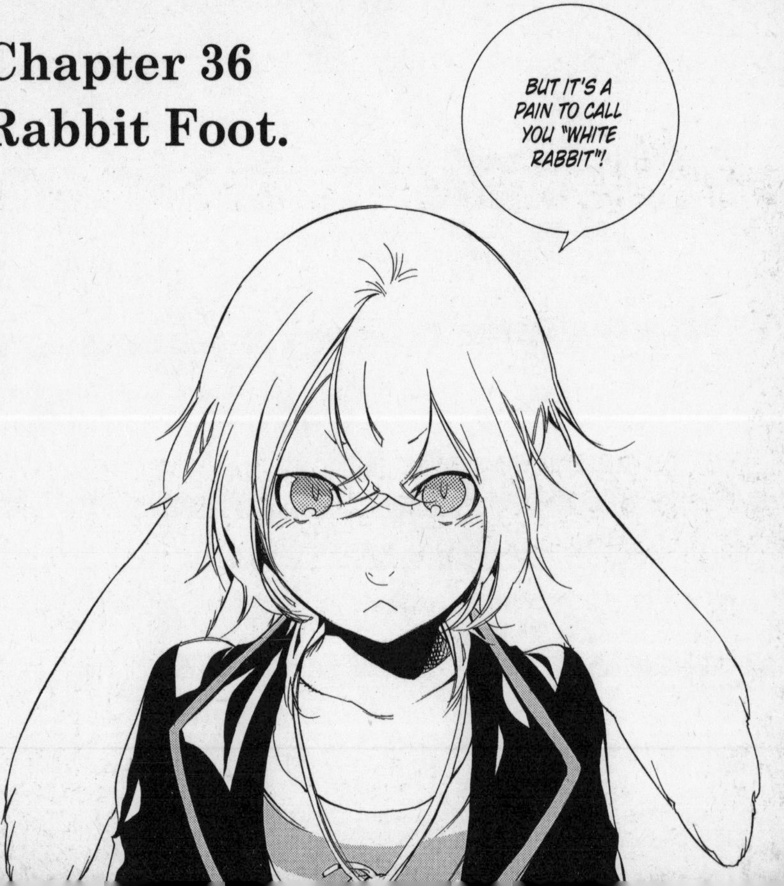
BUT IT'S A PAIN TO CALL YOU "WHITE RABBIT"!

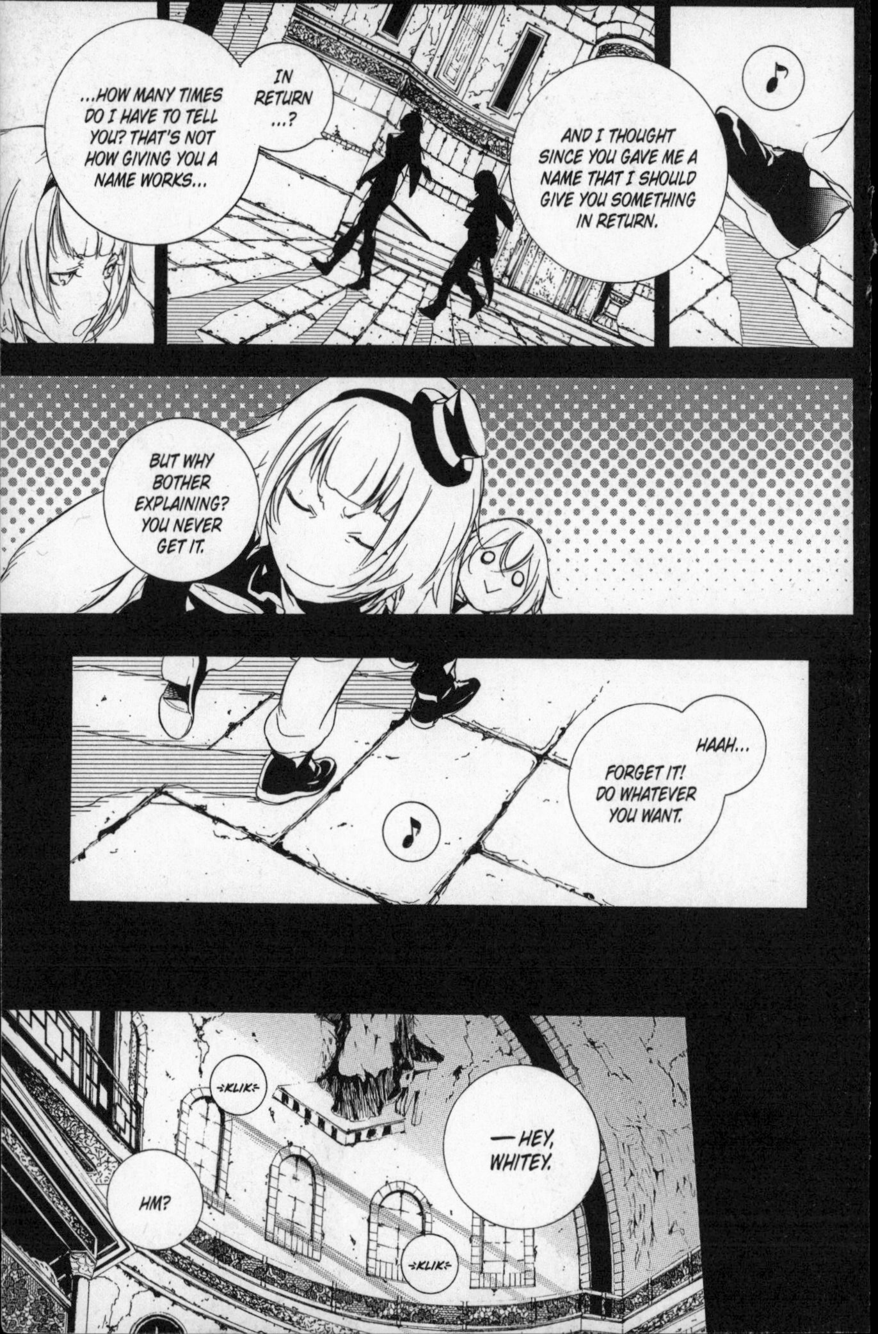
♪
AND I THOUGHT SINCE YOU GAVE ME A NAME THAT I SHOULD GIVE YOU SOMETHING IN RETURN.
IN RETURN ...?
...HOW MANY TIMES DO I HAVE TO TELL YOU? THAT'S NOT HOW GIVING YOU A NAME WORKS...
BUT WHY BOTHER EXPLAINING? YOU NEVER GET IT.
HAAH... FORGET IT! DO WHATEVER YOU WANT.
♪
KLIK
—HEY, WHITEY.
HM?
KLIK

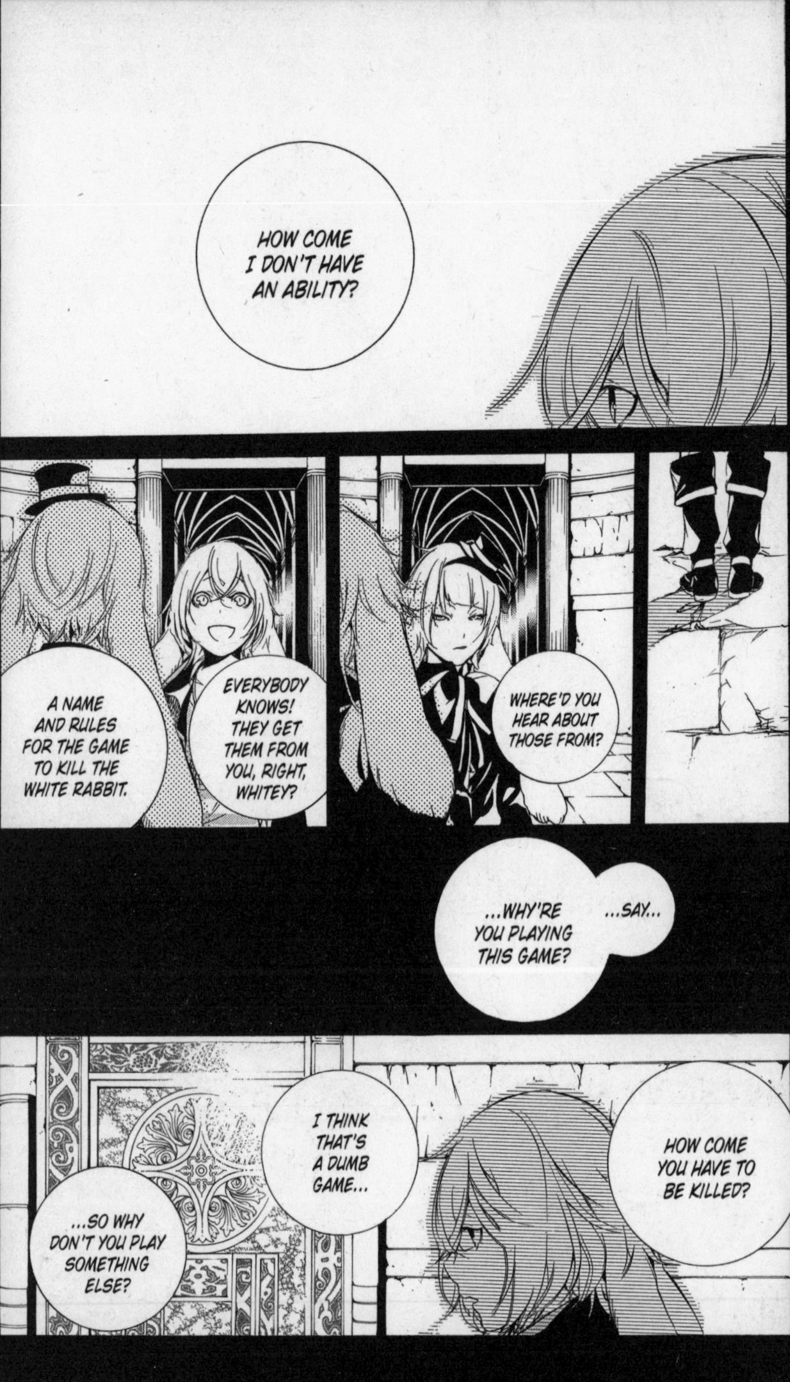
HOW COME I DON'T HAVE AN ABILITY?
WHERE'D YOU HEAR ABOUT THOSE FROM?
EVERYBODY KNOWS! THEY GET THEM FROM YOU, RIGHT, WHITEY?
A NAME AND RULES FOR THE GAME TO KILL THE WHITE RABBIT.
...SAY...
...WHY'RE YOU PLAYING THIS GAME?
HOW COME YOU HAVE TO BE KILLED?
I THINK THAT'S A DUMB GAME...
...SO WHY DON'T YOU PLAY SOMETHING ELSE?

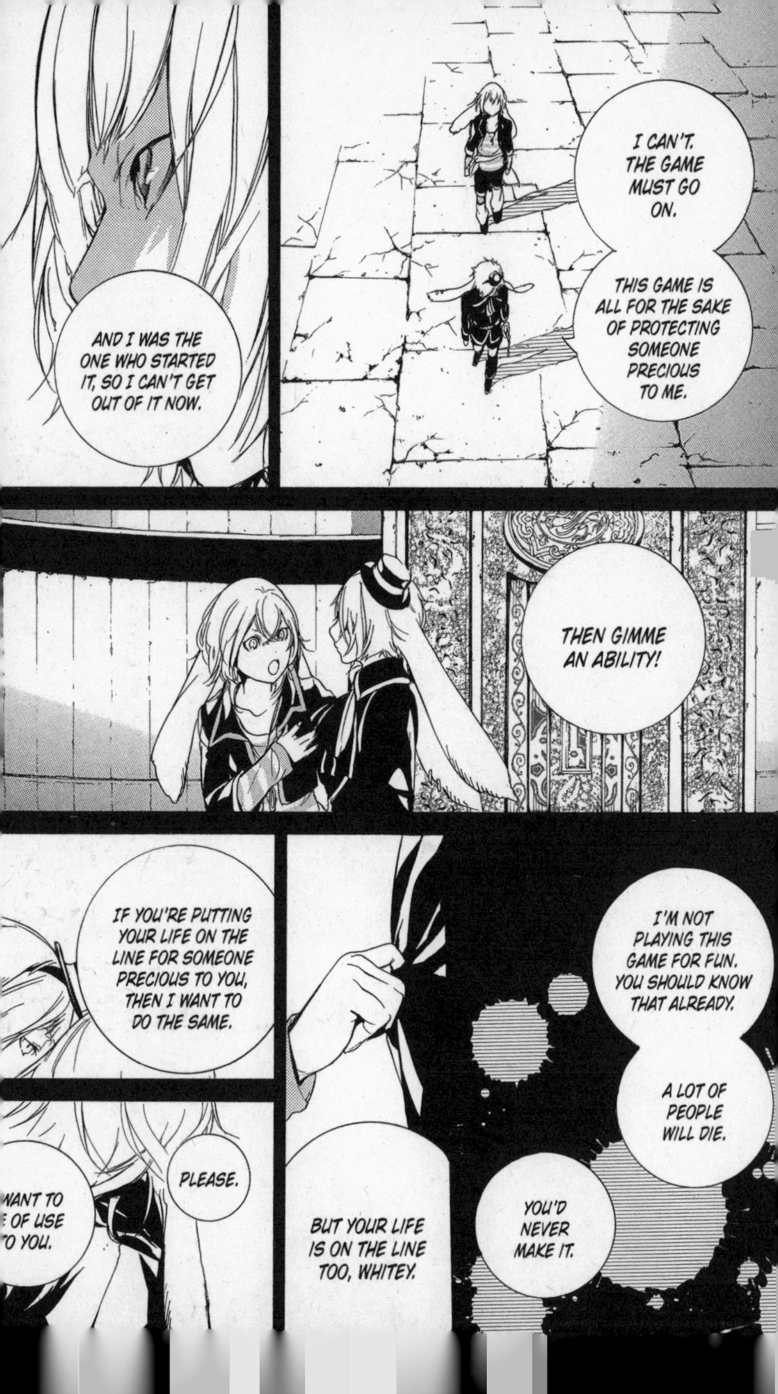
I CAN'T. THE GAME MUST GO ON.
THIS GAME IS ALL FOR THE SAKE OF PROTECTING SOMEONE PRECIOUS TO ME.
AND I WAS THE ONE WHO STARTED IT, SO I CAN'T GET OUT OF IT NOW.
THEN GIMME AN ABILITY!
I'M NOT PLAYING THIS GAME FOR FUN. YOU SHOULD KNOW THAT ALREADY.
A LOT OF PEOPLE WILL DIE.
YOU'D NEVER MAKE IT.
BUT YOUR LIFE IS ON THE LINE TOO, WHITEY.
IF YOU'RE PUTTING YOUR LIFE ON THE LINE FOR SOMEONE PRECIOUS TO YOU, THEN I WANT TO DO THE SAME.
PLEASE.
WANT TO E OF USE O YOU.

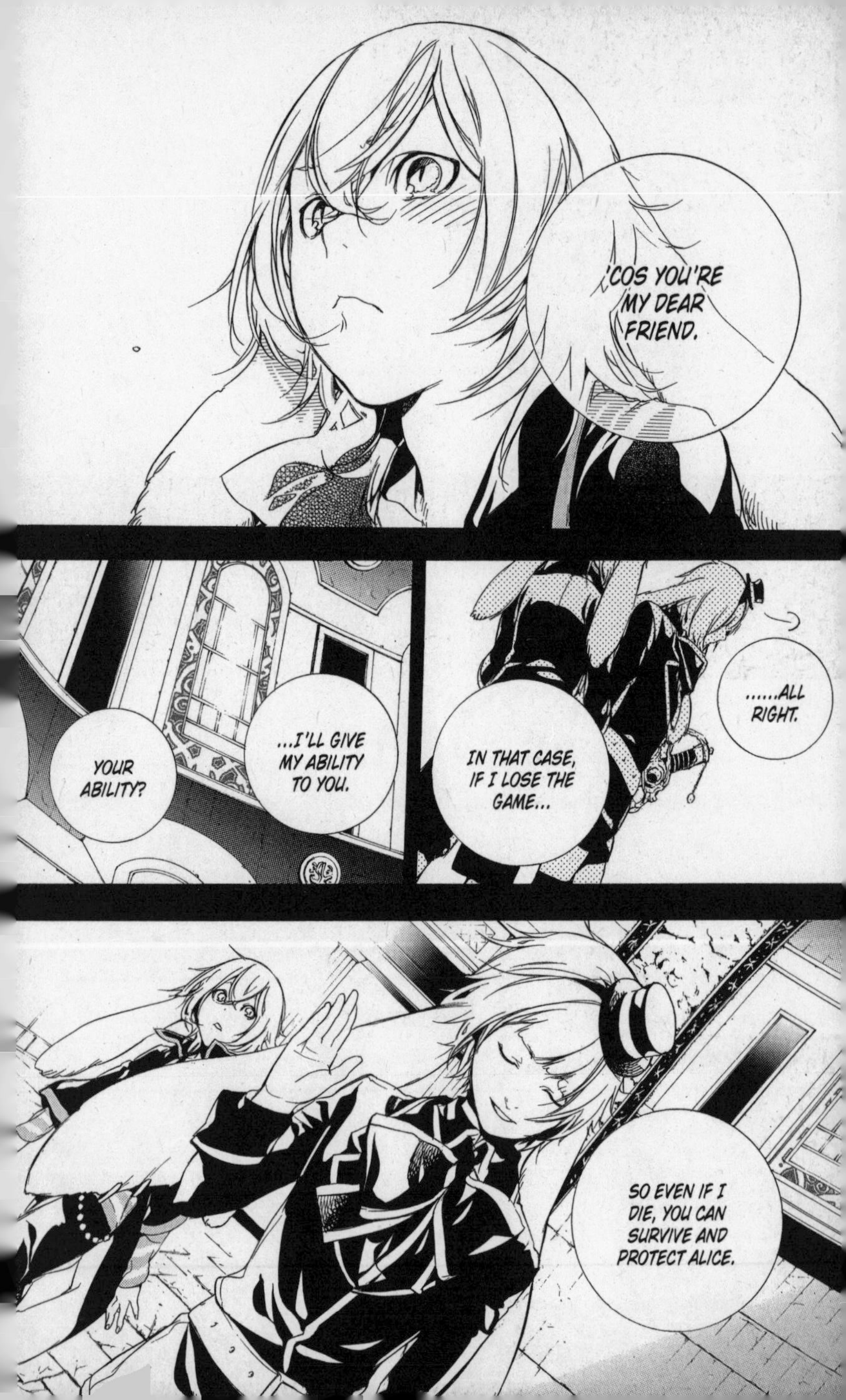
'COS YOU'RE MY DEAR FRIEND.
.....ALL RIGHT.
IN THAT CASE, IF I LOSE THE GAME...
...I'LL GIVE MY ABILITY TO YOU.
YOUR ABILITY?
SO EVEN IF I DIE, YOU CAN SURVIVE AND PROTECT ALICE.

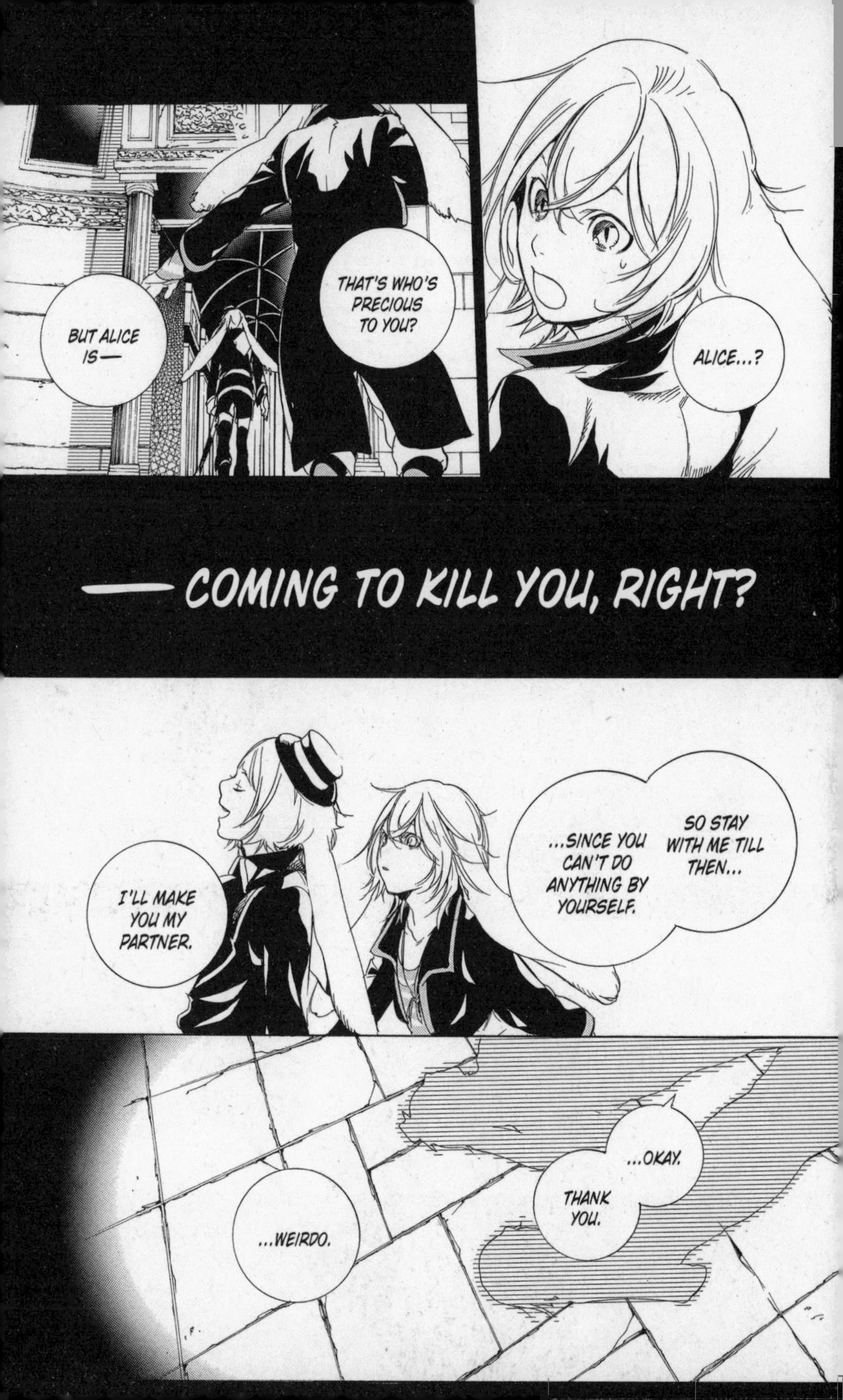
ALICE...?
THAT'S WHO'S PRECIOUS TO YOU?
BUT ALICE IS—
—COMING TO KILL YOU, RIGHT?
SO STAY WITH ME TILL THEN...
...SINCE YOU CAN'T DO ANYTHING BY YOURSELF.
I'LL MAKE YOU MY PARTNER.
...OKAY.
THANK YOU.
...WEIRDO.

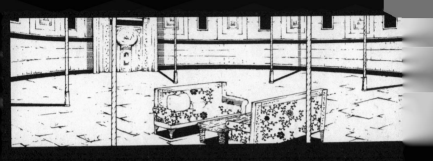

AND MY ABILITY IS A MEANINGLESS ONE. I KNEW THAT, BUT...

...I STILL SMILED AND PRETENDED NOT TO KNOW.

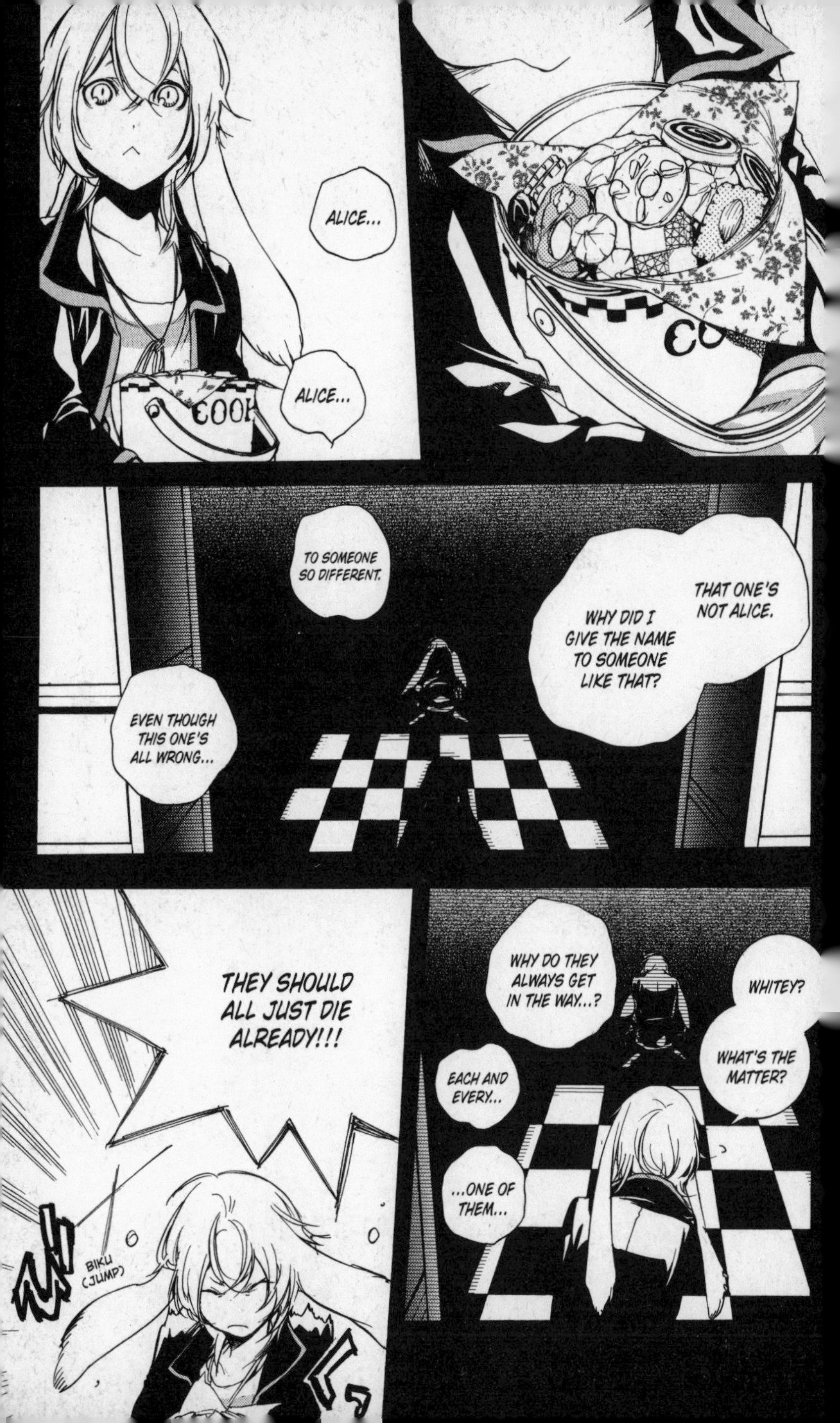
ALICE...
ALICE...
THAT ONE'S NOT ALICE.
WHY DID I GIVE THE NAME TO SOMEONE LIKE THAT?
TO SOMEONE SO DIFFERENT.
EVEN THOUGH THIS ONE'S ALL WRONG...
WHITEY?
WHAT'S THE MATTER?
WHY DO THEY ALWAYS GET IN THE WAY...?
EACH AND EVERY...
...ONE OF THEM...
THEY SHOULD ALL JUST DIE ALREADY!!!
BIKU (JUMP)

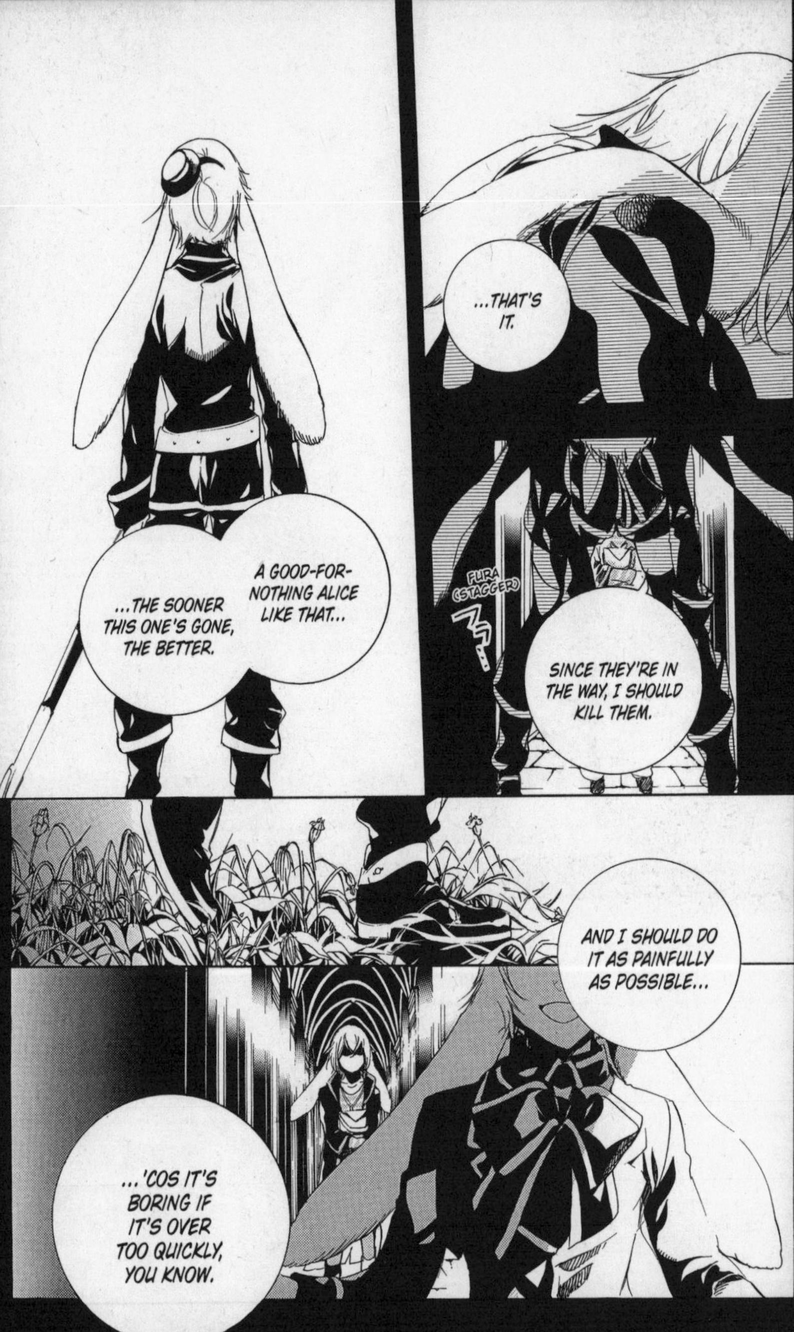
...THAT'S IT.
FURA (STAGGER)
SINCE THEY'RE IN THE WAY, I SHOULD KILL THEM.
A GOOD-FOR-NOTHING ALICE LIKE THAT...
...THE SOONER THIS ONE'S GONE, THE BETTER.
AND I SHOULD DO IT AS PAINFULLY AS POSSIBLE...
...'COS IT'S BORING IF IT'S OVER TOO QUICKLY, YOU KNOW.

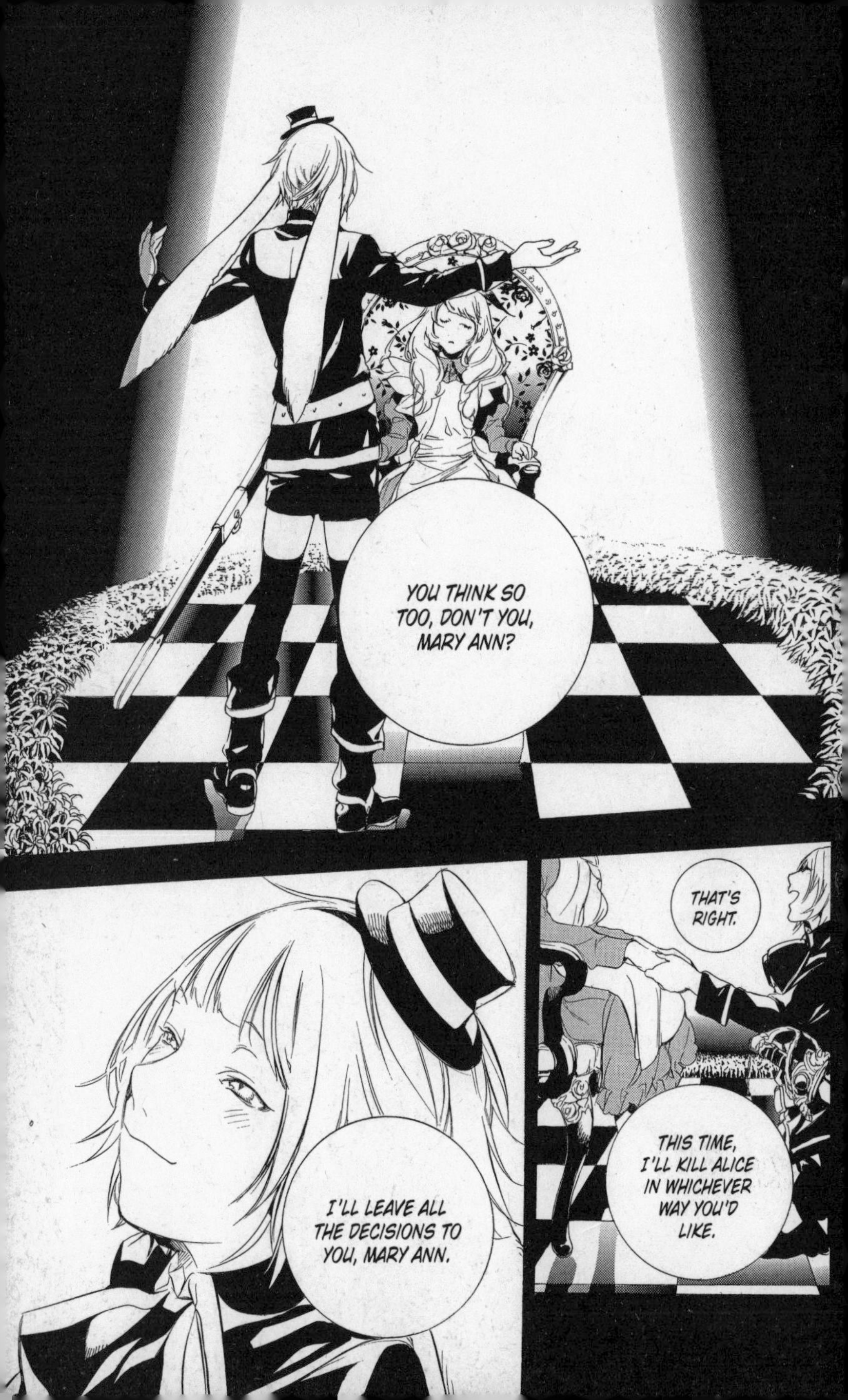
YOU THINK SO TOO, DON'T YOU, MARY ANN?
THAT'S RIGHT.
THIS TIME, I'LL KILL ALICE IN WHICHEVER WAY YOU'D LIKE.
I'LL LEAVE ALL THE DECISIONS TO YOU, MARY ANN.

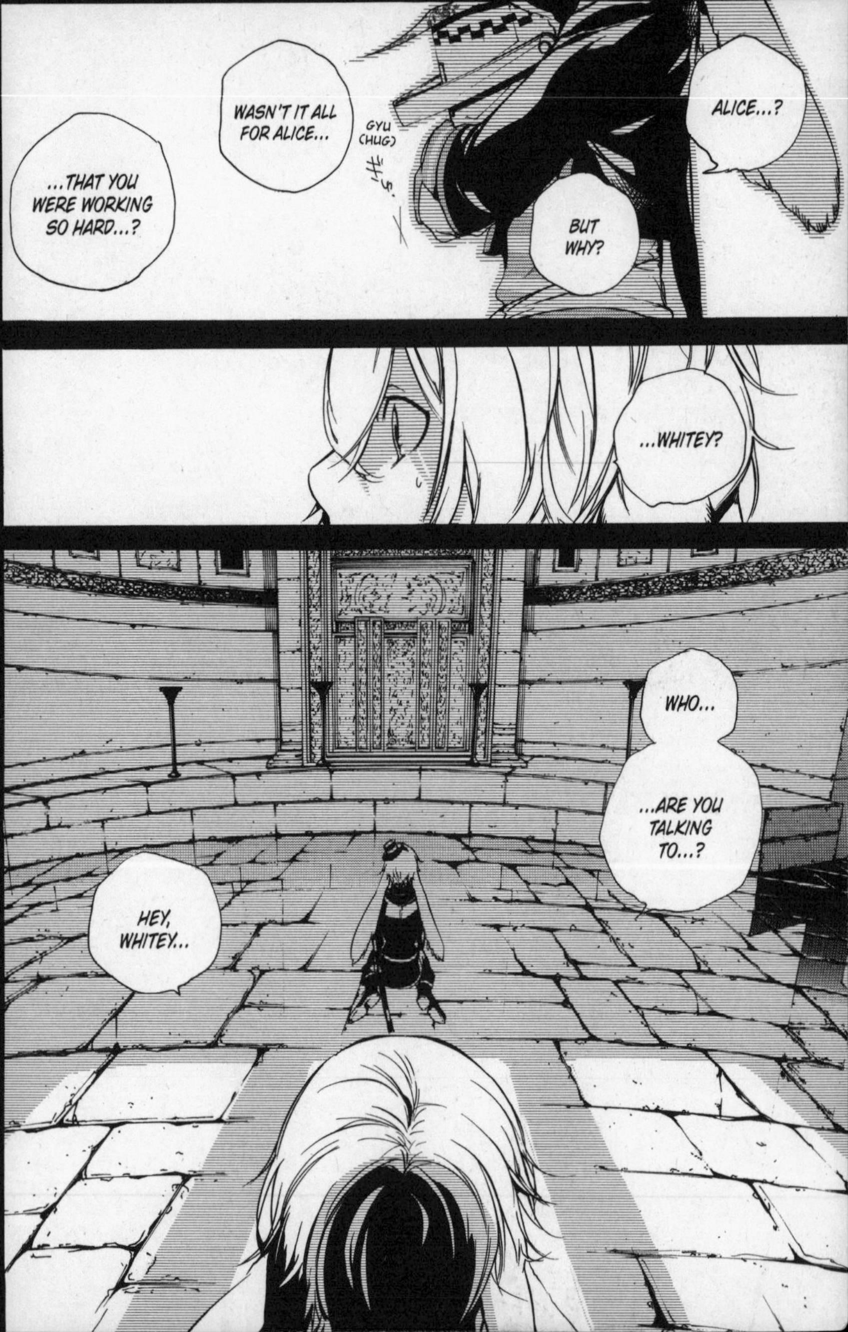
ALICE...?
BUT WHY?
WASN'T IT ALL FOR ALICE...
GYU (HUG)
...THAT YOU WERE WORKING SO HARD...?
...WHITEY?
WHO...
...ARE YOU TALKING TO...?
HEY, WHITEY...

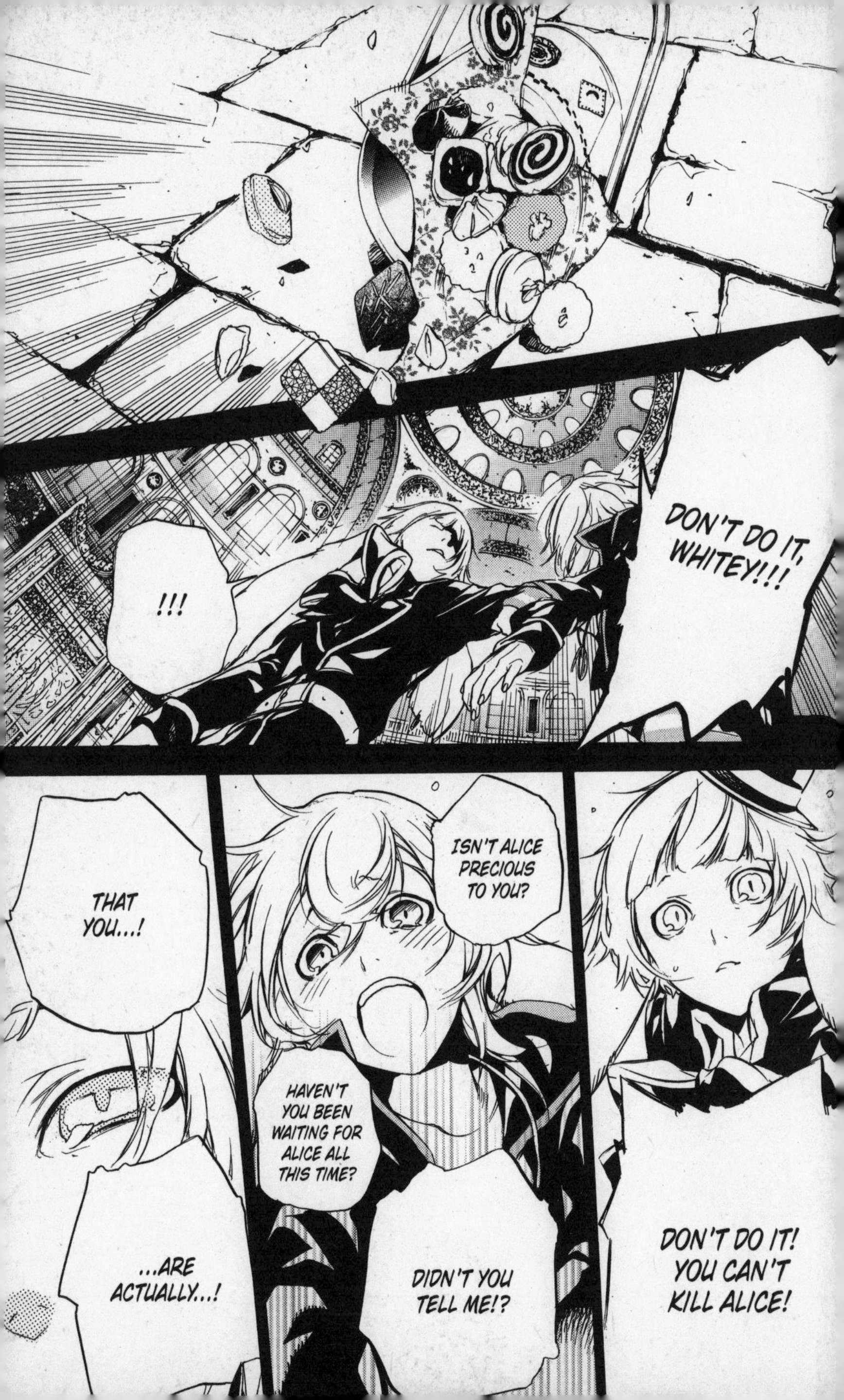
DON'T DO IT, WHITEY!!!
!!!
DON'T DO IT! YOU CAN'T KILL ALICE!
ISN'T ALICE PRECIOUS TO YOU?
HAVEN'T YOU BEEN WAITING FOR ALICE ALL THIS TIME?
DIDN'T YOU TELL ME!?
THAT YOU...!
...ARE ACTUALLY...!

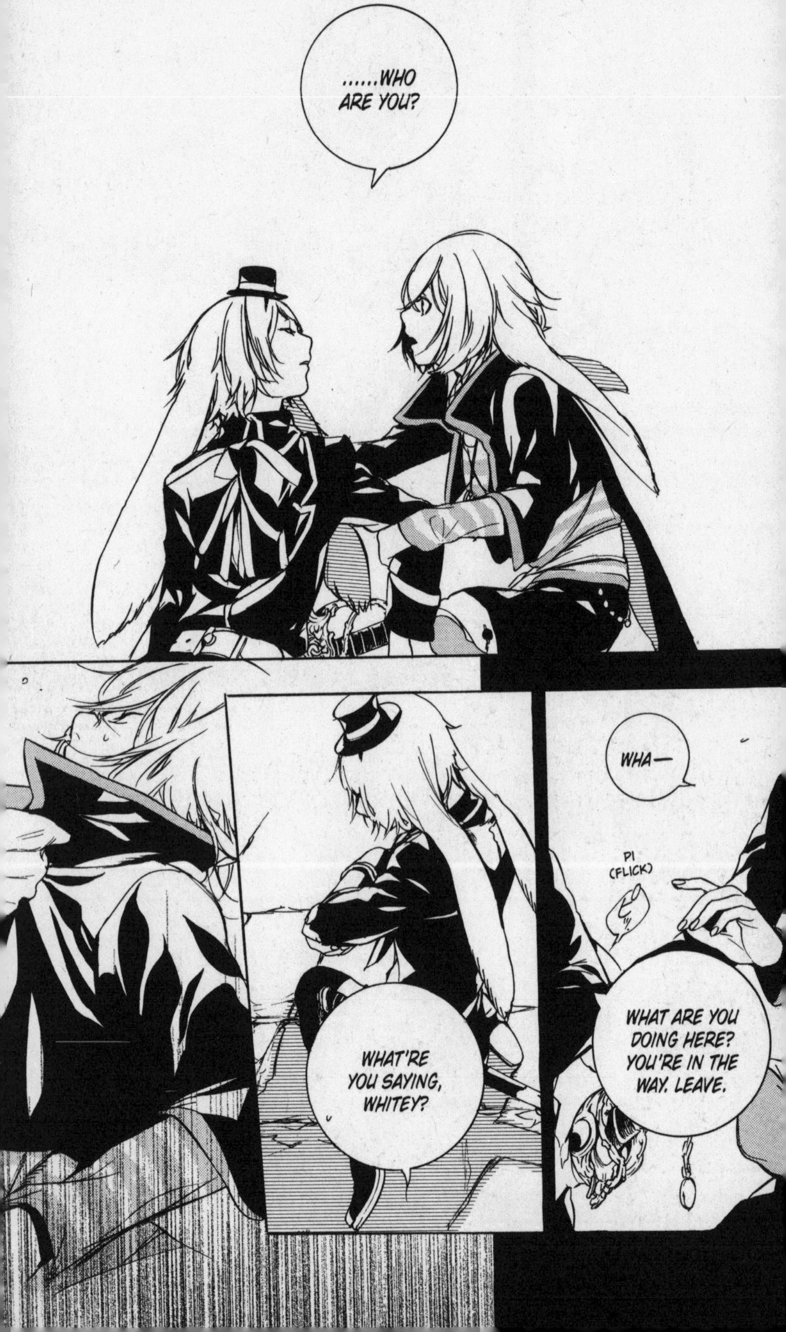
......WHO ARE YOU?
WHA—
PI (FLICK)
WHAT ARE YOU DOING HERE? YOU'RE IN THE WAY. LEAVE.
WHAT'RE YOU SAYING, WHITEY?

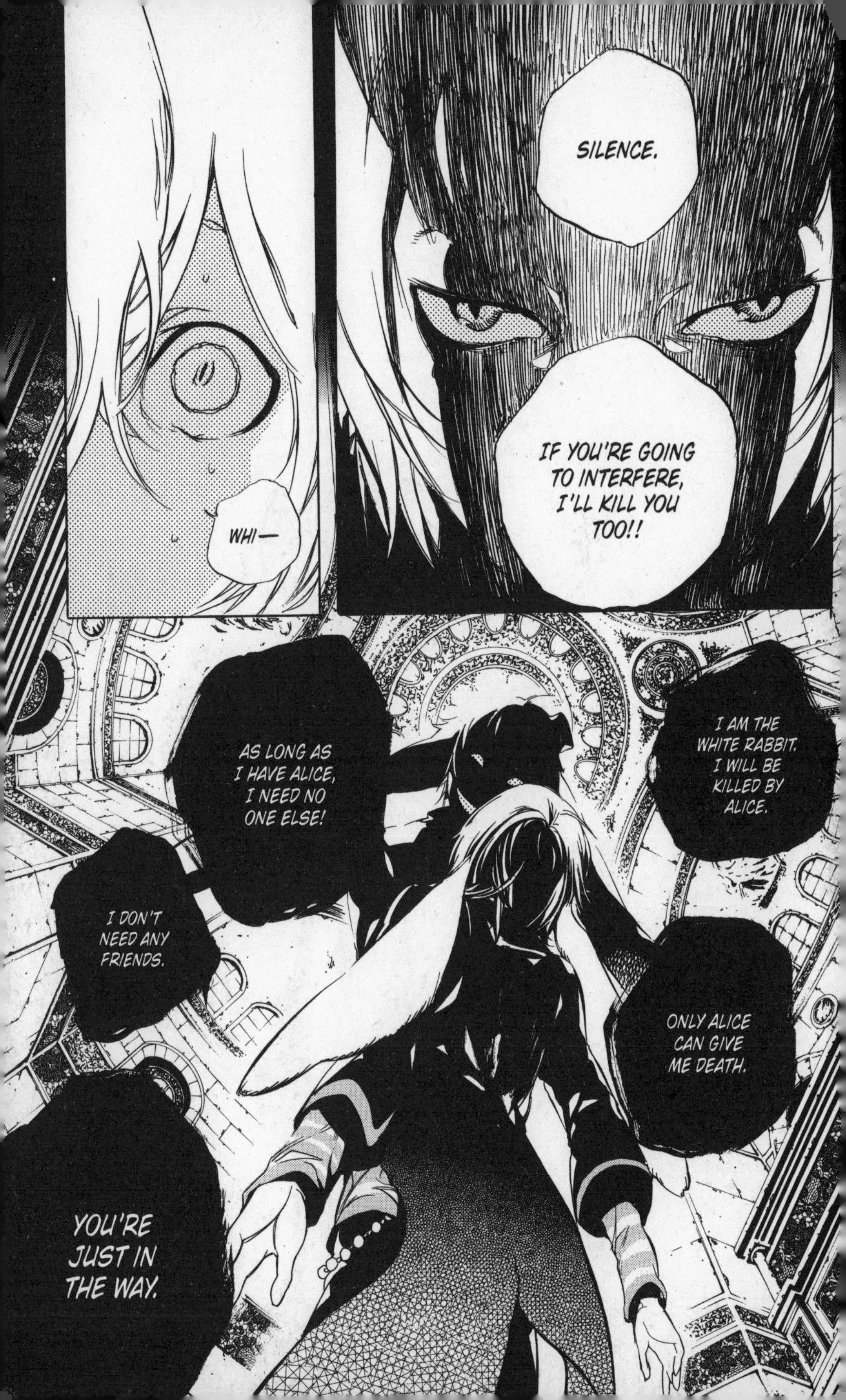
SILENCE.
IF YOU'RE GOING TO INTERFERE, I'LL KILL YOU TOO!!
WHI—
I AM THE WHITE RABBIT. I WILL BE KILLED BY ALICE.
AS LONG AS I HAVE ALICE, I NEED NO ONE ELSE!
ONLY ALICE CAN GIVE ME DEATH.
I DON'T NEED ANY FRIENDS.
YOU'RE JUST IN THE WAY.

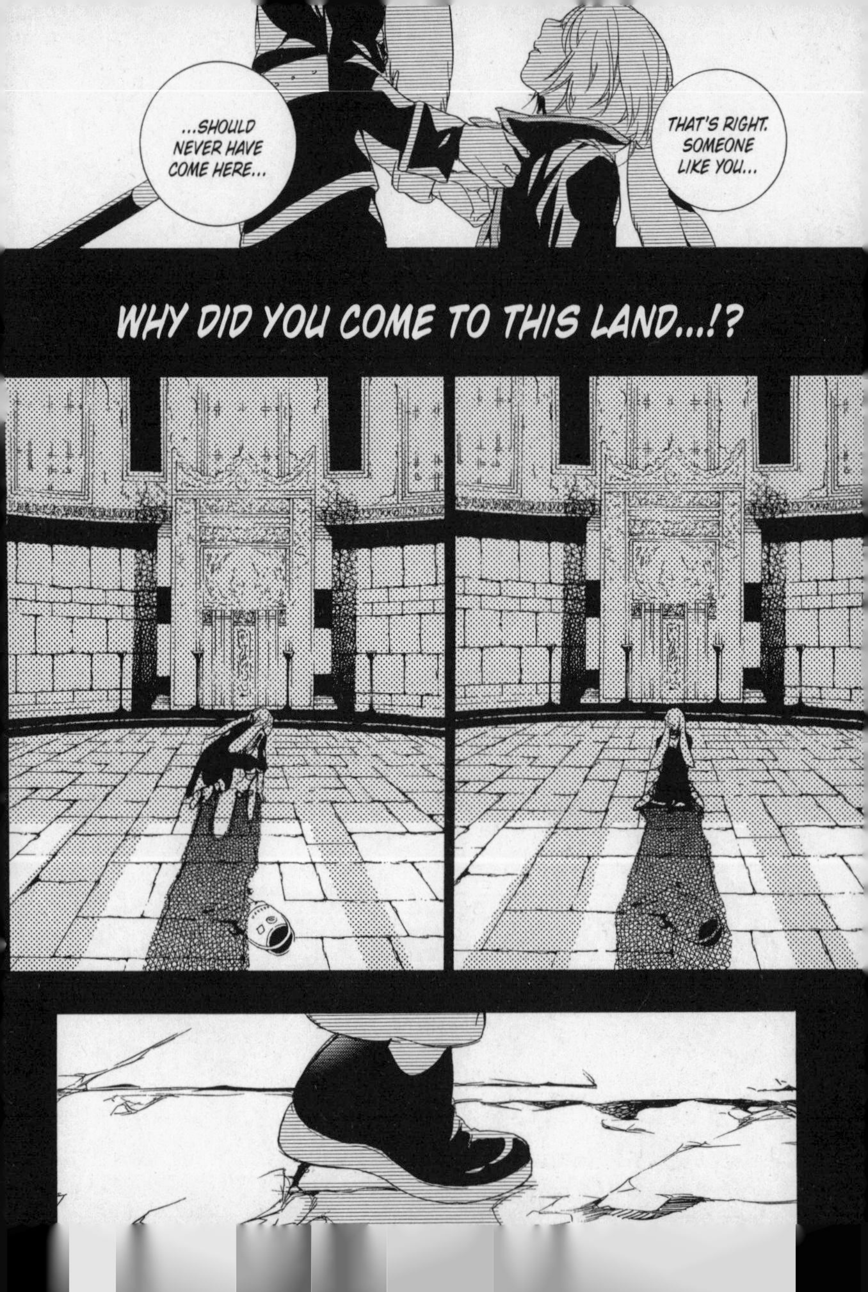
THAT'S RIGHT. SOMEONE LIKE YOU...
...SHOULD NEVER HAVE COME HERE...
WHY DID YOU COME TO THIS LAND...!?

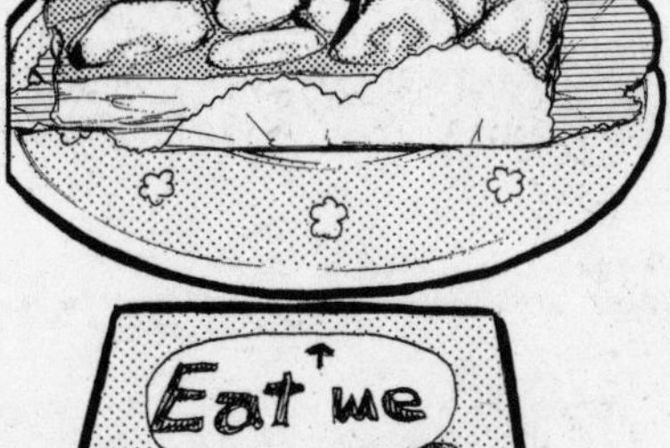
Eat me

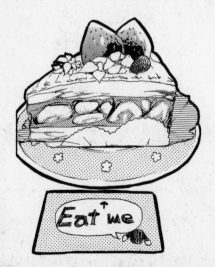

# STAFF

## ORIGINAL WORKS
AI NINOMIYA

## ASSISTANT WORKS
DATENSHI
REIN OFUJI
MIZUKI SAKAMAKI
MARI
SIMA

WHO WOULD YOU WANT AS A BIG SISTER OR BROTHER (AND WHY)?

I BET HE'D ALWAYS LET ME WIN AT GAMES AND STUFF.

JACK

-DATENSHI-

THE 88TH ALICE
I WANNA SECRETLY BORROW HER FASHIONABLE CLOTHES AND THEN GET SCOLDED BY HER FOR IT.

-OFUJI-

THE QUEEN OF HEARTS
HE SEEMS LIKE HE'D BE UNEXPECTEDLY CARING TO FAMILY.

-KATAGIRI-

AS FOR YOU, WHO IS IT GOOD?

Mister Hatter, whose time has begun to move again, is getting more visitors at his house. That was the story this time.

It's not really that interesting, but whenever he's addressing someone he thinks is older than him, Alice uses *anta*, the slightly more respectful "you," but the rest of the time he uses the even ruder *omae*. It's seriously not that interesting an observation, but our hero is unexpectedly one of those sticklers. That's all. How you address someone is as important as their names!

And with that, I hope to see you again in Volume 7!

Ai Ninomiya

# ARE YOU ALICE? 6

### IKUMI KATAGIRI
### AI NINOMIYA

**Translation and Lettering: Alexis Eckerman**

This book is a work of fiction. Names, characters, places, and incidents are the product of the author's imagination or are used fictitiously. Any resemblance to actual events, locales, or persons, living or dead, is coincidental.

Are you Alice? © 2012 by Ai Ninomiya / Ikumi Katagiri. © IM/Re;no, Inc. All rights reserved. First published in Japan in 2012 by ICHIJINSHA. English translation rights arranged with ICHIJINSHA through Tuttle-Mori Agency, Inc., Tokyo.

Translation © 2014 by Hachette Book Group, Inc.

Yen Press
Hachette Book Group
237 Park Avenue, New York, NY 10017

www.HachetteBookGroup.com
www.YenPress.com

Yen Press is an imprint of Hachette Book Group, Inc. The Yen Press name and logo are trademarks of Hachette Book Group, Inc.

First Yen Press Edition: September 2014

ISBN: 978-0-316-28621-3

10 9 8 7 6 5 4 3 2 1

BVG

Printed in the United States of America